VISUAL QUICKSTART GUIDE

RUBY

Larry Ullman

D1609677

Peachpit Press

Visual QuickStart Guide
Ruby
Larry Ullman

Peachpit Press
1249 Eighth Street
Berkeley, CA 94710
510/524-2178
510/524-2221 (fax)

Find us on the Web at: www.peachpit.com
To report errors, please send a note to: errata@peachpit.com
Peachpit Press is a division of Pearson Education.

Copyright © 2009 by Larry Ullman

Editor: Rebecca Gulick
Copy Editor: Bob Campbell
Production Coordinator: Myrna Vladic
Compositor: Debbie Roberti
Indexer: Jack Lewis
Cover Design: Peachpit Press
Technical Reviewer: Fabio Cevasco

ISBN-13: 978-0-321-55385-0
ISBN-10: 0-321-55385-3
9 8 7 6 5 4 3 2 1

Printed and bound in the United States of America

Dedication:

I dedicate this book to all those who freely donate their time, money, and efforts to benefit others. To those who apply their expertise to an open-source technology like Ruby, provide help in an online forum, and assist in their local community, and to so many others, I say thanks.

Bucketfuls of warm fuzzies to:

She without whom I would be so much less of a writer, Rebecca Gulick.

Bob Campbell, for keeping things tidy.

Debbie Roberti and Myrna Vladic, for turning a grab bag of files into a coherent book.

Jack Lewis for creating the index.

Everyone else at Peachpit Press and Pearson, for everything they do!

Fabio Cevasco, for the thorough technical review.

Jessica, Sam, and Zoe, for everything, everything, everything else.

TABLE OF CONTENTS

TABLE OF CONTENTS

INTRODUCTION

If you're looking at this book and reading this introduction, you probably have these two questions:

◆ Should I learn Ruby?

◆ Is this the book for me?

Of course, the answers to these questions depend upon who you are and what your situation is. But the fact that you're curious about Ruby and this book would lead me to suggest that the answer to both question is "Yes!" But I admit I have a biased opinion.

There are a lot of programming languages out there and lots of books on each language. If you quickly read just the next couple of pages, I'll outline my case for Ruby and this book in detail, but know that Ruby is a language that's quite powerful and useful but still remarkably easy to learn. This book, then, has the same aspirations: it's very easy to learn from, and it focuses on providing the most useful information above all.

What Is Ruby?

It's difficult to describe what Ruby *is* without outright convincing you to use it. Such is the problem when you're talking about something special. But I'll try to restrain myself by starting with the more mundane details about Ruby.

Ruby is a dynamic object-oriented programming language that can be used for just about any purpose: text processing, system utilities, Web development, even graphical applications. Ruby was initially created by Yukihiro Matsumoto, aka "Matz," and released to the public in 1995. In 2005 and 2006, largely thanks to the popularity of the Ruby on Rails Web development framework (covered in Chapter 16, "Ruby on Rails"), Ruby came to the forefront of the worldwide computing consciousness. Today, Ruby is one of the ten most-used programming languages, and its user base is predicted to quadruple by 2013.

Unlike C or C++ code, which is compiled into an executable application, Ruby code is most often run through an interpreter. The interpreter works on most operating systems, however, and the large majority of Ruby code is cross-platform compatible without modification.

Last but not least, Ruby is an *open source* project: it's free for anyone to use, modify, or distribute. This also means that Ruby is maintained—and constantly being improved upon—by a broad spectrum of developers around the globe.

While I was writing this book, the stable version of Ruby was 1.8.6 (version 1.8.7, a minor update, was released just as the book went to print). Ruby 1.9 is in development, and many of its features and changes are introduced in this book, although not formally covered.

Why Use Ruby?

Without further ado, my top three reasons for why you should use Ruby:

1. In all likelihood, it can be used for whatever tasks you need to address.

2. It's flexible and powerful, yet still approachable.

3. It's easy to learn, and you'll probably like it (most people do once they get to know it).

I've already mentioned what Ruby can be used for—just about anything, so let's start with the ways in which Ruby is easy.

The first complete script you'll write in this book contains just one line:

```
print "Greetings, planet!"
```

There are no special tags to use, no cryptic invocations, and no semicolons. Plus, you probably already know what that line of code will do. Ruby is specifically designed not to be surprising or confusing; Ruby code should be natural, like the language you speak. Which is not to say that Ruby is simple…

Ruby is a dynamic and extremely flexible language. On the most advanced end of the Ruby-programming spectrum, an application can use *reflection*—the ability to analyze itself—to modify how it behaves while it's running. Not all Ruby programmers need to use this capability, but it's nice to have. Without going to such an extreme, Ruby is flexible in that you can modify key fea-

tures of the language itself, again, while an application is running. For example, your code can modify the definition of the String class—i.e., the representation of any quoted characters—on the fly!

As for Ruby's power, that comes, in part, from its Standard Library, which defines over 9,000 methods that you can use in your code. As if that weren't enough, *RubyGems*—a library of nonstandardized but often more elaborate code—provides many more tools. Quite frequently, a more demanding application can be developed in a matter of minutes, just by researching and using an existing library or gem.

Finally, I will say that Ruby's power, its flexibility, and even its ease of use stem from the fact that Ruby is a pure object-oriented programming (OOP) language. The word "pure" is used there because *everything* in Ruby is an object. In other OOP languages, *most* things are objects, but in Ruby, the number 2 is an object, as is the Boolean value true and the string *Hello, World!* What this means to you, the programmer, is that every piece of information you work with can be treated in the same way and there's tons of functionality built-in to even the simplest snippet of data.

If you're still not convinced Ruby is for you, I encourage you to point your Web browser to http://tryruby.hobix.com. There you'll find a wonderfully done Ruby tutorial that allows you to practice coding in Ruby right in your browser.

WHY USE RUBY?

What You'll Need

The requirements for working with Ruby are both free and minimal: Ruby is just not demanding! For starters, you'll need a computer, but you probably assumed that. It really doesn't matter what kind of computer you have, what operating system it's running, or how much memory and hard disk space you have available. If your computer can run, say, a Web browser, it has all the power you need for programming in Ruby. The most important—in fact, the only—requirement is that you install Ruby itself, but Ruby runs on every operating system that I know of.

To program in Ruby, you'll use a text editor and a command-line interface. Both of these tools are already present on every operating system. Still, you might find you prefer using an Integrated Development Environment (IDE). If so, there are plenty available at a range of prices. NetBeans (`www.netbeans.org`) is a popular open-source—i.e., *free*—choice that runs on most operating systems.

For two of the chapters, you'll need to have a database application installed. In those—Chapter 14, "Databases," and Chapter 16, "Ruby on Rails"—I suggest using the open-source SQLite (`www.sqlite.org`). For a few other chapters, you'll need an Internet connection to follow some of the steps or to execute some of the code.

From you, the reader, nothing is expected except an interest and willingness to learn Ruby. No prior programming language is required; in fact, not knowing one may be beneficial, as Ruby does things differently than programmers coming from other languages might be used to (at the very least, it takes a while to stop placing semicolons at the end of each line).

About This Book

This book attempts to convey the fundamentals of programming with Ruby, without going into overwhelming details or bombarding you with irrelevant technicalities. Unlike many of the other Ruby books out there, this one does not aim to provide documentation on every Ruby feature or library—which can already be found online—nor does the book restrict itself to just dry syntax. Instead, the focus herein is on what you really need to know—in terms of features, libraries, and syntax—and how you would apply that information to real-world situations. This is a lofty and important goal, but I'd like to think the book hits its mark far more than it misses.

This book uses the following conventions:

The step-by-step instructions indicate what code you are to type or what other steps you are to take. The specific text you should type is printed in a unique type style to separate it from the main text. For example:

```
puts 'Hello, World!'
```

Because the column width in this book is narrower than that of the common text editor or IDE, some lines of code printed in the steps have to be broken where they would

not otherwise break in an editor. A small gray arrow indicates when this kind of break occurs. For example:

```
puts 'Hello, world! How are you doing on
→ this rainy Saturday afternoon?'
```

With such code, you should continue to use one line in your scripts, or else you might encounter errors.

In some, but not all chapters, the complete Ruby code is also written as its own separate script and is numbered by line for reference. You shouldn't insert these numbers yourself, because doing so will render your code unusable. Most good text editors and IDEs will number lines for you. In some of these script blocks, extra attention may be drawn to particular lines by highlighting them in bold.

You will also frequently see images showing the results of running some Ruby code, displaying a command you need to enter, or demonstrating a particular subpart of an application. All of the images were taken on either Windows or Mac OS X (the Mac OS X images and steps are similar to those for a Linux user). The exact appearance of an application will change from one computer to the next, but most of the content should be similar, as will all of the functionality.

ABOUT THIS BOOK

Getting Help

Although this book was written with the intent of being the most down-to-earth, get-going-now text around, you may run into problems and desire a little assistance on occasion. If you'd like some help regarding the content of this book, or Ruby in general, you have options. Here are some choices, in order of likelihood for getting a fast response (i.e., the fastest options are listed first):

◆ Search the Internet.

If you have questions about a particular class, method, or concept, Google (or whatever search engine you prefer) will almost always return immediate answers.

◆ Turn to a Ruby Web site.

Ruby's primary Web site—www.ruby-lang.org—is best for downloading Ruby, finding out the latest news, and turning up links to other sites. Of those, you'll definitely want to bookmark www.ruby-doc.org, home to the official Ruby documentation. You may find you prefer the documentation as displayed at www.apidock.com/ruby/, so check it out as well.

◆ Use a Ruby newsgroup or forum.

The ruby-talk mailing list and the comp.lang.ruby Usenet group are the all-stars here, and the two are mirrored. Links to both can be found at Ruby's main site. If you ask a question *wisely* (see the sidebar), you should get the answer you need in a relatively short time.

◆ Check out this book's supporting Web site.

This book's official Web site can be found at www.DMCInsights.com/ruby/. There you'll find all the scripts from the book, links to other resources, extra features, and a list of any printing errors. You can also contact me directly through this site, although it'll always be faster if you first...

◆ Use this book's support forum.

At www.DMCInsights.com/phorum/list.php?22, readers can post questions, get answers, see what others are doing, and so forth. I moderate this forum personally, which means I'll answer your question if someone doesn't beat me to the punch.

Asking Questions the Smart Way

Whether you're posting a message to the book's support forum, sending me an email, or asking a question in a newsgroup, knowing how to most effectively ask a question improves the quality of the response you'll receive as well as the speed with which you'll get your answer. To receive the best answer in the shortest amount of time, follow these steps:

1. Search the Internet, read the manuals, and browse any applicable documentation.

2. Ask your question in the most appropriate forum (newsgroup, mailing list, and so on).

3. Use a clear and concise subject.

4. Describe your problem in detail, show any relevant code, describe what went wrong, include what operating system you're running, and say what development environment (IDE, compiler, etc.) you're using.

For more tips and an enlightening read, see Eric Steven Raymond's "How to Ask Questions the Smart Way" at www.catb.org/~esr/faqs/smart-questions.html. The 10 minutes you spend on it will save you hours in the future!

GETTING STARTED

This chapter begins by discussing how to install Ruby on Windows, Mac OS X, and Linux. That's something you'll likely need to do before following any of the examples in this book (an exception being Mac OS X users, whose operating system comes with Ruby already).

Installing Ruby is something you'll only do a very limited number of times, so, in a way, the remaining topics in this chapter are actually more important. Of those, the first demonstrates how to test your Ruby installation. Doing so not only confirms that you have Ruby properly installed, but also reveals the version in use. The next topic is how to access Ruby's documentation. Finally, the chapter discusses and demonstrates `irb`, the interactive Ruby utility. You'll use this program extensively in the book, particularly within the first few chapters, to practice simple lines of Ruby code.

Installation on Windows

The Ruby programming language does not
come pre-installed on Windows, so you'll
need to install your own copy before you
can follow any of the steps in this book.
Fortunately, Ruby is free and easily added
to your system.

My assumption is that you've installed any
number of applications on Windows before,
so you really don't need me going through
all the details. I expect that you know to
read and agree to a license agreement and
whether something should be added to your
Start menu or not. In these steps, therefore,
I don't discuss every facet of the installation
process, instead just highlighting the most
important ones or those that are particular
to Ruby and may be unfamiliar to you.

There are many ways to install Ruby on
Windows. In these next steps, I'll show you
how to use the One-Click Installer, which
is the easiest and preferred method for
Windows users.

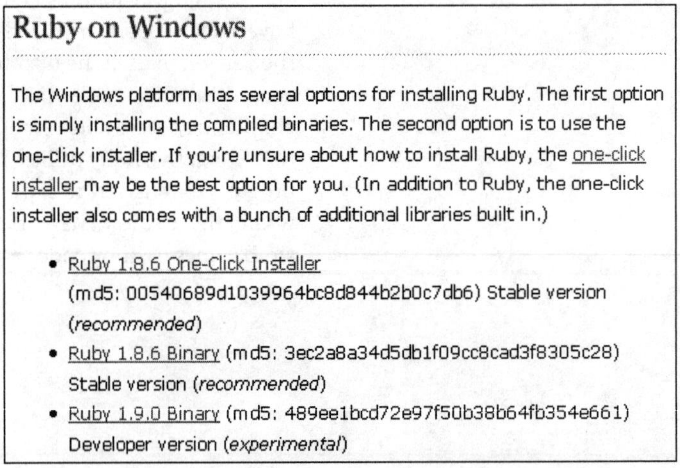

Ruby on Windows

The Windows platform has several options for installing Ruby. The first option
is simply installing the compiled binaries. The second option is to use the
one-click installer. If you're unsure about how to install Ruby, the one-click
installer may be the best option for you. (In addition to Ruby, the one-click
installer also comes with a bunch of additional libraries built in.)

- Ruby 1.8.6 One-Click Installer
  (md5: 00540689d1039964bc8d844b2b0c7db6) Stable version
  (*recommended*)
- Ruby 1.8.6 Binary (md5: 3ec2a8a34d5db1f09cc8cad3f8305c28)
  Stable version (*recommended*)
- Ruby 1.9.0 Binary (md5: 489ee1bcd72e97f50b38b64fb354e661)
  Developer version (*experimental*)

Figure 1.1 The Windows-specific options for installing Ruby.

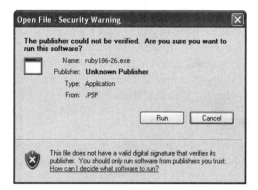

Figure 1.2 Click Run if you see this prompt.

Figure 1.3 The first page of the Ruby Setup Wizard.

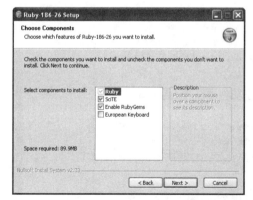

Figure 1.4 Along with Ruby itself, also install SciTE and RubyGems.

To install Ruby on Windows:

1. In your Web browser, head to www.ruby-lang.org.

   This is the official Web site for the Ruby programming language.

2. Click Downloads.

3. In the section entitled Ruby on Windows (**Figure 1.1**), click the Ruby One-Click Installer link to download the file.

   At the time of this writing, the version downloaded is 1.8.6.

4. After the file has been completely downloaded, double-click it to begin the installation process.

5. If you see a Security Warning (**Figure 1.2**), click Run.

   This Ruby Setup Wizard (**Figure 1.3**) should then start.

6. When given the option to select the components to be installed (**Figure 1.4**), make sure that SciTE and RubyGems are also checked.

   This is the default configuration. SciTE is a text editor that you can use to write Ruby scripts (although you can use any other text editor as well). RubyGems are libraries of extra code that you'll commonly use in your Ruby applications. This topic is introduced in Chapter 12, "RubyGems."

7. When the installation process is complete, click Next, and then Finish on the final page.

8. Head to the section "Testing an Installation" of this chapter to learn what to do next.

INSTALLATION ON WINDOWS

Installation on Mac OS X

As mentioned in the introduction to this chapter, Mac OS X comes with Ruby pre-installed. On the current version of Mac OS X, 10.5 or Leopard (at the time of this writing), the most current version of Ruby—1.8.6—is included. You can check to see if Ruby is already installed, and what version, by following the steps in the section "Testing an Installation" of this chapter. You should do that now, before following these installation instructions, because your Ruby install may already be up to date.

If you do need to install Ruby on Mac OS X, there are several ways of doing so, all of which require that you have already installed Apple's Xcode application and corresponding Developer Tools (freely available from http://developer.apple.com). Once you've done that, one option for installing Ruby is to use MacPorts (www.macports.org), a free application that makes it easier to set up open-source software on a Mac. Simply download the MacPorts disk image file from the Web site and then run the package installer. Once you've added MacPorts, installing Ruby is simply a matter of executing this command within the Terminal application:

```
port install ruby
```

Another option is to build Ruby from the source code. This is a little more advanced but not too complicated. Just follow these steps:

To install Ruby on Mac OS X:

1. In your Web browser, head to www.ruby-lang.org.
   This is the official Web site for the Ruby programming language.

2. Click Downloads.

3. In the section entitled Ruby Source Code (**Figure 1.5**), click the recommended stable version link to download the file.
   At the time of this writing, the Ruby source code link name is *Ruby 1.8.6-p114*.

Ruby Source Code

Installing from the source code is a great solution for when you are comfortable enough with your platform and perhaps need specific settings for your environment. It's also a good solution in the event that there are no other premade packages for your platform.

- Ruby 1.8.6-p114 (md5: 500a9f11613d6c8ab6dcf12bec1b3ed3) Stable Version (*recommended*)
- Stable Snapshot This is tar'ed and gzip'ed file of the latest stable CVS. It should be better than the last stable release.
- Nightly Snapshot This is tar'ed and gzip'ed file of the latest CVS. It may contain unfixed problems.

For information about the Ruby Subversion repository, see our Ruby Core page.

Figure 1.5 The Ruby source code can be installed on practically every operating system.

4. Double-click the downloaded file to expand it.

The downloaded file will have a name like `ruby-1.8.6-p114.tar.gz`. This is a compressed format that needs to be decompressed. Double-clicking it within the Finder will accomplish that, resulting in a folder called `ruby-1.8.6-p114`.

5. Open the Terminal application.

You'll find this within the `/Applications/Utilities` folder.

6. Type `cd`, followed by a space.

Don't press Return or do anything else yet! The `cd` command changes the current directory; it'll be used to move into the Ruby folder created in Step 4 (by default, the Terminal opens in your home folder, which may not be where the downloaded file is).

7. Go to the Finder, grab the Ruby folder (created in Step 4), drag it into the Terminal window, and drop it.

The end result will be a complete `cd` command pointing to the Ruby folder (**Figure 1.6**). Once you've done this, press Return to execute the command.

8. Type the following and press Return (**Figure 1.7**):

`./configure`

To build software from the source files, execute the `configure` command. This command is used to dictate how the software should be put together. The period and slash preceding this command say to execute the `configure` command found within the current directory.

If an error occurs, the configuration will stop abruptly and an error message will indicate the problem. You'll need to search online (for your operating system) to find the solution. If you have problems or questions, you can also use the book's corresponding forum (head to `www.DMCInsights.com/phorum/`).

9. Assuming you saw no errors, type `make` and press Return.

The `make` command builds the software per the configuration already declared. Executing this command could take some time (feel free to use other applications in the interim). Again, if an error occurs, make note of the error message, perform a search, and/or use the support forum.

continues on next page

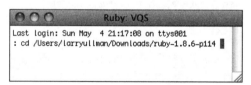

Figure 1.6 The proper command to move into the folder of Ruby source code.

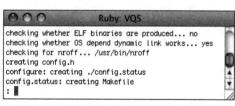

Figure 1.7 The end result after successfully configuring Ruby.

INSTALLATION ON MAC OS X

10. Assuming no errors, type `sudo make install` and press Return.

    This is the final step, performing the actual installation. You'll need to enter your administrative password at the prompt.

11. Head to the section "Testing an Installation" of this chapter to learn what to do next.

✔ Tips

■ To change where Ruby is installed (for example, so as not to conflict with an existing installation), use

   `./configure --prefix=/usr/local`

   You can change `/usr/local` to wherever you'd like Ruby to be installed.

■ For added features, Ruby can be installed along with the `readline` utility. This tool makes it easier to edit and retrieve commands. Search the Web (using *ruby readline mac*) for instructions.

■ From a command line (like the Terminal), you can also expand an archived *.tar.gz* folder using:

   `tar -xzvf rubyFileName.tar.gz`

■ Fink (`www.finkproject.org`) is another application that makes it easier to set up open-source software on a Mac. At the time of this writing, no ready-made version is available for Leopard, however.

Installation on Linux

The exact steps you take to install Ruby on Linux (or Unix) depend upon what distribution you're using. Installation on Red Hat Linux can be accomplished using the Red Hat Package Manager (`rpm`):

`rpm -Uhv ruby-*.rpm`

Debian and Ubuntu environments can use `apt-get`:

`sudo apt-get install ruby irb ri`
`→ rdoc gem`

Of course, you can also build Ruby from the source following the steps outlined in the Mac OS X instructions.

However you install Ruby, just make sure that you also install `ri`, `irb`, `rdoc`, and `gem`, all of which are necessary to follow along with this book's content. (As of Ruby 1.9, `ri`, `irb`, and `gem` are installed with Ruby; in earlier versions they must each be installed separately.)

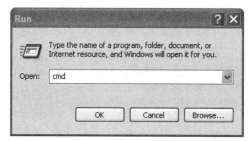

Figure 1.8 Get to the console interface on Windows by entering cmd in this Run dialog.

Figure 1.9 A DOS prompt or console window (although the default appearance is white text on a black background).

Testing an Installation

To confirm that Ruby is installed on your computer, you'll need to invoke the Ruby interpreter. This is a command-line utility, meaning that you'll invoke it using a *DOS prompt* (also called a *console window*) on Windows or a Terminal application on Mac OS X and Linux.

There are two good reasons it's imperative that you test your Ruby installation:

1. So that you know you have a working version of Ruby installed (and what version that is).

2. Because the Ruby interpreter will also be used to run Ruby scripts (as introduced in the next chapter).

The following sequence will show you how to access a command-line interface and invoke the Ruby interpreter.

To use the Ruby interpreter:

1. Access your computer via a command-line interface.

   On Windows, select the Run option in the Start menu, and then enter cmd in the text box (**Figure 1.8**). **Figure 1.9** shows the result.

   Mac OS X, Linux, and Unix users just need to open the Terminal application (Mac users can find this within the /Applications/Utilities folder).

continues on next page

2. Type the following and press Return or Enter (**Figure 1.10**):

```
ruby --version
```

This command, if it works, will confirm that Ruby has been successfully installed. It will also report the version of Ruby that was invoked.

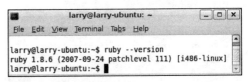

Figure 1.10 Confirmation that my Ubuntu Linux computer is running Ruby 1.8.6.

3. Type the following and press Return or Enter (**Figure 1.11**):

```
ruby --help
```

To learn more about how the Ruby interpreter can be used, run this command.

✔ Tip

■ The Ruby interpreter can execute code using

```
ruby -e 'code to execute'
```

Normally you'll use the interpreter to execute scripts, though. The interactive Ruby utility (irb) is better for handling small snippets of code.

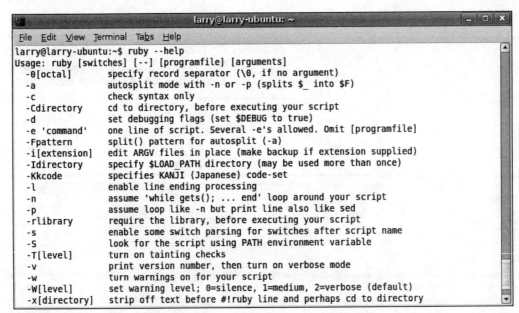

Figure 1.11 The first part of the Ruby help file, showing some of the available options.

Ruby Documentation

You cannot program in Ruby without installing the Ruby interpreter, but almost as important is being able to access Ruby's documentation. If you have Internet access, the best option is to visit www.ruby-doc.org in your Web browser. There's lots of good information there, ranging from basic documentation to tutorials and lists of books.

If you're running Windows, you can run the fxri application, which is installed along with Ruby (**Figure 1.12**). The left-hand column displays a list of topics for which there is documentation (the documentation itself will appear at the top of the right-hand column). There's also a search box to help narrow down the topic list.

A third method for accessing Ruby documentation is to use the command-line ri

utility. It's a quick way to view details about a particular class or method. To use it, enter ri, followed by the name of a class or method on which you want information:

```
ri ClassName
ri method_name
ri ClassName.method_name
ri ClassName::class_method_name
ri ClassName#instance_method_name
```

What is meant by *ClassName* versus *method_name* versus *class_method_name* versus *instance_method_name* is probably not clear to you now, but it will be in time. For now, rest assured that if it's not clear as to what you are referring, ri will let you know.

Within the ri interface (once documentation has been presented), press *f* to move forward a page, *b* to move back a page, and *q* to quit.

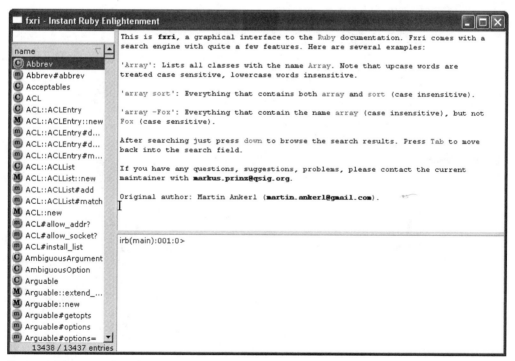

Figure 1.12 The extremely useful fxri application on Windows.

To view Ruby documentation:

1. Access your computer from a command-line interface.

See Step 1 under "Testing an Installation" if you need details on how to do this.

2. Type ri and press Return/Enter (**Figure 1.13**).

It will likely be a couple of moments before anything happens, Then the result will be documentation on how to use the utility. Press *f* to move forward a page, *b* to move back a page, and *q* to quit.

You will need to press *q* to exit ri in order to continue following these steps.

3. Type ri String and press Return/Enter (**Figure 1.14**).

This will show the documentation for the String class. A *class* is a blueprint for a thing, and is the basis of object-oriented programming. So the String class defines how Ruby handles quoted characters and text.

Make sure that you use a capital *S* in *String*, or else the result will be a list of Ruby terms that have the word *string* in them.

Press *q* to exit ri in order to continue following these steps.

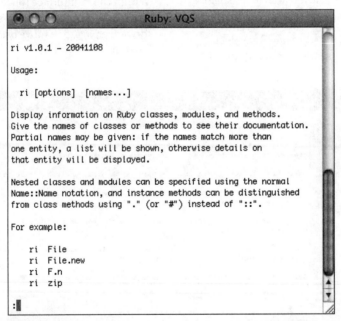

```
ri v1.0.1 - 20041108

Usage:

  ri [options]  [names...]

Display information on Ruby classes, modules, and methods.
Give the names of classes or methods to see their documentation.
Partial names may be given: if the names match more than
one entity, a list will be shown, otherwise details on
that entity will be displayed.

Nested classes and modules can be specified using the normal
Name::Name notation, and instance methods can be distinguished
from class methods using "." (or "#") instead of "::".

For example:

    ri  File
    ri  File.new
    ri  F.n
    ri  zip

:
```

Figure 1.13 The ri help file.

4. Type ri Date.year and press Return/
Enter (**Figure 1.15**).

To view the documentation for a method,
which is to say a *function*, defined within
a class, use the syntax ri *ClassName.
method_name*. Of course, you can find the
list of methods defined in a class by using
ri *ClassName*.

Press *q* to exit ri in order to continue following these steps.

✔ Tips

- You can also view Ruby documentation
  by searching the Web or heading directly
  to www.ruby-doc.org.

- The ri utility gets its information from a
  utility called *RDoc*. This program generates Ruby documentation in both HTML
  and ri formats.

- The command ri is short for *Ruby Index*
  or *Ruby Information* or *Ruby Interactive*
  (no one's exactly sure which).

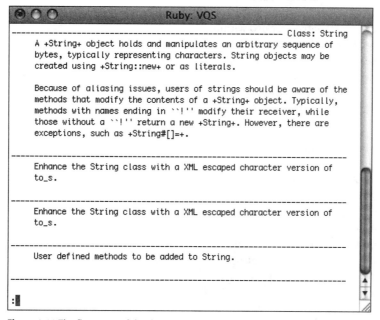

Figure 1.14 The first page of the documentation for the common String class.

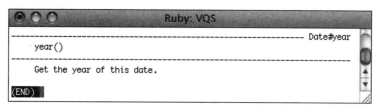

Figure 1.15 The documentation for the year method of the Date class.

Interactive Ruby

The third and final command-line utility that you will use in this book, and in your Ruby programming, is the interactive Ruby shell, known as irb. This application creates an environment in which you can test Ruby code. For the purposes of this book, irb will frequently be used to demonstrate new concepts. For the purposes of any Ruby developer, irb provides a great way to experiment with snippets of code.

The premise is simple: enter an expression, such as 2 + 2, and irb will display the result. But irb can be used for more than just simple statements. Variables defined within irb can be used later in that same session, as can methods or classes. Of course, you may not know what methods or classes are yet (Chapter 6, "Creating Methods," and Chapter 7, "Creating Classes," get into these two subjects), but keep reading.

Note that in these steps (and in the rest of the book), you'll see images taken on both Windows and Mac OS X. The point in doing so is to make all readers (or most, anyway) comfortable with what they should see. Furthermore, doing so demonstrates that Ruby is generally cross-platform safe and that what works in irb on one operating system should also work in irb on another.

To use irb:

1. Access your computer from a command-line interface.

   Step 1 in the section "Testing Your Installation" discuss how to do this on Windows, Mac OS X, and Linux.

2. Type irb and press Return/Enter.

   This will start a new irb session. You'll see that the prompt changes to reflect this.

3. Type 2 + 2 and press Return/Enter (**Figure 1.16**).

   Although I haven't formally covered math in Ruby yet, this should be easy enough to follow. Note that irb displays the result of this statement (which is 4).

4. Type 2 + and press Return/Enter (**Figure 1.17**).

   This is an incomplete statement that has no result. As you can see in the figure, the prompt changes, indicating that the statement has not yet been completed.

continues on next page

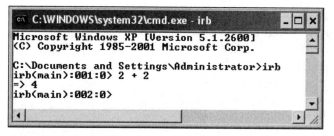

Figure 1.16 Performing simple math within irb (on Windows).

```
C:\WINDOWS\system32\cmd.exe - irb
Microsoft Windows XP [Version 5.1.2600]
(C) Copyright 1985-2001 Microsoft Corp.

C:\Documents and Settings\Administrator>irb
irb(main):001:0> 2 + 2
=> 4
irb(main):002:0> 2 +
irb(main):003:0*
```

Figure 1.17 The asterisk at the end of the prompt means that the previous statement is incomplete (and therefore no result is yet shown).

INTERACTIVE RUBY

5. Type 2 and press Return/Enter.

This completes the statement begun in Step 4. At this point, irb can display the result.

6. Type name = 'larry' and press Return/Enter (**Figure 1.18**).

This line creates a String object with a value of *larry* (feel free, of course, to use your own name instead). As you can see in the figure, irb returns the result of the expression, which is the string *larry*.

7. Type name.upcase and press Return/Enter (**Figure 1.19**).

The upcase method of the String class returns every letter in the string in its uppercase format. If you've never done any object-oriented programming before, this syntax may be new to you. To call the method (or function) on an object, use *object_name.method_name*. So applying the upcase method to the name object results in name.upcase.

8. Press Control+L to clear the console.

After you do this, the previous work will no longer be visible. However, you'll still be in irb and your code history will remain (meaning, for example, that declared variables will still exist).

Unfortunately, this only works for Mac OS X and Unix; there is no keyboard command to clear the screen when using irb on Windows.

9. Type exit or quit and press Return/Enter to leave irb and return to the normal prompt.

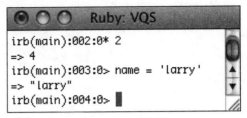

Figure 1.18 Using irb on Mac OS X.

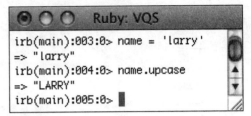

Figure 1.19 The result of applying the upcase method to the string variable.

INTERACTIVE RUBY

✔ Tips

■ If the `readline` utility was also installed, `irb` can take advantage of tab completion. To enable this within an `irb` session, enter the following:

```
require 'irb/completion'
```

Or start `irb` using

```
irb --readline
```

To use tab completion, type part of a keyword, and then press Tab. If there is only one matching keyword for what you've typed, the rest of the keyword should be automatically completed. If there are multiple possible matches, press Tab a second time to see the possible options.

■ The `readline` utility also allows you to navigate through your command history using the up and down arrow keys.

■ You can create multiple `irb` sessions by invoking `irb` within the `irb` shell. The `jobs` command lists every running `irb` session. Type `fg` *n* to switch to a different session (where *n* is the identifying session number indicated by the `jobs` command).

■ The interactive Ruby shell can also be used to execute Ruby scripts, displaying the results as it runs.

■ The `fxri` application on Windows (see the lower-right area of Figure 1.12) includes an interactive Ruby shell. Using `fxri` therefore saves you a trip to the command line and places both the testing environment and the documentation in one window.

INTERACTIVE RUBY

Customizing irb

As you'll use the interactive Ruby shell frequently, you might find it worth your while to
change its default behavior. Some of the ways
you would customize irb's look and behavior
involve adding arguments when invoking the
utility. For example, the --simple-prompt
option changes the prompt used:

```
irb --simple-prompt
```

Or you can use --prompt to indicate the
prompt style to use. Follow this with *null*,
default, *classic*, *simple*, *xmp*, or *inf-ruby*:

```
irb --prompt xmp
```

You can also customize irb by creating an
initialization file. This is just a plain text file
of Ruby code that's read by irb when it's
invoked. As an example, irb can take advantage of tab completion (see the first tip in
the preceding section). To always enable this
feature, place this line in an initialization file:

```
require 'irb/completion'
```

Other ways you can change some of irb's
configuration in an initialization file involve
updating corresponding values in the IRB.
conf hash (hashes are discussed in detail in
Chapter 4, "Arrays, Ranges, and Hashes").
To always use a certain prompt in irb, you
would add this code to your initialization file:

```
IRB.conf[:PROMPT_MODE] = :SIMPLE
```

To best demonstrate how you would use this
information, let's walk through the process
of creating an irb initialization file.

Script 1.1 This script will be run when irb is invoked, thereby changing how it behaves.

```
         ●●●              📄 Script
1    # Script 1.1 - .irbrc
2    # irb initialization (configuration) script
3
4    # Include support for tab completion:
5    require 'irb/completion'
6
7    # Change the prompt:
8    IRB.conf[:PROMPT_MODE] = :SIMPLE
```

To customize irb:

1. Create a new, blank document in your text editor or IDE (**Script 1.1**).

This will be your first Ruby script. You can create it in any program that can make a plain text file.

2. Add the following on the first two lines:

```
# Script 1.1 - .irbrc
# irb initialization (configuration)
→ script
```

Both lines are comments, indicating the name and purpose of the file. Comments in Ruby code are preceded by a number (or pound) sign.

For easier cross-reference purposes, every script in the book will begin with a comment indicating its corresponding script number.

3. On a subsequent line, add:

```
require 'irb/completion'
```

As already stated, this line enables tab completion support with irb.

4. On a subsequent line, add:

```
IRB.conf[:PROMPT_MODE] = :SIMPLE
```

The default irb prompt can be daunting, especially to those new to Ruby. Instead, this line tells irb to start with a simple prompt (you'll see the difference between the two prompts soon).

5. Save the file.

If you're running Mac OS X or Linux, save the file in your home directory with the name .irbrc (yes, starting with a period).

If you're running Windows, save the file in your home directory with the name irbrc (without a period or extension).

By home directory on Windows, I mean C:\Documents and Settings*username*, where *username* is your actual username.

continues on next page

CUSTOMIZING IRB

6. If you're running Windows, tell `irb` where to find the initialization file.

Windows users have to also do the following:

1. Close all existing console windows.

2. Right-click My Computer and select Properties.

3. In the Advanced tab (**Figure 1.20**), click Environment Variables.

4. In the Environment Variables dialog (**Figure 1.21**), click New in the User Variables section (the top section of the dialog).

5. In the New User Variable dialog, enter *IRBRC* as the Variable name and the full path to the file saved in Step 5 as the Variable value (**Figure 1.22**). Windows Explorer can help reveal this last value (in my case it was `C:\Documents and Settings\Administrator\irbrc`).

6. Click OK in all three dialogs to close them.

7. Access your computer from a command-line interface.

Step 1 in the section "Testing Your Installation" discusses how to do this on Windows, Mac OS X, and Linux.

8. Type `irb` and press Return/Enter.

You should see that `irb` now uses a simple prompt.

✔ Tip

■ There are tons of `irb` configuration recommendations to be found online. Two specific add-ons are Wirble (`http://pablotron.org/software/wirble/`) and Utility Belt (`http://utilitybelt.rubyforge.org/`).

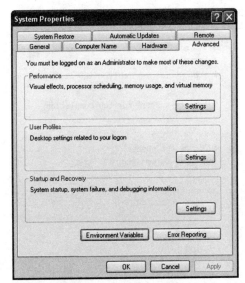

Figure 1.20 The Advanced tab of the System Properties dialog.

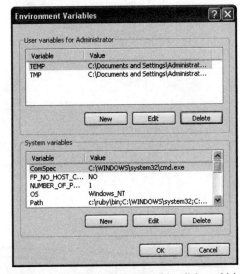

Figure 1.21 The Environment Variables dialog, which lists both user-specific and system-wide variables.

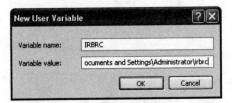

Figure 1.22 The dialog for adding a new variable.

2

SIMPLE SCRIPTS

This chapter covers everything you'll need to know when it comes to writing and executing Ruby scripts. Although the interactive Ruby shell (`irb`), covered in Chapter 1, "Getting Started," is a wonderful learning and practice tool, running saved files of Ruby code is the greater goal.

Along with the steps for creating a simple Ruby script, you'll learn multiple ways of running it, how to output data (text and numbers), and how to take keyboard-supplied input. The chapter concludes by discussing Ruby's syntax for adding comments to code. The information presented here is pretty simple but will be required for many of the later chapters.

Creating a Basic Script

A Ruby script is a plain text file that can be created in most text editors or Integrated Development Environments (IDEs). As for the script's basic syntax, there is none! Ruby does not require opening and closing tags like PHP or a main function like Java, C, or C++.

Most programming books use the common *Hello, world!* example to demonstrate a basic script. Rather than rehash something you'll find everywhere, this first script will be a novel and impressive *Greetings, planet!* example instead: When the script is executed, it will output that message.

One way to generate output in Ruby is to use the aptly named print method:

```
print "Whatever text"
```

Do note that unlike other programming languages you may have seen or used, Ruby does not require semicolons to terminate a line. Instead, the newline character (i.e., the pressing of Return or Enter at the end of the line) indicates the end of a statement to be executed. (There's actually a little more to how Ruby treats newlines and statements, but let's go with this for now.)

I'll also add, before walking through these next steps, that Ruby scripts are normally given an .rb extension. This isn't obligatory, but it does clearly indicate the programming language of a script without having to look at its contents.

To create a basic Ruby script:

1. Begin a new text file in your editor or IDE (**Script 2.1**).

   You can use any application you want here, although some are better than others. For Windows, you can use the plain text editor SciTE, which can be installed with Ruby (see Chapter 1), or Notepad, which comes with the operating system. For Linux, vi, vim, and emacs are popular editors. For Mac OS X, you might consider BBEdit or TextWrangler from Bare Bones (www.barebones.com), or TextMate (www.macromates.com).

   If you'd prefer to use an IDE, NetBeans (www.netbeans.org) is a popular choice. It's an open-source project that runs on most operating systems. It does require that you've installed the Java Development Kit (JDK, available for free from http://java.sun.com).

Script 2.1 A very basic Ruby script, which outputs a message.

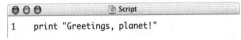

```
1    print "Greetings, planet!"
```

2. As the very first line, type:

```
print "Greetings, planet!"
```

And that's all there is to it! As long as you type this all on one line and use the same quotation mark type to both open and close the text, it should work without error.

3. Save the file as greetings.rb.

You likely want to create a special folder for all of your Ruby scripts (maybe even containing subfolders for each chapter in this book). Make sure you save the file in a plain text format without any additional extensions (hidden or otherwise).

✔ Tips

■ If you're using Notepad on Windows, you'll need to change the Save as type value to *All Files* (**Figure 2.1**) or else Notepad will add .txt to the file's name. For this reason, among others, you may not want to use Notepad. Notepad++ (http://notepad-plus.sourceforge.net) is a good alternative.

■ Using an IDE with Ruby support, such as NetBeans, can have many benefits, including debugging tools and the ability to execute a script without leaving the application (e.g., in NetBeans, choose Run Main Project from within the Run menu or press F6). Some text editors, like SciTE and BBEdit, also have this feature.

Figure 2.1 Notepad's Save As dialog; change the Save as type option to use the .rb extension.

CREATING A BASIC SCRIPT

Execution on Windows

Ruby is a scripting language, meaning that an executable—the installed ruby.exe on Windows—is used to run a script, executing the code it finds therein. There are several ways of executing a Ruby script on Windows, each of which is quite simple.

To execute a script:

◆ Select Tools > Go in SciTE.

The Ruby One Click installer for Windows can also install the SciTE text editor. If you're using this program to write your Ruby scripts, you can quickly and easily run a script by choosing Tools > Go or by pressing F5. Make sure you've saved the file prior to doing this.

The result will appear on the right side of the application (**Figure 2.2**).

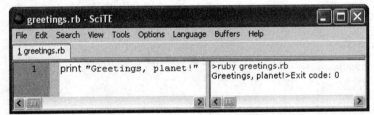

Figure 2.2 The Ruby script on the left and the result of its execution on the right, as viewed in SciTE on Windows.

◆ Select Run > Run Main Project in NetBeans.

If you're using the NetBeans IDE, you can also run a script without leaving the application. Choose Run Main Project from within the Run menu (even a simple script will be part of a project) or press F6.

The result will appear at the bottom of the application (**Figure 2.3**).

◆ If you're using a text editor, use the command line to execute the script.

To do so, follow the steps in the section "Command-Line Execution" of this chapter (next).

✔ Tip

■ If you installed Ruby using the One Click Installer, or otherwise took steps to associate .rb files with the Ruby executable, you can also run Ruby scripts on Windows by double-clicking the actual file. If you do so, a console window will open, run the script, and close. Unfortunately, with an example that doesn't do much, it'll all happen in a blink of an eye.

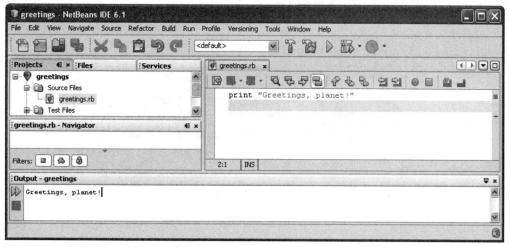

Figure 2.3 The Ruby script at the top right and the result of its execution on the bottom, as viewed in NetBeans on Windows.

EXECUTION ON WINDOWS

Command-Line Execution

Ruby is a scripting language, meaning that an executable—the Ruby interpreter—is used to run a script, executing the code it finds therein. If you're using a plain text editor to write your Ruby scripts, you'll likely need to execute it from a command-line interface. This may be the case for most Mac OS X, Unix, and Linux users, as well as some on Windows.

Before getting into the steps, let me point out that while it is worthwhile to know how to execute a Ruby script from a command-line interface, also do a quick check to see if your text editor or IDE has the ability to execute scripts you create. If so, that'll likely be the fastest and most foolproof option.

To execute a script:

1. Access your computer via a command-line interface.

   Chapter 1 has instructions, if you don't already know what steps to take.

2. At the prompt, change to the directory where the script was saved by typing `cd /path/to/folder` (**Figure 2.4**).

   Note that you must enter the actual path to the folder. One shortcut is to drag the folder (i.e., from the Finder on Mac OS X or Windows Explorer on Windows) and drop it into the console window.

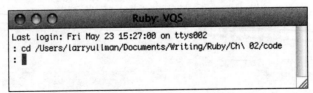

Figure 2.4 Moving into the proper directory (on Mac OS X).

Viewing Ruby Warnings

When using the command-line Ruby interpreter to execute a script (e.g., `ruby scriptname.rb`), you can pass arguments to the Ruby interpreter to change how it runs. The most important of these is `-w`, which enables warnings. When you use this, the Ruby interpreter will notify you of issues in the code that may (or may not) be indicative of a problem.

Alternatively, you can change the warning level under which a script is run: use `ruby -W# scriptname.rb`, where # is the warning level. The default level is 1. To run a Ruby script without seeing any warnings, use `ruby -W0 scriptname.rb`. However, doing so will mean that there may be problems in your code that you're just ignoring (it doesn't actually make the problems go away).

3. Type `ruby -w greetings.rb` and press Enter or Return (**Figure 2.5**).

The command-line Ruby interpreter is demonstrated in Chapter 1 as a way of testing the installation and seeing your version of Ruby. Here it's used to execute a Ruby script. The `-w` argument means that Ruby should notify you of any warnings: code issues that may be a problem. For more on warnings, see the sidebar "Viewing Ruby Warnings." If these steps don't work for you, see the tips for potential causes.

✔ Tips

■ If you see an error that the file cannot be found, you're probably not in the same directory as the Ruby script or it doesn't have the correct name or extension.

■ If you see an error that the Ruby command is not found, the Ruby executable is probably not installed or not in your system's path.

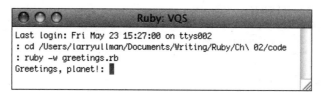

Figure 2.5 The result of successfully executing the Ruby script.

COMMAND-LINE EXECUTION

Making Scripts Executable

For Mac OS X, Unix, and Linux computers, there's one final way to execute a Ruby script. This method still uses the command line but does not invoke the Ruby interpreter directly. Instead, text will be added to the first line of the script to indicate that the Ruby interpreter should be used to execute its code:

```
#!/usr/bin/ruby -w
```

This is called a *shebang* line (named so because of the first two characters).

After adding this line to the script, you can then change the script's properties so that it's executable, and then run the script directly.

To directly execute a script:

1. Access your computer via a command-line interface.

Again, Chapter 1 has instructions, if you don't already know what steps to take.

2. Type `which ruby` and press Return (**Figure 2.6**).

This command will reveal the version of Ruby being used by the terminal sessions. You'll need to know this value so that you can add it to the Ruby script.

3. Open `greetings.rb` (Script 2.1) in your text editor or IDE, if it is not already.

4. Before the `print` line, add (**Script 2.2**):

```
#!/usr/bin/ruby -w
```

Change the value between the shebang and the *-w* so that it matches what was returned in Step 2.

5. Save the file.

For the purposes of these steps and to distinguish this version from the original, I'll save this file as `greetings2.rb`.

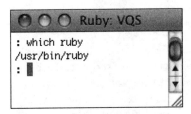

Figure 2.6 Finding the location of the Ruby executable on Mac OS X.

Script 2.2 The shebang line is added to Script 2.1 so that it can be executed without overtly invoking the command-line Ruby interpreter.

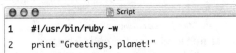

```
1    #!/usr/bin/ruby -w
2    print "Greetings, planet!"
```

6. Back in the terminal application, change to the directory where the script was saved by typing `cd /path/to/folder`.

Again, use your actual path value here.

7. Type `chmod +x greetings2.rb`.

The `chmod` command changes the ownership and permissions properties of a file or directory (i.e., who can do what with it). The *+x* option says that executable status should be added to the item's existing permissions.

8. Run the script by typing `./greetings2.rb` (**Figure 2.7**).

You can run a program from a command line by just typing its name. However, because the operating system likely doesn't know to look in this directory for executables, you have to preface the script's name with `./`, which loosely means "run the `greetings2.rb` script found within this directory."

✔ Tip

■ Alternatively, you can change the she-bang line to `#!/usr/bin/env ruby`. This indicates that the system's Ruby should be used, wherever it may be found. Using this method will make your script more portable across Unix and Mac OS X systems, but you cannot run the Ruby interpreter with the invaluable `-w` flag this way without taking some extra steps.

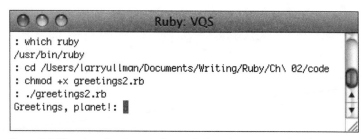

```
: which ruby
/usr/bin/ruby
: cd /Users/larryullman/Documents/Writing/Ruby/Ch\ 02/code
: chmod +x greetings2.rb
: ./greetings2.rb
Greetings, planet!:
```

Figure 2.7 After changing the script's permissions, I can execute it without explicitly calling the Ruby interpreter.

MAKING SCRIPTS EXECUTABLE

Creating Output

In the first section of this chapter, I introduce the print method as a way of creating output. Although print is easily understood and works just fine, it's actually not the most commonly used method in Ruby for this purpose. That honor goes to puts:

```
puts "Whatever text."
```

What differentiates puts from print is that puts will append a newline (\n) character to the output, saving you from having to do so yourself. It's even smart enough *not* to add a second newline character if the output already ends with one:

```
puts "Whatever text.\n"
```

To really appreciate the effect this has, the next example will use both methods and the corresponding output will highlight their differences.

To use puts:

1. Create a new Ruby script in your text editor or IDE (**Script 2.3**).

   If you want to execute the script using the technique outlined in the section "Making Scripts Executable" of this chapter, you'll need to add the proper shebang line. You will not see those in any more of this book's scripts, however, as I normally invoke the Ruby interpreter directly or use an application's built-in hook to run a script.

Script 2.3 These four calls to the puts and print methods will demonstrate how they differ in the output they generate.

```
1  puts "- puts -"
2  print "- print -"
3  puts "- puts -"
4  print "- print -"
```

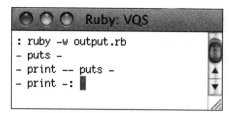

Figure 2.8 The result of executing `output.rb` (Script 2.3).

2. Add these lines:

```
puts "- puts -"
print "- print -"
puts "- puts -"
print "- print -"
```

This is very trivial, of course, but the point is to demonstrate how these two methods differ. Each outputs the name of the method being used, along with spaces and hyphens.

3. Save the script as `output.rb`.

4. Run the script using any of the techniques already covered (**Figure 2.8**).

As you can see in the output, each call to `puts` results in the following `print` output being placed on a subsequent line. Conversely, the first call to `print` results in the second `puts` output appearing immediately thereafter (on the same line). The script ends after the second call to `print`, so the cursor appears immediately after that text.

✔ Tips

■ You'll almost always use `puts` for generating output unless you specifically want the next output, prompt, or whatever to follow on the same line.

■ The `p` method also appends newlines to output, like `puts`, but is commonly used for dumping the values of variables.

■ Just to be clear, you can also use `print`, `puts`, and `p` methods within `irb`, not solely in Ruby scripts.

CREATING OUTPUT

29

Taking Input

Just as you can use the `puts` method to generate output, a script can take input by invoking `gets`. To use this method, assign its invocation to a variable:

```
input = gets
```

When that line of code is executed, a cursor will appear in the output, awaiting user action. Once the user presses Enter or Return, whatever the user typed—including that Enter or Return character—is assigned to the `input` variable.

If you're reading this book sequentially, you haven't been formally introduced to variables as of yet (that begins in Chapter 3, "Simple Types"). For now, I'll just explain that the name of the variable can contain letters, numbers, and underscores. The first character cannot be a number and should not be a capital letter (which is used to create a special type called a constant).

To demonstrate this concept, the next Ruby script will prompt the user for their name, accept what the user types, and then greet them by name (**Figure 2.9**).

To take input:

1. Create a new Ruby script in your text editor or IDE (**Script 2.4**).

2. Prompt the user for their name.

   ```
   puts "What is your name?"
   ```

   Before expecting the user to input anything, an application should indicate what it's looking for. Because the `puts` method is used to print the prompt, the cursor (for the user's input) will appear on the next line.

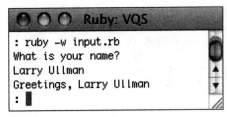

Figure 2.9 This next Ruby script will be interactive.

Script 2.4 This script generates a prompt, reads in the user-typed response, and then uses that response in a greeting.

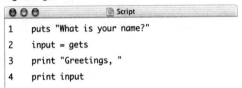

```
1    puts "What is your name?"
2    input = gets
3    print "Greetings, "
4    print input
```

TAKING INPUT

3. Get the user input.

```
input = gets
```

As already stated, this line will create a cursor in the output and await the user's response. Whatever the user types will be assigned to the input variable.

4. Greet the user by name.

```
print "Greetings, "
```

```
print input
```

To greet the user by name, the word *Greetings*, followed by a comma and a space is first outputted. Then the input variable is outputted. Because the print method is being used here, the person's name (whatever they typed) will appear on the same line as *Greetings* (see Figure 2.9).

5. Save the file as input.rb and run it.

Figure 2.9 shows the result when running the script from the command line. **Figure 2.10** shows the result when running the script within NetBeans. You can also run this within SciTE, but you'll need to click in the output area to enter your input, even though you won't see a prompt there.

✔ Tips

■ Even though the print method does not append newlines to the output, this script's greeting still concludes with a newline character. This is evident in Figure 2.9, where the colon prompt (after the script terminates) is on its own line. That newline is part of the input variable's value (outputted by print), which the user supplied when they pressed Enter or Return. The String class's chomp method, which you'll learn about in Chapter 3, can be used to remove a user-supplied newline.

■ The gets method actually reads in data from the *standard input*. If you execute this script using any of the techniques outlined in this chapter, the standard input will be the keyboard. On the other hand, you could execute the script while providing it with input:

```
ruby -w input.rb < textfile.txt
```

In that case, the contents of textfile.txt (located in the same directory as the Ruby script) will be used as the input.

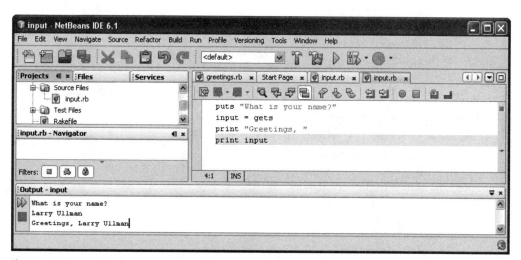

Figure 2.10 The result of executing input.rb within NetBeans.

Making Comments

Proper programming involves not just input, output, variables, control structures, and the like, but also documentation. Even if the end user will likely never see a script's comments, proper documentation is critical, never to be taken for granted. As accessible as Ruby is, there will come a time when you'll need to revisit some work you've done and will be thankful for any notes that you left.

Comments in Ruby begin with the pound or number sign (#):

```
# This is a comment.
```

Anything on the line after that character is a comment, which means it won't be executed by Ruby.

Comments can also be placed after an executed statement:

```
puts "Hello" # Say 'Hello'
```

To demonstrate this, and to reinforce the difference between puts and print, let's rewrite the preceding example, switching the use of those two methods. The script will contain plenty of comments along the way.

To use comments:

1. Begin a new Ruby script in your text editor or IDE (**Script 2.5**).

   ```
   # Script 2.5 - comments.rb
   # Note: the uses of print and puts are
   # reversed for demo purposes.
   # Compare with Script 2.4 - input.rb
   ```

   The scripts in this book will use a comment like the first one—indicating its number and name—as the very first line. Doing so will make it easier to follow when viewing the scripts in the book or in the downloaded versions (available at www.DMCInsights.com/ruby/).

Script 2.5 This script further highlights the differences between the puts and print methods, as well as demonstrates how to add comments to Ruby code.

```
1   # Script 2.5 - comments.rb
2
3   # Note: the uses of print and puts are
4   # reversed for demo purposes.
5   # Compare with Script 2.4 - input.rb
6
7   # Ask the user for their name:
8   print "What is your name?"
9
10  # Read in the input:
11  input = gets
12
13  # Print a greeting:
14  puts "Greetings, "
15
16  # Reprint the user input:
17  puts input
```

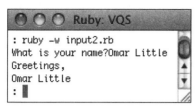

Figure 2.11 If you print the prompt, the user input will appear immediately after it. If you use puts for the greeting, the input will appear on a subsequent line.

Then I have a multiline comment that explains why I've chosen to use print and puts this way (even though the output won't look as good as it does in input.rb). You might also want to add comments indicating who created the script, when, for what purpose, what contingencies exist, what assumptions are made, and so forth.

2. Prompt the user and read in their response:

```
# Ask the user for their name:
print "What is your name?"
# Read in the input:
input = gets
```

Aside from switching when print is used and when puts is used, the non-comment code is the same as that in input.rb (Script 2.4).

3. Greet the user by name.

```
# Print a greeting:
puts "Greetings, "
# Reprint the user input:
puts input
```

Again, unlike in the preceding script, puts is being used here to generate the greeting.

4. Save the script as comments.rb and execute it (**Figure 2.11**).

continues on next page

MAKING COMMENTS

✔ Tips

■ In order to save valuable book space, the scripts in this book may not be as thoroughly documented as I would otherwise recommend. Add comments to your own work as liberally as you would like. You'll also note that throughout the rest of the book, comments that appear in the scripts will normally be omitted from the steps.

■ I also tend to omit comments when executing code within `irb`. The impermanence of an `irb` session makes typing comments practically useless.

■ Ruby does not support multiline comments using `/*` and `*/` as you would find in C, JavaScript, PHP, and other languages. You can create a multiline comment by using `=begin` as the first item on a line. The comment will continue until `=end` is found (also first thing on a line). This option is commonly used to create documentation to be handled by external tools, like RDoc.

SIMPLE TYPES

In this chapter the book starts covering the various types of data that one might work with in Ruby. Although everything in Ruby is, in fact, an object, knowing what you can do with, for example, an object of type String, and how that differs from an object of type Fixnum (a numeric type) is important. This chapter addresses what I call *simple types*: objects that will contain but a single value—one number, one string of text, one moment in time.

In order to pick these concepts up most quickly, the examples will be demonstrated using the command line irb (or fxri on Windows, if you prefer). If you'd rather create Ruby scripts, you can always take the information in this chapter to come up with your own practice scripts.

Creating Numbers

In order to work with any variable type, you first need to know how to create one. Unlike many other programming languages, Ruby does not require that you *declare* variables: indicate that a variable of a specific type exists. Instead, a variable in Ruby is often first referenced when it's assigned a value. Doing so makes use of the assignment operator, which is a single equals sign. The basic syntax is

```
identifier = value
```

A variable's *identifier*, which is to say its name, consists of letters, numbers, and underscores. Variable names cannot start with a number, and, most importantly, they are case sensitive. Variable names should not begin with a capital letter, as that naming scheme is reserved for constants (covered later in this chapter).

With all this in mind, these are valid numeric variables:

```
age = 2
weight = 24.6
```

The first is an integer (an object of type `Fixnum`) and the second is a floating point (an object of type `Float`). Do note that floats must always include at least one digit before the decimal point, even if that digit is a zero: `0.9`, not `.9`.

You can assign values to multiple variables in one statement using *parallel assignment*:

```
x, y = 1, 2
```

Using commas to separate the variables and the values while still using the assignment operator, that line has the result of assigning `1` to `x` and `2` to `y`. You can assign the same value to multiple variables using this syntax:

```
x = y = z = 2
```

To play around with this, try these next steps within `irb` or `fxri` (on Windows). See Chapter 1, "Getting Started," for a reminder of how to access these tools. These steps will also make use of the `puts` method, introduced in Chapter 2, "Simple Scripts."

Helpful Hints

This chapter uses some object-oriented terms that may be unfamiliar to you. I'll highlight a couple of points here.

First, a *class* is a blueprint for a thing and an *object* is a variable of a certain class type. The class defines what an object can know (or store) and do. Actions are accomplished by invoking *methods*, which are functions built into or inherited by a class (inheritance is when one class is derived from another).

Methods are called in Ruby using the dot syntax:

```
object.method
```

Sometimes methods can be called without specifying the object, like `puts`:

```
puts 'Hello, World!'
```

The name of a method indicates what the method does. Conventionally, methods that end with a question mark return a true or false value and methods that end with an exclamation point alter the value of the object.

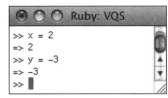

Figure 3.1 Two variables are created within irb.

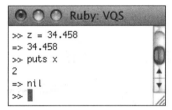

Figure 3.2 A floating-point variable is created, called z. Then the value of the x variable is displaayed.

---

irb vs. Scripts

When you create and run a Ruby script, the only output will be *results* generated by the code. This includes executed puts or other printing statements and, unfortunately, error messages.

By comparison, irb automatically displays the *returned value* of each executed statement as well. As you can see in Figure 3.1, when executing assignment statements, the assigned value is also returned. So the *result* of x = 2 is x being assigned that value. That value is also *returned* by the statement, so irb displays it.

As another example, the *result* of a puts statement is the displaying of whatever text and/or variable values. The value *returned* by uses of puts is nil. As you can see in Figure 3.2, the line puts x first displays the value of x (the result) and then displays nil (the returned value). Again, this is how irb works, if you were to use puts x in a script, only the 2 would be outputted. And the line x = 2 in a script would generate no output.

To create variables:

1. Create an integer variable:

   x = 2

2. Create a negative integer variable (**Figure 3.1**):

   y = -3

   Negation is indicated by prefacing a number with a minus sign. As you can see in the figure, irb immediately displays the assigned value for each variable; see the sidebar "irb vs. Scripts" for more on this behavior.

3. Create a floating-point variable:

   z = 34.458

   Like integers, floats can be positive or negative.

4. Print a variable's value (**Figure 3.2**):

   puts x

   The puts method when used like this outputs a variable's value. See the sidebar "irb vs. Scripts" for why the figure also shows the value nil.

✔ Tips

- Numbers that begin with a zero (aside from just zero itself) are non-base-10 numbers. For example, 0144 is base-8 (octal) for 100. Numbers that begin with 0x or 0X are in hexadecimal format; those beginning with 0b or 0B are in binary.

- Computers are notorious for their difficulty in accurately representing floating-point numbers. One work-around is to use integers (for example, representing 1.09 as 109, then performing division when necessary); another is to use the Ruby Standard Library's BigDecimal class. Chapter 9, "Modules and Includes," introduces Ruby's standard libraries.

CREATING NUMBERS

Performing Arithmetic

You can perform arithmetic with numbers in
Ruby using the basic operators you'd expect
to see: + (addition), - (subtraction), * (multiplication), and / (division):

```
x = 5
x = x + 2 # x equals 7
```

The four basic arithmetic operators can also
be used with the assignment operator as a
shortcut for common calculations:

```
x = 5
x += 5 # x equals 10
x /= 5 # x equals 2
```

You cannot use these shortcuts when performing parallel assignment, however:

```
x, y += 2 # Bad!
```

Arithmetic in Ruby is rather straightforward,
except when it comes to division. When you
divide one integer by another, the result will
be an integer, having dropped any remainder:

```
x = 20
x /= 7 # x equals 2!
```

The fix for this is to use at least one floating-
point number in such operations:

```
20 / 7.0 # 2.857…
20.0 / 7 # 2.857…
20.0 / 7.0 # 2.857…
```

Along with these four arithmetic operators
are the exponential operator (**), which
returns a number to a given power, and the
modulus operator (%), which returns the
remainder of a division:

```
x = 7
y = x % 2 # y equals 1
```

Overflow and Underflow

Programming languages allot a certain
amount of memory for each type of data
placed in a variable. When the value of
the data assigned to that variable requires
more memory than was allotted, the data
cannot be adequately represented. This is
overflow (when a value becomes too large)
and *underflow* (when a value becomes too
small). Such problems can lead to bugs or
even major security concerns.

Unlike other programming languages,
Ruby can handle large integers without a
problem. Depending upon the computer,
the maximum value of a Fixnum integer
will be about 1,073,741,823 (it could
be slightly different, depending upon
the computer and operating system).
Variables assigned a value larger than that
will automatically be converted to Bignum
objects, which have no maximum value.
Conversely, Bignum types whose value
decreases below the Fixnum max will be
converted to Fixnum objects.

Floating-point numbers can still suffer
from overflow and underflow. Normally,
overflows result in special positive or negative infinity values; underflows result in
zero. The maximum float value is stored
in the Float::MAX constant; the minimum
in Float::MIN (constants are discussed
toward the end of the chapter).

To perform arithmetic:

1. Create two numeric variables:

```
x = 2
y = 3.0
```

2. Display the result of adding, subtracting, multiplying, and dividing them (**Figure 3.3**):

```
puts x + y
puts x - y
puts x * y
puts x / y
```

As you can see in the figure, when one of two numbers used in arithmetic is a float, the result will always be a float.

3. Display the remainder of dividing the greater number by the smaller one:

```
puts y % x
```

Using the values from Step 1, the remainder of dividing y by x is 1.0. The remainder of dividing x by y would be 2.0 (because y cannot go into x even one time).

4. Display 2 to the eighth power (**Figure 3.4**):

```
puts 2**8
```

This line shows that arithmetic can be accomplished using any numeric value, not just those assigned to variables.

✔ Tips

■ As in math, dividing a number by zero is not allowed in Ruby. Dividing an integer by zero generates a ZeroDivisionError, dividing a float by zero returns the value Infinity, dividing 0.0 by 0.0 returns NaN (short for *Not a Number*).

■ Ruby handles the division of negative numbers differently than C and Java do. Integer division is rounded toward negative infinity, not zero. Whereas -5/3.0 is 1.6667, -5/3 returns -2, not -1.

■ The arithmetic operators in Ruby have the same order of precedence as they do in math and most programming languages. Exponents have highest precedence; followed by the unary minus operator (-, the negation of a number); then multiplication, division, and modulus; with addition and subtraction at the bottom. For example:

```
3 * 4 - 2 # 10, not 6
```

```
>> x = 2
=> 2
>> y = 3.0
=> 3.0
>> puts x + y
5.0
=> nil
>> puts x - y
-1.0
=> nil
>> puts x * y
6.0
=> nil
>> puts x / y
0.666666666666667
=> nil
>>I
```

Figure 3.3 The result of several calculations, as performed using fxri on Windows.

```
>> puts y % x
1.0
=> nil
>> puts 2**8
256
=> nil
>>I
```

Figure 3.4 More math!

Numeric Methods

Basic arithmetic is only a subset of what you can do with numbers in Ruby. The numeric types have several built-in methods that can be used for various purposes. **Table 3.1** lists some of these, indicating whether they can be used with both integers (i.e., Fixnums and Bignums) and floats, or just floating-point numbers. The purpose of each method should be fairly clear from its name (and the examples you'll soon see).

```
x = -2
puts x.abs # 2
```

For more details on invoking methods, see the "Calling Ruby Methods" sidebar.

Other useful math-related methods are defined within the Math module. These include sqrt, log, sin, cos, tan, and more. Two constants—PI and E—are also defined there. Chapter 9, "Modules and Includes," discusses the topic of modules in detail, but for now just know that you can make use of these methods and constants by referring to Math.*method* and Math::*CONSTANT*:

```
x = Math.sqrt(144) # 12
radius = 10.4
area = Math::PI * (radius ** 2)
```

Alternative, you can include the Math module, then refer to its methods and constants directly:

```
include Math
x = sqrt(144) # 12
radius = 10.4
area = PI * (radius ** 2)
```

Table 3.1

Numeric Methods	
METHOD	WORKS WITH...
abs	Both
ceil	Both
floor	Both
round	Both
truncate	Both
integer?	Both
nonzero?	Both
zero?	Both
finite?	Floats
infinite?	Floats

Calling Ruby Methods

Methods in Ruby can be called in different ways, and differently than you might call methods or functions in other languages. When calling methods without any arguments, the method's parentheses are normally omitted: just rand, not rand(). When calling methods with one argument, you can use or omit the parentheses: rand 100 is the same as rand(100). When calling methods with multiple arguments, you can sometimes get away without using parentheses, but it's more foolproof to include them: some_method(x, y). You could run into problems if you were to write some_method x, y, as Ruby could interpret that differently than you intended in some situations.

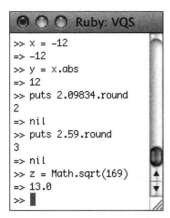

Figure 3.5 A smattering of numeric methods, used in different ways.

Finally, to generate a random number, call the `rand` method. If called without any arguments, it'll return a random (or random enough) float greater than or equal to `0.0` and less than `1.0`. If provided with a maximum value, it'll return an integer greater than or equal to `0` and less than (but not equal to) that maximum.

For more information on these or other methods, check out the Ruby documentation (see Chapter 1 about using `ri` or visit `www.ruby-doc.org`).

To use numeric methods:

1. Assign the absolute value of a number to a variable:

   ```
   x = -12
   y = x.abs
   ```

   Alternatively, you could write just:

   ```
   y = -12.abs
   ```

2. Round two floats:

   ```
   puts 2.09834.round
   puts 2.59.round
   ```

   Although the two periods in both lines may look a little confusing, the examples just apply the `round` method to literal floating-point values.

3. Assign the square root of 169 to a variable (**Figure 3.5**):

   ```
   z = Math.sqrt(169)
   ```

   As you can see in the figure, the `sqrt` method always returns a float.

continues on next page

NUMERIC METHODS

4. Generate two random integers greater than or equal to 0 and less than 10 (**Figure 3.6**):

```
puts rand(10)
puts rand(10)
```

5. Generate two random integers greater than or equal to 1 and less than *or equal to* 10 (**Figure 3.7**).

```
puts rand(10) + 1
puts rand(10) + 1
```

By adding 1 to the random number, the minimum possible value is increased to 1 (from 0) and the maximum is increased to 10.

✔ Tips

■ If you call the rand method providing it with a value 0, it has the same effect as using no value at all, returning a float between 0 and 1.

■ Ruby 1.9 adds the even? and odd? methods, which can be used with integers. Each returns a Boolean value indicating if the number is even or odd.

■ Because everything in Ruby can be done in many different ways, some numeric methods duplicate the basic arithmetic operators. For example, div performs division, modulo returns the remainder of a division, and power! returns the exponential calculation.

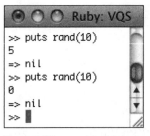

Figure 3.6 Two random integers.

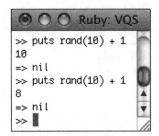

Figure 3.7 By using arithmetic, you can change the range of possible random numbers.

Creating Strings

Along with numbers, strings are a common scalar (single-valued) data type. A string is any quoted sequence of characters:

```
name = 'Zoe'
addr = '100 Main Street'
```

You can quote the string using either single or double quotation marks, but the same mark type must be used to both open and close the string (the next section of the chapter will further distinguish these two options).

One of the most useful manipulations of strings is *concatenation*: appending one string onto another. You can accomplish this in Ruby in two ways; the first is like Java or JavaScript:

```
msg = 'Hello'
msg = msg + ', World!'
```

Note that this last line could be shortened to just

```
msg += ', World!'
```

The second way to concatenate a string is to use <<, which is similar to C++:

```
msg = 'Hello'
msg << ', World!'
```

The end result of both operator usages—msg having a value of *Hello, World!*—is the same, but how that result is accomplished differs. It's a technical distinction and has to do with the way Ruby treats strings, but using + will result in a new string object being created, whose value is the concatenation of the two given strings. When you use <<, the same object is updated.

Ruby 1.9 and Unicode

Perhaps the most significant change between Ruby 1.8 and 1.9 is support for Unicode and multibyte characters. It's an advanced subject but one that's important in an increasingly global world. English and many Western European languages can be written using the 256 characters in the ASCII set, where each character requires only one byte. The characters in most other languages require more than one byte to be represented in a computer. Unicode is a standard that maps every possible character in every language to an associated code (ASCII is a subset of Unicode).

Ruby prior to version 1.9 relied upon ASCII for variable, method, and class names, as well as the values that can be manipulated. By taking on the Herculean task of supporting Unicode, Ruby 1.9 and later will be able to work equally well with characters from practically any of the world's thousands of languages.

To create and use strings:

1. Store your first and last names in two variables:

   first_name = 'Larry'

   last_name = 'Ullman'

   Feel free to use *your* name here. You can also use single or double quotation marks, so long as your name doesn't contain an apostrophe (in which case you should use double quotation marks).

2. Create a new variable by concatenating the other two:

   full_name = first_name + ' ' +
   → last_name

   You could also do it this way:

   full_name = first_name

   full_name << ' ' << last_name

   Note that whichever concatenation operator you use, you also need to append a space between the two names.

3. Output the value of this new variable (**Figure 3.8**):

   puts full_name

✔ Tips

■ Just as you can "add" strings together using +, you can multiply them using *:

   str = 'spam'

   str * 2 # returns 'spamspam'

   Subtraction and division do not work with strings, however.

■ One way of seeing that a new object is created when + is used to append text to an existing string is by invoking the object_id method. It returns an identifying value for the named object (**Figure 3.9**).

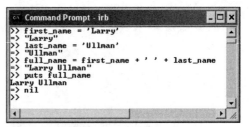

Figure 3.8 The creation of two strings, followed by the creation of a third using concatenation.

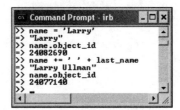

Figure 3.9 The object_id value of a string variable changes after using + because a new object is created.

CREATING STRINGS

Interpolation and Escaping

Two very important concepts when it comes to strings are *interpolation* and *escaping*. Interpolation is the act of replacing one part of a string with the result of an expression; it is best understood by an example. Say you wanted to print a variable's value within a context. This would not work:

```
name = 'Larry'
puts "Hello, name"
```

There's no way for Ruby to distinguish between the intent of printing the value of the name variable and just printing the text *name*. To indicate that a variable's value should be printed, use the number (or pound) sign, followed by the variable's name within curly braces (**Figure 3.10**):

```
puts "Hello, #{name}"
```

It's important to note that interpolation only works within double-quoted strings. But this means it can also be used when printing or creating a string:

```
msg = "Hello, #{name}"
```

As mentioned, interpolation actually inserts the result of an expression into a string. In the preceding two examples, the result is just the variable's value, but you could do more (**Figure 3.11**):

```
price = 10.99
qty = 5
puts "The total of purchasing #{qty}
→ widgets at $#{price} each comes to
→ $#{price * qty}"
```

A nice feature of interpolation is that non-string values are automatically converted to strings as needed, as Figure 3.11 also demonstrates.

```
>> name = 'Larry'
=> "Larry"
>> puts "Hello, name"
Hello, name
=> nil
>> puts "Hello, #{name}"
Hello, Larry
=> nil
>>
```

Figure 3.10 Two different puts statements show how to (bottom), and how not to (top), incorporate variables into a string.

```
>> price = 10.99
=> 10.99
>> qty = 5
=> 5
>> puts "The total of purchasing #{qty} widgets at $#{price} each
   comes to $#{price * qty}"
The total of purchasing 5 widgets at $10.99 each comes to $54.95
=> nil
>>
```

Figure 3.11 The results of mathematical calculations can be inserted into strings.

Escaping refers to preceding certain characters with a backslash to create meaningful *escape sequences* (**Table 3.2**). If you're reading this book sequentially, you'll have already seen references to \n, which generates a newline character (i.e., the result of pressing Enter). Another common use of the backslash is to place a quotation mark in a string delineated by that same quotation mark:

```
puts "I said, \"How are you?\""
name = 'Peter O\'Toole'
```

For the most part, escaping applies to strings within double quotation marks. Only \' and \\ have meaning within single quotation marks.

To use interpolation and escaping:

1. Create a string that contains a single or double quotation mark:

   ```
   text = 'It\'s not that hard.'
   ```

   There are at least two ways of doing this. The first is to escape the conflicting mark, as shown. The other option would be to use the alternative type of quotation mark as the string's boundaries:

   ```
   text = "It's not that hard."
   ```

2. Add a newline character to the string:

   ```
   text << "\n"
   ```

   You can use either + or << to add more characters to the string (see the preceding section of the chapter). Remember, however, that you must use double quotation marks around the newline character; '\n' is just the literal backslash followed by an *n*.

Table 3.2

Escape Sequences	
SEQUENCE	MEANING
\'	Single quotation mark
\"	Double quotation mark
\\	Backslash
\n	Newline
\r	Carriage return
\t	Tab

Figure 3.12 A simple demonstration of interpolation and escaping. Note the extra blank line (before *string end*), created by the newline appended to the string variable.

3. Print the string within the context of another string (**Figure 3.12**):

```
puts "string start--\n#{text}\n--
→ string end"
```

This is obviously all rather trivial, but it should hopefully help with comprehension of interpolation and escaping. To distinguish between the printed text message and the value of the variable, dashes and newlines separate the two.

✔ Tips

- Strings placed within backticks (`` ` ``) are system commands, to be executed by the computer.

  ```
  list = `dir` # Windows
  list = `ls` # Mac OS X and Unix
  ```

- As of Ruby 1.9, the escape sequence \u can be followed by a Unicode character's code point—normally four hexadecimal digits—in order to insert that character into the string. See the sidebar "Ruby 1.9 and Unicode" for more.

- Ruby does have the printf and sprintf methods, used to format and print or return a string. If you're used to using these in other programming languages, you can use them in Ruby, too.

- There are more escape sequences than are listed in Table 3.2, but those are the most important. Many of the others create non-printing characters.

- To print numbers as part of a concatenated string, they must be converted to strings using the to_s method:

  ```
  puts 'The value of x is: ' + x.to_s
  ```

  Alternatively, you could write:

  ```
  puts "The value of x is: #{x}"
  ```

  See the "Type Conversions" sidebar later in the chapter for more.

Common String Methods

Just as the numeric types have plenty of methods that can be used to manipulate values, so does the `String` class. In fact, this class contains dozens and dozens of methods. In this chapter I'll highlight a few (**Table 3.3**) and how they might be used. You'll also come across several other string methods in Chapter 10, "Regular Expressions," and throughout the rest of the book.

Most of the methods listed in Table 3.3 are defined in two ways, for example, `capitalize` and `capitalize!` In Ruby, methods that end with an exclamation mark normally alter the object's value, whereas those without exclamation marks return the effect of the method without making a permanent change. As an example of what this means (**Figure 3.13**):

```
str = 'this is a test'
str.capitalize
puts str
str.capitalize!
puts str
```

The methods listed in the table are all easy to use and understand, so I'll address a couple of others separately. First, there is `include?`, which returns a Boolean value indicating if the string includes the given character or string:

```
'watermelon'.include? "mel" #true
'watermelon'.include? "Z" #false
```

If you want to fetch a substring, you can use the `slice` method. It can take many types of arguments, from integers to a `Range` (see Chapter 4, "Arrays, Ranges, and Hashes") to a regular expression (see Chapter 10). The method will return a slice of the string (the `slice!` method will return the slice and remove it from the string). For example, you can use integers to indicate where in the string to start the slice and how many characters from there to fetch. The first character in a string is indexed at 0, so to get the second and third characters, you would write

```
str = 'brautigan'
str.slice(1, 2) # ra
```

Table 3.3

String Methods	
NAME	PURPOSE
length	Counts characters in a string
capitalize	Capitalizes the string
chomp	Removes ending \n, \r, or \r\n
chop	Removes the last character
concat	Same as <<
downcase	Converts the string to lowercase
empty?	Returns true if the string is empty
lstrip	Removes leading white space
reverse	Reverses the order of the string
rstrip	Removes trailing white space
strip	Removes both leading and trailing white space
upcase	Capitalizes every letter

Figure 3.13 As a Ruby convention, the version of a method whose name ends with an exclamation mark will actually update the value of a string (or any object).

Or if you want to fetch three characters, starting from the fourth-to-the-last character, use a negative index:

```
str.slice(-4, 3) # iga
```

To find where a character or string is in another string, use `index`. It returns the numerical position of the first occurrence (or `nil` if it wasn't found):

```
str = '99 Luftballons'
str.index('ll') # 9
```

You can insert a character or substring within a string using `insert`. Its first argument is the indexed position where the insertion should begin; the second argument is the text to be inserted. A negative index counts from the end of the string, inserting the new string after the character found there:

```
str = 'cat'
str.insert(2, 'bine') # cabinet
str.insert(-1, 'ry') # cabinetry
```

Note that this method does alter the variable's value, even though its name doesn't follow the convention of ending with an exclamation mark.

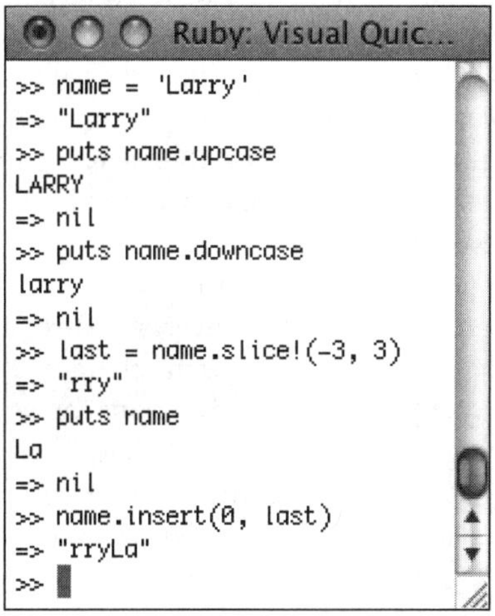

Figure 3.14 Some simple string manipulations, including slicing a substring out and inserting it back in at the beginning.

To use string methods:

1. Create a variable that represents your name:
```
name = 'Larry'
```

2. Print your name in different cases:
```
puts name.upcase

puts name.downcase
```
Note that neither of these uses of the methods affects the original value, each returns a converted version of the value to be outputted by `puts`.

3. Remove the last three letters from the name:
```
last = name.slice!(-3, 3)

puts name
```
The `slice!` method will return the last three characters from the string and assign them to the `last` variable. If `slice` was used instead, `last` would have the same value (*rry*) but `name` would still have its original value.

4. Add those last three letters back in as the first three letters (**Figure 3.14**):
```
name.insert(0, last)
```
All of this isn't terribly useful, but hopefully it shows you how to apply methods to strings. In later chapters, you'll use strings and their methods in more practical ways (this example could be the basis for a program that translates text into Pig Latin).

✔ Tips

- The `chomp` method is often used to remove the carriage return or newline added to user input read in via `gets`.

- Ruby 1.9 adds additional string methods, including `bytesize`, `start_with?`, and `end_with?`.

- The `split` method is used to break a string up into pieces. As it returns an array—a topic not yet covered, I've saved its demonstration for the next chapter.

Creating Multiline Strings

Most of the string examples thus far were rather short, containing but one line of text. You can create multiline strings in Ruby using several different methods, starting by simply entering the text over multiple lines:

```
addr = '100 Main Street
Anytown, IL 12345'
```

It doesn't matter in such cases whether you use single or double quotation marks, but understand that the newline character (after *Street* and before *Anytown*) will be part of that string.

Multiline strings can also be created by using %q, followed by a delimiter of your choosing:

```
poem = %q{If I were to life my life
in catfish forms…}
```

You can use any character as the delimiter, so long as it does not appear in the string itself (or, if it does, it's escaped by preceding it with a backslash). Still, using matching opening and closing curly braces is common. Using %q creates a string as if you had used single quotation marks, but without the need to escape any single quotation marks that appear within the string. This does mean that you cannot use interpolation with it.

Using %Q or just %, followed by a delimiter, is the same as using double quotation marks, meaning you can make use of interpolation:

```
msg = %Q{Name: #{name}
Address: #{addr}}
```

That syntax might look a little confusing (and no, the curly braces around the variable names won't actually conflict with the curly braces used to delimit the string), but as an example, if you were putting variables within HTML, this syntax is quite helpful:

```
msg = %Q{<span class="title">#{title}
→ </span>
<p class="article">#{article}</p>}
```

One last alterative is to use the *here document* (or *heredoc*) syntax. To isolate the string, start by using <<, followed immediately—without a space—by some characters that will indicate the boundaries of the string. Those characters can appear in the string itself, in certain circumstances, but it's best if they don't. Then the actual string starts on the next line:

```
poem = <<EOS
in scaffolds of skin and whiskers
at the bottom of a pond
EOS
```

The closing delimiter—EOS (*End Of String*)—must appear as the first thing on the line, without even a space before it, and with nothing else coming after it, including comments. Note that the newline character after the opening delimiter (i.e., between <<*EOS* and *in*) is not part of the string but the one before the closing delimiter (between *pond* and *EOS*) will be.

Type Conversions

Sometimes you'll have a value that's of one type—an integer (Fixnum or Bignum), decimal (Float), or string—that you'll need to use as another type. For example, say a script asks the user for their age. The value, read in using gets, will be a string, even if it's a string containing a number (e.g., "25"). To use that input as an integer, you'll need to convert it (after chopping off the trailing newline character). Ruby supports several functions for converting data from one type to another: to_s, to_i, and to_f create strings, integers, and floats, respectively. With the age example, you would use:

```
input = gets
age = input.chomp.to_i
```

To use multiline strings:

1. Create a multiline string using one of the methods already described:

   ```
   poem = %q{I have eaten
   the plums
   that were in
   the icebox}
   ```

   These are the first four lines of the poem "This Is Just To Say" by William Carlos Williams. You can use something else here if you'd like.

2. Print the number of characters in the string (**Figure 3.15**):

   ```
   puts poem.length
   ```

   The length method returns the number of characters in a string. It does count the newlines (\n counts as one character).

3. Print just the first line of the string:

   ```
   puts poem.slice(0, poem.index("\n"))
   ```

   This is an application of two methods discussed in the last section of the chapter. The slice method returns a substring. Its first argument is the starting index (beginning at 0), and its second is the number of characters to return from there. So to return just the first line, use the index method to find out where the first newline character is, and use that returned value as the second argument to slice.

continues on next page

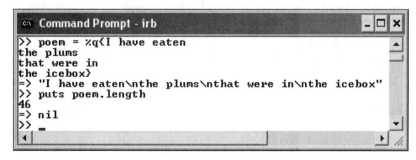

Figure 3.15 A longer string is created over the course of several lines, then the number of characters it contains is printed.

4. See if the string contains an upper- or lowercase *T* (**Figure 3.16**).

```
puts poem.upcase.include?('T')
```

Here I've chained together two string methods to achieve the desired result. There are a couple of ways of finding either a lower- or an uppercase letter in a string. Using the information already covered, one option is to convert the entire string to either upper- or lowercase (here, to uppercase, using upcase) and then looking for the same case letter within that result (using include?).

✔ Tips

- If you use <<- to begin a heredoc block, there can be white space before the terminating mark.

- Just like newlines, any tabs and spaces within a quoted block will also be part of the string. This includes any indentations.

- Both %q and %Q can be used to create single-line strings.

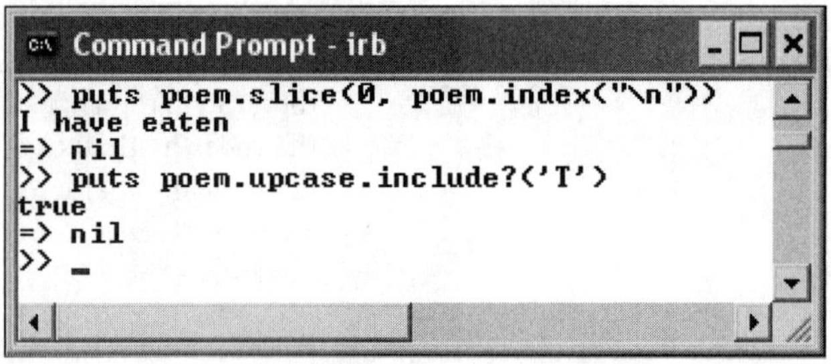

CREATING MULTILINE STRINGS

```
Command Prompt - irb
>> puts poem.slice(0, poem.index("\n"))
I have eaten
=> nil
>> puts poem.upcase.include?('T')
true
=> nil
>> _
```

Figure 3.16 The top puts command prints the first line of the multiline string. The bottom puts command reports that the letter *T*—in either upper- or lowercase—is present within the string.

Symbols

Like constants, symbols are not variables in that they don't have changeable values. In fact, symbols don't have values at all. A symbol is just that: a representation of something. As an example, say you're creating an application that manages to-do lists. For each item on the list, you'll want to assign a priority: *high*, *medium*, *low*, *none*. You might create a `Task` object type (this will mean more after Chapter 7, "Creating Classes") and assign to its `priority` attribute one of those strings:

```
t1 = Task.new('Need to do this')
t1.priority = 'high'
```

This will work, but each time a task is assigned a priority, a separate string object is created (even if the string values are the same). This is inefficient. The alternative is to use symbols.

Symbols have identifiers like variables but begin with a colon. Note that no value is ever assigned to a symbol; instead, a symbol is used as a value for something else:

```
t1 = Task.new('Need to do this')
t1.priority = :high
```

This approach will result in a more efficient application.

A couple last thoughts on symbols: first, symbols are often used as the keys for hashes, discussed in Chapter 4. Second, although symbols generally are named like variables, symbols can have spaces in them if placed within quotes. This is perfectly valid:

```
car = :'Toyota Prius'
```

Finally, symbols can be converted to strings using the `to_s` method and strings can be converted to symbols using `to_sym` or `intern`.

Using Constants

The topic of constants is included in this chapter because it's a simple type in the sense that a constant contains a single value, normally a number or a string. Constants are quite different from variables, however, in that once they are assigned a value, that value should never change.

A constant's name abides by the same rules as variables, consisting of letters, numbers, and the underscore. Constants must begin with a capital letter, though, which is how they are distinguished from variables:

```
BASE = 100 # Constant
Something = 'b' # Constant
dozen = 12 # Variable
```

Even though constants need only begin with one capital letter, they are often written in all caps. You'll notice that, also like variables, constants are assigned values using the assignment operator. For that matter, they can be interpolated within a string just the same:

```
puts "The result is #{BASE * dozen}"
```

Classes and modules often define their own constants. For example, the `Math` module has two: `PI` and `E`. To refer to a constant in a module, use the scope resolution operator (`::`). This example was used earlier in the chapter:

```
area = Math::PI * (radius ** 2)
```

As a demonstration of using constants, this next example will convert a temperature in degrees Celsius to degrees Fahrenheit.

To create and use constants:

1. Create two constants:
```
TO_F_RATIO = 1.8
TO_F_ADD = 32
```
These two numbers are used in the formula to convert temperature from degrees Celsius to degrees Fahrenheit. Because these values will never change in that calculation, they make good candidates for constants.

2. Create a variable:
```
temp_c = 16
```
This variable represents the temperature in degrees Celsius. Because TO_F_RATIO, which will be multiplied by this variable, is a float, it will make no difference whether this variable is an integer or a float.

3. Calculate the temperature in degrees Fahrenheit:
```
temp_f = (temp_c * TO_F_RATIO) +
→ TO_F_ADD
```
To convert degrees Celsius to degrees Fahrenheit, multiply it by 9/5 (or 1.8), then add 32. Because multiplication has a

higher order of precedence than addition, the parentheses here aren't required, but I almost always prefer to use parentheses so that I know for certain which calculations happen first.

4. Print the converted temperature (**Figure 3.17**).
```
puts "#{temp_c} degrees Celsius
→ is #{temp_f} degrees Fahrenheit"
```
Alternatively, you could put the entire calculation (used to assign a value to the temp_f variable) within the second #{} block.

✔ Tips

■ In Ruby 1.8 and earlier, you can change the value of a constant but doing so generates a warning. Later versions of Ruby may prevent changing a constant's value and generate actual errors when that is attempted. No matter the version of Ruby you're using, you should not attempt to change a constant's value.

■ Conventionally, multiword constants in Ruby are written as either TwoWords or TWO_WORDS (I'll stick with this latter approach).

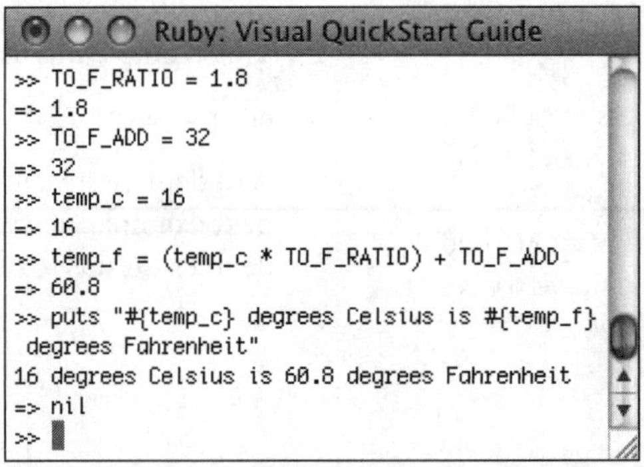

Figure 3.17 A temperature is converted from degrees Celsius to degrees Fahrenheit in part by using constants.

USING CONSTANTS

Dates and Times

The last types to discuss in this chapter are dates and times. Both can be represented by a Time object. To create one, storing the current moment, do this:

```
t = Time.now
```

The value of the Time object will be an integer representing the number of seconds and microseconds since the *epoch*, a special moment in computer time, marked as midnight between December 31, 1969 and January 1, 1970. One of the nice things about Time objects is that they are automatically converted to strings when printed:

```
puts t # Thu Jun 05 00:17:21 -0400 2008
```

(The -0400 is the offset from UTC, *Coordinated Universal Time*.)

Because the value is an integer, you can add or subtract time using basic arithmetic (**Figure 3.18**):

```
puts t + (60 * 60) # Add one hour.
```

If you want to create a Time object for a particular date and/or time, you can use the local method:

```
t = Time.local(year, month, day, hour,
→ minutes, seconds, microseconds)
```

Every argument after *year* is optional and each expects a numeric value, although *month* can also take three-letter abbreviations (*Jan, Feb*, etc.). The result of that method call is a Time object for the computer's time zone for the given parameters. If you'd like to create a UTC (Coordinated Universal Time) Time object, use the utc method instead. It takes the same arguments:

```
t = Time.utc(year, month, day, hour,
→ minutes, seconds, microseconds)
```

If you already have an integer that represents the number of seconds since the epoch (for example, pulled from a database), you can create a Time object for that moment using at:

```
stamp = 1212629552;
t = Time.at(stamp)
```

Other methods built into the Time class are used to return different values for the given time (**Table 3.4**).

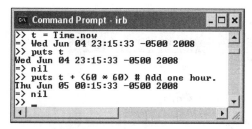

Figure 3.18 The current moment in time and what the date and time will be in an hour.

Table 3.4

Time Methods	
NAME	RETURNS
year	The year as four digits
month	The month as a number
day	The day of the month
yday	The day of the year (1–366)
wday	The day of the week (Sunday is 0)
hour	The hour (24-hour format)
min	The minutes
sec	The seconds
usec	The microseconds
zone	The associated time zone
utc?	True if it's in UTC time zone

To use dates and times:

1. Create a variable representing the current time:

```
t = Time.now
```

2. Print the current month, day, and year (**Figure 3.19**):

```
puts "Today is #{t.month}
→ /#{t.day}/#{t.year}"
```

To do this, just call the appropriate Time object methods within a puts statement.

3. Print the computer's time zone:

```
puts "The computer's time zone
→ is #{t.zone}."
```

As Table 3.4 says, the zone method returns the computer's time zone. This value will be an abbreviation like *EDT* (meaning United States Eastern Daylight Saving Time).

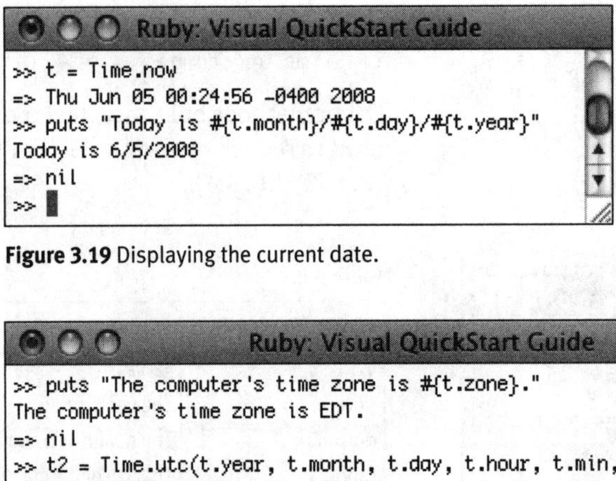

```
Ruby: Visual QuickStart Guide
>> t = Time.now
=> Thu Jun 05 00:24:56 -0400 2008
>> puts "Today is #{t.month}/#{t.day}/#{t.year}"
Today is 6/5/2008
=> nil
>>
```

Figure 3.19 Displaying the current date.

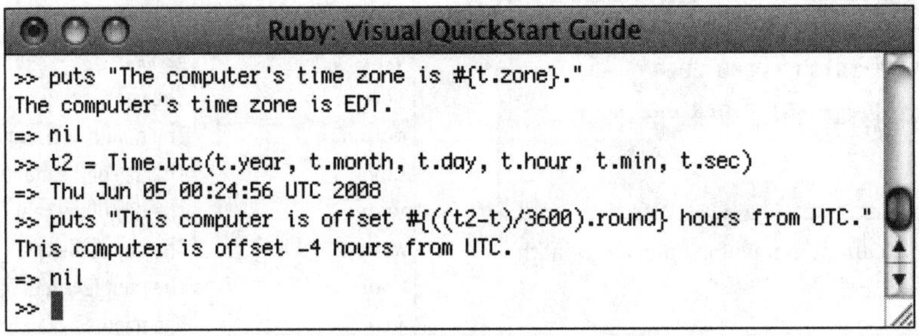

```
Ruby: Visual QuickStart Guide
>> puts "The computer's time zone is #{t.zone}."
The computer's time zone is EDT.
=> nil
>> t2 = Time.utc(t.year, t.month, t.day, t.hour, t.min, t.sec)
=> Thu Jun 05 00:24:56 UTC 2008
>> puts "This computer is offset #{((t2-t)/3600).round} hours from UTC."
This computer is offset -4 hours from UTC.
=> nil
>>
```

Figure 3.20 Some math and use of several Time methods returns the computer's offset from UTC.

DATES AND TIMES

4. Determine the computer's offset from UTC (**Figure 3.20**):

```
t2 = Time.utc(t.year, t.month,
→ t.day, t.hour, t.min, t.sec)
puts "This computer is offset
→ #{((t2-t)/3600).round} hours
→ from UTC."
```

This is another example showing how you can apply several of the ideas covered in this chapter. The offset between two time zones will be the number of hours by which they differ at any given moment. The `t` variable already represents the current moment for this computer (or the moment when it was created). To get the UTC representation of that same moment, call the `utc` method, providing it with values returned by the corresponding `Time` methods. Then subtract the one timestamp from the other, divide by `3600` (`60` seconds times `60` minutes) and round it off. This isn't perfect (e.g., it doesn't properly handle time zones that are offset by fractions of an hour) but is still a fairly sharp application of the `Time` class features.

✔ Tips

- Depending upon the operating system, the allowed date range of a `Time` object may end around 2038. For more sophisticated date and time representations, use the `Date` or `DateTime` class, found in Ruby's Standard Library.

- To retrieve the `Time` value as an integer (i.e., the number of seconds since the epoch), apply the `to_i` method:

```
t = Time.now
puts t.to_i
```

Other Simple Types

There are couple other "simple types" in Ruby that don't get full coverage in this chapter: `true`, `false`, and `nil`. These are objects of types `TrueClass`, `FalseClass`, and `NilClass`. Ruby uses these object types all the time—for example, as the result of conditionals and method invocations—but, ironically, they aren't often used in and of themselves.

DATES AND TIMES

ARRAYS, RANGES, AND HASHES

Chapter 3, "Simple Types," concentrates on the most basic kinds of data used in Ruby, primarily numbers and strings. I call these *simple types* because such variables represent only a single value. In this chapter you'll learn ways to represent multiple values using just one variable. These more complex data types include arrays, ranges, and hashes.

In the examples, you'll learn how to create variables of these types, add and remove values, and manipulate them using different methods. In Chapter 5, "Control Structures," you'll see how to iterate through these types, accessing the individual values one at a time. How to create and use the most important complex data type—*objects*—will be discussed in Chapter 7, "Creating Classes."

Creating Arrays

An array can be thought of as a list of values all placed under one heading (i.e., within one variable). Whereas a string might store a single thought, like something you need to purchase from the grocery store—*kiwis*, an array can be the entire shopping list: *kiwis*, *cereal*, *milk*, etc.

An array's name abides by the same rules as any other variable: it may contain only letters, numbers, and underscores, and it cannot begin with a number or uppercase letter. Arrays can also be assigned values using the assignment operator. However, since arrays store multiple values, a slightly different syntax is used to assigning them:

```
numbers = [1, 2, 3]
groceries = ['kiwis', 'cereal', 'milk']
```

The array's *elements*, which is to say its values, are put between square brackets, each separated from the next by a comma.

Arrays can contain a mixture of types:

```
stuff = ['b', 39.4, 8, 'mayonnaise']
```

Arrays can also be created using %w or %W, followed by the values within matching delineators:

```
labels = %w{hot mild cold}
```

In this syntax, the %w indicates that white space separates the array's elements, so commas between the values, and quotation marks around the strings are not necessary. This syntax is like creating strings using %q and %Q (like %Q, %W treats the values as if in a double-quoted string).

You can easily print an entire array using puts (**Figure 4.1**):

```
puts numbers
puts groceries
```

If you'd like to print, or do anything with, just a single item from the array, refer to the element's indexed position: where the item is found within the list. Arrays use numeric indexes, with the first item found at 0. Referring to specific elements uses the square brackets again, with the integer index value between them:

```
puts groceries[2] # "milk"
```

Figure 4.1 The puts method will print out every value in an array, each on its own line.

You can also change an element's value using this syntax:

```
groceries[2] = 'soy milk'
```

Finally, Ruby has a neat feature where a negative number can be used to count backward from the end of an array. The number -1 refers to the last item in an array:

```
puts stuff[-1] # "mayonnaise"
```

```
puts numbers[-1] # 3
```

The number -2 refers to the second to last element:

```
puts stuff[-2] # 8
```

And so on.

To create and use arrays:

1. Create an array of strings:

   ```
   names = ['Jack', 'Kate', 'Charlie',
   → 'Claire']
   ```

   The names array stores four strings, indexed from 0 to 3.

2. Create an array of floats:

   ```
   grades = [3.6, 2.34, 2.84, 4.0, 3.03]
   ```

3. Print out a specific item in each array (**Figure 4.2**):

   ```
   puts names[1]
   ```

   ```
   puts grades[-1]
   ```

   The second item in the names array is printed (because the first element is indexed at 0). Then the last item in the grades array is printed.

continues on next page

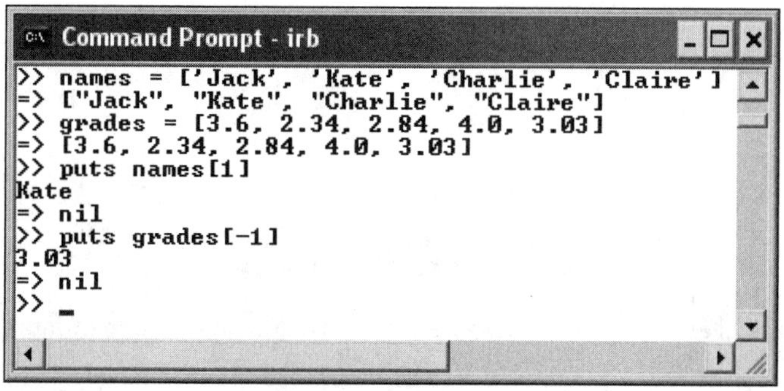

Figure 4.2 Two arrays are created, and then individual elements from each are printed.

CREATING ARRAYS

4. Replace one of the names and print out the array's contents (**Figure 4.3**):

```
names[3] = 'John'
```

```
puts names
```

The first line replaces the value of the fourth element in the array with *John*. Then the entire array is printed out.

✔ Tips

- You can create an empty array, to be populated later, using empty square brackets:

```
my_array = []
```

Or use the new method of the Array class:

```
my_array = Array.new
```

- Arrays in Ruby always begin indexing at 0. Unlike in some other programming languages, you cannot force the index to begin at another number.

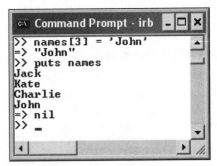

Figure 4.3 Existing array elements can be altered by assigning them new values (compare the final name with that in Figure 4.1).

Multidimensional Arrays

A multidimensional array is just an array that uses other arrays for one or more of its values. For instance:

```
a = [[1, 2, 3, 4], ["a", "b", "c"]]
```

Now a is a multidimensional array whose outermost array has two elements. The first element, a[0], is an array of four integers. The second element, a[1], is an array of three strings.

```
puts a[0] # [1, 2, 3, 4]
```

To refer to one of those numbers or letters (i.e., to the inner array values), use two sets of square brackets:

```
a[0][3] # 4
a[1][2] # "c"
```

There's no limit to how nested an array can be; just keep adding square brackets and indexes to get to an individual value.

Table 4.1

Array Methods	
METHOD	RETURNS…
empty?	True if the array is empty
first	The first value in the array
include?	True if the array includes the given value
index	The index number of a given value
inspect	The array in a printable format
last	The last value in the array
length	The number of items in the array
reverse	The array in reverse order
sort	The array sorted
uniq	The unique values in the array

Common Array Methods

There's way more that you can do with arrays besides creating them and printing their values. The Array class defines and inherits a couple dozen methods that serve various purposes (**Table 4.1**). Some more array methods, in particular each and map, will be discussed in Chapter 5. Both are used to walk through an array one element at a time.

The methods listed in Table 4.1 are easy to understand and use (as the next sequence of steps will show), so I'll devote extra time to some others. To return a subset of an array, use slice. Its first argument is the indexed position of the item to be returned. Its second (and optional) argument is the number of items to return from that point forward:

```
n = ["a", "b", "c", "d", "e"]
n.slice(0) # "a"
n.slice(2, 2) # ["c", "d"]
```

Note that this method will return the matching subset without affecting the original array. If you want to permanently remove the elements, still returning them in the process, use slice!.

The slice method does the same thing as using the square brackets after the array's name. Placing a single digit within square brackets returns a single element:

```
n[0] # "a"
```

Using [x,y] returns y elements starting at position x:

```
n[2, 2] # ["c", "d"]
```

Or you can use first and last to return the first or last x number of elements:

```
n.last # "e"
n.last(2) # ["d, e"]
n.first(3) # ["a", "b", "c"]
```

Finally, in the process of demonstrating the use of some of these methods, I'll frequently invoke `inspect`. This method, which can be used with many types of objects, returns the variable to which it's applied in a more accessible format. With arrays, this means the contents will be displayed on one line, instead of over several.

To use array methods:

1. Create two arrays:

   ```
   numbers = [0.4, 23.0, 23.3, 0.4, 5.2]
   dwarfs = ['Doc', 'Sleepy',
   → 'Bashful', 'Grumpy', 'Happy',
   → 'Sneezy', 'Dopey']
   ```

   The first array is a list of floats, two of which have the same value. The second array is the seven dwarfs that stumbled upon Snow White.

2. Check for specific values in each array:

   ```
   puts numbers.include?(23.0)
   puts dwarfs.include?('Donner')
   ```

   The `include?` method returns a Boolean value indicating if a given value is present in an array.

3. Find the location of specific values in each array (**Figure 4.4**):

   ```
   puts dwarfs.index('Grumpy')
   puts numbers.index(0.4)
   puts numbers.rindex(0.4)
   puts dwarfs.index('Papa Smurf')
   ```

   The `index` method returns the integer location of a value, if found in the array. Note that it returns the location of the *first* found value, so in the `numbers` array, calling `index` points to the first element. Conversely, `rindex` finds the *last* found value. If the value isn't in the array, as is the case with *Papa Smurf*, `nil` is returned.

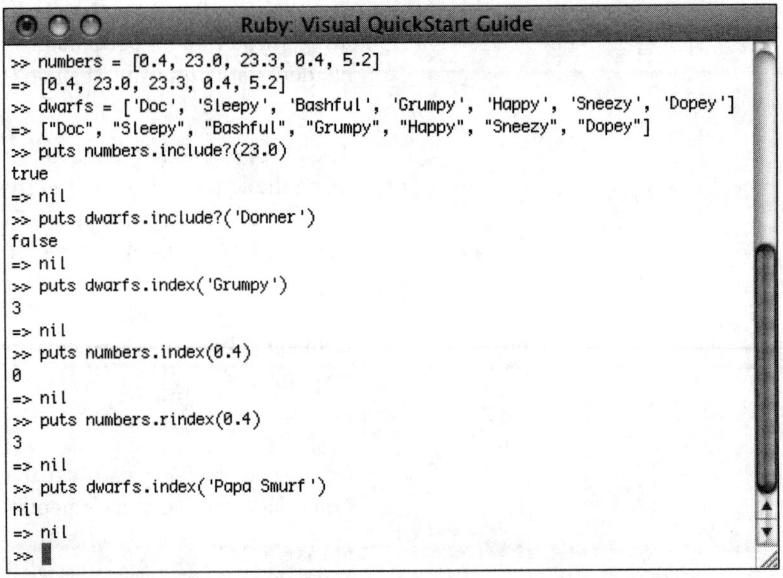

Figure 4.4 Thanks to Ruby and `include?`, I can easily see that *Donner* wasn't one of the Seven Dwarfs! Other examples use the `index` method, which returns the location of a given value in an array.

4. Re-order and display the arrays (**Figure 4.5**):

   `puts numbers.sort.inspect`

   `puts dwarfs.sort.reverse.inspect`

   The `sort` method will arrange a list of numbers in increasing order and arrange strings in alphabetical order. The `reverse` method is applied to the sorted `dwarfs` array to turn it into a reverse-alphabetical order list. In both cases, `inspect` is called so that the array is printed more succinctly (rather than over multiple lines, as would ordinarily be the case).

5. Cut some values from an array (**Figure 4.6**):

   `puts dwarfs.length`

   `oops = dwarfs.slice!(2, 2)`

   `puts dwarfs.length`

   To see the full effect of `slice!`, the `length` method is first called to show the number of items in the array. Then the `oops` array is created (after an accident in the mine), assigning to it two of the dwarfs. Finally, the `length` method is called again to confirm that the `dwarfs` array is now down two elements.

   Note that the `oops` array now contains the values of those two elements (indexed at `0` and `1`) and that the last two elements in the dwarfs array have been reindexed (in other words, there's no gap in the integer locations). Finally, if `slice` had been used instead of `slice!`, `oops` would still contain the same two names but the `dwarfs` array would retain all seven values.

continues on next page

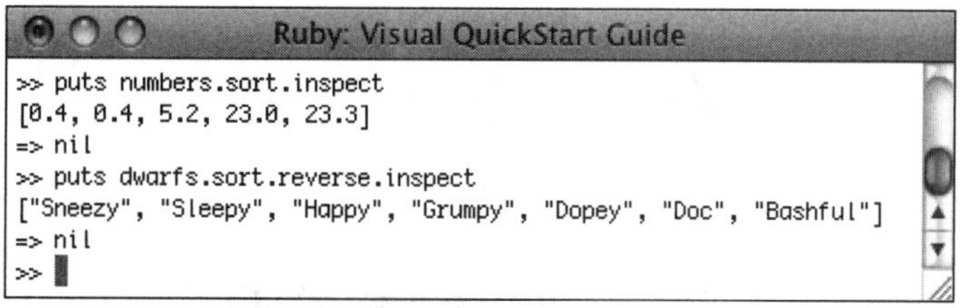

```
Ruby: Visual QuickStart Guide
>> puts numbers.sort.inspect
[0.4, 0.4, 5.2, 23.0, 23.3]
=> nil
>> puts dwarfs.sort.reverse.inspect
["Sneezy", "Sleepy", "Happy", "Grumpy", "Dopey", "Doc", "Bashful"]
=> nil
>>
```

Figure 4.5 The two arrays, redisplayed in different order.

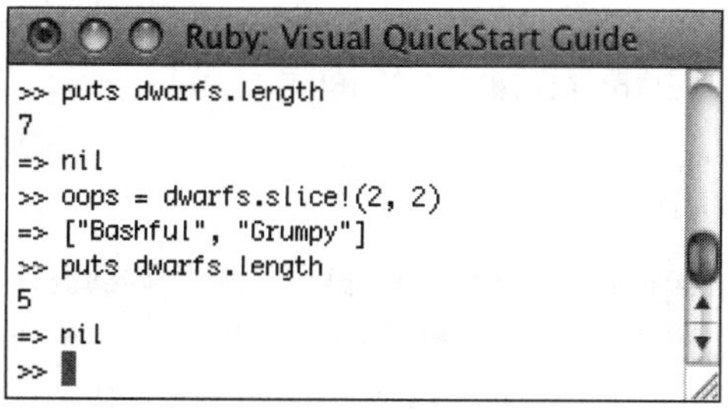

```
Ruby: Visual QuickStart Guide
>> puts dwarfs.length
7
=> nil
>> oops = dwarfs.slice!(2, 2)
=> ["Bashful", "Grumpy"]
>> puts dwarfs.length
5
=> nil
>>
```

Figure 4.6 The `length` method returns the number of elements in an array, and the `slice!` method cuts a subsection out of an array (poor Bashful, poor Grumpy).

6. Return only the unique values in an array (**Figure 4.7**):

```ruby
puts numbers.uniq.inspect
puts numbers.length
puts numbers.uniq.length
```

The uniq method returns an array of unique values (without impacting the original array). With the numbers variable, which has two 0.4 values in it, the returned unique array contains one less element. To confirm this, the length method is called on both versions of the array.

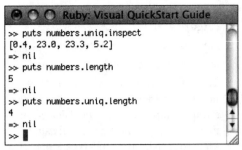

Figure 4.7 To find only the unique values in an array, apply the uniq method.

✔ Tips

■ The size method is an alias for length.

■ Ruby 1.9 adds the shuffle method, for randomly mixing up an array's order.

Command-Line Arguments

When executing a Ruby script from the command line (as demonstrated in Chapter 2, "Simple Scripts," it's possible to pass arguments to the script. For example:

```
ruby -w scriptname.rb 'Hello, World!' 2 'cat'
```

You've seen this in other situations, like in Chapter 1, "Getting Started," where the --version argument was passed when invoking the Ruby executable.

To refer to command-line arguments in the script, use ARGV. ARGV is a special constant in Ruby, which is assigned an array of values. Within the scriptname.rb example shown here, you would have:

```
ARGV[0] # "Hello, World!"
ARGV[1] # 2
ARGV[2] # "cat"
```

This is notably different from the way C and C++ handle command-line arguments. In those languages, the first item in the arguments array is the name of the script being called.

Adding Elements

The first section of the chapter shows the most basic and common way to create an array, but there are alternatives (in Ruby, there are always alternatives). You can start by creating a new empty array by doing either

```
a = Array.new
```

or

```
a = []
```

Then you can add values to the array using <<:

```
a << 32
a << 'carrot'
```

If you'd prefer to use a method instead of an operator, either of these is equivalent to the preceding line:

```
a.push 'carrot'
a.push('carrot')
```

(The sole difference is in how methods can be invoked. See the sidebar "Calling Ruby Methods" in Chapter 3.)

Whether you use << or push, the new item is added at the end of the array. Conversely, unshift adds elements to the beginning of the array:

```
a = [2, 3, 4]
a.unshift(1) # [1, 2, 3, 4]
```

The insert method can be used to add an element anywhere. Its first argument is the index position for the new item; the second is the value itself:

```
a.insert(2, 2.5) # [1, 2, 2.5, 3, 4]
```

ADDING ELEMENTS

To add array elements:

1. Create an array:

   ```
   writers = []
   ```

   You can also use

   ```
   writers = Array.new
   ```

2. Add some elements to the end of the array (**Figure 4.8**):

   ```
   writers << 'Sedaris'
   writers << 'McEwan' << 'Diaz'
   writers.push('Bank')
   puts writers.inspect
   ```

   The first two lines demonstrate two different uses of the << operator. The second just shows that you can add multiple elements in one statement using this approach.

   The third line invokes the push method for the same effect. Finally, the contents of the array are displayed.

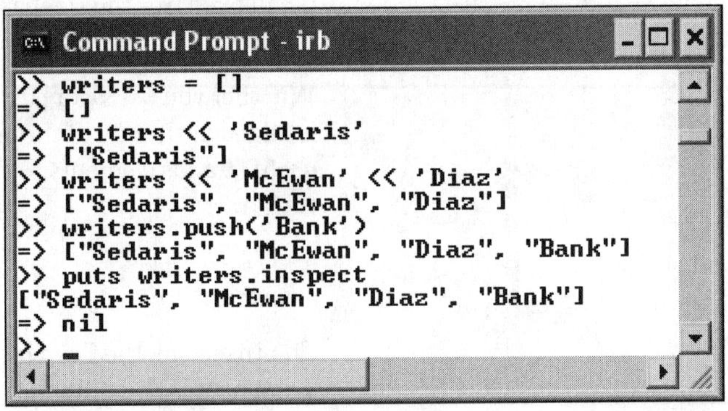

Figure 4.8 Four elements are added to an array.

3. Add an element to the beginning of the array (**Figure 4.9**):

```
writers.unshift('Hodgman')
```

```
puts writers.inspect
```

The new array element will be added as the first value in the array, shifting every other element back one position.

4. Insert elements into the middle of the array (**Figure 4.10**):

```
writers.insert(3, 'Vowell')
```

```
writers.insert(1, 'Stewart')
```

```
puts writers.inspect
```

The first line adds a new name as the fourth element in the array (remember: arrays are indexed starting at 0). The second adds a new name as the second element. In both cases, subsequent elements are pushed back (you could use the index method to confirm the location of values).

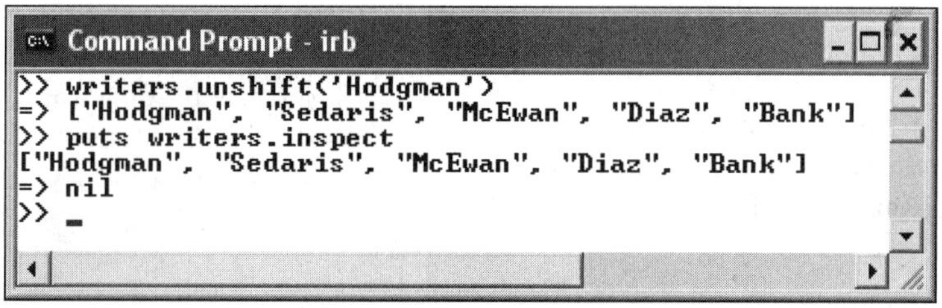

Figure 4.9 The unshift method can be used to add an element to the beginning of an array.

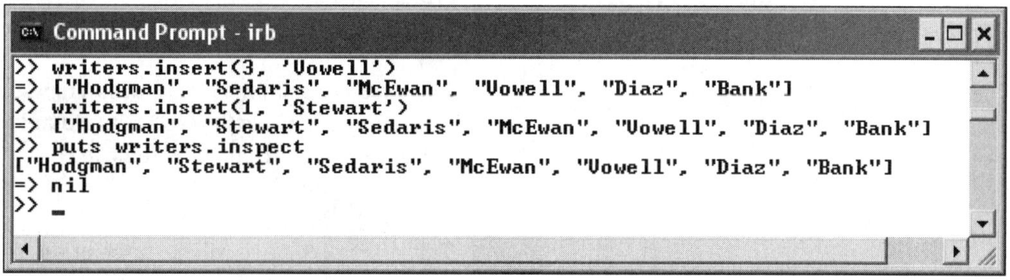

Figure 4.10 To add values anywhere in an array, call the insert method.

Removing Elements

Just as you can add new elements to existing arrays, you can remove elements, too. To remove the last element from the array, use pop:

```
a = [1, 2]
a.pop # a = [1]
```

To remove an item from the beginning of the array, use shift:

```
a = [1, 2, 3, 4]
a.shift # a = [2, 3, 4]
```

To remove an item from the middle of the array, use delete_at, providing it the index position of the item to be deleted:

```
a = [1, 2, 3, 4, 5, 6]
a.delete_at(2) # a = [1, 2, 4, 5, 6]
```

To remove an item from the array based upon its value, use delete:

```
pets = ['cat', 'dog', 'rabbit', 'parrot']
a.delete('dog')
# pets = ['cat', 'rabbit', 'parrot']
```

Each of these methods not only removes the element from the array but also returns the removed value (just like slice!).

Multiple Array Interactions

If you have two (or more) arrays, what you can do with them is even more interesting. The +, &, and | operators perform *difference*, *intersection*, and *union*, respectively. Start with two arrays:

```
a = [1, 2, 3, 4]
b = [4, 5, 6]
```

The *difference* between the two will be a copy of a with any elements also in b removed:

```
a - b # [1, 2, 3]
```

The *intersection* of the two returns a new array containing only those elements found in both (with any duplicates removed):

```
a & b # [4]
```

The *union* of the two will be the creation of a new array containing every unique element found in both:

```
a | b # [1, 2, 3, 4, 5, 6]
```

To remove elements:

1. Create a new array:

   ```
   groceries = %w{milk kiwis carrots
   → tofu steak beets salt turnips}
   ```

   Using the %w technique discussed in the first section of the chapter, I'll quickly create a list of words (the %w means that each array element is separated by a space, so that quotes are not required).

2. Remove the second item from the array (**Figure 4.11**):

   ```
   groceries.delete_at(1)
   puts groceries.inspect
   ```

3. Remove tofu from the list:

   ```
   groceries.delete('tofu')
   puts groceries.inspect
   ```

4. Remove the first and last items (**Figure 4.12**).

   ```
   groceries.pop
   groceries.shift
   puts groceries.inspect
   ```

```
>> groceries = %w{milk kiwis carrots tofu steak beets salt turnips}
=> ["milk", "kiwis", "carrots", "tofu", "steak", "beets", "salt", "turnips"]
>> groceries.delete_at(1)
=> "kiwis"
>> puts groceries.inspect
["milk", "carrots", "tofu", "steak", "beets", "salt", "turnips"]
=> nil
>>
```

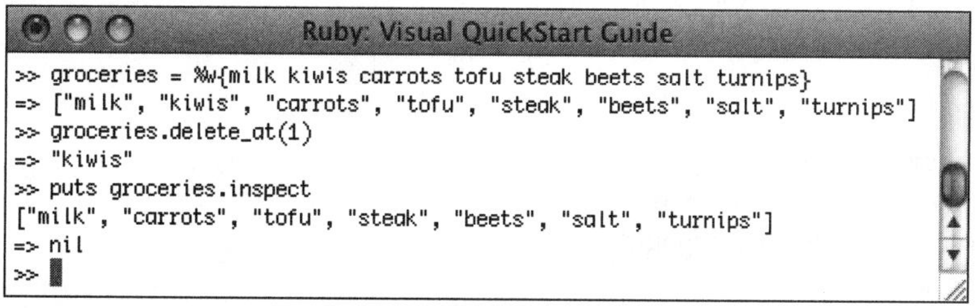

Figure 4.11 An array is created and one value removed.

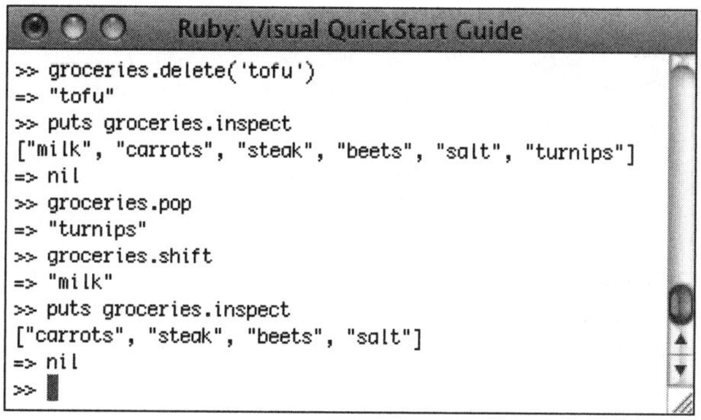

```
>> groceries.delete('tofu')
=> "tofu"
>> puts groceries.inspect
["milk", "carrots", "steak", "beets", "salt", "turnips"]
=> nil
>> groceries.pop
=> "turnips"
>> groceries.shift
=> "milk"
>> puts groceries.inspect
["carrots", "steak", "beets", "salt"]
=> nil
>>
```

Figure 4.12 More array elements are removed using three different methods.

Arrays and Strings

Conversions between arrays and strings are quite common, so I want to give a little extra attention to the topic here. Remember that an array is a list of values, whereas a string is any quoted character (or group of characters). The `to_s` method will convert an array to a string by combining all of the values:

```
a = [1, 2, 3, 4]
a.to_s # Returns "1234"
```

The `join` method does the same thing, but it takes an optional *glue* argument—a character (or character combination) to be placed between the array items within the string:

```
a.join('-') # Returns "1-2-3-4"
```

Turning a string into an array requires the `scan` or `split` method. I'll demonstrate `split` here, and you'll learn more about `scan` in Chapter 10, "Regular Expressions." The `split` method breaks up a string into an array using another string (or a regular expression pattern) as the indicator of where to make the breaks. Its default separator is any white space (spaces, tabs, carriage returns, and newlines):

```
vowels = 'a e i o u'
vowels.split
```

Now `vowels` is an array of five elements: *a*, *e*, *i*, *o*, and *u*. Multiple continuous spaces are ignored in such situations, as are leading and terminating white space.

If you'd like to use a different separator, provide that as an argument to the `split` method:

```
poem = %q{line 1
line 2
line 3}
poem.split("\n")
```

After calling split on the newline character, the poem string will be turned into an array of three elements (**Figure 4.13**). Note that the separator will be removed from the values.

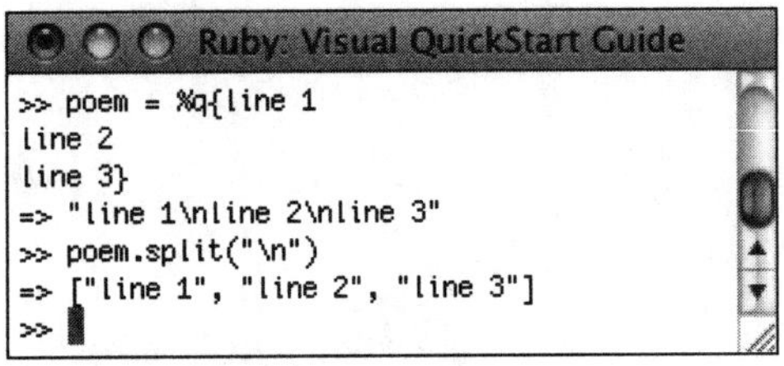

Figure 4.13 Strings can be broken on any character or character sequence you want, including newlines.

To convert arrays and strings:

1. Create a string containing some words:

   ```
   list = 'giraffe, cat, cow, bird, dog,
   → rabbit, walrus'
   ```

   For the sake of this example, let's say this list of words (which was maybe read in from a file or inputted by the user) needs to be sorted, counted, and returned in alphabetical order. As a string there's no way to do that.

2. Turn the string into an array:

   ```
   list_array = list.split(', ')
   ```

   The string will be turned into an array by splitting it up using a combination of commas plus a space. The returned value—the array—is assigned to list_array.

3. Count the number of words (**Figure 4.14**):

   ```
   puts list_array.length
   ```

4. Turn the array back into a string, this time in alphabetical order (**Figure 4.15**).

   ```
   list = list_array.sort.join(', ')
   ```

   First the list array is sorted, and then join is applied, inserting a comma plus a space between each element to create the string. This final value of list could also be created in one step, using

   ```
   list = list.split(', ').sort.join(', ')
   ```

✔ Tips

- The ability to convert between arrays and strings relies upon using separators (or glue) that won't appear within the individual values.

- To break a string into an array by individual characters, use ' ', "", or // as the separator:

   ```
   word = 'text'
   word.split(//) # ['t', 'e', 'x', 't']
   ```

```
>> list = 'giraffe, cat, cow, bird, dog, rabbit, walrus'
=> "giraffe, cat, cow, bird, dog, rabbit, walrus"
>> list_array = list.split(', ')
=> ["giraffe", "cat", "cow", "bird", "dog", "rabbit", "walrus"]
>> puts list_array.length
7
=> nil
>>
```

Figure 4.14 A string of comma-separated words is turned into an array, then counted.

```
>> list = list_array.sort.join(', ')
=> "bird, cat, cow, dog, giraffe, rabbit, walrus"
>>
```

Figure 4.15 The array is sorted alphabetically and then turned back into a string using join.

Using Ranges

A *range* is like a variation of an array, one that's sequential and much, much easier to create. Ranges use the same naming scheme as arrays and other variables and are assigned values using the assignment operator. But the value of a range is created by separating the beginning and end points of the range by either two or three periods:

```
numbers = 1...10
letters = 'A'..'Z'
```

If two dots are used, the range includes both the starting and ending values. If three dots are used, the range includes the starting value but not the ending value (so the `numbers` range represents the integers 1 through 9).

One interesting thing about a range is that it's not actually populated like an array. If you were to output a range, you'd see just how it was created (**Figure 4.16**):

```
puts numbers
puts letters
```

One way to make a range more useful is by applying the `to_a` method to convert it to an array (**Figure 4.17**):

```
puts numbers.to_a
```

To see if a value is found within a range, use the `include?` method:

```
numbers.include?(9) # true
letters.include?('B') # true
letters.include?('b') # false
```

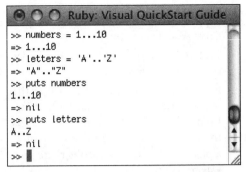

Figure 4.16 Calling `puts` with ranges prints out their definition, not the values they implicitly contain.

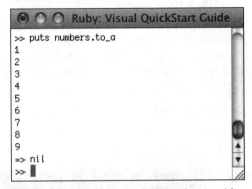

Figure 4.17 The values within a range can be printed (or used in other ways) by converting it to an array first.

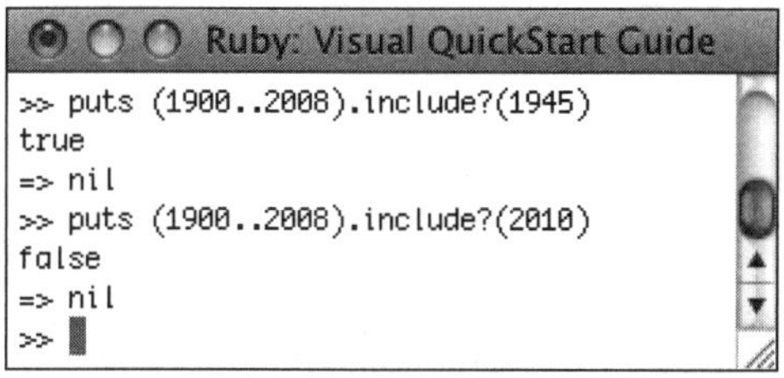

```
>> puts (1900..2008).include?(1945)
true
=> nil
>> puts (1900..2008).include?(2010)
false
=> nil
>>
```

Figure 4.18 One common use of ranges is to see if a value falls within an allowed set.

Ranges are most often used for comparisons (e.g., to see if a number is within a certain series) or iterations (e.g., looping through something ten times). You can create ranges using different data types, but in reality you'll only want to do so with numbers and simple strings. The reason why is quite technical, but it has to do with Ruby's ability to sequence the values. For example, it's easy to make a range from A to Z, to check if a letter is within that range, and to print out each character in the range. The same goes for integers. And Ruby can easily check if a float is within a given range:

```
gpa = 0.0..4.0
gpa.include?(3.2) # true
```

However, Ruby could not convert that floating-point range to an array and iterate through it because there'd be a virtually infinite list of values.

Two final thoughts on ranges before walking through some examples: First, ranges can be used without variables, but doing so requires wrapping the range within parentheses:

```
puts (1..10).to_a
```

Second, ranges can be used to indicate a subset of an array:

```
a = [1, 2, 3, 4, 5, 6]
puts a[0..2]
```

The **puts** line will print the numbers 1, 2, and 3, which are the elements indexed at 0, 1, and 2).

To use ranges:

1. See if a year is within a valid range (**Figure 4.18**):

   ```
   puts (1900..2008).include?(1945)
   puts (1900..2008).include?(2010)
   ```

   A year is just an integer, so it can easily be checked against a range of given values.

   continues on next page

2. Create a string containing every lower-case letter in reverse order (**Figure 4.19**):

`letters = ('a'..'z').to_a.reverse.join`

The range `'a'..'z'` will create the necessary 26 letters (you couldn't use `'z'..'a'`, as ranges must use incremental values). This range is then converted to an array, placed in reverse order, and then turned into a string using `join`.

3. Find the next five letters starting at the middle of the alphabet (**Figure 4.20**):

`letters = ('a'..'z').to_a`

`puts letters[13..17]`

Alternatively, you could write this all on one line:

`puts ('a'..'z').to_a[13..17]`

Or

`puts ('a'..'z').to_a[13...18]`

Or

`puts ('a'..'z').to_a[13, 5]`

(Did I mention there's more than one way to do things in Ruby?)

✔ Tips

■ Ruby 1.9 introduces a new `Range` method called `cover?`. It can be used instead of `include?` and will generally provide faster results.

■ Ranges cannot be defined so that they exclude their beginning value. If you need to do that, just use the next logical initial value instead.

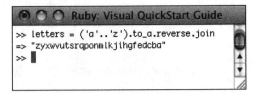

Figure 4.19 By creating a range and converting it to an array, it can easily be manipulated, including turning it into a string.

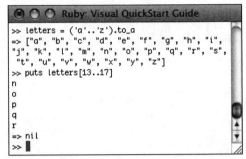

Figure 4.20 Here ranges are used both to create the initial array and to find a subset of it.

Creating a Hash

A hash is like an array in many ways, except a hash uses associated keys (in some languages these are called *associative arrays*). Whereas arrays use numeric indexes, from 0 to `array.length - 1`, hashes use meaningful indexes, normally strings or symbols.

To create a hash, use this syntax:

```
my_hash = {'key' => 'value'}
```

To create a hash with multiple elements, separate each *key-value* pair with a comma:

```
states = {'MD' => 'Maryland', 'IA' =>
→ 'Iowa'}
```

To refer to a hash element, use its key, just as you would an index position in an array:

```
puts states['MD']
```

Referring to a hash key that doesn't exist returns the value `nil`:

```
puts states['QC'] # nil
```

To add items to a hash, you can simply do this:

```
states['IL'] = 'Illinois'
```

In situations where the keys are representative of values and don't need to be used as strings themselves, symbols make a logical choice:

```
me = {:name => 'Larry', :age => 87}
```

To practice using hashes, this next sequence of steps will build up a *multidimensional hash*: a hash where its element values are also hashes.

To use hashes:

1. Create two hashes:

   ```
   english = {:name => 'Grammar',
   → :teacher => 'Ms. Krabapple'}
   science = {:name => 'Physics',
   → :teacher => 'Mr. Frink'}
   ```

   Both hashes contain two elements, one indexed at `:name` and the other at `:teacher`.

2. Create a multidimensional hash (**Figure 4.21**):

   ```
   classes = {'english' => english,
   → 'science' => science}
   ```

   To create a multidimensional hash, a new variable is created using the *key-value* syntax. In this case, however, the values are other hashes. You don't need to create the `english` and `science` hash variables as I do in Step 1, but for the sake of learning, it keeps the syntax cleaner and easier to follow.

continues on next page

```
Command Prompt - irb                                              _ □ ×
>> english = {:name => 'Grammar', :teacher => 'Ms. Krabapple'}
=> {:name=>"Grammar", :teacher=>"Ms. Krabapple"}
>> science = {:name => 'Physics', :teacher => 'Mr. Frink'}
=> {:name=>"Physics", :teacher=>"Mr. Frink"}
>> classes = {'english' => english, 'science' => science}
=> {"science"=>{:name=>"Physics", :teacher=>"Mr. Frink"}, "english"=>{:name=>"Gr
ammar", :teacher=>"Ms. Krabapple"}}
>> _
```

Figure 4.21 The multidimensional `classes` hash contains two elements, each of which is a hash that also has two elements.

3. Print the name of the person that teaches the English course:

```
puts classes['english'][:teacher]
```

When working with multidimensional hashes, refer to the first dimension's key within square brackets, followed by the second dimension's key with square brackets. In this case, the first dimension uses strings for keys while the second uses symbols.

4. Print the name of the science course (**Figure 4.22**):

```
puts classes['science'][:name]
```

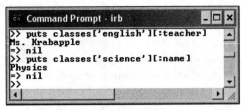

Figure 4.22 The values of two specific hash elements are printed.

✔ Tips

- Alternatively, the `classes` hash could have been created as an array using:

  ```
  class = [english, science]
  ```

  To then refer to a specific teacher or class, you would write

  ```
  puts classes[0][:teacher]
  puts classes[1][:name]
  ```

- Ruby 1.9 supports an alternative syntax for creating hashes with symbols for keys:

  ```
  states = {MD: 'Maryland', IA: 'Iowa'}
  ```

  is the same as

  ```
  states = {:MD => 'Maryland', :IA =>
  'Iowa'}
  ```

- Hashes in Ruby 1.8 and earlier do not necessarily retain the order of the elements as they were created. Hashes in Ruby 1.9 and later will remember the order of the elements.

CREATING A HASH

Common Hash Methods

Many of the methods used with hashes are the same as those used with arrays. These include `each` (discussed in Chapter 5), `delete`, `length`, `index`, `shift`, and `sort`. Start with this hash:

```
states = {'MD' => 'Maryland', 'IA' =>
→'Iowa', 'IL' => 'Illinois'}
```

The `delete` method is provided the key of element to be deleted:

```
states.delete('IL')
```

It returns the value deleted in the process.

To find the key associated with a particular value, use `index`:

```
abbr = states.index('Maryland') # "MD"
```

The `shift` method cuts the first key-value pair from a hash, returning both as an array:

```
md = states.shift # ["MD", "Maryland"]
```

The `length` (and synonymous `size`) methods return the number of elements in the hash:

```
count = states.length
```

The `sort` method differs from the array's `sort` method in that it sorts the elements in the hash by key (hashes can be sorted by value, but doing so requires special syntax not yet covered).

Because hashes have a key-value relationship, there are other methods particular to hashes, not present in arrays. The `keys` method returns an array of the keys in the hash; `values` returns an array of the values.

To see if a value is in a hash, use `has_value?` or the synonym `value?`:

```
puts states.has_value?('Quebec') # false
```

Similarly, `has_key?`—like its synonyms `key?`, `include?`, and `member?`—returns a Boolean value indicating if the hash has a given key:

```
puts states.has_key?('MD') # true
```

Finally, the `invert` method swaps all the keys and values. The relationship between the two will be maintained, but their roles will be switched (**Figure 4.23**).

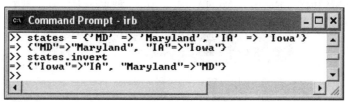

Figure 4.23 A demonstration of how the `invert` function works. Note that it returns the inverted hash without affecting the original.

To use hash methods:

1. Create a new hash:

   ```
   stooges = {'Moe' => 190, 'Larry' =>
   → 190, 'Curly' => 145}
   ```

   This hash stores the names of the Three Stooges characters (some of them, anyway), along with the number of shorts in which they appeared (approximately).

2. Sort the hash by key in alphabetical order (**Figure 4.24**):

   ```
   puts stooges.sort
   ```

   As you can see in Figure 4.24, when `puts` is called on an entire hash, both the keys and the values will be printed.

3. Replace Curly with Shemp:

   ```
   stooges.delete('Curly')
   stooges['Shemp'] = 32
   ```

   To remove a hash element, call `delete`, providing it with the key of the element to be deleted. To add a new element, use the hash name, followed by the new key within square brackets, assigning that a value.

4. Print out the current contents of the hash (**Figure 4.25**):

   ```
   puts stooges.inspect
   ```

✔ Tip

- The `clear` method empties a hash of all its elements.

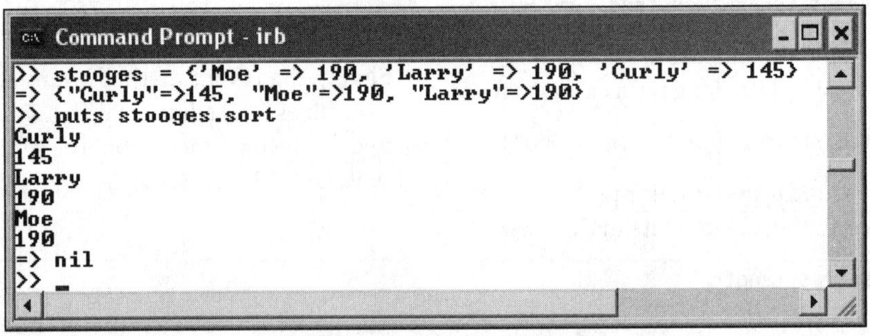

Figure 4.24 The creation and sorting of a hash, which is then printed.

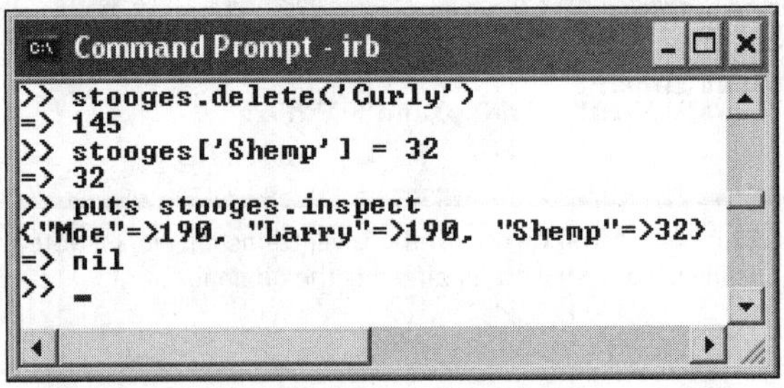

Figure 4.25 One Stooge left, another was added, and the whole hash was printed using `inspect`.

CONTROL STRUCTURES

Chapters 3, "Simple Types," and 4, "Arrays, Ranges, and Hashes," introduce the fundamental, built-in types of data you'll work with in Ruby. This chapter delves into another facet of programming: control structures. This topic includes operators, conditionals, loops, and iterators. What all of these have in common is their ability to alter the logical flow of Ruby code.

Operators

Many control structures, as well as other kinds of statements, rely upon various operators. Chapters 3 and 4 introduced some of these, including the assignment, arithmetic, array, and hash operators. **Table 5.1** adds to those the comparison and logical operators. These operators can be used in a statement that will return a Boolean value:

```
puts 2 > 3 # false
puts 3 > 2 && 3 < 4 # true
```

Most of the operators listed in Table 5.1 are easy to understand, but I do want to highlight the equality operator, which is two equals signs together. This is different from a single equals sign, which is the assignment operator:

```
x = 2 # Assignment
x == 2 # Equality
```

The comparison operator (<=>) returns a negative value if the left-hand operand is less than the right-hand operand, a positive value if the left-hand operand is greater than the right-hand operand, and 0 if the two have the same value:

```
puts 'cat' <=> 'dog' # -1
```

One use of this operator is in sorting a list by comparing the values it contains.

When using multiple operators within the same statement, one has to factor in *precedence*. Operator precedence affects the order in which operators are executed. In basic math, you learn that multiplication and division have higher precedence than addition and subtraction. So:

```
2 + 3 * 4 # 14, not 20
8 / 4 - 2 # 0, not 4
```

Table 5.1

Basic Operators	
OPERATOR	**MEANING**
<	less than
>	greater than
<=	less than or equal to
>=	greater than or equal to
==	equal to
===	identical
!=	not equal to
<=>	comparison
&&	and
||	or

Table 5.2

Operator Precedence	
OPERATOR	DESCRIPTION
[ ]	element reference
**	exponent
! + -	not, unary plus, unary minus
* / %	multiplication, division, modulus
+ -	plus, minus
>> <<	right shift, left shift
< <= => >	comparison
<=> == === !=	equality
&&	logical and
||	logical or
.. ...	range
? :	ternary
=	assignment (plus += etc.)

Table 5.2 lists Ruby's precedence order, from high to low, for several operators (some are omitted, like the bitwise operators). Note that plus and minus are listed both as unary operators, which indicate the sign of a number, and binary operators, for addition and subtraction.

Personally, I find that it's more foolproof and clearer to use parentheses, rather than relying upon precedence, so you're more likely to see me write equations using parentheses, even when not strictly necessary:

```
2 + (3 * 4) # still 14
```

Using operators alone, there are not many practical things you can do, but to test a couple of ideas, let's run a few examples within irb. Each will use puts to display the result of an expression. That value—the result of an expression—will be an important concept to keep in mind throughout the rest of the chapter.

To use operators:

1. Create some variables:

```
x = 2
y = 2.0
z = '2'
```

To play with some of the operators and types, I'll use an integer, a float, and a string. Each has a different representation of the value 2.

As you'll see when you execute these lines, each statement returns a value, namely, the value assigned to the variable.

continues on next page

2. Check if the variables are equal and identical (**Figure 5.1**):

```
puts x == y
puts x === y
puts x == z
```

These are trivial examples, but testing for equality will be used frequently in your programming.

3. Check if the variables are equal as strings (**Figure 5.2**):

```
puts x.to_s == z
puts y.to_s == z
```

The to_s method will return an object's value as a string, so that a string comparison can be made.

✔ Tips

■ Two other operators are =~ and !~. They are used to determine if a regular expression pattern is (=~) or is not (!~) matched by a given string. You'll see these in Chapter 10, "Regular Expressions."

■ Conventionally, methods that end with a question mark return a Boolean value. Such methods can often be used instead of operators. This—

```
puts 16.between?(0,35) # true
```

—is the same as—

```
puts 0 <= 16 && 16 <= 35
```

■ The eql? method returns true if two values are the same and of the same type:

```
puts 2.eql?(2.0) # false
puts 2.eql?(2) # true
```

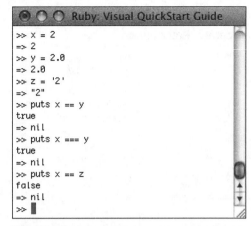

Figure 5.1 The two numeric types are equal and identical, but neither is equal to the string.

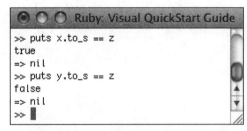

Figure 5.2 As strings, the x and z variables are equal, but y and z are not (because y is *2.0* as a string).

```
>> if defined? a_var then
?>   puts a_var
>> end
=> nil
>> a_var = 'trout'
=> "trout"
>> if defined? a_var then
?>   puts a_var
>> end
trout
=> nil
>> ▌
```

Figure 5.3 If the a_var variable hasn't been defined, the result of this conditional is nil. After the variable is assigned a value, the condition becomes true and the variable's value is printed.

Basic Conditionals

The if-then conditional is at the heart of any programming language. By using an if (the then is often omitted), the execution of one or more statements can take place only under explicit conditions. An if conditional in Ruby can be written in two different formats. The first is to use a block structure, concluding with the keyword end:

```
if condition then
    do this
end
```

As an example, this next bit of code will invoke the defined? method so that it only prints the value of a variable if the variable exists (**Figure 5.3**):

```
if defined? a_var then
    puts a_var
end
```

The syntax is rather straightforward, although you might be surprised to see that the condition is not placed within parentheses, as in some other languages. But you must use the keyword then to separate the condition from the executable statements, or otherwise follow the condition with a newline. So either the preceding example or these next two will work:

```
if defined? a_var then puts a_var end
if defined? a_var
    puts a_var
end
```

However, this will not work:

```
if defined? a_var puts a_var end # Error!
```

As in these examples, when creating an if conditional over multiple lines, the statements to be executed—and you can have as many as you'd like—are normally indented to indicate their subservient relationship.

BASIC CONDITIONALS

Conventionally, Ruby uses two spaces for indentation. This style of formatting isn't required but makes for more legible code.

To use conditionals, one must know how to distinguish between true and false. A condition in Ruby is considered to be true if it evaluates to anything other than `false` or `nil`. This means that the values `0`, `0.0`, and `'0'` are all true, unlike in some other programming languages. Testing for the existence of a variable, as in Figure 5.3, is a simple enough condition, but you can also use the operators in Table 5.1 to make other kinds of tests.

As an example, in the United States, Social Security tax is paid, at a rate of 2.9 percent, on the first $102,000 of income:

```
if income <= 102000
    ss = income * 0.029
end
```

Being Ruby, where things are often simplified as much as possible, `if` conditionals are normally written as a single line when there's only one resulting executable statement. In such cases, the condition can be written after the statement to be executed. The preceding example could be written more succinctly as

```
ss = income * 0.029 if income <= 102000
```

This is the second way you might use an `if` conditional: acting as a modifier of another expression. The earlier example, which tests for the existence of a variable, could also be written as:

```
puts a_var if defined? a_var
```

Finally, as mentioned in the previous set of tips, conditions can make use of methods that return a Boolean value:

```
puts 'valid' if user_input.between?(0,35)
```

To use conditionals:

1. Check if an array contains any duplicate values (**Figure 5.4**):

```
a = [1, 2, 2, 3, 4]
if a.uniq.length != a.length then
    puts 'The array contains duplicate
    ⇢ values!'
end
```

First, an array is created. Then the if conditional applies some of the know-how covered in Chapter 4. To determine if an array contains duplicate values, you could just apply uniq!, which returns nil if no duplicates are found, but that would permanently alter the array by removing any duplicate values. Instead, apply length to the array returned by uniq, then compare this to the size of the original array.

2. Repeat the code in Step 1 with an array that does not contain any duplicates.

```
a = [1, 2, 3, 4]
if a.uniq.length != a.length then
    puts 'The array contains duplicate
    ⇢ values!'
end
```

In this case, nothing will happen because the condition is not true. Therefore, the puts statement is never executed.

continues on next page

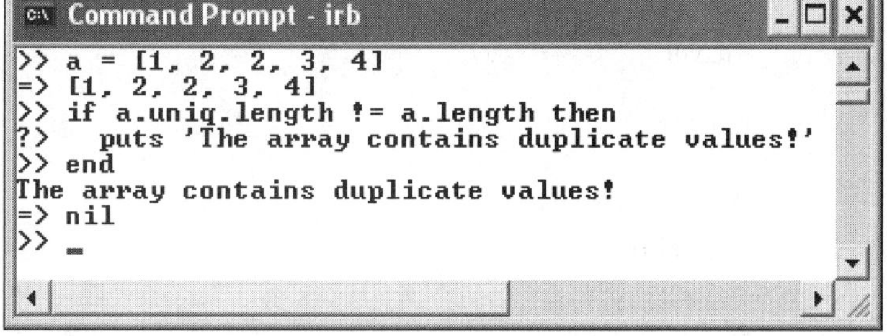

BASIC CONDITIONALS

```
>> a = [1, 2, 2, 3, 4]
=> [1, 2, 2, 3, 4]
>> if a.uniq.length != a.length then
?>    puts 'The array contains duplicate values!'
>> end
The array contains duplicate values!
=> nil
>>
```

Figure 5.4 The combination of two methods and the not equals operator is used to determine if an array contains duplicate values.

3. Print a value if it's within a given range:

```
num = 54
puts num if (0..100).include?(num)
```

The `include?` method, which can be used with arrays, ranges, and hashes, returns `true` if a given value is found within the set of values. Here it's used in an `if` conditional that modifies the `puts num` expression. So the number will be printed only if it's found within that range.

4. Repeat Step 3 with a value that's not within the range (**Figure 5.5**):

```
num = 154
puts num if (0..100).include?(num)
```

As in Step 2, the `puts` statement will not be executed, as the condition is false.

✔ Tips

- The `irb` prompt changes when you're typing code within the confines of a control structure (see Figures 5.3 and 5.4).

- In Ruby, only the values `false` and `nil` are considered to be false. Any other value is considered to be true, including the number `0`, an empty string, or `NaN` (meaning *not a number*).

- You can use a semicolon in place of the keyword `then`. Ruby 1.8 (but not Ruby 1.9 and later) also allows you to use a colon instead of `then`.

- A common cause of problems is inadvertent use of the assignment operator (=) in place of the equality operator (==). Fortunately, Ruby is smart enough to trigger a warning should you attempt to use the assignment operator as part of a condition.

```
Command Prompt - irb
>> num = 54
=> 54
>> puts num if (0..100).include?(num)
54
=> nil
>> num = 154
=> 154
>> puts num if (0..100).include?(num)
=> nil
>>
```

Figure 5.5 The `include?` method, which returns a Boolean value, is used to see if a specific value is within a range of numbers.

Extended Conditionals

The if conditional is a basic control structure, but it can be expanded as needed. An if statement is often paired with an else, which takes effect when the given condition is not true.

```
if condition then
    do this
else
    do this instead
end
```

Unlike the statements that follow the condition, those that follow the else do not need to be on their own line. However, it is standard to do exactly that unless you're putting the entire construct on a single line.

If you'd like to test for a second condition, add an elsif clause (note there's only one *e* in *elsif*):

```
if condition1 then
    do this
elsif condition2 then
    do this instead
end
```

You can have multiple elsif clauses and you can use else with an if-elsif, but the else must always come last. The else will act like a default case, always taking effect if the control structure gets to that point

(i.e., if none of the preceding conditions are true). Also note that the keyword then is optional after a condition (an if or elsif) so long as a newline is present.

Before getting into some more examples, there's one more thing to point out. Control structures in Ruby are actually *expressions* in that they return values. You can take advantage of this in your programming. For example, the following code would assign an appropriate value to the variable:

```
ss = if income <= 102000
        income * 0.029
elsif income > 102000
        102000 * 0.029
else
        0
end
```

This is just a different way of writing

```
if income <= 102000
    ss = income * 0.029
elsif income > 102000
    ss = 102000 * 0.029
else
    ss = 0
end
```

This may seem a little strange, particularly if you've used other programming languages before, but little shortcuts like this is what Ruby's all about.

To use elsif and else:

1. Create a grade point average–specific message (**Figure 5.6**):

```
gpa = 3.75
msg = if gpa >= 3.9 then
   'summa cum laude'
elsif gpa >= 3.75 then
   'magna cum laude'
elsif gpa >= 3.5 then
   'cum laude'
else
   'graduating'
end
```

The premise behind this example is to create a message associated with a person's grade point average. So the msg variable will be assigned the value returned by this conditional. The first condition checks if the gpa variable is greater than or equal to 3.9, meaning that the person is graduating with highest honors (depending upon the school's grade point system, of course). Two more conditions test for magna cum laude and cum laude. If none of these conditions are true, then the else clause takes effect.

2. Rerun the code in Step 1 using different grade point values.

3. Add only a new value to an array (**Figure 5.7**):

```
pets = ['cat', 'dog', 'bird']
new_pet = 'naked mole rat'
if pets.include?(new_pet)
   puts "#{new_pet} is already
   → listed."
else
   pets << new_pet
   puts pets.inspect
end
```

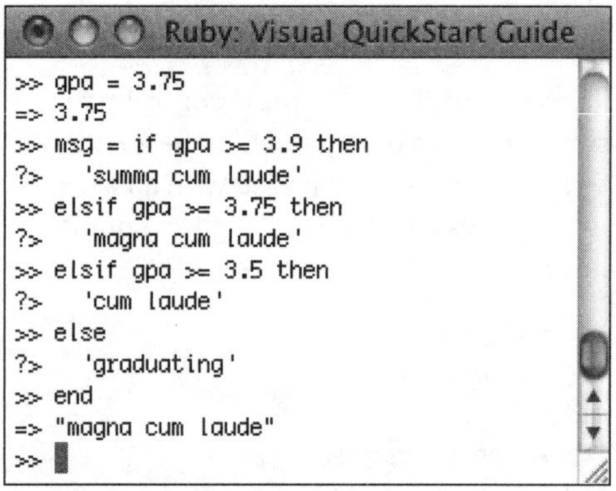

Figure 5.6 An if-elsif-elsif-else conditional is used to assign a value to a variable.

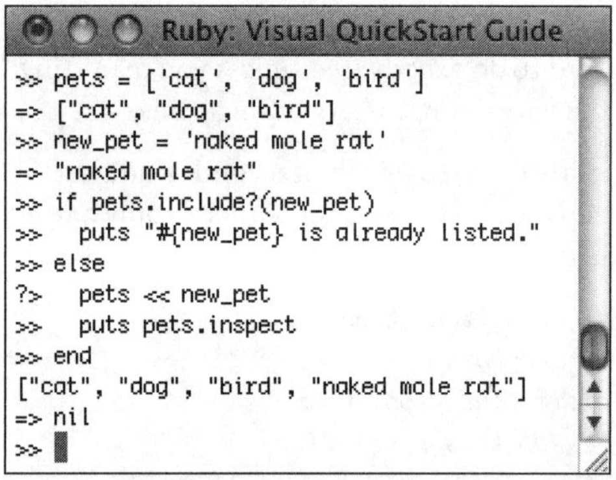

Figure 5.7 Only a unique value will be added to the array, after which the array's contents will be reprinted.

```
>> pets = ['cat', 'dog', 'bird']
=> ["cat", "dog", "bird"]
>> new_pet = 'dog'
=> "dog"
>> if pets.include?(new_pet)
>>    puts "#{new_pet} is already listed."
>> else
?>    pets << new_pet
>>    puts pets.inspect
>> end
dog is already listed.
=> nil
>>
```

Figure 5.8 The message, printed because the condition is true, says that the string is already present in the array.

When a value is added to an array, no check is made to see if the value is already present, a condition you may want to ensure in some situations. To accomplish that, first an array is created, then a string variable. The if condition checks if that string value is already within the array. If so, a message saying as much is printed. Otherwise, the new value is added to the array and the entire array is reprinted.

4. Rerun the code in Step 3 using an existing value (**Figure 5.8**):

```
pets = ['cat', 'dog', 'bird']
new_pet = 'dog'
if pets.include?(new_pet)
    puts "#{new_pet} is already
    ↪ listed."
else
    pets << new_pet
    puts pets.inspect
end
```

With this code, the string value won't be added to the array, and a message saying that the value is already present will be printed.

✔ **Tip**

■ Note that you cannot use else or elsif clauses when using this syntax:
```
ss = income * 0.029 if income
↪ <= 102000
```

The unless Conditional

Conditionals can also be created using unless, which means *if not*. For instance, this example performs division unless the denominator equals zero:

```
x = y / z unless z == 0
```

Normally, which you use—if or unless—is a matter of semantics and personal preference (i.e., which you find easier to read and comprehend). Like if, an unless conditional can be written over multiple lines or on a single line. Both can use either newlines or the keyword then to differentiate between the condition and the statements to be executed. An unless conditional can also have an else clause, but it cannot use elsif.

The Conditional Operator

Ruby supports the ability to write if-else conditionals using ?:, the *conditional operator* (which can also be called the *ternary* or *trinary* operator). The syntax is a little different, but its compactness makes it very useful:

```
condition ? return_if_true :
→ return_if_false
```

The condition is tested, and if it is true, the value (or result of a statement) after the question mark is returned. If the condition is false, the value (or result of a statement) after the colon is returned. This syntax is commonly used to assign a value to a variable:

```
x = y >= 0 ? y : -y
```

That example, which needlessly replicates the *abs* (absolute value) method, assigns to x either the value of y or the opposite of the value of y, depending upon whether y is greater than or equal to 0.

The conditional operator can also be used to adjust what text is printed (**Figure 5.9**):

```
puts "You purchased #{qty} #{qty > 1 ?
→ 'widgets' : 'widget'}"
```

This works, in part, because you can place full expressions within #{} in double-quoted strings.

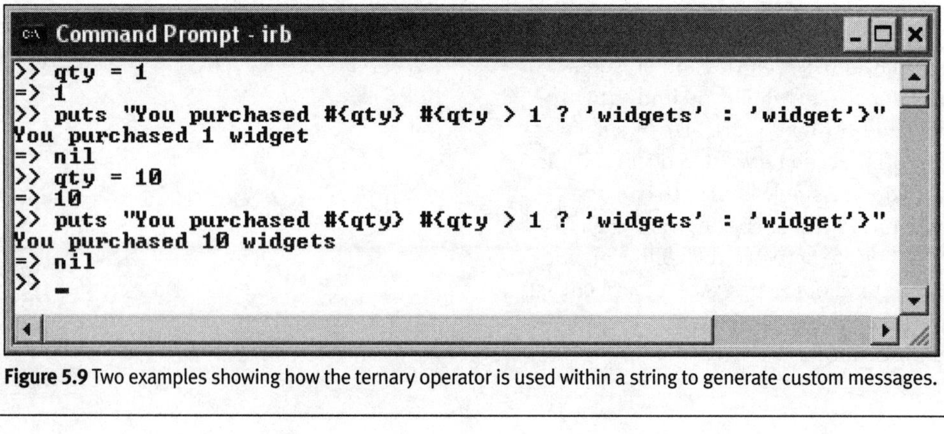

Figure 5.9 Two examples showing how the ternary operator is used within a string to generate custom messages.

Rewritten using `if`, these two examples might look like

```
x = if y >= 0 then y else -y end
```

and

```
print "You purchased #{qty} widget"
print 's' if qty > 1
puts
```

(The second example uses `print`, and then `puts`, to properly control where newlines are added.)

The conditional operator has relatively low precedence (see Table 5.2), which means that parentheses are not often required. As always, using parentheses to make the logic clear and explicit is still a good idea. So, if you'd like to make the absolute value line easier to read, you can optionally do

```
x = (y >= 0) ? y : -y
```

or

```
x = (y >= 0 ? y : -y)
```

Most importantly, both the `defined?` method and the assignment operators have lower precedence than the conditional operator, so you must use parentheses when invoking them:

```
x = (defined? d) ? d : (d = 88)
```

That somewhat cryptic line checks to see if a variable called `d` is defined. If it is, then `x` is assigned its value. If `d` is not defined, `d` will be assigned the value **88** (for whatever reason), *as will* `x`, because the returned value of the statement `d = 88` is **88**.

To use the conditional operator:

1. Print the value of a variable only if it's been defined:

```
puts (defined? some_var) ? some_var :
→ 'some_var is undefined'
```

As has already been demonstrated, the defined? method returns true if the given variable has been defined. This line, therefore, prints a variable's value, if it has one, or prints a message saying that the variable hasn't been defined otherwise.

2. Retry the conditional in Step 1 after defining the variable (**Figure 5.10**):

```
some_var = 2346.3

puts (defined? some_var) ? some_var :
→ 'some_var is undefined'
```

3. Only perform division if the denominator isn't zero:

```
x = 32.2
y = 0
puts (y == 0) ? 'division by zero'
→ : (x / y)
```

Division by zero is a bad thing in math and in programming. To prevent that from being attempted, the condition checks if the denominator is equal to zero. If so, a message is printed. Otherwise, the division takes place and that result is printed.

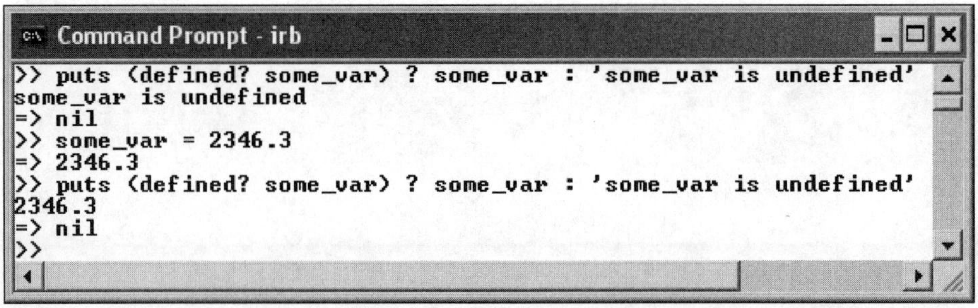

```
>> puts (defined? some_var) ? some_var : 'some_var is undefined'
some_var is undefined
=> nil
>> some_var = 2346.3
=> 2346.3
>> puts (defined? some_var) ? some_var : 'some_var is undefined'
2346.3
=> nil
>>
```

Figure 5.10 If a variable is not defined, a message saying that is printed. Otherwise, the variable's value is printed.

THE CONDITIONAL OPERATOR

4. Retry the conditional in Step 3 using a non-zero value for y (**Figure 5.11**):

```
x = 32.2
y = 5
puts (y == 0) ? 'division by zero'
→ : (x / y)
```

✔ Tips

■ When looking at the figures, remember that the `puts` method returns the value `nil`. So some of the `nil`s you'll see are the result of executing a `puts`, not the result of a conditional.

■ You can only execute a single statement when using the conditional operator. If multiple things need to happen if a condition is or is not true, you'll need to use a standard `if-then-else` instead.

■ Ruby 1.9 allows the colon and third part of the ternary expression to be placed on another line, so long as a space follows the colon. If no space were used, the colon would be treated as the start of a symbol, causing a problem.

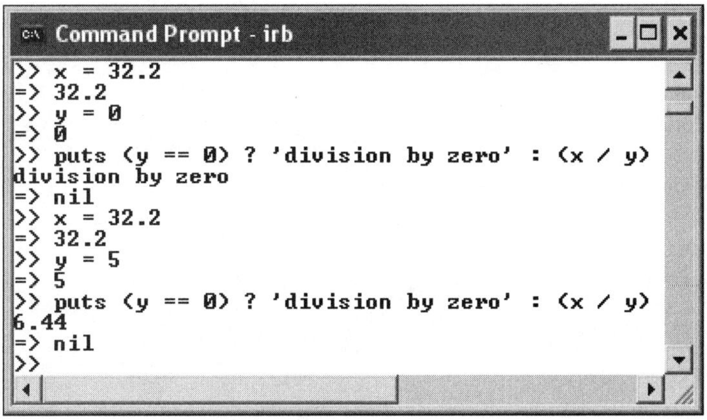

```
>> x = 32.2
=> 32.2
>> y = 0
=> 0
>> puts (y == 0) ? 'division by zero' : (x / y)
division by zero
=> nil
>> x = 32.2
=> 32.2
>> y = 5
=> 5
>> puts (y == 0) ? 'division by zero' : (x / y)
6.44
=> nil
>>
```

Figure 5.11 Division will not take place if the denominator equals 0.

Case Statements

The final type of conditional to be discussed is case. A case statement compares the value of a variable or the result of a statement against multiple possible values. When a match is made, the associated statements are executed. The basic syntax is

```
case exp
when value1
    do this
when value2
    do this instead
end
```

A case statement can have as many when comparisons as you'd like. They can also have an else clause, which must come last, that takes effect should none of the when values match.

Frequently a case is used to compare a variable against several logical values. When doing this, the expression is just the variable itself:

```
case gender
when 'M'
    print 'Mr. '
when 'F'
    print 'Mrs. '
else
    print 'Mr./Mrs. '
end
```

Because the executed statements within a case return results, a case can be used to assign a value to a variable, just as you've seen with an if conditional:

```
salutation = case gender
when 'M'
    'Mr. '
when 'F'
    'Mrs. '
else
    'Mr./Mrs. '
end
```

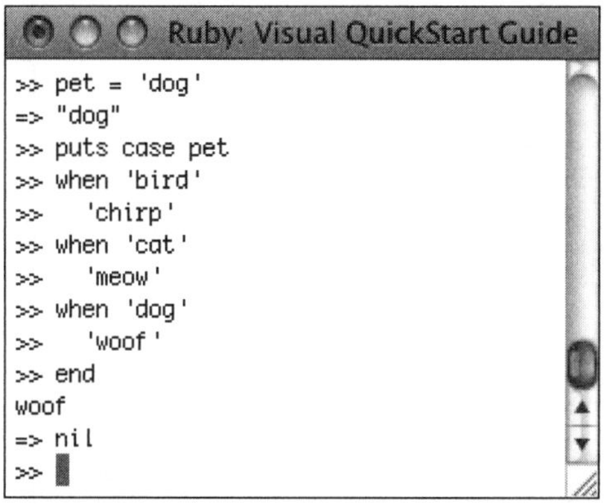

```
⊙ ○ ○   Ruby: Visual QuickStart Guide
>> pet = 'dog'
=> "dog"
>> puts case pet
>> when 'bird'
>>    'chirp'
>> when 'cat'
>>    'meow'
>> when 'dog'
>>    'woof'
>> end
woof
=> nil
>> █
```

Figure 5.12 The noise associated with an animal will be printed if there's a when clause whose value matches the pet variable.

Before practicing this, there's one last idea to mention. Instead of using singular values for the case comparisons, you can use ranges to easily see if a variable is within a group of values:

```
case x
when 0..9
    puts 'this'
when 10..19
    puts 'that'
end
```

To use case statements:

1. Print a pet-associated message (**Figure 5.12**):

```
pet = 'dog'
puts case pet
when 'bird'
    'chirp'
when 'cat'
    'meow'
when 'dog'
    'woof'
end
```

Another obviously trivial example, but it's an effective demonstration of the syntax. By using a case statement immediately after puts, the result of the case will be printed (because it's returned to puts).

This case statement has no else clause, which is perfectly fine.

2. Repeat the code in Step 1 using a different value for pet.

If you use a pet value that doesn't match up with one of the cases, the value nil will be printed, because that's what the case will return. An else clause would prevent that from happening.

continues on next page

3. Assign a letter grade based upon a numeric score (**Figure 5.13**):

```
score = 75
grade = case score
when 0...60
  'F'
when 60...70
  'D'
when 70...80
  'C'
when 80...90
  'B'
when 90..100
  'A'
else
  'n/a'
end
```

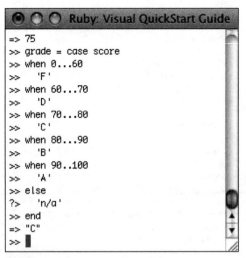

Figure 5.13 A *case* statement that uses ranges assigns the correct letter grade associated with a numerical score.

First a variable called score is assigned a numeric value (it could be a float, too). Then grade will be assigned the result returned by the case. For each when, a range is created. The first four ranges use the exclusionary three periods. This means, for example, that the first range is actually from 0 to 59, but it's written as 0 to 60, which I find slightly easier to read. The exception is the final when statement, which does include 100.

4. Change the value of score and rerun the case statement from Step 3.

For any value of score between 0 and 100, the correct grade will be assigned. If score has a value outside of that range, including non-numeric values, it's considered to be illegitimate and the grade variable is assigned a value of *n/a* (short for *not applicable*).

✔ Tips

■ A single statement associated with a when can be placed on the same line as the when if it's preceded by a colon:

```
salutation = case gender
when 'M': 'Mr. '
when 'F': 'Mrs. '
else 'Mr./Mrs. '
end
```

Single else statements can always be placed immediately after the else keyword, without needing a colon.

■ To have multiple possible values have the same result, separate the values by commas:

```
puts case gender
when 'M', 'm': 'Mr. '
when 'F', 'f': 'Mrs. '
else
   'Mr./Mrs. '
end
```

Basic Loops

Ruby does support loops, although *iterators*—to be covered next—are more frequently used. Still, it's worth knowing the loop types and syntax.

The two basic loops are `while` and `for`. The distinction between the two can be subtle: a `while` loop is executed as long as a condition is true; a `for` loop is executed for a certain number of times. Normally `while` is used in circumstances where the number of executions won't be known at the outset, whereas a `for` loop is used when that value would be known. In Ruby, this means a `for` loop is reserved for arrays, ranges, and hashes (objects that have an `each` method). However, iterators are a better choice in such situations, so I'll leave further discussion of `for` loops to the "for Loops" sidebar.

The syntax of a `while` loop is

```
while condition do
    statements
end
```

The first time the loop is encountered, the condition will be checked for truth. If it is true, the statements within the loop will be executed, and then the process is repeated until the condition becomes false (**Figure 5.14**). It's critical that the statements within the loop eventually do something that will make the condition be false, or else you'll have an infinite loop.

This simple example prints the numbers 1 through 10:

```
n = 1
while n <= 10 do
    puts n
    n += 1
end
```

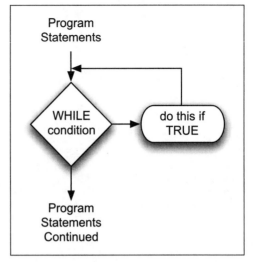

Figure 5.14 The logical flow of a `while` loop.

BASIC LOOPS

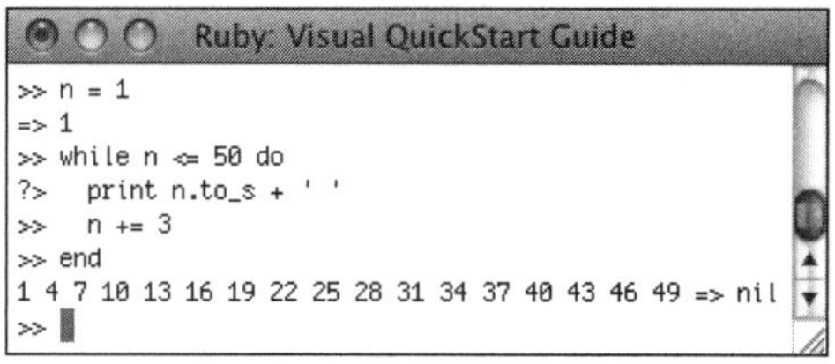

Figure 5.15 Using a while loop, a set of numbers can be quickly found and printed.

Of course, that could be more succinctly written as puts (1..10).to_a, but that's beside the point for now.

An until loop is just the opposite of while: it runs so long as a condition isn't true:

```
until condition do
    statements
end
```

For instance:

```
n = 1
until n > 10 do
    puts n
    n += 1
end
```

For both while and until, the do keyword is optional so long as a newline follows the condition.

Much of what one might do with a while loop requires knowledge not yet covered, so to just demonstrate the syntax a couple more times, let's practice with some relatively simple examples.

To use loops:

1. Count from 1 to 50 by threes (**Figure 5.15**):

```
n = 1
while n <= 50 do
    print n.to_s + ' '
    n += 3
end
```

To accomplish this, a number is first given a value of 1. The loop will be executed as long as the number is less than or equal to 50. Within the loop, the number is first printed and then incremented by three.

continues on next page

BASIC LOOPS

So that the resulting display takes up less space, I use print, separating each number by a space. This does require converting each number to a string, however.

2. Find the largest square less than 100 (**Figure 5.16**):

```ruby
n = 1
while (n**2) < 100
    n += 1
end
n -= 1
puts "The largest square less than
→ 100 is #{n**2} (#{n} * #{n})."
```

Figure 5.16 A while loop and some basic math quickly finds the largest square under a given limit.

For Loops

The for loop is one way to access every element within a collection, like an array or hash. The syntax is

```ruby
for var_name in collection_name do
    statements
end
```

As an example, take an array of the numbers 1 through 10:

```ruby
a = (1..10).to_a
for e in a
    puts e
end
```

For each value in the array, the loop will be called once, assigning the current value to the variable **e**. The loop's contents can then use the element's value (e) as needed.

With hashes, elements contain both keys and values. To access both, use two variables, separated by commas:

```ruby
h = {'a' => 1, 'b' => 2, 'c' => 3}
for k, v in h do
    puts "#{k} is #{v}"
end
```

That code will print out the key and corresponding value for each element in the hash.

I'm showing the for loop's syntax here in case you run across it elsewhere, but the fact is that iterators are a better and more common way to access the contents of arrays, ranges, and hashes.

The goal here is to determine what the maximum number whose square—that number to the second power—is still less than 100. To start, the number is given a value of 1. The condition then checks if the number to the second power is less than 100. If so, the number is incremented. This process will continue until n**2 is equal to or greater than 100.

Because the loop's condition will be false when the number has been incremented to a point where its square is greater than or equal to 100, after the loop terminates, I need to subtract 1 from the current value of n. For example, I know that the condition will be false when n equals 10 (because 10 * 10 equals 100), so subtracting 1 shows that 9 has the largest square less than 100 (specifically, 81).

The number and its square are then printed.

3. Change the while loop to find the largest square less than 1000 (**Figure 5.17**):

   Just change the one number in the while loop's condition (plus the same number within the puts statement) to make this work!

✔ Tips

- If you include the do keyword and there's only one statement to be executed, a while or until loop can go on one line:

  while *condition* do *statement* end

- A less common way of creating loops in Ruby starts with the keyword loop. The loop's statements are repeatedly executed until the loop is terminated using a break statement:

  ```
  loop do
      statements
      break if condition
  end
  ```

```
● ○ ○          Ruby: Visual QuickStart Guide
>> n = 1
=> 1
>> while (n**2) < 1000
>>    n += 1
>> end
=> nil
>> n -= 1
=> 31
>> puts "The largest square less than 1000 is #{n**2} (#{n} * #{n})."
The largest square less than 1000 is 961 (31 * 31).
=> nil
>>
```

Figure 5.17 Unlike the example in Figure 5.16, this answer I didn't know off the top of my head!

Numeric Iterators

Iterators are a fundamental and important control structure in Ruby. In practice, iterators are often used to perform some task multiple times, like a loop, although the full power and meaning of an iterator eclipses that simple notion. For now, though, think of iterators as methods that execute some code some number of times when applied to objects.

Iterators are tied to *blocks*, which are created using the keywords do and end:

```
object.iterator do
    statements
end
```

Blocks can also be written on a single line, in which case the curly braces are conventionally used:

```
object.iterator { statement }
```

Whichever syntax you use, when placing a block after a method call, the keyword do or the opening curly bracket must be on the same line as the method invocation. You cannot do this:

```
object.iterator
{ statements } # Error!
```

There are many iterators in Ruby; you choose one to suit the object upon which the action is being taken and what, exactly, you want to do with that object's values. As a trivial example, this will print out *Hello, World!* five times:

```
5.times { puts 'Hello, World!' }
```

When using iterators, you'll normally want to do something with the values being accessed in each iteration. To do so, write the block so that it takes a parameter by placing a variable name within vertical bars (also called *pipes*) as the first thing within the block. You could do this with the times method, but as a

Figure 5.18 The first example counts from 0 to 20 by twos. The second counts from 0 to 1.0 by tenths.

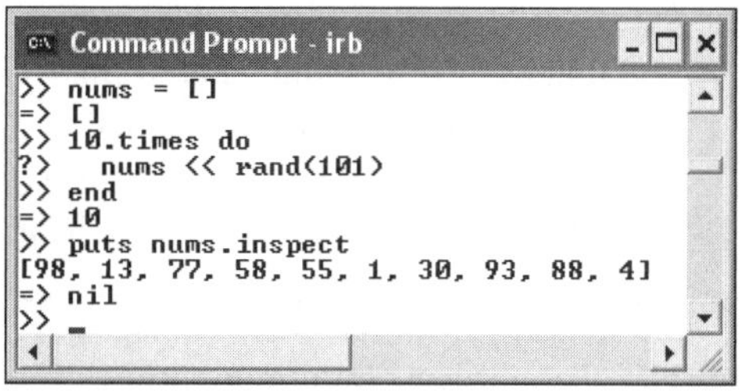

Figure 5.19 The `times` iterator is used to populate an array with ten random numbers.

better example, the `upto` and `downto` methods run from one integer value to another:

```
1.upto(10) { |num| puts num }
10.downto(1) { |num| puts num }
```

The first line counts from 1 to 10; the other counts down from 10 to 1.

Finally, the `step` method can be used on both integers and floats. Its first argument is the upper limit (as with `upto`), and its second is the increments to use (**Figure 5.18**):

```
0.step(20, 2) { |num| puts num}
0.step(1.0, 0.1) { |num| puts num}
```

To use numeric iterators:

1. Create an array of ten random numbers between 0 and 100 (**Figure 5.19**):

   ```
   nums = []
   10.times do
      nums << rand(101)
   end
   puts nums.inspect
   ```

   First, an empty array is created, called `nums`. Then, for ten iterations, a block is executed. Within the block, the `rand` method is called. When provided with a numeric argument, this method will return a semi-random number between 0 and up to (but not including) that argument value. So to allow for a maximum value of 100, the argument's value must be 101. The integer returned by the `rand` method will be pushed onto the array.

   Alternatively, the `fill` method of the array class could be used for this same purpose, as you'll see in the chapter's next sequence of steps.

continues on next page

NUMERIC ITERATORS

2. List all the odd numbers between 1 and 100 (**Figure 5.20**):

```
1.upto(100) {|n| print n.to_s + ' '
→ if n % 2 != 0 }
```

To iterate incrementally from one number to another, use upto. Within the block, the current number is received as n, and this value is printed only if the remainder of dividing the number by 2 does not equal 0. As with an earlier example, I use print, the conversion of the number to a string, plus a space, to display the list over one long line.

3. List all the odd numbers between 1 and 100 without using the modulus operator (**Figure 5.21**):

```
1.step(100, 2) { |n| print n.to_s
→ + ' ' }
```

Since you know that 1 is an odd number and that every other number after that is also odd, you can just use step to find this list, starting at one and incrementing by twos.

✔ Tips

■ Not all iterators in Ruby loop through a series of values. An iterator is just a method that can call a block of code. Normally that block of code is executed multiple times, but that's not necessarily always the case.

■ Some methods in Ruby take blocks as their argument. In other words, the value passed to the method when it's called is a block of code to be executed within that method.

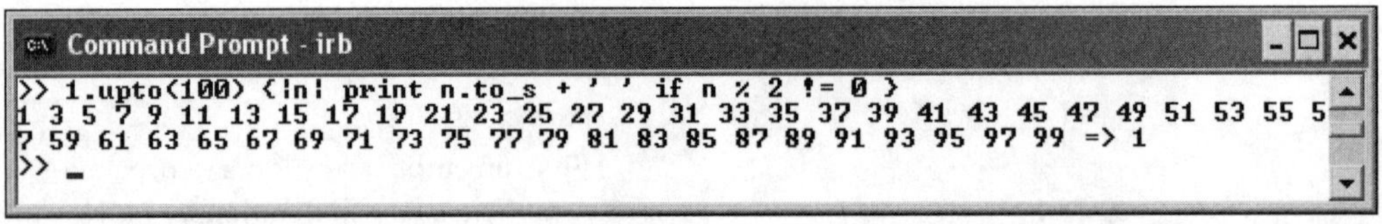

Figure 5.20 The upto iterator loops to a given value. Within each loop, only odd numbers are printed.

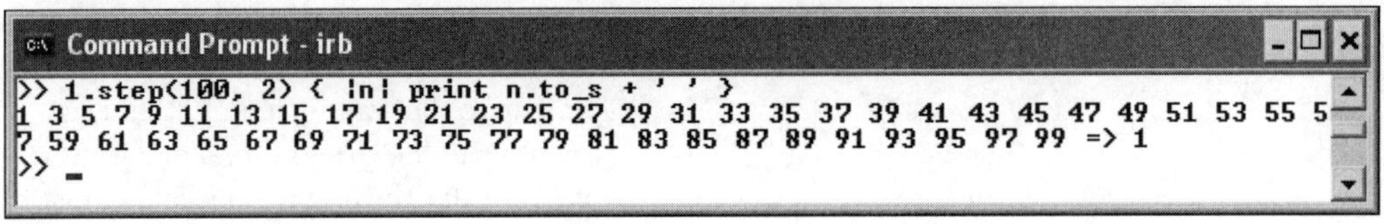

Figure 5.21 An alternate way to find a list of odd numbers.

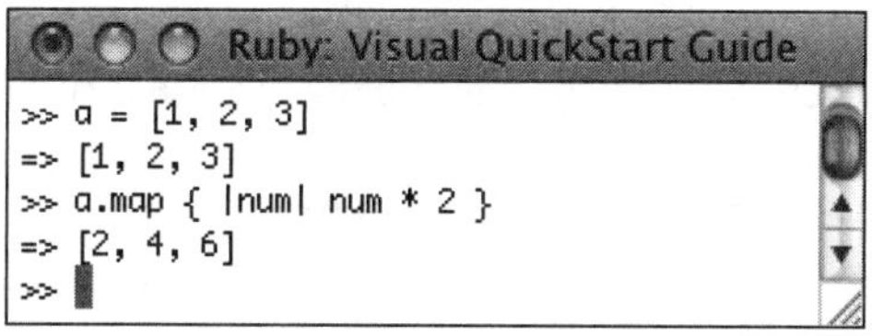

Figure 5.22 The map iterator is used to return an array of values. Here, the new array's values are each double the values in the first array.

break, next, redo, retry, return, and yield

There are a handful of statements in Ruby, used singularly like keywords, that also affect the flow of code execution. The break statement stops the execution of the current loop or iterator. It might be used to terminate the control structure should some condition become true. The next statement terminates the current execution of the loop or iterator, advancing on to the next iteration (i.e., unlike with break, the loop or iterator is not permanently stopped).

The redo statement restarts the current iteration of the loop. The retry statement restarts the entire loop or iterator from the beginning.

The return statement is used to return a value from a method. It also has the effect of terminating the execution of the method. The yield statement is used by methods to yield control, and a value, to a block that uses it. The yield is therefore used by any method that qualifies as an iterator. You'll see examples of both return and yield in the next chapter.

Collection Iterators

The preceding section of the chapter introduces the topics of iterators and blocks, demonstrating the numeric iterators in the process. These are easiest to comprehend but just the tip of the proverbial iterator iceberg.

With collections of data—arrays, ranges, and hashes, each is a standard iterator. This method call is followed by code within a block that will be executed once for every element in the array, range, or hash. As demonstrated with the numeric iterators, the block can be written to take a parameter so that it can use the current array element:

```
a = [1, 2, 3]
a.each { |num| puts num }
```

Another important iterator is map (and its synonym collect). This method also walks through a set one element at a time but, in the process, creates a new array containing the values returned by the block. This code returns an array with the values 2, 4, and 6 (**Figure 5.22**):

```
a = [1, 2, 3]
a.map { |num| num * 2 }
```

To make the changes to the given array, use map! or collect! instead (remember that methods whose names end with exclamation points conventionally alter the object to which they are replied). Note that you don't have to write num = num * 2 within the code block, as the result of the code block will be automatically assigned as elements in the new array.

The fill method can be used in many ways, including as an iterator. Its purpose is to populate an array with values. To use it as an iterator, provide a starting index position, plus a number of elements to create, and then follow it with the block that returns the values to be used:

```
a = Array.new
a.fill(0, 5) { |i| i*2 }
```

That line creates an array five elements long whose values are 0, 2, 4, 6, and 8. The block is executed five times, receiving the index position as an argument with each iteration. That index position—0 through 4—is then doubled. This doubled value is used as the element's value for the array at that position.

The preceding are just a couple of the array iterators (the tips reference some more), but I also want to mention two iterators used with ranges: each and step. The each method works just like each with arrays:

```ruby
(0..100).each {|n| print n.to_s + ' '
→ if n % 2 != 0 }
```

And step works similarly to the numeric step iterator, although it only takes one argument: the incrementation unit (**Figure 5.23**):

```ruby
(0..20).step(2) { |num| print num.to_s
→ + ' '}
```

Hashes can make use of many of the same iterators as arrays; with hashes, however, you have two important pieces of information for each element: the key and the value. For that reason, blocks handling hashes should be written to take two parameters:

```ruby
h = {'a' => 1, 'b' => 2, 'c' => 3}
h.each do |k, v|
    puts "#{k} = #{v}"
end
```

Instead of using each, each_pair is a slightly more efficient way to iterate through hashes. Here's that same code written using each_pair and placed on a single line:

```ruby
h = {'a' => 1, 'b' => 2, 'c' => 3}
h.each_pair { |k, v| puts "#{k} = #{v}" }
```

Another useful hash interator is select (it can also be used with arrays). It returns an array of values for which the code block returns true (**Figure 5.24**):

```ruby
h = {'moe' => 102, 'larry' => 125,
→ 'curly' => 86}
h.select { |k, v| v > 100 }
```

```
>> (0..100).each {|n| print n.to_s + ' ' if n % 2 != 0 }
1 3 5 7 9 11 13 15 17 19 21 23 25 27 29 31 33 35 37 39 41
 43 45 47 49 51 53 55 57 59 61 63 65 67 69 71 73 75 77 79
 81 83 85 87 89 91 93 95 97 99 => 0..100
>> (0..20).step(2) { |num| print num.to_s + ' '}
0 2 4 6 8 10 12 14 16 18 20 => 0..20
>>
```

Figure 5.23 The first example prints every odd number between 0 and 100. The second counts from 0 to 20 by twos.

```
>> h = {'a' => 1, 'b' => 2, 'c' => 3}
=> {"a"=>1, "b"=>2, "c"=>3}
>> h.each_pair { |k, v| puts "#{k} = #{v}" }
a = 1
b = 2
c = 3
=> {"a"=>1, "b"=>2, "c"=>3}
>> h = {'moe' => 102, 'larry' => 125, 'curly' => 86}
=> {"moe"=>102, "curly"=>86, "larry"=>125}
>> h.select { |k, v| v > 100 }
=> [["moe", 102], ["larry", 125]]
>>
```

Figure 5.24 The first example just shows how to iterate through an entire hash, printing each element's key and value. The second example uses select to return only hash elements whose value is greater than 100.

Before running through a few more examples, I should clarify that the names given to a block's parameters have the same restrictions as any other variable. I frequently use n, i, num, k, and v, but those are not required.

To use collection iterators:

1. Create an array of the squares from 1 to 100 (**Figure 5.25**):

```
squares = (1..10).to_a.map { |n|
→ n**2 }
```

A range is first created and then converted to an array, to create an array of the numbers 1 through 10. Then the map iterator is applied to this array. This method returns an array of values. The values themselves are the numbers to the second power.

You could also accomplish this using the fill method:

```
squares = Array.new
squares.fill(0, 10) { |i| (i + 1)
→ ** 2 }
```

In this case, you have to create a new, empty array first. Then to fill the array, you must add 1 to the index position—which goes from 0 to 9—prior to squaring the number.

In either example, the numbers 1 through 10 are used as the basis because I already know that the square of 10 is 100.

2. Print every even number between 1 and 100 that's also divisible by 3 (**Figure 5.26**):

```
(3..100).step(3) { |n| print n.to_s
→ + ' ' if n % 2 == 0 }
```

The range goes from 3 to 100, because I know that 3 is the first number that's divisible by 3. By using the step method, the iterator will loop in increments of 3, instead of one at a time. The block associated with the iterator will only print the number if the remainder of dividing it by 2 is 0. (This is another rather trivial example, but...)

continues on next page

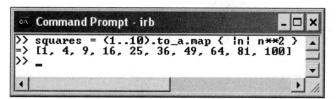

```
>> squares = (1..10).to_a.map { |n| n**2 }
=> [1, 4, 9, 16, 25, 36, 49, 64, 81, 100]
>>
```

Figure 5.25 An array of ten squares is created (in one line!) using a range, the to_a method, and map.

```
>> (3..100).step(3) { |n| print n.to_s + ' ' if n % 2 == 0 }
6 12 18 24 30 36 42 48 54 60 66 72 78 84 90 96 => 3..100
>>
```

Figure 5.26 Every even number divisible by three (aka every number divisible by six) between 0 and 100.

3. Display a list of states and their abbreviations (**Figure 5.27**):

```
states = {'AL' => 'Alabama', 'AK' =>
→ 'Alaska', 'AZ' => 'Arizona', 'AR'
→ => 'Arkansas'}
states.each_pair do |k, v|
    puts "The abbreviation for #{v}
    → is #{k}."
end
```

First, the hash is created. It uses the states' abbreviations as its keys and the corresponding state names for its values. I'm only using the first few, but you can flesh this out if you feel the need. Then the each_pair iterator is called. Within it, the keys and values are assigned to k and v, which are both used in a puts statement.

✔ Tips

■ The count method can use a block so that only element values that return true (from the block) will be counted. The following only counts the odd values in the array:

```
a = [1, 2, 3, 4, 5]
a.count{ |num| num % 2 != 0 }
```

■ The delete_if method can use a block so that only element values that return true (from the block) will be deleted. The following only deletes the even values in the array:

```
a = [1, 2, 3, 4, 5]
a.delete_if{ |num| num % 2 == 0 }
```

■ Other iterators that can be applied to collections include sort, reject, and inject.

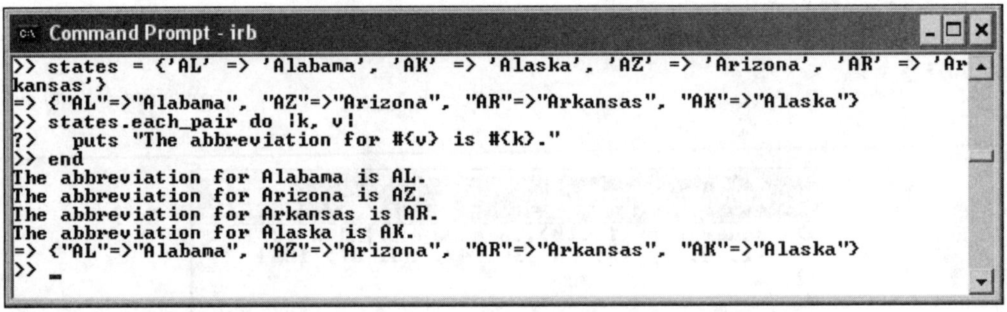

Figure 5.27 Walking through a hash using the each_pair method.

CREATING METHODS

Methods, or *functions* as they're called in non-object-oriented situations, are a crucial part of any programming language. A *function* is just a name given to the encapsulation of some code; when that function is part of a *class*, it's called a *method*. The ability to define and use methods and functions makes any programming endeavor that much easier and, in OOP languages like Ruby, makes the creation of classes and objects meaningful.

Ruby comes with hundreds of methods already defined, like `puts` and `include?`. Several dozen have already been demonstrated and put to use in the chapters leading up to this one. Here, the focus is on *defining and using your own methods*. You'll learn how to create simple methods, how to return values from methods, how to accept arguments, and how to provide default argument values. Those subjects cover the basics of method definitions. The last three sections of the chapter walk through the more sophisticated concepts of referencing the object to which a method is applied, creating methods that take variable-length arguments, and using methods with blocks.

Simple Methods

A method is defined using the keywords `def` and `end` to frame a section of code:

```
def method_name
    method code
end
```

The method's name will primarily contain letters, numbers, and the underscore. As you'll see, there are a few other special characters that may be part (or all) of the method's name, but stick to alphanumeric characters and the underscore to start. Conventionally, method names always begin with a lowercase letter and use underscores to break up words: *print_this*, not *printThis* or *PrintThis*.

The functionality of the method, which is to say the code that will be executed when the method is called, goes between the method's name and `end`.

Using just the information provided, there's not much that a method can do, but let's walk through an example using `irb` (or `fxri` on Windows, if you'd rather), just to make sure the basics make sense.

To create a method:

1. Begin defining a new method:

   ```
   def say_hello
   ```

   The keyword `def` begins the definition. The name of this method is `say_hello`.

2. Add the method's content:

   ```
   puts 'Hello, World!'
   ```

   This method performs the critical task of printing a *Hello, World!* message. (If it wasn't so important, why would so many books use it as an example?)

   The functionality of a method is normally indented two spaces from the `def` and `end` lines, although that's not syntactically required.

Creating Aliases

Ruby supports the ability to create aliases for methods: alternative names for the same functionality:

```
alias new_name original_name
```

So the `say_hello` method could also be invoked using `print_hello` after executing this statement:

```
alias print_hello say_hello
```

One reason to use aliases is to give a method a more natural label. For example, the `collect` method has an alias, `map`, which matches what people coming from other languages might be used to.

Another reason for using an alias is that you want to expand a method's definition while still being able to invoke its original definition. If you redefine a method after creating an alias to it, the alias will execute the method as it was previously declared.

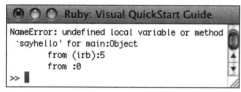

```
>> def say_hello
>>   puts 'Hello, World!'
>> end
=> nil
>>
```

Figure 6.1 The creation of a very simple method.

```
>> def say_hello
>>   puts 'Hello, World!'
>> end
=> nil
>> say_hello
Hello, World!
=> nil
>>
```

Figure 6.2 After defining your own method, you can call it as you would any other method in Ruby.

```
NameError: undefined local variable or method
 `sayhello' for main:Object
        from (irb):5
        from :0
>>
```

Figure 6.3 References to variables or methods that have not been defined, possibly because of a spelling or capitalization error, result in errors like the one seen here.

3. Complete the method (**Figure 6.1**):

end

That's it!

4. Invoke the method (**Figure 6.2**):

say_hello

Again, that's all there is to it.

5. Continue calling the method until your heart's content.

✔ Tips

- If you see an *undefined local variable or method* error (**Figure 6.3**), you likely misspelled the method when defining or calling it. Also remember that Ruby is case sensitive, so *say_hello* is not the same as *say_Hello*.

- The methods you define within irb will only exist for that session. Once you exit irb, you'll need to redefine the methods before calling them again. In later chapters, this book will return to writing Ruby scripts, so that more complex definitions won't need to be retyped.

- Methods can be removed using the undef keyword:

undef *method_name*

However, it's more common to redefine a method than it is to outright delete it.

- If you define a method with the same name as that of an existing method, the new definition will replace the method's previous definition.

SIMPLE METHODS

Returning Values

Many methods return some sort of value as part of their functionality. For example, the `length` (and its alias, `size`) method returns the number of elements in an array or hash (as well as the number of characters in a string).

To return a value from a method, you can use the `return` statement, followed by the value to be returned. This value could be a literal number or string, but it will most likely be a variable or other object type (like `true` and `false`).

```
def get_two
    return 2
end
```

It's important to know that the `return` statement will terminate the execution of the method. Any code after the `return` will not be run.

When a method returns a value, the code that invokes the method is normally written to use that value (**Figure 6.4**):

```
two = get_two
puts get_two * get_two
```

Although you *can* use the `return` keyword, it's often optional and, therefore, omitted. Methods in Ruby will automatically return the value of the last expression they execute. This code is therefore the same as the preceding:

```
def get_two
    2
end
```

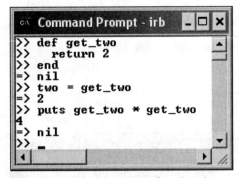

Figure 6.4 A method that returns the value 2 is defined and then invoked in two different ways.

To return the value of a variable, just use the variable's name as the final statement:

```
def get_three
    n = 3
    n
end
```

Even if a method omits the `return` keyword (which, again, is standard in Ruby), such methods are still invoked in the same way:

```
three = get_three
puts get_three + get_two
```

Because methods return the result of their final expressions, the `return` keyword is normally used in situations where the method needs to return a value and terminate prior to its last statement. For example, if a method requires something in order to perform a task, it might return `nil` if its requirements are not met:

```
def theoretical_example
    return nil if condition
    # code if OK
end
```

Before getting into another example, there's one more related concept to address. Methods that return a Boolean value—`true` and `false` (and possibly `nil`)—conventionally have question marks at the end of their names:

```
def always_true?
    true
end
```

You've already seen this several times over: `include?`, `empty?`, and so on.

To return values from methods:

1. Redefine the say_hello method:

```
def say_hello
    'Hello, World!'
end
```

There are two interesting things going on here. First, if you're continuing an existing irb session from the last sequence of steps, you'll see that Ruby allows you to redefine existing methods. This new definition will replace the original one. Second, this method returns the string *Hello, World!* by having it be the last (actually, only) result executed within the method.

2. Invoke the say_hello method (**Figure 6.5**):

```
puts say_hello
msg = say_hello
puts msg.class
```

Since the method now returns a string, the method invocation can be used in places where a string is expected. This includes as an argument to puts or in assigning a value to a variable. To further prove that msg is now a string, the variable's class method is called, printing the result.

3. Define another method:

```
def is_false?
    false
end
```

This needless method always returns the value false. It'll be used just to demonstrate how methods that return Boolean values might be defined and used (although, technically, such methods would return either true or false, and this one returns only false).

Figure 6.5 The method, which returns a string, is invoked in two different ways.

RETURNING VALUES

Figure 6.6 Another method is defined; this one returns the Boolean value false. One logical use of such functions is in conditionals.

Returning Multiple Values

Methods can be written so that they return multiple values. One way of doing so uses the return statement and separates the values by commas:

```
def return_one_two
    return 1, 2
end
```

Since the values being returned together constitute an array, you can omit the return keyword and use array syntax instead:

```
def return_one_two
    [1, 2]
end
```

When calling a method that returns multiple values, you can use *parallel assignment* to assign the returned values to individual variables:

```
one, two = return_one_two
puts one # 1
```

Alternatively, you can receive the result as an array:

```
both = return_one_two
puts both[0] # 1
```

Either of these ways for invoking the method will work regardless of how the method returns the values.

4. Invoke the is_false? method (**Figure 6.6**):

```
puts say_hello if !is_false?
```

This line says that the value returned from the say_hello method should be printed if the negation (the exclamation mark) of the value returned from the is_false? method is true. Since that method always returns false, its negation will always be true, and the puts statement will be executed.

Again, this is a rather silly example, but it goes to show how the methods you define may be used exactly like those built into Ruby.

✔ Tips

■ The use of ? in method names that return Boolean values is suggested, not required.

■ Methods that conclude with ? may be written so that they return values other than just true and false (or nil).

Taking Arguments

Along with returning values, methods often take *arguments* (also called *parameters*): values passed to the method when it is called. The method then uses those values to do whatever it needs to do. For example, the `Array` class' `delete_at` method takes one argument: the index position of the element to be deleted from the array.

To have a method take arguments, place variable names within parentheses after the method's name:

```
def method_name(some_var)
    method code
end
```

A method can take as many arguments as it needs; just separate each variable from the next with a comma:

```
def add(n1, n2)
    n1 + n2
end
```

That method replicates the functionality of the numeric addition operator. To call a method that takes arguments, you need to pass it a value for each variable in the method's definition:

```
four = add(2, 2)
```

To take arguments:

1. Start redefining the `subtotal` method:

   `def subtotal(price, qty)`

   This method, called `subtotal`, takes two arguments, assigned to `price` and `qty`. The method will use those variables to calculate and return a subtotal.

2. Validate the argument values:

   `return nil if price.to_f <= 0 ||`
   `→ qty.to_f <= 0`

   Methods, like applications, shouldn't be written under the assumption that they'll be used properly. In this case, no calculations should be performed if either value isn't positive. For that matter, both values must be numbers, so the `to_f` method is applied.

   This method will therefore return the value `nil` if either number, when converted to a float, is less than or equal to `0`. Note that non-numeric values, when converted to floats, will become `0.0`.

3. Complete the method (**Figure 6.7**):

   `price.to_f * qty.to_f`

   `end`

   The method needs to multiply the two values and return the result. It can do this all in one line, as the result of the last executed statement in a method will be returned automatically.

   continues on next page

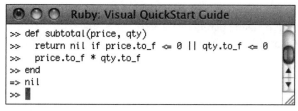

Figure 6.7 The complete method definition, which takes two values, validates them, and then returns their product.

4. Invoke the method (**Figure 6.8**):

```ruby
puts subtotal(12.93, 3)
puts subtotal(456.82, 6)
puts subtotal('cat', 4)
puts subtotal(-25.00, 100)
```

Each call to the method will be used as an argument to `puts`, so that the value returned is printed. You could instead assign the value to a variable or do whatever else needs to be done. The first two lines show how the method would be properly used; the last two show the result if improperly used.

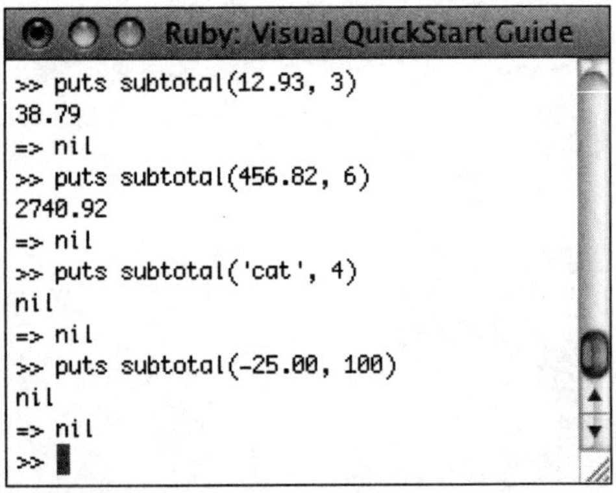

Figure 6.8 Two correct and two incorrect uses of the subtotal method.

✔ Tips

- All methods in Ruby, including those you define, will generate an error if not provided with the required number of arguments (**Figure 6.9**).

- To take advantage of the `subtotal` method's validation routine, call the method like so:

```ruby
puts subtotal('cat', 4) if
→ subtotal('cat', 4)
```

Because the method returns `nil` if it receives invalid values, that line will attempt to print the subtotal only if the method is properly invoked.

- The parentheses after a method's name in its definition are not required if the method takes no arguments. Similarly, you don't have to use parentheses when calling a method that takes no arguments. In fact, you don't even need to use parentheses when calling a method that takes arguments, but by using parentheses you can help avoid confusion and potential bugs.

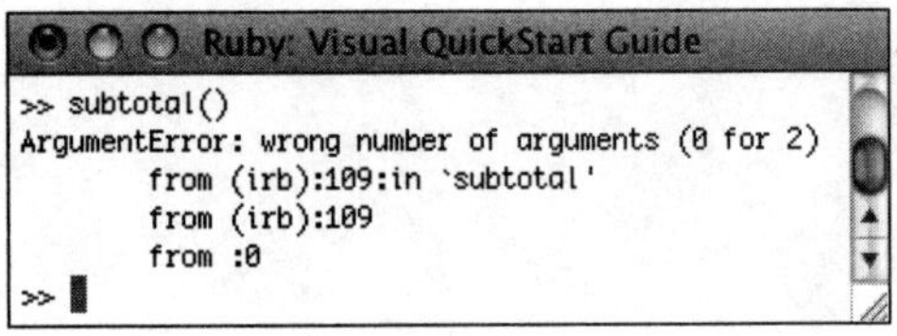

Figure 6.9 Calling the new subtotal method with more or less than exactly two arguments generates an error.

Default Argument Values

Method arguments can also have default values. Just assign a value to the argument in the method's definition:

```
def get_user_input(prompt = 'OK to
→ continue? [Y/N] ')
    print prompt
    gets
end
```

If a value is provided for that argument when the method is called, the new value will be used. Otherwise, the default value applies (**Figure 6.10**).

When using default argument values, those arguments must be listed after any arguments without default values in the method's definition (this is the case in Ruby 1.8 and earlier):

```
def print_countdown(start, finish = 0)
    until start == finish do
        puts start
        start -= 1
    end
end
```

That function prints a countdown (as the name suggests), starting at start (e.g., 10) and stopping at either 0 or whatever value is supplied when the method is invoked.

Finally, unlike in many other languages, the default value assigned to a parameter can actually be the result of an expression:

```
def add_record(info, ts = Time.now)
    # method code
end
```

The expression that assigns a default value can even make use of values assigned to preceding arguments:

```
def do_something(str, len = str.length)
    # method code
end
```

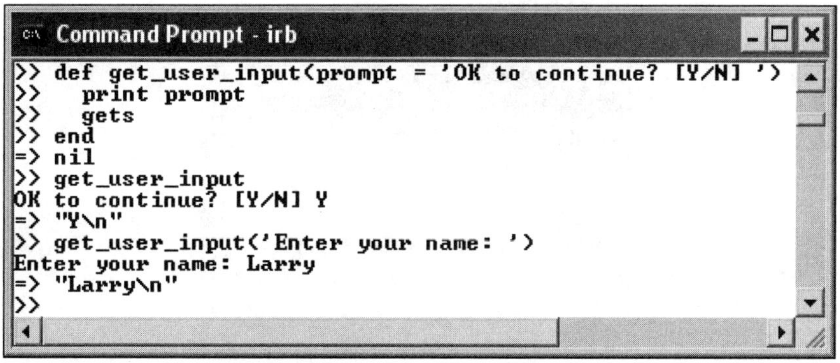

Figure 6.10 When invoked without any arguments, the method uses a default prompt. When invoked with an argument, it uses that as the prompt.

To set default argument values:

1. Start redefining the subtotal method:

   `def subtotal(price, qty = 1)`

   This new version of the subtotal method still takes two arguments, but now the qty argument is optional. It defaults to a value of 1.

2. Complete the method (**Figure 6.11**):

   ```
       return nil if price.to_f <= 0 ||
   → qty.to_f <= 0
       price.to_f * qty.to_f
   end
   ```

   The rest of the method's code is the same as it was before.

3. Invoke the method (**Figure 6.12**):

   `puts subtotal(12.93)`

   `puts subtotal(12.93, 3)`

   `puts subtotal(456.82, 6)`

   Because the qty argument in the method's definition has a default value, you can omit that when invoking the method, so long as you intend for the qty to be 1. If you provide the method with two values when you call it, that second value will be used instead of the default.

✔ Tip

■ Ruby 1.9 allows arguments without default values to be listed after those with default values. I think it's still best to place the arguments with default values last.

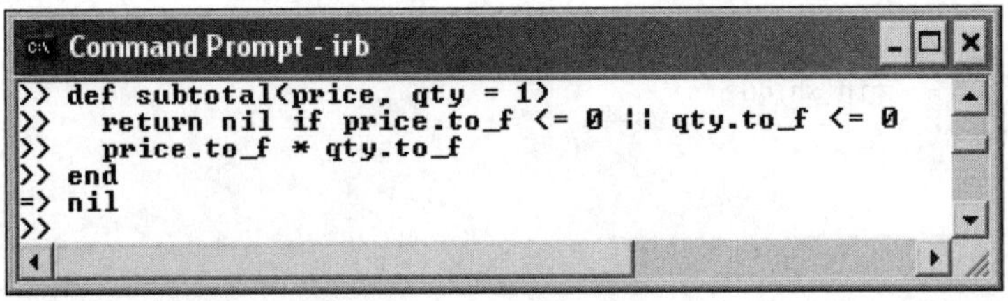

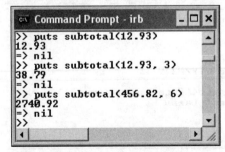

Figure 6.11 The new version of the subtotal method has a default value for the qty argument, making it optional.

Figure 6.12 The new version of the subtotal method can be called in two ways: with or without a quantity value.

Using self

One important attribute of methods is that they don't exist in a vacuum (i.e., by themselves). Unlike functions, methods are associated with classes, which means they are normally applied to an object. The examples thus far in the chapter have presented a procedural approach to methods (by necessity), but that's not how methods are actually used in Ruby. For instance, the `length` method is applied to a string, array, or hash in this way:

```
msg = 'Hello, World!'
puts msg.length
```

or just

```
'Hello, World!'.length
```

In such cases, the object to which the method is being applied is not passed to the method as an argument. Instead, the object is available within the method via the keyword `self`:

```
def add(n)
    self + n
end
puts 2.add(2) # 4
```

That version of the *add* method takes one argument: the amount to be added to the object on which it is called. It returns the value of that object plus the argument's value. Note that this method does not change the original object! Methods defined outside of a class, like those in this chapter, can access the value of `self` but cannot change it.

To apply methods to objects:

1. Start redefining the `subtotal` method:

   ```
   def subtotal(qty = 1)
   ```

   To demonstrate how one might use `self`, let's create another version of the `subtotal` method. This time, the item's price will come from the object invoking the method, but its quantity will still be a method argument and have a default value.

2. Complete the method (**Figure 6.13**):

   ```
   return nil if self.to_f <= 0 ||
   → qty.to_f <= 0
   self.to_f * qty.to_f
   ```
   end

   As I said, the item's price will be found in the object to which this method is applied, so previous uses of `price` are changed to `self`.

continues on next page

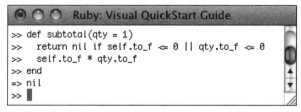

Figure 6.13 This method uses the `self` keyword to refer to the object to which it was applied.

USING SELF

3. Create a couple of variables:

```
book = 39.99
car = 16789
```

These two objects will represent two different things being purchased (in theoretical computer-example world). Each is assigned its associated price. The fact that one object is a float and the other is an integer makes no difference in this case because the method will convert their values to floats.

4. Apply the method to the variables (**Figure 6.14**):

```
puts book.subtotal(3)
puts car.subtotal
puts car.subtotal(7)
```

The method can now be invoked using the dot syntax: *object_name.method_name*. If a quantity other than the default 1 is being used, then that new value is placed within parentheses after the method call.

✔ Tip

■ Methods defined outside of any class, as is the case for every example in this chapter, become part of Ruby's `Object` class. For this reason, such methods are like global functions that can be applied to any object.

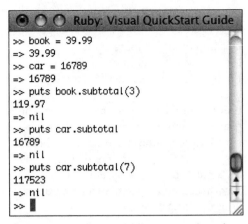

Figure 6.14 Two objects, of different types, have the subtotal method applied to them.

```
C:\ Command Prompt - irb        _ □ ×
>> def show_args(a, b, *c)
>>    puts "a = #{a}"
>>    puts "b = #{b}"
>>    puts "c = #{c.inspect}"
>> end
=> nil
>> show_args(1, 2, 3)
a = 1
b = 2
c = [3]
=> nil
>> show_args(1, 2, 3, 4)
a = 1
b = 2
c = [3, 4]
=> nil
>> show_args(1, 2)
a = 1
b = 2
c = []
=> nil
>>
```

Figure 6.15 This show_args method demonstrates how values passed to a method with variable-length arguments are assigned.

Variable-Length Arguments

The last topic to discuss with respect to the arguments that a method can take is *variable-length arguments*. This phrase refers to the notion that methods can be written so that they can take a variable number of values when called. To do so, prefix an argument's name with an asterisk:

```
def method_name(var1, *var2)
    # method code
end
```

Note that you can prefix only one variable in this manner, and that the asterisked argument should follow the standard (i.e., non-asterisked) ones. It should also come after any arguments with default values.

When a method is defined like this, if there are more values sent to the method than the method has variables for, the extra values are assigned to the asterisked argument as an array (**Figure 6.15**). As you can see in the figure, the asterisked argument is optional: if no values are provided for it, it becomes an empty array.

To test this out, let's rewrite the subtotal method one last time so that it can take an optional quantity, tax rate, and shipping charge. The method could be written using default values for each—

```
def subtotal(qty = 1, tax = 0, ship = 0)
```

—but let's use variable-length arguments instead.

To accept variable-length arguments:

1. Start redefining the subtotal method:

```
def subtotal(*args)
```

Every value sent to this function will be received in the args variable.

2. Begin defining a case statement:

```
case args.length
    when 0
        qty = 1
        tax = 0
        ship = 0
```

Because this method can be called with literally any number of arguments, it needs some system for pulling out the values from the array, based upon how many values were sent to the method. That is accomplished using a case statement, which takes the array's size—the number of elements it contains—as its condition.

The first case is true when no arguments are sent to the method. If so, qty is given a default value of 1, and tax and ship are assigned default values of 0.

3. Add two more cases:

```
when 1
    qty = args[0]
    tax = 0
    ship = 0
when 2
    qty = args[0]
    tax = args[1]
    ship = 0
```

If one argument is provided, that will be used as the quantity and the other two variables still get default values. If two arguments are provided, the qty and tax values are determined, but ship still uses 0.

```
>> def subtotal(*args)
>>   case args.length
>>     when 0
>>       qty = 1
>>       tax = 0
>>       ship = 0
>>     when 1
>>       qty = args[0]
>>       tax = 0
>>       ship = 0
>>     when 2
>>       qty = args[0]
>>       tax = args[1]
>>       ship = 0
>>     else
?>       qty = args[0]
>>       tax = args[1]
>>       ship = args[2]
>>   end
```

Figure 6.16 The beginning of the method definition, which includes the case statement for pulling the values out of the argument array.

4. Complete the case (**Figure 6.16**):
```
else
  qty = args[0]
  tax = args[1]
  ship = args[2]
end
```

If more than two arguments are received, then the ship variable is also assigned a value: the third element in the args array. If more than three arguments were passed to the method, the extraneous values are ignored. You could instead report an error, return nil, or otherwise indicate that the method was improperly used.

5. Validate the data:
```
return nil if self.to_f <= 0 ||
→ qty.to_f <= 0 || tax.to_f < 0 ||
→ ship.to_f < 0
```

The method still needs to confirm that all values received are acceptable as floats. The price, found in self, and quantity must be positive. The other two variables cannot be negative but can equal 0 (because that's their default value).

6. Complete the method (**Figure 6.17**):
```
total = self.to_f * qty.to_f
total += (total * tax.to_f)
total + ship.to_f
end
```

continues on next page

```
>>     tax = args[1]
>>     ship = args[2]
>>   end
>>   return nil if self.to_f <= 0 || qty.to_f <= 0 || tax.to_f < 0 || ship.to_f
< 0
>>   total = self.to_f * qty.to_f
>>   total += total * tax.to_f
>>   total + ship.to_f
>> end
=> nil
>>
```

Figure 6.17 The rest of the method definition, with the validation routine and calculations.

VARIABLE-LENGTH ARGUMENTS

After assigning values to variables from the received arguments, and after validating those values, the last thing the method has to do is calculate and return the total. First, the price is multiplied by the quantity. Then the amount of tax is added to the total, found by multiplying the tax rate times the total. Finally, the shipping is added to the total and the result of that expression is returned by the method.

All of these calculations could be done in one line, but I wanted to keep the individual steps more clear.

7. Invoke the method (**Figure 6.18**):

```
book = 39.99
puts book.subtotal
puts book.subtotal(3)
puts book.subtotal(3, 0.0575)
puts book.subtotal(3, 0.0575, 5.00)
```

Because the method is written quite flexibly, it can be called in several different ways. The first value passed to the method will always be assigned to the qty variable; the second to tax (this should be a decimal, like 0.0575 for a tax of 5.75%); and the third to ship (the shipping costs).

✔ Tips

■ One improvement you could make to this method would be to format the returned subtotal so that it always has just two digits after the decimal point. The format method can accomplish that.

■ You can pass an array to a method and have its elements assigned to individual arguments by invoking * when calling the method:

```
def some_method(a, b, c)
    # method code
end
my_array = [1, 2, 3]
some_method(*my_array)
```

In that example, a will be assigned 1; b, 2; and c, 3.

■ The asterisk, when used with arrays for method arguments, is called the *splat* operator.

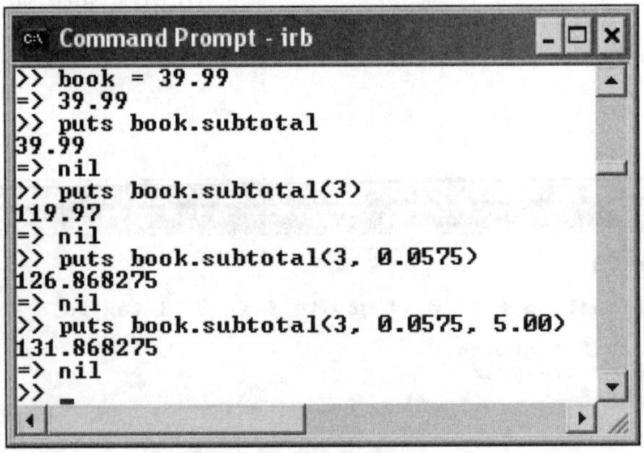

Figure 6.18 By using similar numbers, you can see how the addition of extra arguments changes the returned value.

VARIABLE-LENGTH ARGUMENTS

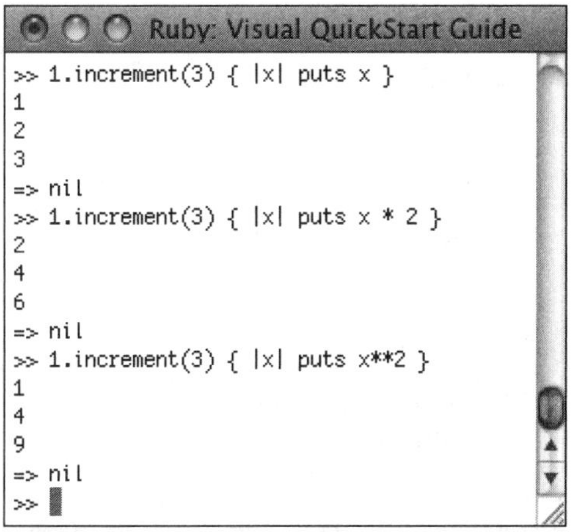

Figure 6.19 By changing the block associated with a method, you can manipulate the values generated by the method.

Methods and Blocks

The final subject in this chapter on defining and using your own methods involves *blocks*. This topic was introduced in Chapter 5, "Control Structures," in the discussion of *iterators*. Iterators are methods that are followed by a block. In order for a method to make use of that block, it has to invoke the `yield` keyword, which temporarily cedes control to the block, passing it one or more values at the same time. This can be a tough concept to grasp, but it's an important one, so I'll provide a couple of examples plus an illustration.

Say you define a method like so:

```
def increment(stop)
    start = self
    while start <= stop
      yield start
      start += 1
    end
end
```

This method essentially mimics the `upto` method, incrementing by ones from `self` to `stop`. However, instead of printing or doing something else with the numbers within the loop, the numbers are yielded so that the programmer can define what should be done with them. For instance (**Figure 6.19**):

```
1.increment(3) { |x| puts x }
```

or

```
1.increment(3) { |x| puts x * 2 }
```

or

```
1.increment(3) { |x| puts x**2 }
```

In the one case, the numbers yielded by the method are printed as is; in the next, the numbers are doubled; and in the third, the numbers are squared: all without changing the method's definition! **Figure 6.20** shows the logical flow of this method and its associated block.

Again, it may take a while to understand and appreciate the `yield` statement and blocks, but the potential here is vast. Anytime you have a method that will return a series of values—not just multiple values one time, but several values over time, tying the method into a block makes sense. It may also help your understanding of this topic to revisit the iterators sections in Chapter 5.

This next example will use a method and the `yield` statement to generate a list of *Lucas numbers*. Lucas numbers are like *Fibonacci numbers*: each number is the sum of the previous two numbers. The Fibonacci sequence starts with 0 and 1; Lucas starts at 2 and 1. If you're not familiar with these concepts, that's fine; the point is that both are perfect examples of how one might make use of blocks with methods.

To use yield:

1. Begin a new method:

```
def lucas(num)
  a = 2
  b = 1
```

The method will be called `lucas`. It takes one argument, the total number of Lucas numbers to return. Within the method, two variables are initialized at 2 and 1, the first two values in the Lucas sequence. To follow the logic for calculating Lucas numbers, remember that the *a* variable will always represent the current number; *b* will always represent the next number.

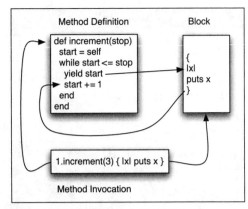

Figure 6.20 Each time the `yield` statement is executed, the value of `start` is passed to the block (and assigned to x). Once the block has completed its tasks, control is returned to the method, to the point after the `yield` statement.

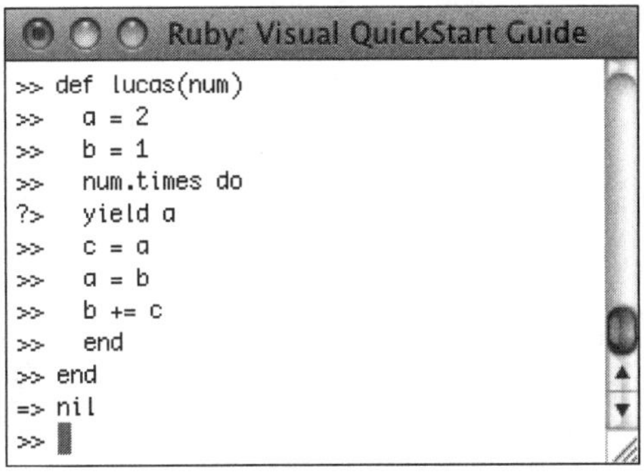

```
>> def lucas(num)
>>   a = 2
>>   b = 1
>>   num.times do
?>   yield a
>>   c = a
>>   a = b
>>   b += c
>>   end
>> end
=> nil
>> █
```

Figure 6.21 The definition of the lucas method, which yields a value to an associated block.

2. Invoke the times iterator:

```
num.times do
    yield a
```

Because the method needs to return num numbers, invoking the times method makes sense (a while loop would also work). Within the times block, the value of a is yielded. So at this point in the method, whatever value a has will be sent to the block associated with this method's call.

3. Complete the times block:

```
c = a
a = b
b += c
```

This is the hard part of calculating a Lucas sequence. First, the current value of a needs to be assigned to a third variable (because that value will be overridden on the next line). Then a, which represents the current Lucas number, is assigned the value of b, which is the next Lucas number. Finally, the new next Lucas number, b, is assigned a new value by adding the previous value of a, which was assigned to c, to the value of b.

4. Complete the method definition (**Figure 6.21**):

```
    end
end
```

The first end terminates the times block. The second terminates the method definition.

continues on next page

METHODS AND BLOCKS

5. Invoke the method (**Figure 6.22**):

```
lucas(10) { |x| puts x }
```

Remember that this method requires a block. This particular block receives one argument, returned by the method and assigned to x, which is then printed.

6. Print only the odd numbers in the first fifteen Lucas numbers (**Figure 6.23**):

```
lucas(15) { |x| puts x if x%2 != 0 }
```

As another example of how the method can be used, the block is changed (as is the argument passed to the method). The method itself yields the first fifteen Lucas numbers to the block, but only the odd ones—those that have a remainder when divided by two—are printed.

✔ Tips

■ The three assignment lines within the times block can actually be simplified to just:

```
a, b = b, a+b
```

This works because of how Ruby handles parallel assignment. I opted not to use this shortcut because it may be more confusing.

■ Methods can also be defined so that they accept a block as an argument. Doing so creates a Proc, to be discussed in Chapter 17, "Dynamic Programming."

■ Methods that expect blocks will generate errors if called without one (**Figure 6.24**). To prevent that, you can invoke block_given? within the method:

```
...
num.times do
    yield a if block_given?
...
```

■ A method can yield multiple values using

```
yield a, b
```

The block associated with the method would then be written to take multiple arguments:

```
obj_name.iterator_name { | x, y | #
→ do whatever }
```

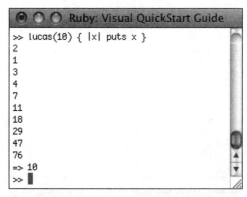

Figure 6.22 A basic invocation of the newly defined lucas method.

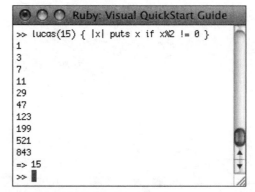

Figure 6.23 Another use of the lucas method.

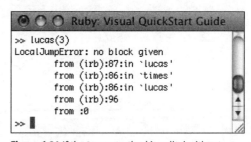

Figure 6.24 If the lucas method is called without providing a block, its executed yield statement will create this error.

CREATING CLASSES

Classes are the foundation of object-oriented programming (OOP). A *class* is a blueprint; an *object* is an *instance* of a class. Since everything in Ruby is an object, even a basic *Hello, World!* example makes use of OOP. Although Ruby provides tons of functionality through its built-in classes, you'll eventually want or need to start creating your own.

This chapter introduces the basics of defining and using classes in Ruby. Herein you'll learn about the syntax, about class variables, and how to write several different types of methods that classes commonly use. You'll also be introduced to two concepts that separate Ruby from many other OOP languages. The first is the ease with which you can redefine existing Ruby classes. The second is called *duck typing*. I'll put off further discussion of it until the chapter's end.

Chapter 8, "Inheritance and More," is the companion to this chapter. The focus there is on defining classes that are derived from other classes.

Simple Classes

Procedural programming approaches an application by defining the *steps* that need to be taken. Conversely, object-oriented programming focuses on the *data* being used by an application. With this approach, a class needs to represent the application's data in terms of both the information that needs to be stored and the sorts of tasks that will be done with the data. Information can be represented in variables (called *attributes* or *properties* when in classes) and functions (called *methods*). As a theoretical but approachable example, think of a person: a person has attributes—name, age, etc.—and methods—eating, sleeping, and so forth.

A basic class definition begins with the keyword `class`, followed by the name of the class. The code for the class comes next, and the class definition terminates with the `end` keyword.

```
class ClassName
    # class code
end
```

The name of the class can contain letters, numbers, and the underscore, but class names generally only contain letters. Class names are constants, so they must begin with an uppercase letter. Conventionally, they use uppercase letters to separate words: *ClassName*, not *className* or *Class_name*.

Methods within a class are defined using the same syntax and techniques as those outlined in Chapter 6, "Creating Methods." Method definitions are normally indented two spaces from the class' definition, but that's not syntactically required.

For example, suppose you loved the *Hello, World!* example so much that you thought it deserved to be its own class:

```
class HelloWorld
    def say_hello
        puts "Hello, World!"
    end
end
```

Once you've defined a class, you can create an object of that type by using *ClassName*`.new`. That line invokes the class's `new` method, which every class automatically has, without it being formally defined by you.

```
hw = HelloWorld.new
```

The Struct Class

If you need to store multiple pieces of information in a class-like structure but don't need to define associated methods, you can create a `Struct` instead. To define one, use `Struct.new`, providing it with a structure name and the variables (as symbols) it should include:

```
Book = Struct.new('Book', :title, :author, :isbn)
```

Then you can create a new variable of this type:

```
rubyvqs = Book.new('Ruby: VQS', 'Larry Ullman', ' 978-0-321-55385-0')
```

From that point on, you can use the dot syntax to access any values:

```
puts rubyvqs.title # Ruby: VQS
```

Alternatively, you can treat the variable as if it's a hash:

```
puts rubyvqs[:title] # Ruby: VQS
```

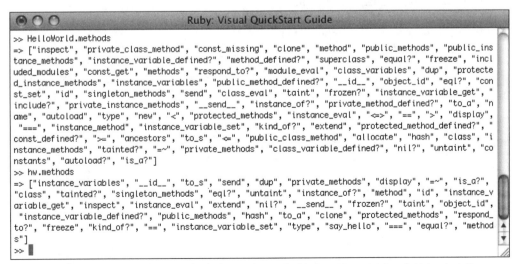

```
>> class HelloWorld
>>   def say_hello
>>     puts "Hello, World!"
>>   end
>> end
=> nil
>> hw = HelloWorld.new
=> #<HelloWorld:0x79cac>
>> hw.say_hello
Hello, World!
=> nil
>>
```

Figure 7.1 When a new class is created, Ruby returns the value nil. When an object of that class is created, Ruby returns the class type and a reference to where it's stored in memory (the 0x29cac part). The class' methods can be invoked through the object.

Use the dot syntax to invoke a class' methods (**Figure 7.1**):

```
hw.say_hello
```

Ruby also has tons of methods that can be called by any class. Like the new method, these other methods are automatically *inherited* by classes you create (Chapter 8 goes into inheritance in detail). For example, the class method returns the class of the current object:

```
hw.class # HelloWorld
```

To see the list of methods that a class supports, invoke *ClassName*.methods. To see the list of methods that a specific object supports, invoke *obj_name*.methods (**Figure 7.2**) or *ClassName*.instance_methods.

Over the course of this chapter, you'll create a couple of different classes—some will be more useful for understanding the theories behind OOP, and others will be more practical. For these initial examples, I'll continue to use irb for simplicity's sake; later examples will be Ruby scripts. If you'd rather use Ruby scripts for every example, feel free (following the steps in Chapter 2, "Simple Scripts").

```
>> HelloWorld.methods
=> ["inspect", "private_class_method", "const_missing", "clone", "method", "public_methods", "public_ins
tance_methods", "instance_variable_defined?", "method_defined?", "superclass", "equal?", "freeze", "incl
uded_modules", "const_get", "methods", "respond_to?", "module_eval", "class_variables", "dup", "protecte
d_instance_methods", "instance_variables", "public_method_defined?", "__id__", "object_id", "eql?", "con
st_set", "id", "singleton_methods", "send", "class_eval", "taint", "frozen?", "instance_variable_get", "
include?", "private_instance_methods", "__send__", "instance_of?", "private_method_defined?", "to_a", "n
ame", "autoload", "type", "new", "<", "protected_methods", "instance_eval", "<=>", "==", ">", "display",
 "===", "instance_method", "instance_variable_set", "kind_of?", "extend", "protected_method_defined?", "
const_defined?", ">=", "ancestors", "to_s", "<=", "public_class_method", "allocate", "hash", "class", "i
nstance_methods", "tainted?", "=~", "private_methods", "class_variable_defined?", "nil?", "untaint", "co
nstants", "autoload?", "is_a?"]
>> hw.methods
=> ["instance_variables", "__id__", "to_s", "send", "dup", "private_methods", "display", "=~", "is_a?",
"class", "tainted?", "singleton_methods", "eql?", "untaint", "instance_of?", "method", "id", "instance_v
ariable_get", "inspect", "instance_eval", "extend", "nil?", "__send__", "frozen?", "taint", "object_id",
 "instance_variable_defined?", "public_methods", "hash", "to_a", "clone", "protected_methods", "respond_
to?", "freeze", "kind_of?", "==", "instance_variable_set", "type", "say_hello", "===", "equal?", "method
s"]
>>
```

Figure 7.2 The top section lists the 75 methods that can be used with the HelloWorld class (which only defines one method itself). The bottom array is the list of 42 methods that a HelloWorld object can invoke.

To create a class:

1. Begin defining a new class:

   ```
   class Dog
   ```

   This class is called **Dog** and will provide a way to represent, um, dogs in Ruby code.

2. Add a couple of methods:

   ```
   def speak
      "woof"
   end
   def play
      "fetch"
   end
   def sleep
      "sleep"
   end
   ```

   These are just three very simple definitions that reflect some of what dogs can do. Each method returns a one-word string. For more on method definitions, see Chapter 6.

3. Complete the class definition (**Figure 7.3**):

   ```
   end
   ```

   If I was writing this code within a Ruby script, I might be inclined to add a comment here to indicate that this **end** terminates the class definition (as opposed to a method definition).

```
>> class Dog
>>    def speak
>>       "woof"
>>    end
>>    def play
>>       "fetch"
>>    end
>>    def sleep
>>       "sleep"
>>    end
>> end
=> nil
>> █
```

Figure 7.3 The definition of the Dog class.

SIMPLE CLASSES

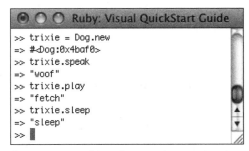

```
>> trixie = Dog.new
=> #<Dog:0x4baf0>
>> trixie.speak
=> "woof"
>> trixie.play
=> "fetch"
>> trixie.sleep
=> "sleep"
>>
```

Figure 7.4 A new object of type Dog is created, and then its methods are invoked.

4. Make use of the class (**Figure 7.4**):

```
trixie = Dog.new
trixie.speak
trixie.play
trixie.sleep
```

The first line creates a new object of type Dog. The object is a variable called *trixie*. The object's methods can then be invoked using the dot syntax. Because each method returns a string, the result of calling each is just the string itself. Alternatively, you can print the result of each method call:

```
puts trixie.speak
```

✔ Tips

■ Methods defined outside of any class, like those in Chapter 6, are automatically defined as part of the Object class. Because every class automatically inherits from the Object class, these methods are therefore inherited by every class.

■ Methods defined like speak, play, and sleep within a class are called *instance methods*.

SIMPLE CLASSES

Instance Variables

When working outside of a class, the variables are normally *local* variables, like those defined and used in the chapters preceding this one. Within a class definition, variables of a different type can be created, called *instance variables*. Such variables belong to the class, and therefore, to objects created of that class type. Instance variables use the same naming scheme as other variables, except that their names begin with @.

In a Dog class, instance variables might store a specific dog's name, age, breed, gender, and so forth. Classes often define *getter* and *setter* methods for accessing instance variables. Setter methods take a value as an argument and assign it to an instance variable. Getter methods return the stored value. These next two methods could be placed within the Dog class definition for those purposes:

```
def set_name(n)
    @name = n
end
def get_name
    @name
end
```

Such a version of the class would be used like so (**Figure 7.5**):

```
trixie = Dog.new
trixie.set_name('trixie')
puts "My dog's name is #{trixie.get_name}."
```

Any method can make use of an instance variable, of course:

```
def sleep
    "#@name is sleeping"
end
```

In the sleep method, a new twist on *interpolation* (the insertion of a statement's returned value within a double-quoted string) is introduced. To interpolate regular variables, you must use #{var_name}, but to interpolate instance variables, you can use just #@var_name.

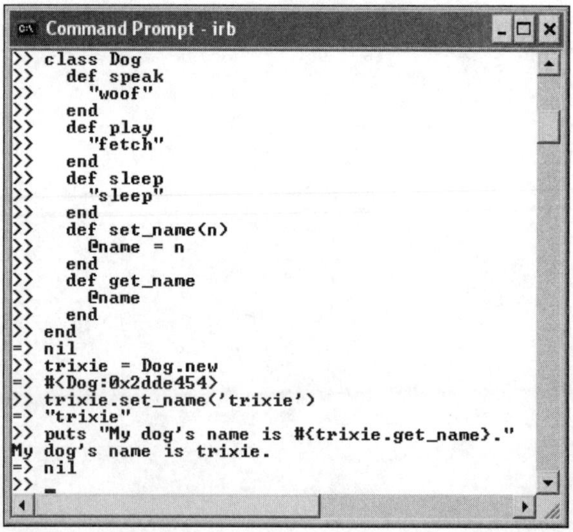

Figure 7.5 One getter method and one setter method are added to the Dog class for access to the @name variable.

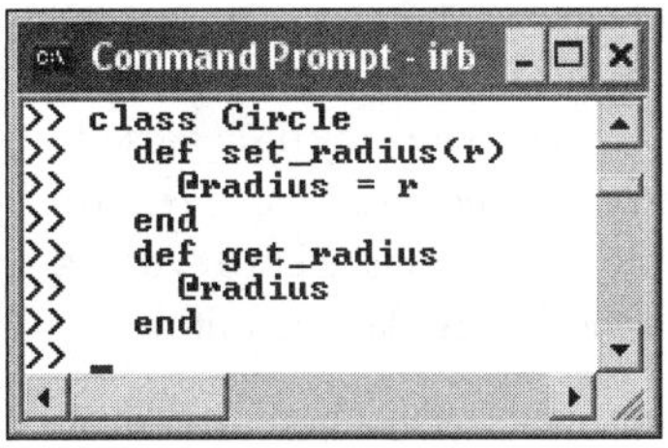

Figure 7.6 The beginning of the Circle class definition, with a getter and a setter for the @radius variable.

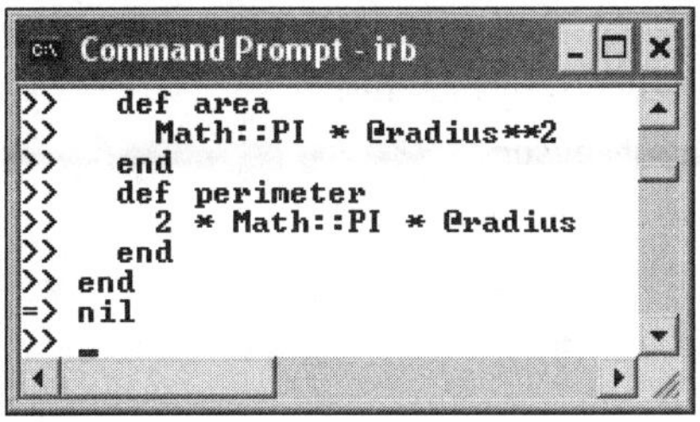

Figure 7.7 The conclusion of the Circle class definition, with one method for returning the circle's area and another that returns its perimeter.

To use instance variables:

1. Begin defining a new class:

   ```
   class Circle
   ```

   This class, called `Circle`, will represent geometric circles.

2. Define a setter method:

   ```
   def set_radius(r)
       @radius = r
   end
   ```

   This method assigns to the instance variable `@radius`, the value submitted to the method when invoked.

3. Define a getter method (**Figure 7.6**):

   ```
   def get_radius
       @radius
   end
   ```

   This method just returns the circle's radius value. Remember that the result of the last statement executed in a method will be returned (see Chapter 6). So just using the variable's name as that last statement has the effect of returning the variable's value.

4. Define two more methods:

   ```
   def area
       Math::PI * @radius**2
   end
   def perimeter
       2 * Math::PI * @radius
   end
   ```

   These two methods calculate and return the area and perimeter of the circle. To do so, they make use of the class' `@radius` variable and the `PI` constant, found within the `Math` module.

   For the calculation of the area, the exponential operator has higher precedence than multiplication, but if you want to be more explicit, you could write

   ```
   Math::PI * (@radius**2)
   ```

5. Complete the class (**Figure 7.7**):

   ```
   end
   ```

continues on next page

6. Create a new circle and assign a value to its radius:

```
c = Circle.new
c.set_radius(4.59)
```

The first line creates a new object of type Circle. The second line invokes the class' set_radius method so that the value 4.59 is assigned to the class' @radius variable.

7. Print the circle's geometric properties (**Figure 7.8**):

```
puts "A circle with a radius of
→ #{c.get_radius} has a perimeter
→ of #{c.perimeter} and an area
→ of #{c.area}."
```

Three of the object's methods are invoked to print the corresponding values.

✔ Tips

■ *Instance variables* can only be accessed within *instance methods*. This means that, for example, you cannot refer to @radius outside of the Circle class definition.

■ You do not need to declare or initialize any kind of variable in Ruby prior to using it. This is also true for class instance variables. In fact, you *shouldn't* attempt to declare or initialize instance variables outside of a method. You don't want to do something like this:

```
class Person
  @name = null # Bad!
  def set_name(n)
    @name = n
```

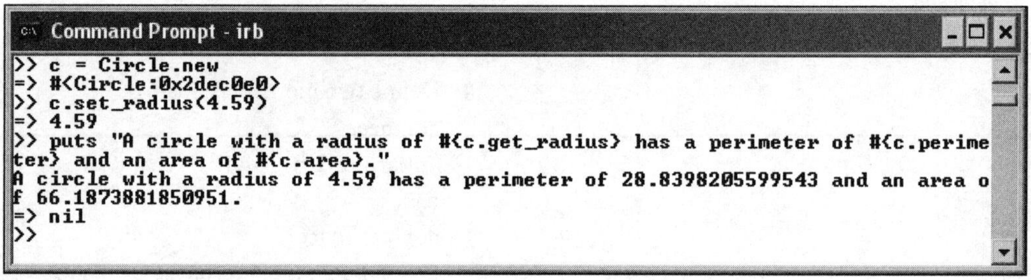

Figure 7.8 Sample usage of the Circle class.

Using Accessors

As I say several times over in this book, Ruby is all about making things easy (or easier, at least) for the programmer. And since having setters and getters in a class is common, Ruby provides a shortcut for creating them. Within the class definition, after naming the class but before defining any methods, you can use the keywords `attr_reader` and `attr_accessor` to identify the variables for which getter and setter methods should exist.

```
class ClassName
    attr_accessor :var1, :var2, :var3
    # other methods
end
```

As you can see in that example, you use the keyword `attr_accessor` or `attr_reader`, followed by a space, followed by symbols representing the instance variables. Symbols should be separated by commas. So the definition of the `Dog` class would begin:

```
class Dog
    attr_accessor :name, :breed, :gender
```

Be certain to note that the syntax uses `:name`, `:breed`, and `:gender`, not `@name`, `@breed`, and `@gender`.

When you use `attr_accessor`, a getter and a setter method will be created for each listed variable. With that `Dog` class definition (if completed), you could then do this (**Figure 7.9**):

```
d = Dog.new
d.name = 'trixie'
d.breed = 'Yorky'
d.gender = 'female'
puts "My dog, #{d.name}, is a
→ #{d.gender} #{d.breed}."
```

Those lines show how you can easily assign values to instance variables (i.e., *set* them) and retrieve their values (i.e., *get* them, as in the `puts` statement). If you use the keyword `attr_reader` instead, only getter methods will be created, meaning you could do this—

```
puts object_name.variable_name
```

but not—

```
object_name.variable_name = value
```

Let's update the `Circle` class with this in mind. If you're using `irb` for these examples, one interesting point will also be made by these next steps: in Ruby you can alter existing classes on the fly!

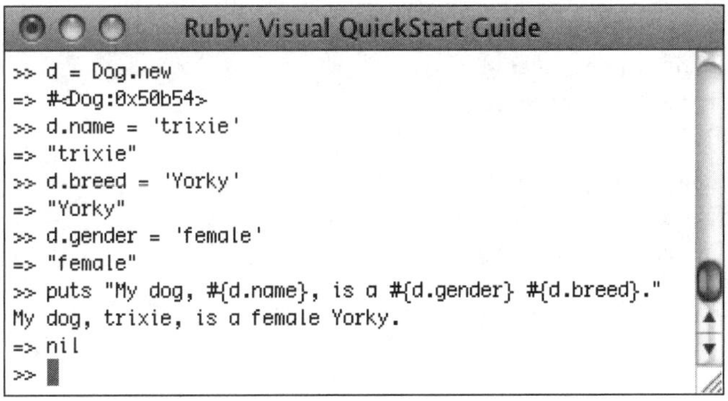

Figure 7.9 Thanks to `attr_accessor`, it's easy to access instance variables for both assigning and retrieving their values.

To use accessors:

1. Add an accessor to the Circle class:

```
class Circle
    attr_accessor :radius
end
```

These three lines say, in layman's terms, take the existing definition of Circle and update it so that you have a getter and a setter for the @radius variable.

If you're using irb to practice these steps, and you had previously entered the Circle class definition, then the class still has the set_radius, get_radius, area, and perimeter methods. If you're not using irb or have not previously entered this class' definition, then you need to add the definitions for the area and perimeter methods to this code.

2. Create a new circle and assign a value to its radius (**Figure 7.10**):

```
c = Circle.new
c.radius = 123.481
```

The first line creates a new object of type Circle. The second line assigns a value to the class' @radius variable in a more direct and obvious way.

3. Print the circle's geometric properties (**Figure 7.11**):

```
puts "A circle with a radius of
→ #{c.radius} has a perimeter
→ of #{c.perimeter} and an area
→ of #{c.area}."
```

This line is similar to that used in the previous set of steps, but now the radius is returned by invoking just c.radius.

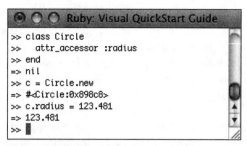

Figure 7.10 A quick update of the Circle class, and a new object of that type is created.

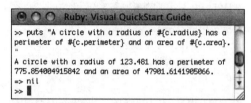

Figure 7.11 Because of the attribute reader, the puts line can now refer to c.radius to retrieve the circle's radius.

✔ **Tips**

■ The getter and setter methods auto-generated by this line:

```
attr_accessor :varname
```

are equivalent to

```
def varname
   @varname
end
def varname=(value)
   @varname = value
end
```

■ The `attr_reader` and `attr_accessor` keywords are actually methods defined in the `Module` class, of which `Class` is a derived subclass (see Chapter 8).

■ Ruby also has an `attr` method. In Ruby 1.8 and earlier, it creates a reader for a single variable if you do this:

```
attr :var_name
```

If used like so, it creates both a getter and a setter:

```
attr :var_name, true
```

In Ruby 1.9, `attr` can be used just the same as in earlier versions or as a aliases to `attr_reader`.

■ The `attr_reader` and `attr_accessor` methods create simple getters and setters. If you need smarter or more flexible getters and setters, you'll need to define them yourself. For example, a more exacting getter in the `Circle` class could confirm that the radius value is a number greater than 0.

■ Using `attr_reader` and `attr_accessor` is an example of *metaprogramming*: where Ruby will generate some code for you.

Creating Constructors

In most object-oriented languages, there is a method that's automatically invoked when an object of that class is created. Other languages call such methods *constructors*, but Ruby also calls them *initializers* because they always have the name `initialize`. (In Java and C++, a constructor is a method with the same name as the class.)

```ruby
class ClassName
    def initialize
        # do whatever
    end
end
```

This method will automatically be invoked when an object of that class type is created using *ClassName*.new. Normally the `initialize` method is used to assign values to the class' main attributes, in which case it's written to accept arguments:

```ruby
class Dog
    def initialize(name)
        @name = name
    end
end
d = Dog.new('trixie')
```

The Dog class as defined there has only one method, `initialize`. As it stands, this means that each Dog object's @name variable can be assigned a value but there's no system in place for retrieving that value (i.e., there's no getter for @name). One solution is to use `attr_reader` to have Ruby create the getter(s) for you.

```ruby
class Dog
    attr_reader :name
    def initialize(name)
        @name = name
    end
end
d = Dog.new('trixie')
puts "My dog's name is #{d.name}."
```

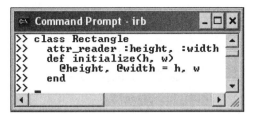

Figure 7.12 The beginning of the `Rectangle` class definition, with getters for its two variables and a constructor that assigns values to those variables.

To create constructors:

1. Begin a new class definition:

   ```
   class Rectangle
       attr_reader :height, :width
   ```

   This is a new class, called `Rectangle`, used to represent the geometric shape. The class has two instance variables, `height` and `width`, used to represent the dimensions of the rectangle. Getter methods will be generated for both, thanks to this use of `attr_reader`.

2. Define the constructor (**Figure 7.12**):

   ```
   def initialize(h, w)
       @height, @width = h, w
   end
   ```

   The `initialize` method takes two arguments, assigned to h and w. Using parallel assignment, the value passed to h will be assigned to `@height` and the value passed to w will be assigned to `@width`.

3. Define two more methods:

   ```
   def area
       @height * @width
   end
   def perimeter
       (@height + @width) * 2
   end
   ```

   Like the same-named methods within the `Circle` class, these two methods will return the shape's area and perimeter.

continues on next page

CREATING CONSTRUCTORS

4. Define another method (**Figure 7.13**):

```
def is_square?
  if @height == @width then
    true
  else
    false
  end
end
```

This method returns a Boolean value indicating if the rectangle is also a square or not. It follows the standard Ruby convention of ending method names with a question mark when they return Boolean values.

5. Complete the class:

```
end
```

6. Create a Rectangle object:

```
r = Rectangle.new(10, 34)
```

Because the class has a constructor that takes two arguments, two values need to be passed to the new method when an object of this class is created. This rectangle will have a height of 10 units and a width of 34.

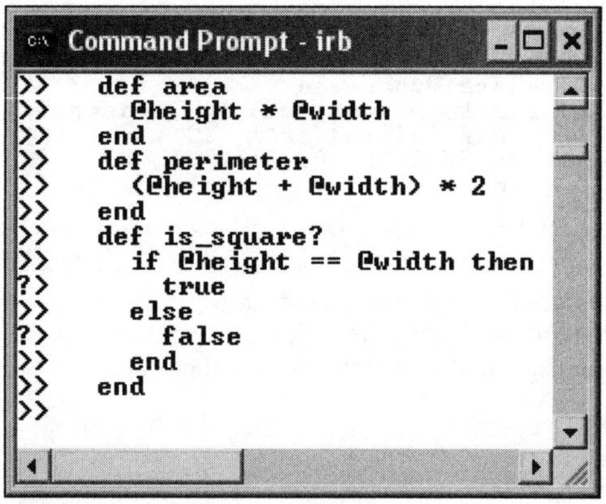

Figure 7.13 Three more methods added to the Rectangle class provide basic geometrical information.

7. Use the object's methods (**Figure 7.14**):

```
puts "A rectangle with a height
→ of #{r.height} and a width of
→ #{r.width} has a perimeter
→ of #{r.perimeter} and an area
→ of #{r.area}."

puts "The rectangle #{r.is_square? ?
→ 'is' : 'is not'} a square."
```

The first puts statement shows how you can use the class' auto-generated getters to retrieve the rectangle's dimensions. That statement also invokes the perimeter and area methods.

The second puts statement uses the is_square? method with a conditional (or ternary) operator to print either *The rectangle is a square.* or *The rectangle is not a square.* For more on the syntax of this operator, see Chapter 5, "Control Structures."

8. Create a new rectangle and repeat the lines from Step 7 (**Figure 7.15**):

```
r = Rectangle.new(14, 14)

puts "A rectangle with a height
→ of #{r.height} and a width of
→ #{r.width} has a perimeter of
→ #{r.perimeter} and an area
→ of #{r.area}."

puts "The rectangle #{r.is_square? ?
→ 'is' : 'is not'} a square."
```

I would recommend trying with another rectangle that is also a square just to see the results. You can create a new Rectangle object or overwrite the existing r variable.

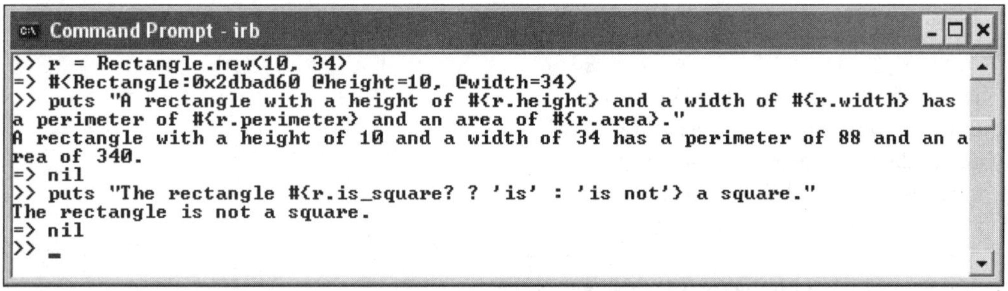

Figure 7.14 An object of type Rectangle is created, and then five of its methods are invoked.

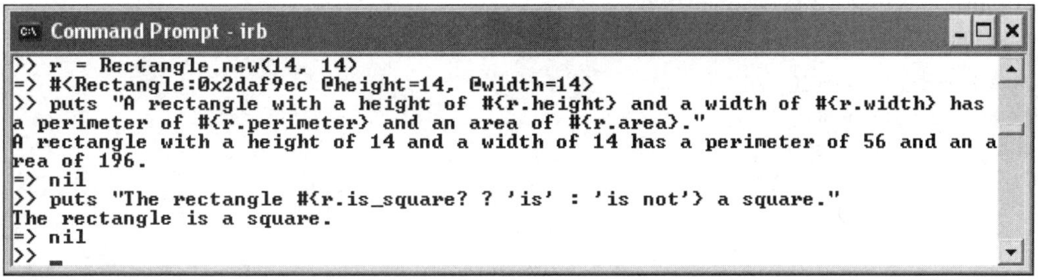

Figure 7.15 A new Rectangle object is created. This one happens to also be a square.

Defining Operators

Just as objects have methods that perform certain tasks, they also often support operators—arithmetic, assignment, and logical—whose functionality you may want to define. To do so, create a method whose name is the operator involved: +, -, ==, etc. These kinds of operators are used in pairs—4 - 2, some_string + some_other_string, so the associated method needs to work with two objects. The first object will be the left-hand operand (4 and some_string in the examples). This object is available within a method by referring to self (see Chapter 6 for more on this concept) or to the class' instance variables. The right-hand operand (2 and some_other_string) should be accepted as the method's lone argument:

```
class ClassName
    def *(rh)
        # Do whatever with self and rh.
    end
end
```

That's the basic syntax for implementing the multiplication operator for a class. It's up to you, the class' designer, to determine what exactly the method should do when that operator is used. For that matter, you can opt to leave an operator undefined, in which case attempts to use it with that object type will result in an error (**Figure 7.16**).

For instance, take the addition of two Rectangle objects:

```
r1 = Rectangle.new(10, 20)
r2 = Rectangle.new(6, 8)
puts r1 + r2
```

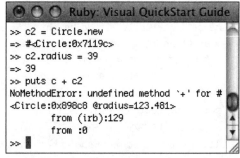

Figure 7.16 If a class doesn't define a method for a given operator, using that operator on objects of that type generate a NoMethodError.

DEFINING OPERATORS

```
>> c2 = Circle.new
=> #<Circle:0x4c554>
>> c2.set_radius(10)
=> 10
>> puts c2 == c
false
=> nil
>> puts c = c2
#<Circle:0x4c554>
=> nil
>> puts c
#<Circle:0x4c554>
=> nil
>> puts c.area
314.159265358979
=> nil
>>
```

Figure 7.17 This code uses two `Circle` objects to demonstrate the ability to use the assignment and equality operators without either being defined within the class.

Now, should the result be the sum of their two areas (`200 + 48 = 248`) or the sum of their perimeters (`60 + 28 = 88`)? Or should the operation calculate the sum of the two heights and the sum of the two widths:

```
def +(rh)
    @height += rh.height
    @width += rh.width
    self
end
```

With the `Rectangle` example, each approach has its problems. But, again, it's up to you to decide how such things are best handled, if at all: it may not make sense for a class to allow for addition or subtraction or multiplication or division.

Another decision to be made is whether an operation returns a new object or updates the current one (see the "Updating the Current Object" sidebar on page 153). The preceding example updates the values in the current object and returns it. To create and return a new object instead, the method would look like:

```
def +(rh)
    Rectangle.new(@height + rh.height,
    → @width + rh.width)
end
```

Toward this end, some object types use two operators and methods: one that modifies the current object and one that leaves the current object untouched, returning a new object in its place. For example, the `String` class has two forms of concatenation: +, which returns a new object, and <<, which alters the current one.

Classes may also want to define their own version of the assignment and logical operators. Ruby will automatically generate the assignment (=) and equality operators (==) for you (**Figure 7.17**), but you may want to change what each does.

Conversely, the comparison operator, <=>, is not defined unless you do so. By creating a <=> method, you can make the objects of that class type be both comparable and sortable. Just return -1 to indicate that the left-hand operand is smaller, 1 to indicate that the right-hand operand is smaller, and 0 to indicate that the objects have the same value. For example, to base the comparison of two Rectangles on their respective areas:

```
def <=>(rh)
    if self.area < rh.area then -1
    elsif self.area > rh.area then 1
    else 0 end
end
```

As a fairly real-world example of how one might use this knowledge, I'm going to turn to a hobby of mine: woodworking. When starting a new project, I need to know how many board feet of materials I have to see if I have enough wood. The total board feet—that I have or that the project requires—is the summation of the length times the width of each board. **Table 7.1** shows some sample data.

In defining the class, I've made a couple of decisions. First, I'll consider two different allotments of wood to be the same if they have equal total board feet. The number of boards is comparatively unimportant, as two boards can be joined together to create one larger board. Secondarily, I am opting to ignore board thickness for simplicity's sake. In the real world, you might have a board that's an inch and a half thick (or 6/4 in wood parlance) and the number of board feet that provides depends upon how thick you need the final pieces. Using boards 3/4 thick would mean you have twice as many board feet; using boards 2/4 means you have three times as much. You could add this into the class, it would just mean a bit more math.

Table 7.1

Total Board Feet

WIDTH	LENGTH	TOTAL
4	30	120
5.5	22	121.0
6	14	84
Total Board Feet		**325**

Script 7.1 The Wood class allows for Wood objects to be added and compared.

```
● ● ●                    📄 Script
1    # Script 7.1 - wood.rb
2
3    # A class for representing
     collections of wood.
4    class Wood
5
6        # Read access for the boards array:
7        attr_reader :boards
8
9        # Constructor can initialize the
         @boards array.
10       def initialize(*args)
11           @boards = args
12       end
13
14       # Method for adding a single board.
15       def add_board(board)
16           @boards.push(board)
17       end
18
19       # Method for returning the total
         board feet.
20       def total
21           t = 0
22           @boards.each { |b| t += (b[:width]
             * b[:length]) }
23           t
24       end
25
26       # Method for seeing if enough
         wood is available
27       # for a given project.
28       def enough?(project)
29           project.total <= self.total
30       end
31
32       # Addition operator:
33       def +(rh)
34           @boards += rh.boards
35           self
36       end
37
38       # Equality operator:
39       def ==(rh)
40           self.total == rh.total
41       end
42
43       # Identity operator:
44       def ===(rh)
45           @boards == rh.boards
46       end
47
```

(script continues on next page)

To define class operators:

1. Create a new Ruby script in your text editor or IDE (**Script 7.1**):

   ```
   # Script 7.1 - wood.rb
   ```

   Since this example will have a fair amount of code, syntax errors will be that much more annoying to hunt down and fix within irb (or fxri). So I'll write this up as a script to be executed. See Chapter 2, "Simple Scripts," for details on writing and executing Ruby files.

2. Start defining the Wood class:

   ```
   class Wood
       attr_reader :boards
       def initialize(*args)
           @boards = args
       end
   ```

   First, a getter is created for the class' @boards variable. Then the class' initialize method is defined so that it can take any number of arguments, received as any array (see Chapter 6 for more on the splat operator). The @boards variable will be an array whose elements are hashes, one for each board. The hashes will use symbols for keys. To create an object containing two boards, you would write:

   ```
   walnut = Wood.new({:width => 5,
   → :length => 26.25}, {:width => 4.75,
   → :length => 32})
   ```

   If no values are provided when creating a new object, then @boards will be an empty array (because args will be an empty array).

continues on next page

3. Define the `add_board` method:

```
def add_board(board)
    @boards.push(board)
end
```

This is just a simple method for adding boards to the collection by pushing the submitted argument onto the array.

4. Define the `total` method:

```
def total
    t = 0
    @boards.each { |b| t += (b[:width]
    → * b[:length]) }
    t
end
```

The `total` method needs to return the total amount of board feet represented by the object. To do so, it initializes a variable at `0` and then iterates through the `@boards` array. The code block associated with the iterator will receive one board (a variable of type `Hash`). It then adds to the `t` variable the result of multiplying the board's width times its length. Finally, the total is returned.

5. Define an `enough?` method:

```
def enough?(project)
    project.total <= self.total
end
```

This method returns a Boolean value indicating if the wood allotment has enough board feet for a given project. To do so, it returns `true` if the total board feet required by the project is less than or equal to the current object's total amount of board feet. This method will be used like so (where `maple` and `table` are both `Wood` objects):

```
puts "Choose another wood!" if
→ !maple.enough?(table)
```

Script 7.1 *continued*

```
48    # Comparison operator:
49    def <=>(rh)
50        if self.total < rh.total then -1
51        elsif self.total > rh.total then 1
52        else 0 end
53    end
54
55    end # End of Wood class.
56
57    # Create a new Wood object:
58    maple = Wood.new({:width => 7,
      :length => 42}, {:width => 4.5,
      :length => 22}, {:width => 6.75,
      :length => 32.5}, {:width => 5,
      :length => 26.25})
59
60    # Create a second Wood object:
61    oak = Wood.new
62    oak.add_board({:width => 5,
      :length => 26.25})
63    oak.add_board({:width => 6.25,
      :length => 27.5})
64
65    # Some tests:
66    print "Total amount of maple: "
67    puts maple.total
68    print "Total amount of oak: "
69    puts oak.total
70    print "maple and oak are equal? "
71    puts maple == oak
72    print "maple compared to oak: "
73    puts maple <=> oak
74
75    # Buy more oak:
76    oak += Wood.new({:width => 7,
      :length => 19}, {:width => 5.5,
      :length => 22.2})
77
78    # Check a project:
79    table = Wood.new({:width => 4.5,
      :length => 22}, {:width => 6.75,
      :length => 32.5}, {:width => 5,
      :length => 26.25}, {:width => 5,
      :length => 26.25})
80    print "Board feet required to make
      a table: "
81    puts table.total
82    print "Do I have enough maple? "
83    puts maple.enough?(table) ? "It's
      a go!": "Sorry!"
84    print "Do I have enough oak? "
85    puts oak.enough?(table) ? "It's
      a go!": "Sorry!"
```

Updating the Current Object

Some class methods will alter objects of that class type when called. These methods conventionally end with an exclamation mark, indicating that they should be used with caution (like the `Array` class' `slice!` method). A method can update an object by changing the value of its instance variables.

```
def double!
    @some_var *= 2
end
```

Another consideration in such methods is the value the method returns. The preceding method returns the value of the class' `@some_var` instance times 2. That's fine unless the method was used on the object like so:

```
my_obj = SomeClassName.new
my_obj = my_obj.double!
```

Now `my_obj` has a value of twice `@some_var` and is no longer an object of type `SomeClassName`. The fix is to have the method return the current version of the object, represented by `self`:

```
def double!
    @some_var *= 2
    self
end
```

If you want to provide a method that performs the same task and returns the result without permanently altering the object (like the `Array` class' `slice` method), have that method create a copy of the object by invoking the `dup` method, and then call the version of the method that does affect the object:

```
def double
    copy = self.dup
    copy.double!
end
```

6. Define the addition operator:

```
def +(rh)
    @boards += rh.boards
    self
end
```

If you have one collection of wood and someone gives you their collection, the two collections would be added together:

```
my_oak += your_oak
```

This use of the + operator adds the right-hand operand's `@boards` array to the current object's `@boards` array. The method returns the current object.

7. Define the equality and identity operators:

```
def ==(rh)
    self.total == rh.total
end
def ===(rh)
    @boards == rh.boards
end
```

To demonstrate how this might be done, even though this is probably never necessary in the real word, the == (equality) and === (identity) operators are given functionality. Equality is defined as the two collections having the same total number of board feet, even if they contain a different number of boards. Identity is a more stringent version of equality. Here it's defined as checking if two `Wood` objects have `@boards` arrays with the same elements.

8. Define the comparison operator:

```
def <=>(rh)
    if self.total < rh.total then -1
    elsif self.total > rh.total then 1
    else 0 end
end
```

continues on next page

If the left-hand operand (the current object) has less total board feet than the right-hand operand, -1 is returned. If the left-hand operand has more total board feet, 1 is returned. If neither is the case, then 0 is returned, as the two objects are considered equal.

9. Complete the class and create a couple new objects of that type:

```
end
maple = Wood.new({:width => 7,
→ :length => 42}, {:width => 4.5,
→ :length => 22}, {:width => 6.75,
→ :length => 32.5], [:width => 5,
→ :length => 26.25})
oak = Wood.new
oak.add_board({:width => 5,
→ :length => 26.25})
oak.add_board({:width => 6.25,
→ :length => 27.5})
```

First I create a Wood object called maple. When the object is created, its boards are assigned. Then I create a second Wood object called oak. At first the object contains no boards, so two are added.

10. Play with the objects:

```
print "Total amount of maple: "
puts maple.total
print "Total amount of oak: "
puts oak.total
print "maple and oak are equal? "
puts maple == oak
print "maple compared to oak: "
puts maple <=> oak
```

Just to see what the objects can do, the total method is invoked and two of their operators used.

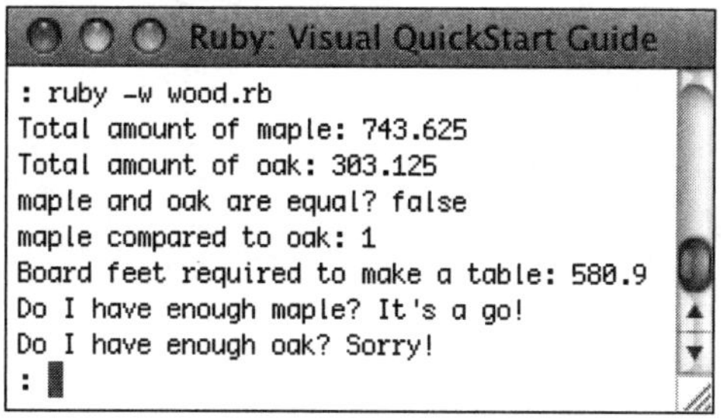

Figure 7.18 The results of running the woods.rb script.

11. Add some more oak:

```
oak += Wood.new({:width => 7,
→ :length => 19}, {:width => 5.5,
→ :length => 22.25})
```

This is a test of using the + operator on objects of this class type.

12. See if there's enough maple or oak for a given project:

```
table = Wood.new({:width => 4.5,
→ :length => 22}, {:width => 6.75,
→ :length => 32.5}, {:width => 5,
→ :length => 26.25}, {:width => 5,
→ :length => 26.25})

puts "Board feet required to make
→ a table: "

puts table.total

print "Do I have enough maple? "

puts maple.enough?(table) ? "It's
→ a go!": "Sorry!"

print "Do I have enough oak? "

puts oak.enough?(table) ? "It's
→ a go!": "Sorry!"
```

A new object of type Wood is created called table. This is a theoretical representation of the boards needed to make, um, a table. With this object, you can then compare its requirements against the stockpiles (the other objects).

13. Save and run the completed script (**Figure 7.18**).

DEFINING OPERATORS

✔ Tips

■ If you need to create a unary minus or plus operator, name the method -@ and +@. You can't use just - and +, as those represent subtraction and addition.

■ Ordinarily you would place a class definition in a separate file, and then include it in scripts that need to use that class. You'll see how to do this in Chapter 9, "Modules and Includes."

■ To allow an object to be treated like an array, define a [ ] method. For example, this next method allows you to refer to a Rectangle's height using obj_name[0] or obj_name[-2] and its width using obj_name[1] or obj_name[-1]:

```
def [](i)
    case i
    when 0, -2: @height
    when 1, -1: @width
    else nil
    end
end
```

If you wanted the object to be treatable as a hash, you would add when cases for :height and 'height', :width and 'width'.

Other Special Methods

With the great power of defining and using your own classes comes the great responsibility of defining them properly. One of those responsibilities includes making them behave, as much as possible, like other Ruby objects. For example, most classes have a to_s method that returns a string version of the object. For numeric types, to_s returns the value in quotes. For arrays, to_s is equivalent to join.

To create your own to_s method, just create a method with that name. Logically, such a method might return the values of the class' variables:

```
class Dog
    def initialize(name)
        @name = name
    end
    def to_s
        @name
    end
end
```

With the Rectangle class, you might place the returned values within a context (**Figure 7.19**):

```
class Rectangle
    attr_reader :height, :width
    def initialize(h, w)
        @height, @width = h, w
    end
    def to_s
        "height: #@height, width: #@width"
    end
    # other methods
end
```

For some classes, it also makes sense to create an each method for iteration. Defining one won't always make sense but can be useful if the class stores multiple values. You'll see an example of this in the next sequence of steps, which defines a class for managing grocery lists. The list is stored within a hash that uses the item as the key and the quantity to purchase as the value. The initialize method creates a new hash. The add method adds an item to the list. The class also implements each and to_s methods so that the grocery list object can be used like a hash when necessary.

```
>> class Rectangle
>>    attr_reader :height, :width
>>    def initialize(h, w)
>>       @height, @width = h, w
>>    end
>>    def to_s
>>       "height: #@height, width: #@width"
>>    end
>>    # other methods
?> end
=> nil
>> r = Rectangle.new(13, 21)
=> #<Rectangle:0x2d9905c @height=13, @width=21>
>> puts r.to_s
height: 13, width: 21
=> nil
>> _
```

Figure 7.19 How a to_s method might work for Rectangle objects.

To create to_s and each methods:

1. Create a new Ruby script in your text editor or IDE (**Script 7.2**):

   # Script 7.2 - groceries.rb

   Again, this example will be written up as a Ruby script.

2. Start defining the GroceryList class:

   ```
   class GroceryList
       def initialize
           @items = Hash.new
       end
   ```

   The class' initalize method takes no arguments and creates a new empty Hash object. Note that I haven't declared any accessors for the hash variable. New values will be added to it using add, and you can view the entire list using each.

3. Define the add method:

   ```
   def add(item, qty = 1)
       @items[item] = qty
   end
   ```

   This method will be used to add items to the list. It takes two arguments: the item and its quantity. The quantity argument has a default value of 1, making it optional. Within the method, the item is added to the hash by adding another element. The item itself is the hash's key; the quantity is the value for that element.

   If the particular item already exists in the hash, its quantity value is updated.

4. Define an each method:

   ```
   def each
       @items.each_pair { |k, v|
       →yield k, v }
   end
   ```

Script 7.2 The GroceryList class provides each and to_s methods so that it behaves more like other Ruby classes.

```
1   # Script 7.2 - groceries.rb
2
3   # Define a new class:
4   class GroceryList
5
6       # Constructor just creates a new
        hash.
7       def initialize
8           @items = Hash.new
9       end
10
11      # Method for adding items to the list.
12      # The quantity value is optional,
        with a default value of 1.
13      # The item's name is used as the key.
14      def add(item, qty = 1)
15          @items[item] = qty
16      end
17
18      # Method for iterating through
        the list.
19      # Yields the key and the value.
20      def each
21          @items.each_pair { |k, v| yield k, v }
22      end
23
24      def to_s
25          str = ''
26          @items.each_pair{ |k, v| str +=
            "#{k}: #{v}, "}
27          str.slice(0, str.length - 2).to_s
28      end
29
30  end # End of GroceryList class.
31
32  # Create a new list:
33  g = GroceryList.new
34
35  # Add some items:
36  g.add('sugar', '5 lbs')
37  g.add('kiwis', 4)
38  g.add('steak')
39
40  # Print the list as a string:
41  puts "List as a string => " + g.to_s
42
43  # Print the list with each item on
        its own line:
44  puts "Grocery List"
45  g.each { |item, qty| puts "#{qty}
        of #{item}" }
```

The **each** method, being an iterator, needs to loop through each element in the hash and yield something to an associated code block. (Iterators always use `yield` and are called with a code block; see Chapters 5 and 6.)

To loop through the hash, the `each_pair` iterator can be used. With each iteration, the hash's key and value will be assigned to the **k** and **v** variables in the code block. These are then yielded by this iterator (to the code block defined when this method is called). This may sound unnecessary and repetitive, but it helps if you think of it like this: `@items` is a hash, so it can use the `Hash` class' `each_pair` (or `each`) method; `GroceryList` is not a `Hash`, so it needs to define its own `each` method (even if it makes use of another iterator).

5. Define a `to_s` method:

```
def to_s
    str = ''
    @items.each_pair { |k, v|
    → str += "#{k}: #{v}, "}
    str.slice(0, str.length -
    → 2).to_s
    end
```

This method will return the hash as a string in the syntax *item: value*, with each item-value pair separated by a comma and a space. An empty string is defined, and then the `each_pair` iterator accesses each element in the hash. Within the associated code block, each pair is concatenated to the string. Then the string is returned, minus its final two characters (the ending comma and space).

Because the `slice` method will return `nil` if the string is empty, the `to_s` method is called on that value to return an empty string instead.

continues on next page

OTHER SPECIAL METHODS

6. Complete the class and create a new object of that type:

```
end
g = GroceryList.new
```

7. Add some items to the list:

```
g.add('sugar', '5 lbs')
g.add('kiwis', 4)
g.add('steak')
```

There's no exact syntax for the item's quantities, so you can use strings or numbers for that. Because the second argument has a default value of 1, it's optional (as in the addition of steak to the list).

8. Print the grocery list as a string:

```
puts "List as a string => " + g.to_s
```

You can use the `to_s` method to get the list as a string. As a string, it can be printed, turned into an array, searched: anything you can do with a standard `String` object.

9. Print the list with each item on its own line:

```
puts "Grocery List"
g.each { |item, qty| puts "#{qty}
→ of #{item}" }
```

First a caption is printed, and then the object's **each** method is invoked. It'll return each item and quantity. Those values will be assigned to `item` and `qty` in this code block, which then prints it within a context.

10. Save and run the completed script (**Figure 7.20**).

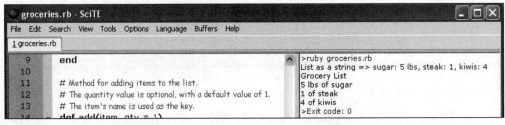

Figure 7.20 The execution of the `groceries.rb` script, as run within SciTE on Windows.

✔ Tips

- Another way to write the to_s method would be to invoke the class' each method:

```
def to_s
  str = ''
  self.each { |k, v| str +=
→ "#{k}: #{v}, "}
  str.slice(0, str.length -
→ 2).to_s
end
```

- Another method you may want to consider declaring is coerce. Such a method switches the arguments in an executed statement:

```
def coerce(rh)
  [self, rh]
end
```

Such a method is necessary if, as an example, a class can be involved in arithmetic with another class type. Say the Wood class handled multiplication, so that you could double or triple your stockpile. In that case, the statement maple * 2 would work but 2 * maple would not (because the Fixnum class wouldn't support multiplying by a Wood object). If the Wood class defined this coerce method, then it could switch the operands around and still perform the arithmetic.

- If the GroceryList class defined an attribute reader for @items—

```
attr_reader :items
```

—then no each method would need to be defined within the class, because you could do this outside of the class:

```
g.items.each { |item, qty| puts
→ "#{qty} of #{item}" }
```

But that would assume the user knew that the class' @items variable existed and that it was a hash. Ideally, classes should be written so that they are usable without knowing, or even having access to, their inner workings. This is called *encapsulation*, and will be discussed more in the next chapter.

OTHER SPECIAL METHODS

Validation and Duck Typing

The Wood class as written in Script 7.1 has a problem in its design: it assumes its methods and operators will be used properly. The enough? method assumes that it receives something with a total method, as does the equality operator. The + and === operators assume that they'll only be applied to an operand that has a boards variable. Either of the following will cause errors (**Figure 7.21**):

```
puts !maple.enough?(439.50)

oak += 35
```

To prevent improper use of a method, you can add validation routines that terminate the execution of the method if certain conditions aren't met. One kind of validation that you can perform is to check what type of object is involved. The instance_of? method returns a Boolean value indicating if a given object is of a certain class type:

```
class ThisClass
    def -(rh)
        return nil unless rh.instance_of?
→ ThisClass
        # It's OK, perform subtraction.
    end
end
```

That method will return the value nil unless the right-hand operand object is also of type ThisClass.

If you want to be more flexible, you can see if an object is of a certain type or any inherited types. The next chapter discusses inheritance in detail, but for now just know that inheritance allows one class to be derived from another class.

```
class Rectangle
    def <=>(rh)
        return nil unless rh.is_a? Shape
        self.area <=> rh.area
    end
end
```

The premise in that example is that a comparison can be made between a Rectangle object and any other object of the Shape class or of a derived class. This might include Rectangle, Circle, and Triangle. A comparison could be made in such cases because any Shape-derived object should have an area method (the comparison suggests that a rectangle is bigger than a circle if its area is bigger than the circle's area). However, if all you really care about is if the object has a certain method, there's an even more liberal way to go.

For instance, say you create a class that generates HTML tables. Such a class could be written so that it turns an array into a table. But why shouldn't it also be able to handle a hash or even a range? In fact, why couldn't it handle a GroceryList object, which is also just a list of values? What such a class

```
>> puts !maple.enough?(439.50)
NoMethodError: undefined method `total' for 439.5:Float
        from (irb):106:in `enough?'
        from (irb):139
        from :0
>> oak += 35
NoMethodError: undefined method `boards' for 35:Fixnum
        from (irb):111:in `+'
        from (irb):140
        from :0
>>
```

Figure 7.21 The kinds of errors you might see if class methods and operators aren't called with the right kinds of arguments or operands.

really requires might just be any object that supports the `each` iterator. To test for that condition, use the `respond_to?` method:

```ruby
class HtmlTable
    # Other class code.
    def make_rows(data)
        return nil unless
        → data.respond_to?('each')
        data.each { # block code }
    end
end
```

This notion of writing code so that it doesn't care about specific types involved so much as what the types can do is called *duck typing*. The name comes from the saying "If it walks like a duck and quacks like a duck, I would call it a duck" (quote originally attributed to James Whitcomb Riley). With something like this `HtmlTable` class the benefit is that you can write the class once and it'll work with any kind of object that has an `each` method. This includes classes defined well after the `HtmlTable` class was created.

Support, and even preference for, duck typing is one of the many ways in which Ruby differs from other programming languages. It illustrates part of the Ruby model: what a thing *can do* is more important than what a thing *is*.

To test this out, let's define two new versions of the `Rectangle` and `Circle` classes, and then see what can be done with them.

To use duck typing:

1. Create a new Ruby script in your text editor or IDE (**Script 7.3**):

   ```
   # Script 7.3 - ducks.rb
   ```

2. Start defining the Rectangle class:

   ```ruby
   class Rectangle
       attr_reader :height, :width
       def initialize(h, w)
           @height, @width = h, w
       end
       def area
           @height * @width
       end
   end
   ```

   Most of this class definition will come from an earlier example. To save space, I won't implement the `perimeter` and `is_square?` methods in this version.

3. Define the + method:

   ```ruby
   def +(rh)
       return nil unless rh.instance_of?
       → Rectangle
       @height += rh.height
       @width += rh.width
       self
   end
   ```

   Addition can be performed only using two Rectangle objects. Within this method, the first line returns `nil`, which therefore exits the method, if the received argument—the right-hand operand—isn't also a Rectangle object. If the `rh.instance_of?` conditional returns `true`, then the addition takes place by adding the two heights together and adding the two widths together. The current object is then returned.

Script 7.3 This script makes use of the `instance_of?` and `responds_to?` methods to control what kinds of objects can be used together.

```ruby
1   # Script 7.3 - ducks.rb
2
3   # Very basic Rectangle definition:
4   class Rectangle
5
6       attr_reader :height, :width
7
8       def initialize(h, w)
9           @height, @width = h, w
10      end
11
12      def area
13          @height * @width
14      end
15
16      # + should only work with other
        Rectangles!
17      def +(rh)
18          return nil unless rh.instance_of?
            Rectangle
19          @height += rh.height
20          @width += rh.width
21          self
22      end
23
24      # Comparison can be with any
        object that
25      # has an "area" method.
26      def <=>(rh)
27          return nil unless rh.respond_to?
            ('area')
28          if (self.area < rh.area) then -1
29          elsif (self.area > rh.area) then 1
30          else 0 end
31      end
32
33  end # End of Rectangle class.
34
35  # Simple Circle definition:
36  class Circle
37      attr_reader :radius
38      def initialize(r)
39          @radius = r
40      end
41      def area
42          Math::PI * @radius**2
43      end
44  end # End of Circle class.
45
```

(script continues on next page)

Script 7.3 *continued*

```
46   # Create the objects:
47   r = Rectangle.new(32, 56)
48   c = Circle.new(8.4)
49
50   # Print their info:
51   puts "The area of r is #{r.area}.
     The area of c is #{c.area}."
52
53   # Print addition:
54   print "The addition of r + c: "
55   puts r + c
56
57   # Print comparison:
58   print "The comparison of r and c: "
59   puts r <=> c
60
```

4. Define the `<=>` method and complete the class:

```
def <=>(rh)
    return nil unless
→ rh.respond_to?('area')
    if (self.area < rh.area) then -1
    elsif (self.area > rh.area)
→ then 1
    else 0 end
end
end
```

The comparison operator uses duck typing to allow it to make comparisons between a `Rectangle` and any object that has an **area** method. The first line within the method terminates the method if the condition is not met. Then -1, 1, or 0 is returned, depending upon the comparison.

5. Define a `Circle` class:

```
class Circle
    attr_reader :radius
    def initialize(r)
        @radius = r
    end
    def area
        Math::PI * @radius**2
    end
end
```

This is a bare-bones version of the `Circle` class, containing only the `initialize` and **area** methods. If you wanted, you could also define `<=>`, exactly like it's defined in the `Rectangle` class, so that `Circle` objects can be the left-hand operand in a comparison.

6. Create objects of both class types:

```
r = Rectangle.new(32, 56)
c = Circle.new(8.4)
```

continues on next page

7. Print each shape's area:

```
puts "The area of r is #{r.area}.
→ The area of c is #{c.area}."
```

8. Print the addition of the two shapes:

```
print "The addition of r + c: "
puts r + c
```

Because the `Rectangle` class requires that the right-hand operand also be of type `Rectangle`, the result of the addition will be `nil` (the value returned by the method).

9. Print the comparison of the two shapes:

```
print "The comparison of r and c: "
puts r <=> c
```

This operator can be used because of duck typing.

10. Save and run the completed script (**Figure 7.22**).

✔ Tips

■ Another way to define methods in a class is to assume that any received input will work (i.e., to treat everything like a duck), and then throw exceptions when the received input won't work. Chapter 11, "Debugging and Error Handling," discusses this approach.

■ Because the `Circle` class doesn't define a comparison operator, you'll see an error if you write the comparison as:

```
c <=> r
```

The solution would be to define the comparison operator in the `Circle` class or a coerce method in `Rectangle`.

```
○ ○ ○        Ruby: Visual QuickStart Guide
: ruby —w ducks.rb
The area of r is 1792. The area of c is 221.670777637296.
The addition of r + c: nil
The comparison of r and c: 1
: █
```

Figure 7.22 By watching for the types of objects being used, scripts can be more or less restrictive in what they allow to be done.

INHERITANCE AND MORE

Chapter 7, "Creating Classes," walks through the fundamentals of defining and using your own classes. That chapter includes all of the basic syntax, how to use instance variables within the class, and how to define special methods and operators. In this chapter, the subject of OOP is taken one important step further: into the realm of *inheritance*. Inheritance is the act of deriving one class, called the *child* or *subclass*, from another, called the *parent*, *superclass*, or *base class*. The derived class will begin with the same properties as the base class, but those can then be expanded or altered as needed. Inheritance gives OOP its muscle, making it so much more useful.

The chapter begins with the basics of inheritance in Ruby. Subsequent sections cover overriding methods, chaining methods, and class methods. The other two primary topics address access control and class variables. And, of course, there's lots of extra information to be found in the various sidebars and tips.

Basic Inheritance

To understand inheritance, you have to start with a base class:

```
class ParentClass
    def this
        # do whatever
    end
    def that
        # do whatever
    end
end
```

The syntax for deriving a class from that class is:

```
class ChildClass < ParentClass
end
```

The ChildClass definition indicates that it inherits from ParentClass. This means that even though ChildClass doesn't define any of its own methods, it still has two: this and that. You can now do:

```
ex = ChildClass.new
ex.this
ex.that
```

There's no limit to how many classes can be derived from a superclass (**Figure 8.1**) or

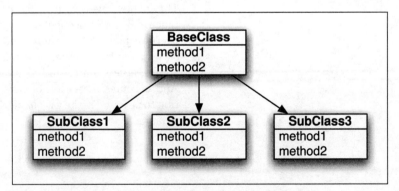

Figure 8.1 Any number of subclasses can inherit from the same base class.

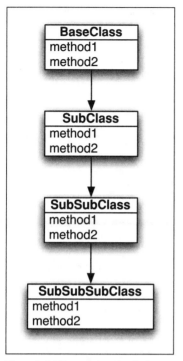

Figure 8.2 Although there's a limit as to what's practical and useful, tiered inheritance can be used to any depth.

how many tiers of inheritance can be created (**Figure 8.2**). However, as a rule of thumb, a well-conceived model probably won't involve more than three levels of inheritance. Here's an extension of ChildClass:

```
class GrandchildClass < ChildClass
end
```

Objects of type GrandchildClass can also invoke the this and that methods, because they are inherited from ChildClass.

Still, there's no point to define a class as just an inherited version of another class: in these examples, there's no difference between ParentClass, ChildClass, and GrandchildClass. Most subclasses distinguish themselves by adding their own method definitions:

```
class ChildClass < ParentClass
    def the_other
    end
end
```

With these definitions, objects of type ParentClass can call a this and a that method; objects of type ChildClass can call this, that, and the_other.

When to Use Inheritance

Comprehension of inheritance involves understanding not only its syntax but also *when to use it*. A class might be a candidate to be a child of another class if it passes the "is a" test. Looking at the examples in Chapter 7, a Dog could be inherited from Pet (because a dog is a pet) and a Rectangle could be inherited from a parent Shape class (because a rectangle is a shape). But the Wood class would not likely inherit anything because a pile of wood is just that.

Second, understand that you should not extend classes defined by other people, including base Ruby classes, unless you fully comprehend them. Without solid knowledge of how a class is designed and written, you're just as likely to undermine its power in the act of deriving another class from it.

To use inheritance:

1. Begin a new Ruby script in your text editor or IDE (**Script 8.1**):

Script 8.1 - pets.rb

This file will define a Pet class and a derived Dog class.

2. Begin defining the Pet class:

class Pet

    attr_reader :name

The Pet class has an instance variable called @name. A getter will be created so that the pet's name can be retrieved outside of the class. This is equivalent to defining a method like so:

def name

    @name

end

See Chapter 7 if you're not familiar with the concepts of attribute readers and attribute accessors.

3. Add the constructor:

def initialize(name)

    @name = name

end

The constructor, always called initialize in Ruby, takes one argument, which will be assigned to the local variable name. This value is then assigned to the instance variable @name.

4. Complete the Pet class definition:

    def sleep

      "#@name is sleeping."

    end

end

The third method in the class (after name and initialize) returns a message saying that the pet is sleeping.

Script 8.1 The Dog class inherits three methods from Pet and then adds one of its own.

```
1   # Script 8.1 - pets.rb
2
3   # Define the Pet class:
4   class Pet
5
6       # Getter for the name:
7       attr_reader :name
8
9       # Constructor sets the pet's name:
10      def initialize(name)
11          @name = name
12      end
13
14      # Pets need to sleep:
15      def sleep
16          "#@name is sleeping."
17      end
18
19  end # End of Pet definition.
20
21  # Dog class is an extension of Pet:
22  class Dog < Pet
23
24      # Dogs also fetch:
25      def fetch
26          "#@name is playing fetch."
27      end
28
29  end # End of Dog definition.
30
31  # Create a new Dog:
32  d = Dog.new('trixie')
33
34  # Do stuff:
35  puts d.sleep
36  puts d.fetch
37  puts "The dog's name is #{d.name}."
```

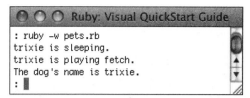

```
: ruby -w pets.rb
trixie is sleeping.
trixie is playing fetch.
The dog's name is trixie.
:
```

Figure 8.3 The execution of `pets.rb` (Script 8.1), shows how a `Dog` object can invoke methods defined in either the `Pet` class or the `Dog` class.

5. Define the `Dog` class:

```
class Dog < Pet
    def fetch
        "#@name is playing fetch."
    end
end
```

The `Dog` class is defined as an extension of `Pet`. So `Dog` starts off inheriting the `initialize`, `name`, and `sleep` methods. To these three, `fetch` is added (something not all pets do). This method also refers to the `@name` variable.

6. Create a `Dog` object:

```
d = Dog.new('trixie')
```

Note that I don't create an object of type `Pet`, but instead create a more specific `Dog` object. When this object is created, the `initialize` method inherited from `Pet` will be called. It will assign the value *trixie* to `@name`.

7. Have the dog do stuff:

```
puts d.sleep
puts d.fetch
puts "The dog's name is #{d.name}."
```

The `sleep` and `name` methods are defined in `Pet`. The `fetch` method is only in `Dog`. But since `Dog` inherits from `Pet`, the `d` object can call them all.

8. Save and run the completed script (**Figure 8.3**).

BASIC INHERITANCE

✔ Tips

- Chapter 7 mentions that you can use *ClassName*.instance_methods to see the methods available to a given class. Passing this method a value of false returns only the non-inherited methods (**Figure 8.4**).

- Ruby does not support multiple inheritance: where a class simultaneously inherits from multiple parent classes (this is different than tiered inheritance as reflected in Figure 8.2). Similar functionality can be achieved by having a class include a module. That topic is covered in Chapter 9, "Modules and Includes."

- Classes that aren't overtly extensions of existing classes end up being subclasses of the Object parent class. In Ruby 1.9 and later, Object is itself a subclass of the parent BasicObject.

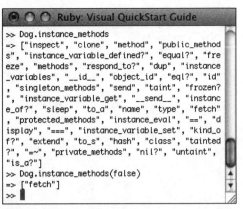

```
>> Dog.instance_methods
=> ["inspect", "clone", "method", "public_method
s", "instance_variable_defined?", "equal?", "fre
eze", "methods", "respond_to?", "dup", "instance
_variables", "__id__", "object_id", "eql?", "id"
, "singleton_methods", "send", "taint", "frozen?
", "instance_variable_get", "__send__", "instanc
e_of?", "sleep", "to_a", "name", "type", "fetch"
, "protected_methods", "instance_eval", "==", "d
isplay", "===", "instance_variable_set", "kind_o
f?", "extend", "to_s", "hash", "class", "tainted
?", "=~", "private_methods", "nil?", "untaint",
"is_a?"]
>> Dog.instance_methods(false)
=> ["fetch"]
>>
```

Figure 8.4 The instance_methods method, inherited by all classes, will return only non-inherited methods, like fetch, if provided with a value of false. The top of the image shows every method available to Dog objects.

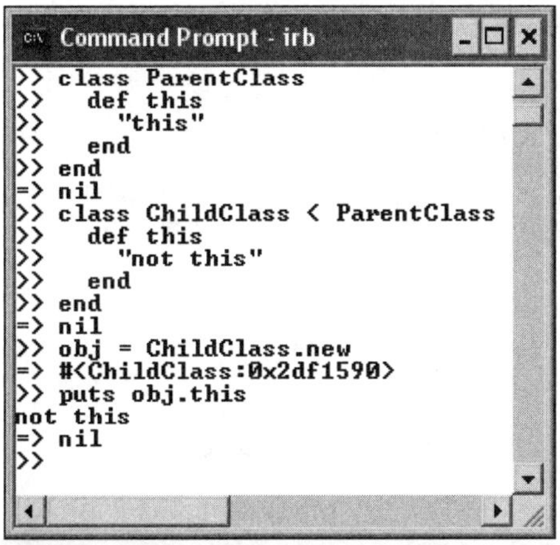

```
>> class ParentClass
>>   def this
>>     "this"
>>   end
>> end
=> nil
>> class ChildClass < ParentClass
>>   def this
>>     "not this"
>>   end
>> end
=> nil
>> obj = ChildClass.new
=> #<ChildClass:0x2df1590>
>> puts obj.this
not this
=> nil
>>
```

Figure 8.5 When a method is overridden, its new definition is used when invoked on an instance of the child class.

Overriding Methods

A child class begins with the same definition as its parent class. From there, the child can be updated by adding its own method definitions, as demonstrated in `pets.rb` (Script 8.1). Subclasses can be further distinguished from their superclasses by redefining methods declared in the parent class. This is called *overriding* a method (**Figure 8.5**):

```
class ParentClass
    def this
        "this"
    end
end
class ChildClass < ParentClass
    def this
        "not this"
    end
end
obj = ChildClass.new
puts obj.this
```

One way of thinking about this concept is that the parent class defines a method's default behavior. The subclass method then changes this behavior if something other than the default is required by objects of the subclass' type.

To override a method:

1. Open pets.rb in your text editor or IDE if it is not already.

To demonstrate the concept of overriding methods, the Pet and Dog classes will be updated so that Pet implements a play method, which is then overridden in Dog.

2. Add a new method to Pet (**Script 8.2**):

```
def play
    "#@name is playing."
end
```

Conceptually, all pets play, but they do so in different ways. The Pet version of the method just says that the pet is playing.

3. Rename the Dog class' fetch method as play:

```
def play
    "#@name is playing fetch."
end
```

The Dog version of the play method is more specific, saying that the dog is playing fetch. If you had a Cat class, which also inherits from Pet, it might do this:

```
def play
    "#@name is playing with string."
end
```

Script 8.2 The play method defined in Pet is overridden in Dog to change its behavior.

```
1    # Script 8.2 - pets2.rb
2
3    # Define the Pet class:
4    class Pet
5        attr_reader :name
6        def initialize(name)
7            @name = name
8        end
9        def sleep
10            "#@name is sleeping."
11        end
12
13        # Pets can also play:
14        def play
15            "#@name is playing."
16        end
17
18    end # End of Pet definition.
19
20    # Dog class is an extension of Pet:
21    class Dog < Pet
22
23        # Dogs fetch to play:
24        def play
25            "#@name is playing fetch."
26        end
27
28    end # End of Dog definition.
29
30    # Create a new Dog:
31    d = Dog.new('trixie')
32
33    # Do stuff:
34    puts d.sleep
35    puts d.play
36    puts "The dog's name is #{d.name}."
```

4. Change the invocation of the `fetch` method to `play`:

   `puts d.play`

5. Save and run the completed script (**Figure 8.6**).

✔ Tips

■ If you created an object of type `Pet`, which you can do, and invoked its `play` method, you'd see the method's original result: *#@name is playing.*

■ Ruby does not support *overloading* methods: multiple definitions of the same method that take different numbers or kinds of arguments.

■ Ruby also does not formally support *abstract* methods. In languages that have this feature, an abstract method is one that is mentioned in a parent class but whose full definition and implementation must be placed in a derived class. One way to create a pseudo-abstract method would be to have the parent class's definition throw an exception (discussed in Chapter 11, "Debugging and Error Handling"). That exception would be seen if a subclass does not override the method.

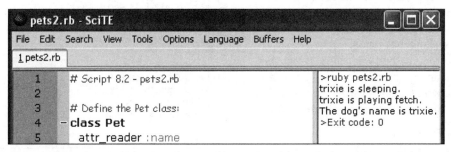

Figure 8.6 When the `Dog` object plays, the overridden version of the method is used instead of the original defined in `Pet`.

OVERRIDING METHODS

Chaining Methods

There are often times when you override a method that it would still be useful to invoke the original method definition. You can do so using *chaining*: the act of calling the parent class' definition of the current method. To do this, use super:

```
class ParentClass
    def this
        # do whatever
    end
end
class ChildClass < ParentClass
    def this
        # do something else
        super # Call ParentClass.this
    end
end
```

One logical place to use chaining is with initialize methods, since such methods perform basic setup that the class requires. In this next example, you'll see how the Horse class performs some initial functionality and then relies upon the Pet constructor to do the rest.

First, though, there's one thing to know. When you use super without any arguments, the values passed to the method that calls super will automatically be passed to the overridden method. In other words, super is like calling the original method exactly as the current method was called, except that the arguments passed along will reflect any changes that might have been made to them in the interim. An example (**Figure 8.7**):

```
class ParentClass
    def put_this(msg)
        puts "ParentClass: #{msg}"
    end
end
```

```
class ChildClass < ParentClass
    def put_this(stuff)
        puts "ChildClass: #{stuff}"
        stuff *= 2
        super
    end
end
ex = ChildClass.new
ex.put_this('test')
```

Alternatively, you can call super as you would any other method, dictating exactly what values are passed:

```
class ChildClass < ParentClass
    def put_this(stuff)
        super('print this')
    end
end
```

Figure 8.7 The value sent to the ChildClass.put_this method—*test*—is automatically passed to the ParentClass.put_this method, thanks to super, but in its altered state (namely, doubled to *testtest*).

Script 8.3 Both methods in the Horse class invoke the corresponding overridden Pet method by calling super.

```
1   # Script 8.3 - horse.rb
2
3   # Define the Pet class:
4   class Pet
5       def initialize(name)
6           @name = name
7       end
8
9       # Returns info about the pet:
10      def to_s
11          "Name: #@name\nType:
            #{self.class}\n"
12      end
13
14  end # End of Pet definition.
15
16  # Horse class is an extension of Pet:
17  class Horse < Pet
18
19      # Constructor takes two args:
20      def initialize(name, hands)
21          @hands = hands
22          super(name)
23      end
24
25      # Update the to_s method:
26      def to_s
27          super + "Size: #@hands hands\n"
28      end
29
30  end # End of Horse definition.
31
32  # Create a new Horse:
33  h = Horse.new('Seabiscuit', 15.2)
34
35  # Print the horse as a string:
36  puts h.to_s
```

To use chaining:

1. Begin a new script in your text editor or IDE (**Script 8.3**):

   `# Script 8.3 - horse.rb`

   For this example, I'll make another variation on the Pet class, which has the benefit of being easy to follow. In this script, Pet will be defined more minimally and will be extended by a Horse class.

2. Begin defining Pet:

   ```
   class Pet
       def initialize(name)
           @name = name
       end
   ```

   The `initialize` method assigns a value to the @name instance variable, as it did in the previous incarnation of the class. I've dropped the `attr_reader` line just to save some space, but you can add it if you'd like.

3. Define a to_s method and complete the class:

   ```
   def to_s
       "Name: #@name\nType:
       → #{self.class}\n"
   end

   end
   ```

   As stated in Chapter 7, most classes should have a to_s method. At the very least, such a method aids in debugging. In the Pet class, the to_s method returns some of the information about the pet: its name and type. You can find the pet type by calling the class method on self. You might think that this would always return Pet, but it will be invoked using objects of a different class types, so it'll reflect the object type on which it was called: Dog, Cat, Horse, etc.

   continues on next page

4. Start defining a `Horse` class:

```
class Horse < Pet
```

The `Horse` class is an extension of `Pet`. (And, yes, not everyone considers a horse to be a pet, but just work with me here.)

5. Define the `initialize` method:

```
def initialize(name, hands)
    @hands = hands
    super(name)
end
```

Every pet has a name, so the `Pet initialize` method takes care of assigning that value. But horses differ from other pets in that they are measured in *hands*. So the `Horse` class' `initialize` method takes two arguments: the horse's name and its size. Within the method, the submitted `hands` value is assigned to the instance variable `@hands`. Then the submitted `name` value is assigned to the `@name` instance variable by passing it to the `Pet initialize` method via a call to `super`.

You could just as easily do this within `Horse`:

```
@name = name
```

But that approach violates the *DRY* principle of Ruby programming: *Don't Repeat Yourself*. Since the parent class already handles the assignation of the `@name` variable, let it continue to do so.

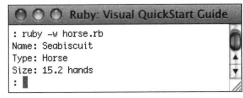

Figure 8.8 The result of invoking the overridden to_s method on a Horse object.

6. Define the to_s method and complete the Horse class:

```
def to_s
    super + "Size: #@hands hands\n"
end
end
```

The to_s method needs to be overridden from its original definition so that it also returns the information about the horse's size. But what the original to_s method does is still useful; so this version will invoke that to_s method and then append the horse's size to the returned result.

7. Create a new horse and print it as a string:

```
h = Horse.new('Seabiscuit', 15.2)
puts h.to_s
```

8. Save and run the completed script (**Figure 8.8**).

✔ Tips

■ As uses of **super**, without any parentheses or arguments, will automatically pass to the parent method the values received by the current one, if you want to pass no values, you need to use **super()**.

■ You can call other parent class methods within subclasses using the syntax *ParentClassName::method_name* or *ParentClassName.method_name*.

Access Control

Access control is used to define the circumstances in which methods can be invoked. The three options are: *public*, *protected*, and *private*. If you're familiar with this concept in other programming languages, do note that Ruby implements access control differently than you might be used to.

Public methods can be invoked using objects of that type, using objects of inherited subtypes, or within a class definition. For example, a Dog object can call the public methods fetch and sleep (the latter defined in Pet):

```
d = Dog.new('trixie')
d.fetch
d.sleep
```

Methods in the Dog class could also directly call methods in Pet.

Private methods are the most restricted; they can be invoked only within a class definition

Instance Variables and Inheritance

Ruby has a subtle distinction from other OOP languages when it comes to inheritance: *instance variables* are not inherited but instance accessor methods are. For example:

```
class Fairy
    attr_accessor :name
end
class Pooka < Fairy
end
```

The Fairy class has two auto-generated methods—name= and name. The first is a setter, used to assign a value to the @name instance variable. The second is a getter, used to return that variable's value. They'd be used like so:

```
obj = Fairy.new
obj.name = 'Harvey'
puts obj.name
```

The Pooka class also has name= and name methods, inherited from Fairy. These methods also access a @name instance variable, but this variable exists only within the Pooka class and is a different entity than @name within Fairy.

and only on the current object. Private methods will be called using just the name of the method (you cannot call a private method using *obj_name.private_method_name*). Unlike in other languages, private methods in Ruby *are* inherited.

Protected methods are like private methods in that they can be called only within a class definition, but they differ in that they can be used on any object of the same or inherited class types. So you can use *obj_name.protected_method_name* in a class definition as long as *obj_name* is of the right class type. Most methods in Ruby will be defined as either public or private; protected is less often used.

As for syntax, there are two ways to declare the accessibility. The first is to write the method definitions after the term `protected` or `private`:

```
class ClassName
    # Define public methods.
    protected
    # Define all protected methods.
    private
    # Define all private methods.
end
```

Methods not given an explicit access level will be public by default, except for the `initialize` method, which is always auto-matically private. Also, if you use one of these keywords, every method defined after the term will have that access level. In this example, both `method1` and `method2` are protected:

```
class ClassName
    protected
    def method1
    end
    def method2
    end
end
```

The second way to declare accessibility is to define the methods, and then use the proper term, followed by symbols representing the methods:

```
class ClassName
    # Define all methods.
    protected :method_name1,
    ➝ :method_name2
    private :method_name3,
    ➝ :method_name4
end
```

The final thing to understand about access control—and this also differs from other languages—is that it only affects methods. The instance variables in a class can never be directly referenced via objects or within derived classes (also see the "Instance Variables and Inheritance" sidebar for more).

To use access control:

1. Begin a new Ruby script in your text editor or IDE (**Script 8.4**):

```
# Script 8.4 - creditcard.rb
```

This example will be a partial class representing credit cards. The class will manage just the debits (charges) and credits (payments), as well as the card's balance and limit. In terms of security, the card's balance is the most important value, so I need to restrict access to it.

2. Begin defining the class:

```
class CreditCard
    attr_reader :balance, :limit
    protected :balance
```

The class needs getter methods for the card's balance and limit. Both will be given values within the `initialize` method. The `@balance` getter method is then marked as protected so that it's only usable within the class definition (i.e., so that it's hidden outside of the class). The method cannot be made private, though, as it'll be used by a comparison operator when contrasting two credit cards.

These first two lines within the class' definition are equivalent to writing:

```
def limit
    @limit
end
protected
def balance
    @balance
end
```

3. Define the `initialize` method:

```
def initialize(limit, bal = 0)
    @limit = limit
    @balance = bal
end
```

Script 8.4 To limit access to key methods in the class, one is protected and two are made private.

```
1   # Script 8.4 - creditcard.rb
2
3   # Partial class for representing
    credit cards:
4   class CreditCard
5
6       # Need getters for the balance
        and limit:
7       attr_reader :balance, :limit
8
9       # Protect the balance getter:
10      protected :balance
11
12      # Constructor sets the card's
        limit and balance:
13      def initialize(limit, bal = 0)
14          @limit = limit
15          @balance = bal
16      end
17
18      # For making charges:
19      def charge(amt)
20          # validation
21          debit(amt)
22      end
23
24      # For making payments:
25      def payment(amt)
26          # validation
27          credit(amt)
28      end
29
30      # Returns the difference between
        the limit and the balance:
31      def available
32          @limit - @balance
33      end
34
35      # Compares two objects by balance:
36      def >(rh)
37          return nil unless rh.respond_to?
            ('balance')
38          @balance > rh.balance
39      end
40
```

(script continues on next page)

Script 8.4 *continued*

```
     ┌──────────────────────────────────┐
     │ ● ● ●            📄 Script        │
     ├──────────────────────────────────┤
41   │    # Private methods impact the
     │    card's balance:
42   │    private
43   │    def debit(amt)
44   │       @balance += amt
45   │    end
46   │    def credit(amt)
47   │       @balance - = amt
48   │    end
49   │
50   │ end # End of CreditCard class.
51   │
52   │ # Create two objects:
53   │ mc = CreditCard.new(2000)
54   │ visa = CreditCard.new(3000, 1200)
55   │
56   │ # Charge the card with the most
     │ available room:
57   │ if mc.available > visa.available then
58   │    mc.charge(225)
59   │    puts "The MasterCard has been
     │    charged $225!"
60   │ else
61   │    visa.charge(225)
62   │    puts "The Visa has been charged $225!"
63   │ end
64   │
65   │ # Pay the card with the highest balance:
66   │ if mc > visa then
67   │    mc.payment(500)
68   │    puts "Payment of $500 has been
     │    sent to the MasterCard!"
69   │ else
70   │    visa.payment(500)
71   │    puts "Payment of $500 has been
     │    sent to the Visa!"
72   │ end
```

This method, called when a new
CreditCard object is created, takes two
arguments: the card's limit and its opening balance. The second argument has a
default value of 0. The received values are
then assigned to instance variables. The
initialize method is always private.

4. Define the charge and payment methods:

```
def charge(amt)
   debit(amt)
end
def payment(amt)
   credit(amt)
end
```

These two methods will have the net effect
of increasing and decreasing the card's
balance. To do so, these methods would
perform a whole lot of validation—making
sure that both receive positive integers,
making sure that the charge won't exceed
the limit, etc.—and then call the debit
and credit methods. Those methods will
perform the actual adjustments on the
balance. For improved security, debit and
credit will be private, so that they can be
called only within this class. The charge
and payment methods, however, are public
(the default access level).

5. Define the available method:

```
def available
   @limit - @balance
end
```

This method returns the difference
between the card's limit and its current
balance: the amount of spending still
possible. It could be called in the charge
method as part of the validation routine:

```
return 'Insufficient funds!' unless
→ amt <= available
```

continues on next page

6. Define the greater-than operator:

```
def >(rh)
   return nil unless
   → rh.respond_to?('balance')
   @balance > rh.balance
end
```

This operator will be used to compare two credit cards by balance, returning true if the current card has a higher balance than the second card (received in rh). Within the method definition, the first line returns the value nil, terminating the method, unless the second object also has a balance method. By using this technique—*duck typing* (see Chapter 7), a credit card could be compared to a loan (if it has a balance method).

Because the balance getter method is protected, this > method can refer to the second object's balance method. If balance were private, this comparison could not be made. If it were public, then the comparison could be made using objects outside of the class definition, which may not be desired.

I have not implemented the <, >=, or <= operators, just to save space. Those definitions would look much like this one, but with the corresponding operator being used within the method.

7. Define the debit and credit methods:

```
private
def debit(amt)
   @balance += amt
end
def credit(amt)
   @balance -= amt
end
```

These two methods are the only ones that actually alter the credit card's balance. For this reason, they're restricted, only being callable within the class definition and on the current object. In the class as defined thus far, only the charge and payment methods invoke these, but they might also be called within a transfer method.

8. Complete the class and create two credit card objects:

```
end # End of CreditCard class.
mc = CreditCard.new(2000)
visa = CreditCard.new(3000, 1200)
```

The mc object is a card with a $2,000 (or 2,000 *whatever currency*) limit and no balance. The visa object has a $3,000 limit and an initial $1,200 balance.

9. Add a charge to the card that has the most available spending room:

```
if mc.available > visa.available then
   mc.charge(225)
   puts "The MasterCard has been
   → charged $225!"
else
   visa.charge(225)
   puts "The Visa has been charged
   → $225!"
end
```

Because the available method is public, objects outside of the class definition can invoke it to determine which card has the most available spending room, even though the card's balance is essentially hidden.

The balance cannot be directly seen or altered using the mc and visa objects because of the access control restrictions.

10. Pay $500 to the card with the highest balance:

```
if mc > visa then
    mc.payment(500)
    puts "Payment of $500 has been
    ⇢ sent to the MasterCard!"
else
    visa.payment(500)
    puts "Payment of $500 has been
    ⇢ sent to the Visa!"
end
```

This conditional makes use of the > operator defined in the class.

11. Save and run the completed script (**Figure 8.9**).

✔ Tips

■ The terms public, protected, and private are actually methods found within the Module class (of which Class is a subclass).

■ Methods defined outside of any class become private methods of the global Object class.

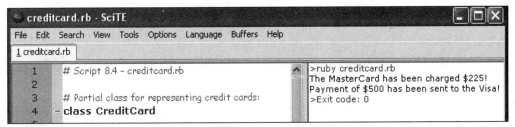

Figure 8.9 The CreditCard class allows certain tasks to be done, but maintains security by encapsulating the most important information and functionality.

Class Variables

Chapter 7 shows how to use variables within a class. The examples all had names that begin with @, like @height in the Rectangle class. Such variables are *instance variables*: variables tied to instances of a class (i.e., objects). Classes can use a second kind of variable, called *class variables*. These variables follow the same rules for their identifiers—letters, numbers, and underscores—but begin with @@. Unlike instance variables, class variables can be assigned values outside of any method definition but can be used by any method:

```
class ClassName
    @@var = value
    def method_name
        # Use @@var
    end
end
```

Class variables are tied to the class itself and not to any specific instance of the class (i.e., not to any particular object of that class type). One possible use of class variables is to track all the objects that exist of that type, including derived types. This next example will do just that.

To use class variables:

1. Begin a new Ruby script in your text editor or IDE (**Script 8.5**):

    This will be another variation on the Pet example. The class will be defined in the most minimal way, and then extended by three different classes.

2. Begin the Pet class definition:

    ```
    class Pet
        @@count = 0
        attr_reader :name
    ```

    The class has one class variable: @@count. Its initial value—the value before any objects are created of type Pet or any subclass—is 0.

Script 8.5 The class variable @@count is used to track how many total Pet objects exist.

```
1   # Script 8.5 - pets3.rb
2
3   # Define the Pet class:
4   class Pet
5
6       # Class variable:
7       @@count = 0
8
9       # Getter for the name:
10      attr_reader :name
11
12      # Constructor sets the pet's name
13      # and increments the count:
14      def initialize(name)
15      @name = name
16          @@count += 1
17      end
18
19      # Returns the total number of pets:
20      def total_pets
21          @@count
22      end
23
24  end # End of Pet definition.
25
26  # Dog class is an extension of Pet:
27  class Dog < Pet
28  end
29
30  # Cat class is an extension of Pet:
31  class Cat < Pet
32  end
33
34  # Fish class is an extension of Pet:
35  class Fish < Pet
36  end
37
38  # Create a new Dog:
39  d = Dog.new('Old Yeller')
40
41  # How many pets do I have?
42  puts "After getting a dog, I have
    #{d.total_pets} pet."
43
44  # Get a cat and a fish:
45  c = Cat.new('Bucky')
46  f = Fish.new('Nemo')
47  puts "After getting a cat and a
    fish, I have #{d.total_pets} pets."
```

3. Define the `initialize` method:

```
def initialize(name)
  @name = name
  @@count += 1
end
```

Each time a new `Pet` object is created (or any subclass type), the Pet `initialize` method will be called, incrementing the class variable `@@count`.

4. Define the `total_pets` method and complete the class:

```
def total_pets
  @@count
end

end # End of Pet definition.
```

The `total_pets` method will simply return the class variable. (This works fine, but as you'll see, a more logical solution would be to use a class method, discussed next in the chapter).

5. Define the `Dog`, `Cat`, and `Fish` classes:

```
class Dog < Pet
end
class Cat < Pet
end
class Fish < Pet
end
```

Each is an inherited version of `Pet`, with no alterations. This is for simple demonstration purposes only.

continues on next page

6. Get a dog and print the total number of pets:

```
d = Dog.new('Old Yeller')

puts "After getting a dog, I have
→ #{d.total_pets} pet."
```

Because the Dog class inherits from Pet, it also has the total_pets method. As you'll see when you run this script, when the Dog object is created, the Pet initialize method is called, and @@count is incremented by 1.

7. Acquire two more pets and print the total again:

```
c = Cat.new('Bucky')

f = Fish.new('Nemo')

puts "After getting a cat and a fish,
→ I have #{d.total_pets} pets."
```

Because Cat and Fish inherit from Pet, the Pet initialize method is called when each of these objects is created. As you'll see when you run this script, @@ count will go from 1 (after d was created) to 2 (after c) to 3 (after f).

In the puts line, you can call the total_ pets method by referring to d, c, or f, because they each have that method and the method returns the class variable shared by all of these objects.

8. Save and run the completed script (**Figure 8.10**).

✔ Tip

■ Both *instance variables* (@var) and *class variables* (@@var) are encapsulated within a class. This means they are not accessible outside of a class, including directly through an object. Both variable types can only be accessed using getter and setter methods defined within the class.

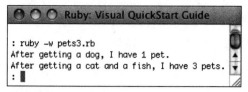

```
: ruby -w pets3.rb
After getting a dog, I have 1 pet.
After getting a cat and a fish, I have 3 pets.
:
```

Figure 8.10 By using a class variable, shared among all inherited class types, the script tracks and reports upon the number of pets in existence.

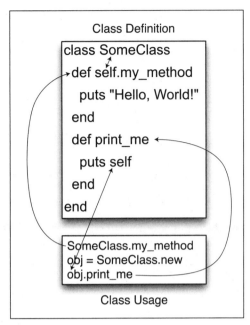

Class Definition

```
class SomeClass
  def self.my_method
    puts "Hello, World!"
  end
  def print_me
    puts self
  end
end
```

```
SomeClass.my_method
obj = SomeClass.new
obj.print_me
```

Class Usage

Figure 8.11 The term self refers to either the class itself or an object of that class type, depending upon where it is used.

Class Methods

Chapter 7 shows how to define several kinds of methods within a class. All were examples of *instance methods*—functions to be called via an object (an instance of a class):

```
r = Rectangle.new(10, 3)
puts r.area
```

An alternative is to define a *class method*—a function to be called via the class itself, not through an object:

```
puts ClassName.method_name
```

To create a class method, define it as you would any other method within the class, but preface the method's name with *ClassName.*:

```
class SomeClass
    def SomeClass.my_method
    end
end
```

Now you can only call my_method through the class, using either SomeClass.my_method or SomeClass::my_method.

Another way of creating a class method is to use the keyword self:

```
class SomeClass
    def self.my_method
    end
end
```

Inside of a class definition but outside of the body of a method definition, self refers to the current class. Within a method definition's body, self refers to the current object invoking the method (**Figure 8.11**). By using self, this version of the definition has the same net result as using SomeClass, but will still be accurate even if you later change the class's name.

Class methods are a logical way to provide access to class variables. In the preceding example (Script 8.5), it doesn't make sense that you'd see how many pets you have by referring to a Dog, Cat, or Fish object. The total_pets method would be better written as:

```
def self.total_pets
    @@count
end
```

Then the method would be called using:

```
puts "I currently have #{Pet.total_pets}
→ pets."
```

Alternatively, you could make use of *class instance variables*: a cross between instance variables and class variables (see the sidebar "Variable Types"). Class instance variables start with a single @, are initialized outside of any method, but can be used only within class methods. This next example, a rewrite of the CreditCard class, will use a class instance variable and a class method.

Variable Types and Scope

Chapter 7 and this chapter show four types of variables that can be used within a class. Where a variable exists and can be referenced is called its *scope*. Here's a quick recap to help avoid confusion…

Variables that don't start with @ and are used within a single method are *local variables*. For example, the arguments passed when a method is invoked are assigned to local variables. *Instance variables* start with @, are not declared or initialized outside of any methods, but can be used within every method. *Class instance variables* start with @, are declared or initialized outside of every method, but can be used only within *class methods*, not within instance methods. *Class variables* start with @@, are declared or initialized outside of every method, and can be used within any method.

Finally, none of these four variable types can be inherited, but class instance variables and class variables are shared among related classes. The @@count variable in Pet (Script 8.5) and the @total_limit variable in CreditCard (Script 8.6) are examples where you might use class and class instance variables.

Script 8.6 By adding a class instance variable and a class method, the CreditCard class can track the sum of the limits of all CreditCard objects.

```
1    # Script 8.6 - creditcard2.rb
2
3    # Partial class for representing
     credit cards:
4    class CreditCard
5
6        # Class instance variable:
7        @total_limit = 0
8
9        attr_reader :balance, :limit
10       protected :balance
11       def initialize(limit, bal = 0)
12           @limit = limit
13           @balance = bal
14       end
15
16       # Returns the total limit:
17       def self.total_limit
18           @total_limit
19       end
20
21       # Adds to the total limit:
22       def self.new(limit, bal = 0)
23           @total_limit += limit
24           super
25       end
26
27       def charge(amt)
28           debit(amt)
29       end
30       def payment(amt)
31           credit(amt)
32       end
33       def available
34           @limit - @balance
35       end
36       def >(rh)
37           return nil unless rh.respond_to?
             ('balance')
38           @balance > rh.balance
39       end
40       private
41       def debit(amt)
42           @balance += amt
43       end
44       def credit(amt)
45           @balance -= amt
46       end
```

(script continues on next page)

To use class methods:

1. Open creditcard.rb (Script 8.4) in your text editor or IDE, if it is not already.

2. Add a class instance variable (**Script 8.6**):
   @total_limit = 0
   This variable will track the capacity of all of the credit cards put together. It starts with just a single **@**, so it's a *class instance variable*, not a *class variable*. Therefore, it can only be referenced within class methods.

   To save space, I've also removed some comments and blank lines from Script 8.4.

3. Add a class method that returns @ total_limit:
   def self.total_limit
       @total_limit
   end
   By naming this method either self. total_limit or CreditCard.total_limit, it becomes a class method, that can only be invoked by referencing the class itself. As a class method, self.total_limit can access the @total_limit class instance variable.

4. Add a class method called new:
   def self.new(limit, bal = 0)
       @total_limit += limit
       super
   end
   This part's a bit tricky, so I'll explain in detail. The @total_limit variable needs to be increased for every new CreditCard object. But it cannot be touched within the initialize method because that's an *instance method*, not a *class method*.

   continues on next page

One solution would be to have the `initialize` method call a class method that updates @total_limit, passing it this new card's limit. Another, more elegant, solution is to create a class method called new.

In Ruby, all classes inherit a method called new from the Class class. It's invoked when an object is created:

`obj = ClassName.new`

The version of new in the CreditCard class overrides the Class version so the CreditCard version of new will be called when a CreditCard object is created. As a class method, it can update @total_limit. However, the original, overridden Class version of new still needs to be called, so the CreditCard new method invokes super to accomplish that.

Script 8.6 *continued*

```
47    end # End of CreditCard class.
48
49    # Create two objects:
50    mc = CreditCard.new(2000)
51    visa = CreditCard.new(3000, 1200)
52
53    # Show the total limit:
54    puts "The limit of all cards is
      #{CreditCard.total_limit}."
55
56    # Add another card and repeat:
57    disc = CreditCard.new(1500)
58    puts "The limit of all cards is
      #{CreditCard.total_limit}."
```

Class Constants

Just as classes can have their own variables (separate from instance variables), they can also have their own constants. Such constants are named and assigned values just like any other kind of constant, but their creation takes place outside of any method definition (but inside the class definition):

```
class ClassName
    CONSTANT_NAME = value
    # methods
end
```

Within the class, the constant can be used just as you would a constant anywhere. This includes referencing constants within the method definitions. Outside of the class, constants are referenced using the scope resolution operator (::):

`puts ClassName::CONSTANT_NAME`

Chapter 3, "Simple Types," had an example of this using the Math::PI constant.

Note that class constants are always public. You cannot make them protected or private. Second, a subclass can redefine a class constant without warning. This is possible because the result will be two different constants: *ParentClass::CONSTANT_NAME* and *ChildClass::CONSTANT_NAME*.

5. After creating the first two `CreditCard` objects, print the total limit:

```
puts "The limit of all cards is
→ #{CreditCard.total_limit}."
```

To retrieve the total of the limits of all of the cards, use `CreditCard.total_limit`. This is an invocation of the `total_limit` class method in the `CreditCard` class.

I've also deleted the existing conditionals and `puts` statements from the previous version of the script.

6. Create another card and reprint the total limit:

```
disc = CreditCard.new(1500)
```

```
puts "The limit of all cards is
→ #{CreditCard.total_limit}."
```

7. Save and run the completed script (**Figure 8.12**).

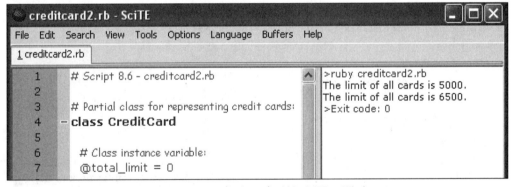

Figure 8.12 The result of running `creditcard2.rb` (Script 8.6) within SciTE on Windows.

✔ Tips

- To change a class method's accessibility, use `private_class_method` and `public_class_method` after its definition:

  ```
  def self.some_method
  end

  private_class_method : some_method
  ```

  Class methods cannot be marked as protected.

- Class methods are also inherited, but it's best if they are still called by referencing the parent object in which they are defined.

- As a reminder, the `ri` utility uses the syntax *ClassName#method_name* to look up the `method_name` instance method in `ClassName`. The syntax *ClassName::method_name* returns information on the `method_name` class method in `ClassName`.

- A third way to create a class method is to use `<<`. Within the class definition you could do:

  ```
  class ClassName
      # regular (instance) methods
      class << self
          # define all class methods
      end
  end
  ```

  Or you could do:

  ```
  class ClassName
      # regular (instance) methods
  end
  class << ClassName
      # class methods
  end
  ```

Updating Existing Classes

As Chapter 7 shows, Ruby allows you to alter existing classes on the fly. In that chapter, one example added additional methods to an already defined `Circle` class. Part of Ruby's power is that you can even alter its built-in classes. For instance, say you want to add a square method to the `Math` class that returns a number squared. To do so, just execute this code:

```
class Math
    def square(x)
      x * x
    end
end
```

This can be shortened a bit to just:

```
def Math.square(x)
    x * x
end
```

You can also use this information, along with method overriding to change existing class methods. For example, if you'd rather that the `Time` class' year method returns the year as two digits, you could make that happen.

The ability to update existing Ruby classes is an important concept as it's how many libraries add functionality: instead of creating new classes for whatever purposes, new methods are just added to `String`, `Array`, `Fixnum`, etc.

9
MODULES AND INCLUDES

Every example in the book up to this point uses either an `irb` session or a single Ruby script. As the demands of your projects grow larger, restricting yourself to placing every line of code within one file (let alone typing it all within `irb`) becomes ever more inefficient. Programming in Ruby should be easy, if not fun! Once you've gone beyond the basics, this means, in part, learning how to modularize and re-use code.

This chapter focuses on two ways you can most efficiently organize and use Ruby code in your projects. The first of these makes use of *modules*. A module is like a class in that it defines methods, variables, and constants. But a module is significantly different from a class in that you do not create instances of modules nor can modules be inherited. Modules are used in Ruby for two purposes: as *namespaces* or as *mixins*.

The second broad topic in the chapter shows how to incorporate existing files to make use of previously written code. You might include a Ruby file you've created or one from the Standard Library.

Modules as Namespaces

A *namespace* is simply the definition of some set of functionality under one umbrella. You might create a namespace module in situations where you want to provide functionality that can be used without creating objects. For example, the `Abbrev` module defines only one method, called *abbrev*, which returns a list of possible abbreviations for a set of words (**Figure 9.1**). This is such a unique and isolated feature that it really doesn't merit being part of a class and having instances.

Of course, you can define methods, variables, and constants outside of any class or module (as the first few chapters of the book do), but when you do so, you run the risk of replacing existing methods, variables, and constants, or having yours overwritten in subsequent code (**Figure 9.2**). When you use a namespace, the methods, variables, and constants will be encapsulated in such a way that they are less likely to conflict with other existing definitions.

To define a namespace module, use a syntax similar to that used to define a class, but begin with the keyword `module`:

```
module ModuleName
    # definition
end
```

Module names abide by the same rules as class names: letters, numbers, and underscores, always starting with a capital letter.

```
>> words = %w{cat dog donut}
=> ["cat", "dog", "donut"]
>> Abbrev::abbrev(words)
=> {"cat"=>"cat", "don"=>"donut", "c"=>"cat", "donut"=>"donut", "dog"=>"dog", "donu"=>"donut", "ca"=>"cat"}
>>
```

Figure 9.1 An example usage of the *abbrev* method from the `Abbrev` module.

Figure 9.2 If a method, like hello, is accidentally redefined, the result of invoking that method could be unexpected and unreliable.

The methods within a namespace module are defined like *class methods*, having each name start with self. or the module's name:

```
module ModuleName
    def self.method_name1
        # method definition
    end
    def ModuleName.method_name2
        # method definition
    end
end
```

Module definitions can also use variables and constants:

```
module ModuleName
    @@var = value
    CONSTANT_NAME = value
end
```

Note that a module's variables are like class variables: their names begin with @@ and they can be referenced within any module method. Because you'll never create a namespace module instance—i.e., an object of a namespace module type—namespace modules don't use the equivalent of instance variables or class instance variables (both of which begin with a single @).

Once a module has been defined, its methods are called using the dot syntax—*ModuleName*.*method_name*—or the scope resolution operator—*ModuleName*::*method_name*. You would refer to a module constant using *ModuleName*::*CONSTANT_NAME*. You cannot directly refer to a module's variables outside of the module, which is equally true for class and instance variables.

To use namespaces:

1. Begin a new Ruby script in your text editor or IDE (**Script 9.1**):

   ```
   # Script 9.1 - helloworld.rb
   ```

   As is often the case, to demonstrate a new concept, sometimes it's best to use a mindless example, like our old friend *Hello, World!*

2. Begin defining a module:

   ```
   module HelloWorld
   ```

   Start with the keyword `module`, and then add the module's name. This one will be called `HelloWorld`. As with classes, the module name you choose should be both descriptive and unique.

3. Define a constant:

   ```
   GREETING = 'Hello, World!'
   ```

   This constant called `GREETING` has a string value.

4. Define a method:

   ```
   def HelloWorld.greet
      puts GREETING
   end
   ```

   This method, called `greet`, prints the value of the constant. This is admittedly a trivial example but has the benefit of being easy to understand.

5. Complete the module.

   ```
   end
   ```

Script 9.1 This simple namespace places the *Hello, World!* functionality under one umbrella.

```
                          Script
1    # Script 9.1 - helloworld.rb
2
3    # Define the HelloWorld module:
4    module HelloWorld
5
6       # Define a constant:
7       GREETING = 'Hello, World!'
8
9       # Define a method:
10      def HelloWorld.greet
11         puts GREETING
12      end
13
14   end # End of HelloWorld module.
15
16   # Use the module:
17   msg = HelloWorld::GREETING
18   puts msg
19   HelloWorld.greet
```

MODULES AS NAMESPACES

6. Use the module:

```
msg = HelloWorld::GREETING
puts msg
HelloWorld.greet
```

The module is used in two different ways. First, the value of the constant is assigned to a local variable, which is then printed. Next, the module's `greet` method is invoked directly.

7. Save and run the completed script (**Figure 9.3**).

✔ Tips

■ The `Class` class in Ruby is actually a subclass of `Module`.

■ Modules can include nested modules or classes:

```
module SomeModule
  class ClassA
    # definition
  end
  class ClassA
    # definition
  end
end
```

To refer to the subclasses, use `SomeModule::ClassA` and `SomeModule::ClassB`. To call those classes' methods, use `SomeModule::ClassA.method_name`.

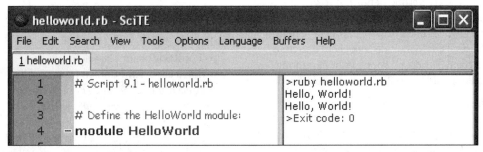

Figure 9.3 Using the `HelloWorld` module, a greeting is printed twice: once using the module's constant, the second time by invoking its method.

Modules as Mixins

As I state in the introduction to this chapter, modules can be used as both *namespaces* and as *mixins*. Namespaces are easy to understand and implement, but mixins are far more useful. Whereas namespaces encapsulate related code, mixins provide a quick way to add functionality to other classes and modules.

To create a mixin, define *instance methods* within a module instead of *class methods*:

```
module ModuleName
    def method_name
        # method definition
    end
end
```

To incorporate a mixin into a class, use `include`:

```
class SomeClass
    include MixinModuleName
    # rest of class definition
end
```

The term `include` is followed by the name of the module to be included, without using any quotation marks. With that code, all of the methods, variables, and constants defined in `MixinModuleName` can be used with objects of type `SomeClass`. See the "Understanding include" sidebar for more.

Two of the best-known and most frequently used mixins in Ruby are `Enumerable` and `Comparable`. The `Enumerable` module uses a class' each method definition to provide different iterators. For instance, the `GroceryList` class (from Chapter 7, "Creating Classes") could include `Enumerable` so that the `count`, `find`, and `sort` methods, among others, could be applied to a shopping list.

The `Comparable` module uses a class' comparison operator (`<=>`) definition to provide `<`, `<=`, `=>`, `>`, and `between?` methods. In this next example, I'll include it in a definition of a `Circle` class so that circles can be compared in various ways.

Understanding include

The `include` keyword, which is actually a private method of the `Module` class, does not work like `include` in other languages. This method includes only modules (not classes) and has nothing to do with including files (as it does in C, C++, and PHP). This means that in order to include a module, the current environment—an `irb` session or a Ruby script—must already have access to the module's definition, which is to say the file in which that module is defined. For some modules, like `Enumerable` and `Comparable`, the definition is always available. For modules you create, you may need to use `require`, discussed later in the chapter, to load the file in which the module is defined.

The `include` method makes the methods and constants defined within a module available within the current context. By that I might mean an `irb` session, Ruby code outside of any class definition, or within a class definition. In other words, `include` brings a module's contents into the current *scope*. By using it within a class, the module's methods and constants become part of that class. By using it outside of a class, you can refer to the module's constants using just `CONSTANT_NAME`.

Script 9.2 By including the Comparable mixin, Circle objects can be compared in numerous ways.

```
1    # Script 9.2 - mixin.rb
2
3    # Define the Circle class:
4    class Circle
5
6        # Include Comparable mixin:
7        include Comparable
8
9        # Accessor for the radius:
10       attr_reader :radius
11
12       # initialize method sets the radius:
13       def initialize(r)
14           @radius = r
15       end
16
17       # Define the comparison operator:
18       def <=>(rh)
19           @radius <=> rh.radius
20       end
21
22   end # End of Circle class.
23
24   # Create four circles:
25   c1 = Circle.new(8)
26   c2 = Circle.new(5)
27   c3 = Circle.new(8)
28   c4 = Circle.new(6)
29
30   # Print some comparisons:
31   puts "c1 is greater than or equal to
     c2: #{c1 >= c2}"
32   puts "c1 is equal to c3: #{c1 == c3}"
33   puts "c4 is between c2 and c1:
     #{c4.between?(c2, c1)}"
```

To use mixins:

1. Begin a new Ruby script in your text editor or IDE (**Script 9.2**):

   ```
   # Script 9.2 - mixin.rb
   ```

2. Begin defining the Circle class:

   ```
   class Circle
   ```

3. Include the Comparable module:

   ```
   include Comparable
   ```

   By adding Comparable to this class definition, instances of this class will be able to use the various comparison operators.

4. Create a getter for the @radius variable and define the initalize method:

   ```
   attr_reader :radius
   def initialize(r)
       @radius = r
   end
   ```

   The @radius instance variable needs to be accessible outside of the class in order to make comparisons using its value. So the attr_reader line will automatically create a method to access @radius through *obj_name*.radius.

   The initialize method takes one argument, the circle's radius. The received value is then assigned to the @radius instance variable.

   For more on any of this code, see Chapter 7.

   continues on next page

MODULES AS MIXINS

5. Define the comparison operator:

```
def <=>(rh)
    @radius <=> rh.radius
end
```

The comparison operator is used in lines like:

```
circle1 <=> circle2
```

To compare two circles, their radii will be compared as numbers. The `@radius` variable will represent the current circle, which is the left-hand operand in the comparison. The right-hand operand will be received as an argument to this method, assigned to `rh`.

6. Complete the class:

```
end # End of Circle class.
```

7. Create four `Circle` objects:

```
c1 = Circle.new(8)
c2 = Circle.new(5)
c3 = Circle.new(8)
c4 = Circle.new(6)
```

Here are four objects of `Circle` type, with three different radius values.

8. Make comparisons using the four circles:

```
puts "c1 is greater than or equal
→ to c2: #{c1 >= c2}"
puts "c1 is equal to c3: #{c1 == c3}"
puts "c4 is between c2 and c1:
→ #{c4.between?(c2, c1)}"
```

Because the `Circle` class defines a `<=>` method (or operator) and includes the `Comparable` mixin, `Circle` objects can be compared using `<`, `<=`, `==`, `=>`, `>`, and `between?`.

9. Save and run the completed script (**Figure 9.4**).

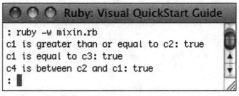

Figure 9.4 The results of comparing four circles in various ways.

✔ Tips

■ Other OOP languages support *multiple inheritance*, where one class simultaneously inherits from multiple, probably unrelated, other classes. Ruby does not support this feature, but mixins can be used to a similar effect.

■ You can include one module within another module or include a module within a class, but you cannot include a class anywhere.

■ It is technically possible for a module to contain *instance variables* if it will be used as a mixin, but the potential problems created by doing so suggest you're likely best off not going that route.

■ You can create *namespaces* using classes instead of modules, but you cannot create classes that are used as *mixins*.

■ To include multiple mixins, separate each by a comma:

```
include ModuleName1, ModuleName2
```

Requiring Files

Although the simple examples in this book up to this point have always used a single Ruby script or an `irb` session, the fact is that projects of any size are normally built by storing distinct groups of code in separate files. Even a simple example, like one in which you define and use a class, would probably use two files: one for the class' definition and another for the invocation and usage of that class. To be able to do something like that, the script that does the actual work must include the secondary file (or files) so that it has access to the necessary definitions and other code.

To include a file, use `require`, providing it with the name of the file to be included:

```
require '/path/to/somefile.rb'
```

Alternatively, you can use `load`, which is discussed in the sidebar "Loading Files." It has a couple different features than `require` but is less often used.

To use `require` (or `load`), provide it with a quoted string that represents either an *absolute* or a *relative* path to the file. An absolute path begins at the root of the computer:

```
require 'C:\ruby\somefile.rb' # Windows
require '/Users/larry/somefile.rb' # Mac
```

An absolute path can also be simulated by referencing the user's home directory, represented by the tilde (~). "User" means the computer user that is executing the script. On Windows, the user's directory is `C:\Documents and Settings\`*username*. On Mac OS X, the user's directory is `/Users/`*username*.

Loading Files

You can include a file using either `require` or `load`. Here's how `load` behaves differently than `require`:

◆ It requires a full filename, including the extension.

◆ It can load the same file multiple times within the same context (`require` won't, unless it's tricked into doing so).

◆ It loads files at the current `$SAFE` level.

With respect to the second point, if you're writing and testing a new module, you can reload it within an `irb` session using `load`. With respect to the last point, see Chapter 17, "Dynamic Programming," for discussion of `$SAFE` levels.

A relative path will not start with the root of the computer—C:\ or /—or the user's home directory. Instead it might be relative to the current script (**Figure 9.5**):

```
require 'fileA.rb' # same dir
require 'dirB/fileB.rb' # inside dirB
require '../fileC.rb' # inside parent dir
require '../dirD/fileD.rb' # inside
→ parallel dir
```

If you use an absolute path, the reference will always be correct for that computer (meaning the code is less portable). If you use a relative

path, the reference will always be correct as long as the relationship between the parent, or *including*, and child, or *included*, files remains the same (making the code more portable).

When using a relative path, you have the option of using the name of the file without the .rb extension. This makes sense if you think about it as a matter of including the something library, which is logically stored in something.rb:

```
require 'something'
```

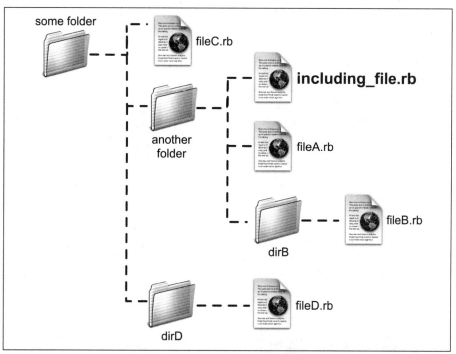

Figure 9.5 A pictorial representation of the relationship between including_file.rb and files it might require.

Ruby will attempt to automatically find the corresponding file by searching through a list of directories, including the current one (represented by a period). That list is stored in a special array with the name $: (**Figure 9.6**). If you prefer a more obvious name, $LOAD_PATH is equivalent.

To demonstrate how to use this feature of Ruby, the preceding example will be rewritten as two scripts. One, circle.rb, will define the Circle class. The second, circles.rb, will include circle.rb and then create and use four Circle objects.

To require files:

1. Begin a new Ruby script in your text editor or IDE (**Script 9.3**):

   ```
   # Script 9.3 - circle.rb
   ```

   This file will use the name circle.rb.

2. Copy the Circle class definition from Script 9.2 and paste it into this new script:

   ```
   class Circle
       include Comparable
       attr_reader :radius
       def initialize(r)
           @radius = r
       end
       def <=>(rh)
           @radius <=> rh.radius
       end
   end # End of Circle class.
   ```

Script 9.3 This script defines a class and is not intended to be executed directly.

```
1    # Script 9.3 - circle.rb
2
3    # Define the Circle class:
4    class Circle
5
6        # Include Comparable mixin:
7        include Comparable
8
9        # Accessors for the radius:
10       attr_reader :radius
11
12       # initialize method sets the radius:
13       def initialize(r)
14           @radius = r
15       end
16
17       # Define the comparison operator:
18       def <=>(rh)
19           @radius <=> rh.radius
20       end
21
22   end # End of Circle class.
```

Figure 9.6 The list of directories in which Ruby will search for included files on my Windows installation.

```
:ruby -e 'puts $:'
c:/ruby/lib/ruby/site_ruby/1.8
c:/ruby/lib/ruby/site_ruby/1.8/i386-msvcrt
c:/ruby/lib/ruby/site_ruby
c:/ruby/lib/ruby/1.8
c:/ruby/lib/ruby/1.8/i386-mswin32
.
:_
```

Script 9.4 This script first requires the file that defines a class and then creates and uses objects of that class type.

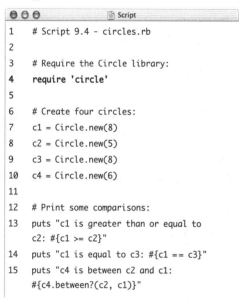

```
    ● ○ ○                📄 Script
1       # Script 9.4 - circles.rb
2
3       # Require the Circle library:
4       require 'circle'
5
6       # Create four circles:
7       c1 = Circle.new(8)
8       c2 = Circle.new(5)
9       c3 = Circle.new(8)
10      c4 = Circle.new(6)
11
12      # Print some comparisons:
13      puts "c1 is greater than or equal to
        c2: #{c1 >= c2}"
14      puts "c1 is equal to c3: #{c1 == c3}"
15      puts "c4 is between c2 and c1:
        #{c4.between?(c2, c1)}"
```

```
● ○ ○   Ruby: Visual QuickStart Guide
: ruby -w circles.rb
c1 is greater than or equal to c2: true
c1 is equal to c3: true
c4 is between c2 and c1: true
:
```

Figure 9.7 The output of this example is the same as that in Figure 9.3, although it uses two logically divided scripts.

3. Save the file as `circle.rb`.

4. Create another new Ruby script in your text editor or IDE (**Script 9.4**):

```
# Script 9.4 - circles.rb
```

This file will include and use the `Circle` class definition.

5. Include `circle.rb`:

```
require 'circle'
```

Assuming that the file `circle.rb` is saved within the current directory (the same directory as this script) or in one of the directories in your computer's search path (see Figure 9.6), this line will include that file, making its code available.

6. Complete the script by copying and pasting the remaining code from `mixin.rb` (Script 9.2):

```
c1 = Circle.new(8)
c2 = Circle.new(5)
c3 = Circle.new(8)
c4 = Circle.new(6)
puts "c1 is greater than or equal
→ to c2: #{c1 >= c2}"
puts "c1 is equal to c3: #{c1 == c3}"
puts "c4 is between c2 and c1:
→ #{c4.between?(c2, c1)}"
```

You can change and update the examples, if you'd prefer.

7. Save and run the completed script (**Figure 9.7**).

Note that you run `circles.rb`, not `circle.rb` (which in itself does not produce any result).

continues on next page

✔ Tips

- The "magic variable" __FILE__ contains the name of the current file, and $0 represents the name of the file initially executed (e.g., circles.rb in this example). You can use this information to have a script behave differently if it's being executed directly or included by another script:

```
if __FILE__ == $0 then # executed
else # required
end
```

- To add a directory to the list that Ruby will search through, push the new value onto the $: array:

```
$:.push('/path/to/dir')
```

or

```
$: << '/path/to/dir'
```

- The $" array represents every loaded file (**Figure 9.8**).

- To use a module you created as a mixin in a class, the script that defines the class has to both require the module file and include the mixin within the class definition. Remember that the require method applies to files, but include applies to code.

- Ruby 1.9 adds new default directories to the load path. This is due in part to the inclusion of RubyGems in the default Ruby installation.

- Because you can update existing Ruby classes during run time, you could, for example, add a method you like to the Array class by placing this in an separate file:

```
class Array
   # new method definition
end
```

Then include that file anytime you want to use your modified Array class.

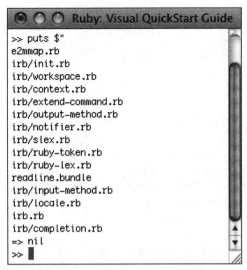

```
>> puts $"
e2mmap.rb
irb/init.rb
irb/workspace.rb
irb/context.rb
irb/extend-command.rb
irb/output-method.rb
irb/notifier.rb
irb/slex.rb
irb/ruby-token.rb
irb/ruby-lex.rb
readline.bundle
irb/input-method.rb
irb/locale.rb
irb.rb
irb/completion.rb
=> nil
>>
```

Figure 9.8 The list of files automatically loaded by my irb session.

Included Files and Scope

In some other languages, code in an included file is executed as if it were part of the parent file. In other words, replacing the require line with the code from the other file has the same net effect. In Ruby, however, code included via require or load has different scope than the parent file's code. Specifically, any local variables defined in the including, or parent, script prior to require or load are not available to the included, or child, file. Second, any local variables defined in the included file are not available to the including file. Global variables and any constants in the including file are available within the included file, though.

REQUIRING FILES

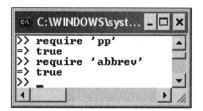

Figure 9.9 By including the two libraries, they can be used throughout the rest of the `irb` session.

Ruby Standard Library

The Ruby Standard Library is a repository of code, written in Ruby, that programmers may find useful at some time or another. The library is automatically included with the Ruby source code and installed when you install Ruby.

To use a library, you must first require it:

```
require 'libraryname'
```

To see the full list of libraries and view their associated documentation, head to www.ruby-doc.org/stdlib/ (the documentation can also be downloaded from that site). For example, the `abbrev` method mentioned earlier in the chapter is defined within the `abbrev` library. To use it, first execute the command `require 'abbrev'` in your `irb` session or Ruby script. Ruby will then load the `abbrev.rb` file, found within one of the search directories. After that, you can use `abbrev` by calling `Abbrev::abbrev` (see Figure 9.1).

In this next example, I'll make use of the `pp` library. This library, whose name stands for *pretty-printer*, provides a method for viewing the values and structure of any object in an easier-to-read way. This example will take place within `irb`, but `pp` can be used in a Ruby script as well.

To use a standard library:

1. Open an `irb` session.

2. Require the `pp` and `abbrev` libraries (**Figure 9.9**):
   ```
   require 'pp'
   require 'abbrev'
   ```

continues on next page

3. Create a list of words:

```
words = %w{cat canary crow}
```

This code creates an array of three elements, each being a word. See Chapter 4, "Arrays, Ranges, and Hashes," for an explanation of the %w syntax.

4. Create a list of possible abbreviations:

```
Abbrev::abbrev(words)
```

As I say in the beginning of the chapter, this method creates a list of unique abbreviations for a set of words. It returns a hash, where the keys are abbreviations and the values are the words they could represent.

5. Display the same list in an easier-to-read format (**Figure 9.10**):

With an array or hash, pp will print the items on individual lines, making the result much more legible.

✔ Tips

■ A more complete sense of the value of pp can be found when printing out the values of more elaborate object types.

■ RubyGems take the idea of a standard library one giant step forward. A *gem* is a package of Ruby code that provides a lot more functionality than a simple library. This topic is discussed in Chapter 12, "RubyGems."

```
C:\WINDOWS\system32\cmd.exe - irb
>> words = %w{cat canary crow}
=> ["cat", "canary", "crow"]
>> Abbrev::abbrev(words)
=> {"cat"=>"cat", "cro"=>"crow", "crow"=>"crow", "canar"=>"canary", "canary"=>"c
anary", "cr"=>"crow", "can"=>"canary", "cana"=>"canary"}
>> pp Abbrev::abbrev(words)
{"cat"=>"cat",
 "cro"=>"crow",
 "crow"=>"crow",
 "canar"=>"canary",
 "canary"=>"canary",
 "cr"=>"crow",
 "can"=>"canary",
 "cana"=>"canary"}
=> nil
>>
```

Figure 9.10 The bottom half of the figure shows how the pp library displays a hash in a nicer format.

REGULAR EXPRESSIONS

Regular expressions are a very important topic in any programming language, but they are also one of the hardest to master, in my experience. The difficulties exist because, more than most other subjects, you'll be faced with cryptic syntax, the need to memorize lots of symbols, and remembering that a symbol's effect can change in certain contexts. And, after all that, the result may still not be foolproof! But this is not to dissuade you from taking on the challenge, only to reassure you that if you don't pick up regular expressions at first, you're not alone.

But what are regular expressions? Think of regular expressions as an elaborate system of comparing strings to patterns. You first identify a pattern based upon what you're looking for, and then use one of Ruby's built-in methods or operators to apply the pattern to a value (regular expressions are applied to strings, even if that means a string with a numeric value). Whereas a basic string comparison could check if the name *John* is in some text, a regular expression could just as easily find *John*, *Jon*, and *Jonathon*, or lowercase versions of those names.

Because the regular expression syntax is so complex, while the methods and operators that use them are simple to understand, the focus in this chapter will primarily be on mastering the pattern-making syntax.

Performing Matches

Although the brunt of this chapter is on the syntax of regular expressions, and specifically the Perl-Compatible Regular Expressions (PCRE) that Ruby implements, you'll need to know what operators and methods make use of regular expressions. To start, there is the *pattern matching operator*, = ~. This operator is used with one `String` and one `Regexp` (the Ruby class that represents regular expressions). Logically, you might use this operator in a condition:

```
puts 'match' if str =~ regex
```

It doesn't matter in what order you place the string and the regular expression:

```
puts 'match' if regex =~ str
```

To create a `Regexp` object, place a pattern—the combination of literal and special characters—between forward slashes. As a simple example, this pattern—**a**—matches a letter *a*. (As a formatting rule in this chapter, I'll define patterns in **bold** and will indicate what the pattern matches in *italics*.) As a `Regexp`, this pattern would be written as /a/. Knowing just this information, you could do:

```
puts 'match' if text =~ /larry/
```

The pattern matching operator will return the indexed position where the matched pattern begins in the string or the value `nil`, if it was not found (**Figure 10.1**).

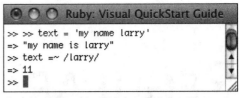

Figure 10.1 Since the "l" in *larry* is the twelfth character in the string, the pattern matching operator returns the value 11 when it's found (because indexes begin at 0).

Strings vs. Regular Expressions

It's important to understand that the initial examples in the chapter perform just literal comparisons because that's all that's been covered to that point. Such examples will work, but if you ever find yourself comparing literal strings, you're best off using a `String` method instead. The `index`, `rindex`, and `include?` methods search for one string within another string:

```
puts 'match' if str.index('larry')
```

The `index` method returns either `nil` (if the substring was not found) or the starting indexed position where it was found. The `rindex` method returns the starting indexed position of the last (or right-most) occurrence of the substring. The `include?` method simply returns a Boolean value indicating if the substring was found or not.

If you want to see if a string is exactly the same as another string, you can use `eql?`, `==`, `<=>`, or `casecmp`. All of these methods and operators are case-sensitive, except for `casecmp`, which is case-insensitive.

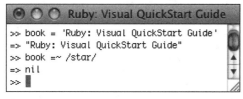

Figure 10.2 If a pattern does not match a string, `nil` will be the result.

An alternative to the pattern matching operator is the `match` method.

```
puts 'match' if text.match(/larry/)
```

The `match` method can also take a string as its argument, which it will convert to a `Regexp`. This line is the same as the preceding bit of code:

```
puts 'match' if text.match('larry')
```

This feature is nice if you tend to forget to add the delimiters or if you want to use a pattern that's not hard-coded. For example, you could create a Ruby script for testing regular expressions that takes user-typed input for the string and pattern, and then uses the latter as the argument to `match`. And, of course, if your keyboard does not have the tilde character (~), then you'll have to use `match` instead.

Unlike the pattern matching operator, the `match` method returns either `nil`, if no match was found, or a `MatchData` object, if a match was found. You'll see how to use this information near the end of the chapter.

To perform matches:

1. In an `irb` session, check the title of this book for the word *star* (**Figure 10.2**):
   ```
   book = 'Ruby: Visual QuickStart Guide'
   book =~ /star/
   ```
   Regular expression patterns are case-sensitive by default, so the conditional will return the value `nil`, as *star* was not found in the book's title.

continues on next page

2. Retest the book's title against *Star* and *tart* (**Figure 10.3**):

```
book =~ /Star/
book =~ /tart/
```

As you should expect, both will work, returning the indexed position for where each begins in the given string.

3. Find the first space in the string:

```
book =~ / /
```

A space can be treated as just another character, so the pattern to match a space is just a space between two slashes. For the book's title, this statement will return the number 5 (because the first space is the sixth character in the string).

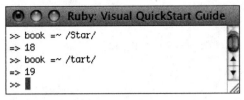

Figure 10.3 Both patterns matched the book's title.

✔ Tips

■ You'll see the term *regular expression* (singular or plural) often abbreviated as *regex* or *regexp*.

■ Instead of using // to create a regular expression, you can invoke the `Regexp` class directly:

```
pattern = Regexp.new('larry')
puts 'match' if text =~ pattern
```

■ Just as you can create strings using `%q` or arrays using `%w`, you can also create regular expressions by using custom delimiters after `%r`:

```
pattern = %r<larry>
```

Table 10.1

Basic Meta-Characters	
CHARACTER	MEANING
\	Escape character
.	Any single character except newline
I	Alternatives (or)
[	Start of a character class
]	End of a character class
(	Start of a subpattern
)	End of a subpattern
{	Start of a quantifier
}	End of a quantifier

Defining Simple Patterns

The first type of character you will use for defining patterns is a *literal*. A literal is a value that is written exactly as it is interpreted, as you've already seen. For example, **a** will match the letter *a*, **ab** will match *ab*, and so forth. Therefore, assuming a case-sensitive search is performed, **rom** will match any of the following strings, since they all contain *rom*:

◆ cd-rom

◆ rommel crossed the desert.

◆ I'm writing a roman à clef.

Along with literals, patterns use *meta-characters*. These are special symbols that have a meaning beyond their literal value (**Table 10.1** lists the most basic of these). While **a** simply means *a*, the period (.) will match any single character except for a newline (. matches *a*, *b*, *c*, the underscore, a space, etc., just not \n). To match any meta-character, you need to escape it, just as you escape a quotation mark to print it. Hence \. will match the period itself. So **1.99** matches *1.99* or *1B99* or *1299* (a *1* followed by any character followed by *99*) but **1\.99** only matches *1.99*.

Regular expressions make use of the pipe (I) as the equivalent of *or*. Therefore, **a|b** will match strings containing either *a* or *b*. (Using the pipe within patterns is called *alternation* or *branching*). So **yes|no** accepts either of those two words in its entirety (the alternation is *not* just between the two letters surrounding it: *s* and *n*).

Once you comprehend the basic symbols, then you can begin to use parentheses to group characters into more involved patterns. Grouping works as you might expect: **(abc)** will match *abc*, **(trout)** will match *trout*. Think of parentheses as being used to establish a new literal of a larger size. Because of precedence rules in PCRE, **yes|no** and **(yes)|(no)** are equivalent. But **(even|heavy) handed** will match either *even handed* or *heavy handed*.

To use simple patterns:

1. Check if a string contains the letters *cat* (**Figure 10.4**).

   `'I like catamarans.' =~ /cat/`

   To do this, use the literal **cat** as the pattern and any number of strings as the subject. Any of the following would be a match: *catalog, catastrophe, my cat left*, etc. For the time being, use all lower-case letters, as **cat** will not match *Cat* or *Catalog*.

   Remember to use delimiters around the pattern, as well (see the figures).

2. Check if a string contains a period or an exclamation mark (**Figure 10.5**).

   `pattern = /\.|!/`

   `'I like birds.' =~ pattern`

   `'I said, "Hi!"' =~ pattern`

   To see if a pattern contains one of two characters, use the pipe to represent *or*. The exclamation mark does not have special meaning in regular expressions, so it can be used in the pattern as is. However, the period does have special meaning, so it must be escaped to be treated literally.

   Since I wanted to use the same pattern in comparisons against two different strings, I assigned the regular expression, including the delimiters, to a variable called `pattern`.

Figure 10.4 Looking for a *cat* in a string.

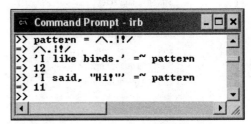

Figure 10.5 This pattern will match any string that contains a period or an exclamation mark.

3. Check if a string contains the word *color* or *colour* (**Figure 10.6**).

```
pattern = /col(o|ou)r/

'What\'s your favorite color?' =~
→ pattern

'What\'s your favourite colour?' =~
→ pattern
```

The pattern to look for the American or British spelling of this word is **col(o|ou)r**. The first three letters—*col*—must be present. This needs to be followed by either an *o* or an *ou*. Finally, an *r* is required.

✔ Tips

■ To match a single backslash, you have to use \\. The reason is that matching a backslash in a regular expression requires you to escape the backslash, resulting in \\.

■ The escape method of the Regexp class will automatically escape meaningful characters in a string:

```
parens = Regexp.escape('()')
```

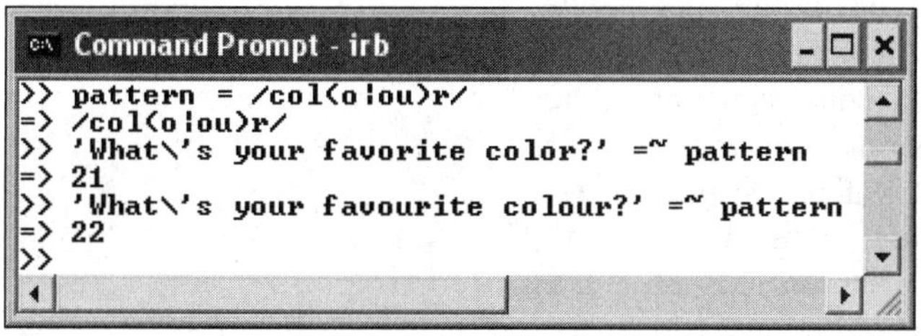

```
>> pattern = /col(o|ou)r/
=> /col(o|ou)r/
>> 'What\'s your favorite color?' =~ pattern
=> 21
>> 'What\'s your favourite colour?' =~ pattern
=> 22
>>
```

Figure 10.6 Using alternation, this pattern checks for two different possible spellings of the same word.

Using Anchors

Like the anchor on a boat, used to tie the boat to a spot in the water, an anchor in a regular expression ties a pattern to a part of a string (**Table 10.2**). Anchors are crucial to validation, as validation normally requires checking the value of an entire string, not just looking for the presence of one string in another. For example, using an email matching pattern *without* anchors will match any string containing an email address. Using an email matching pattern *with* anchors will match a string that contains only a valid email address.

The first two anchors to discuss are \A and \Z. \A anchors a pattern to the beginning of a string, and \Z anchors it to the end of the string. Accordingly, **\Aa** will match any string that begins with an *a*, while **a\Z** will match any string that ends with an *a*. Therefore, **\Aa\Z** will match only *a* (a string that both begins and ends with *a*).

The caret (^) and dollar sign ($) are slight variations on \A and \Z. Whereas \A anchors a pattern to the beginning of a string, the caret anchors it to the beginning of the string *or to the beginning of a line in the string*. Similarly, the dollar sign is an anchor to the end of the string *or to the end of a line in the string*. So, **^a** will match any string that begins with an *a* or has an *a* as the first character on a line, like *this\na that*. And **a$** will match any string that ends with an *a* or has an *a* as the last character on a line, like *I was a\nwalking*.

The remaining two anchors are tied to word boundaries. Here, "word" isn't the same as a word in a language but rather means one or more numbers, letters, and underscores unbroken by spaces or punctuation. This string has four "words": *My pass_code is 1234abc*. To use words as boundaries, there's

Table 10.2

Anchors	
CHARACTER	ANCHORS TO…
\A	The start of the string
\Z	The end of the string
^	The beginning of the string or a line
$	The end of the string or a line
\b	A word
\B	Non-words

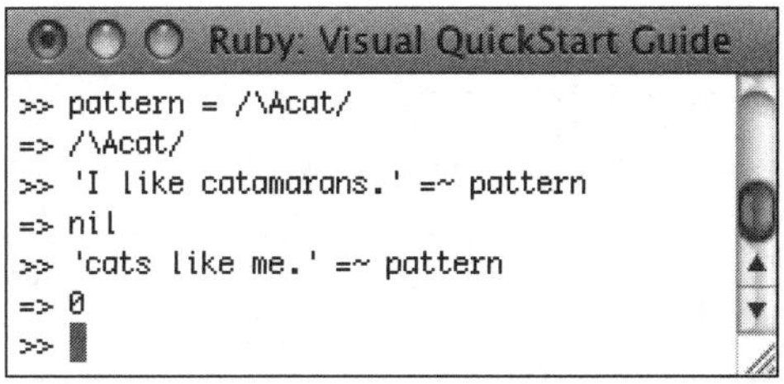

```
● ○ ○    Ruby: Visual QuickStart Guide
>> pattern = /\Acat/
=> /\Acat/
>> 'I like catamarans.' =~ pattern
=> nil
>> 'cats like me.' =~ pattern
=> 0
>>
```

Figure 10.7 The \A anchor means that the pattern must match the beginning of the string.

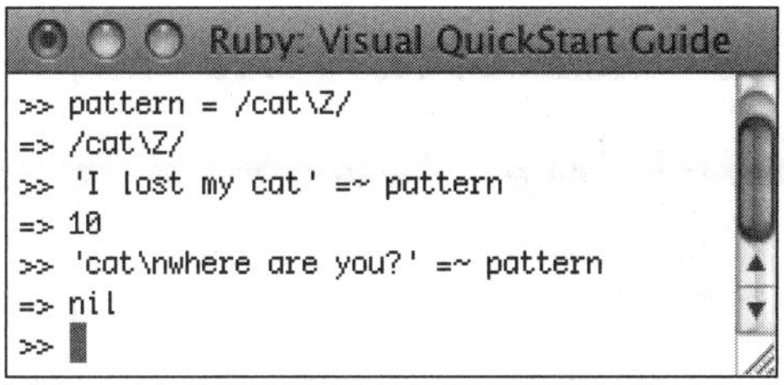

```
● ○ ○    Ruby: Visual QuickStart Guide
>> pattern = /cat\Z/
=> /cat\Z/
>> 'I lost my cat' =~ pattern
=> 10
>> 'cat\nwhere are you?' =~ pattern
=> nil
>>
```

Figure 10.8 The \Z anchor means that the pattern must match the end of the string.

the **\b** shortcut. To use non-word characters as boundaries, there's **\B**. So the pattern **\bfor\b** matches *they've come for you—for* with a word boundary on both sides—but doesn't match *force* or *forebode*. And **\bfor\B** would match *force—for* with a word boundary before it but a non-word boundary after it—but not *they've come for you* or *informal*.

To use anchors:

1. Check if a string starts with the letters *cat* (**Figure 10.7**).

   ```
   pattern = /\Acat/
   'I like catamarans.' =~ pattern
   'cats like me.' =~ pattern
   ```

   To do this, use the literal **cat**, anchored to the beginning of a string, as the pattern and any number of strings as the subject.

2. Check if a string ends with the letters *cat* (**Figure 10.8**).

   ```
   pattern = /cat\Z/
   'I lost my cat' =~ pattern
   'cat\nwhere are you?' =~ pattern
   ```

   This is the opposite of the pattern in Step 1. It only matches strings whose last three letters are *cat*.

continues on next page

3. Check if a string contains the word *cat* as the first or last thing on a line (**Figure 10.9**).

```
pattern = /^cat|cat$/

"I lost my cat\nwhere are you?" =~
→ pattern

'cat, I found you!' =~ pattern
```

By using the caret and the dollar sign, the letters *cat* are acceptable at the beginning of the string, at the beginning of any line, at the end of any line, or at the end of the string.

Note that for this to work, the string must be placed within double quotation marks (because within single quotation marks, \n is just a backslash followed by an *n*).

4. Check if a string contains a word that begins with *cat* but is not just *cat* (**Figure 10.10**).

```
pattern = /\bcat\B/

'I lost my cat' =~ pattern

'This is cataclysmic!' =~ pattern
```

Like the *for* example used to explain word boundaries, this pattern says that the letters *cat* must be preceded by a word boundary and must be followed by a non-word boundary. So the character before *c* cannot be a letter, number, or underscore, and the character after *t* must be a letter, number, or underscore.

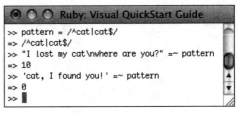

Figure 10.9 Looking for a *cat* as either the first three or last three characters in the string or on any line therein.

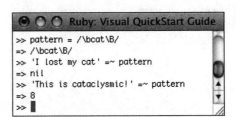

Figure 10.10 A use of the two different word boundary anchors \b and \B.

Table 10.3

Quantifiers	
CHARACTER	MEANING
?	0 or 1
*	0 or more
+	1 or more
{x}	Exactly x occurrences
{x, y}	Between x and y (inclusive)
{x,}	At least x occurrences

Using Quantifiers

Moving forward in the discussion of the various meta-characters, there are three that match multiple occurrences: **a*** will match zero or more *a*'s (no *a*'s, *a*, *aa*, *aaa*, etc.); **a+** matches one or more *a*'s (*a*, *aa*, *aaa*, etc., but there must be at least one); and **a?** will match up to one *a* (*a* or no *a*'s match). These meta-characters all act as *quantifiers* in your patterns, as do the curly braces. **Table 10.3** lists all of the quantifiers.

To match a certain quantity of a thing, put the quantity between curly braces ({}), stating a specific number, just a minimum, or both a minimum and a maximum. Thus, **a{3}** will match *aaa*; **a{3,}** will match *aaa*, *aaaa*, etc. (three or more *a*'s); and **a{3,5}** will match just *aaa*, *aaaa*, and *aaaaa* (between three and five).

Note that quantifiers apply to the character or grouping that came before it, so **a?** matches zero or one *a*'s, **ab?** matches an *a* followed by zero or one *b*'s, but **(ab)?** matches zero or one *ab*'s. Therefore, to match *color* or *colour* (see Figure 10.6), you could also use **colou?r** as the pattern.

To use quantifiers:

1. Check if a string contains the letters *s* and *c*, with one or more letters in between (**Figure 10.11**).

   ```
   'secret phrase' =~ /s.+c/
   'discount' =~ /s.+c/
   ```

   To do this, use **s.+c** as the pattern and any number of strings as the subject. Remember that the period matches any character (except for the newline). Each of the following words would be a match: *success, succulent, sabbatical*, etc. The word *discount* would not match, as there are no letters between the *s* and the *c* (although *discount* would match **s.*c**).

2. Check if a string is either just *cat* or *cats* (**Figure 10.12**).

   ```
   pattern = /\Acats?\Z/
   'cat' =~ pattern
   'cats' =~ pattern
   'I like cats.' =~ pattern
   'cats like me.' =~ pattern
   ```

   To start, if you want to make an exact match, use the anchors. Then you'd have the literal text *cat*, followed by an *s*, followed by a question mark (representing 0 or 1 *s*'s). The final pattern—**\Acats?\Z**—matches *cat* or *cats* but not *my cat left* or *I like cats*.

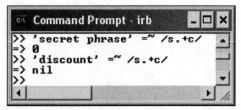

Figure 10.11 The plus sign, when used as a quantifier, requires that one or more of a thing be present. Here it requires that at least one non-newline character appear between the *s* and the *c*.

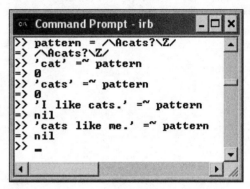

Figure 10.12 You can check for the plural form of many words by adding *s?* to the pattern.

3. Match a five-digit number (**Figure 10.13**).

```
pattern = /\A(0|1|2|3|4|5|6|7|8|9)
→ {5}\Z/
'12345' =~ pattern
'12b45' =~ pattern
'1235' =~ pattern
```

A number can be any one of the integers 0 through 9, so the heart of the pattern is **(0|1|2|3|4|5|6|7|8|9)**. Plainly said, this means: a number is a 0 or a 1 or a 2 or a 3…. To make it a five-digit number, follow this with a quantifier: **(0|1|2|3|4|5|6|7|8|9){5}**. Finally, to match this exactly (as opposed to matching a five-digit number within a string), use the anchors: **\A(0|1|2|3|4|5|6|7|8|9){5}\Z**.

This, of course, is one way to match a United States zip code, a very useful pattern.

✔ Tips

- When using curly braces to specify a number of characters, you must always include the minimum number. The maximum is optional: **a{3}** and **a{3,}** are acceptable, but **a{,3}** is not.

- Although it demonstrates good dedication to programming to learn how to write and execute your own regular expressions, numerous working examples are available already by searching the Internet.

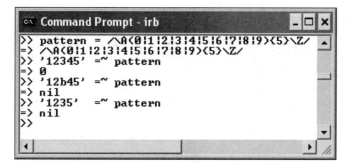

Figure 10.13 A proper test for confirming that a number contains exactly five digits.

Using Character Classes

As the last example demonstrated (Figure 10.13), relying solely upon literals in a pattern can be tiresome. Having to write out all those digits to match any number is silly. Imagine if you wanted to match any four-letter word: **^(a|b|c|d...){4}$** (and that doesn't even take into account uppercase letters)! To make these common references easier, you can use *character classes*.

Classes are created by placing characters within square brackets (**[ ]**). For example, you can match any one vowel with **[aeiou]**. This is equivalent to **(a|e|i|o|u)**. Or you can use the hyphen to indicate a range of characters: **[a-z]** is any single lowercase letter and **[A-Z]** is any uppercase, **[A-Za-z]** is any letter in general, and **[0-9]** matches any digit. As an example, **[a-z]{3}** would match *abc*, *def*, *oiw*, etc.

Within classes, most of the meta-characters are treated as literals, except for three. The backslash is still the escape, but the caret (^) is a negation operator when used as the first character in the class. So **[^aeiou]** will match any non-vowel (the caret escapes everything within the class, not just the first character). The only other meaningful meta-character within a class is the dash, which indicates a range. (If the dash is used as the last character in a class, it's a literal dash.)

Naturally a class can contain both ranges of characters and literal characters. A person's first name, which can contain letters, spaces, apostrophes, and periods, could be represented by **[A-z'.]** (again, the period doesn't need to be escaped within the class, as it loses its meta-meaning there).

Table 10.4

Character Classes

CLASS	SHORTCUT	MEANING
[0-9]	\d	Any digit
[\f\r\t\n\v]	\s	Any white space
[A-Za-z0-9_]	\w	Any word character
[^0-9]	\D	Not a digit
[^\f\r\t\n\v]	\S	Not white space
[^A-Za-z0-9_]	\W	Not a word character

```
⦿ ○ ○       Ruby: Visual QuickStart Guide
>> pattern = /\A(\d{5})(-\d{4})?\Z/
=> /\A(\d{5})(-\d{4})?\Z/
>> '12345' =~ pattern
=> 0
>> '12345-0012' =~ pattern
=> 0
>> '12345-001' =~ pattern
=> nil
>>
```

Figure 10.14 The pattern to match a United States zip code, in either the five-digit or five plus four format.

Along with creating your own classes, there are six already-defined classes that have their own shortcuts (**Table 10.4**). The digit and space classes are easy to understand. As with the \b and \B anchors, the word character class doesn't mean "word" in the language sense but rather as in one or more characters unbroken by spaces or punctuation other than the underscore.

Using this information, the five-digit number (aka zip code) pattern could more easily be written as **\A[0-9]{5}\Z** or **\A\d{5}\Z**. As another example, **can\s?not** will match both *can not* and *cannot* (the word *can*, followed by zero or one space characters, followed by *not*).

To use character classes:

1. Check if a string is formatted as a valid United States zip code (**Figure 10.14**).

   ```
   pattern = /\A(\d{5})(-\d{4})?\Z/
   '12345' =~ pattern
   '12345-0012' =~ pattern
   '12345-001' =~ pattern
   ```

   A United States zip code always starts with five digits (**\d{5}**). But a valid zip code could also have a dash followed by another four digits (**-\d{4}**). To make this last part optional, use the question mark (the 0 or 1 quantifier). This complete pattern is then **\A(\d{5})(-\d{4})?\Z**. To make it all clearer, the first part of the pattern (matching the five digits) is also grouped in parentheses, although this isn't required in this case.

   continues on next page

2. Check if a string contains no spaces (**Figure 10.15**).

```
pattern = /\A\S*\Z/
'this will not pass' =~ pattern
'this_will_pass' =~ pattern
```

The **\S** character class shortcut will match non-space characters. To make sure that the entire string contains no spaces, use the **\A** and **\Z** boundaries: **\A\S\Z**. If you don't use those, then all the pattern is confirming is that the subject contains at least one non-space character. The zero or more quantifier (*) needs to be applied to **\S** to allow for any number of non-space characters.

Alternatively, you could use just \s, which will return an integer if a space *is* found. So such a pattern would be used using opposite logic as the pattern in Figure 10.15.

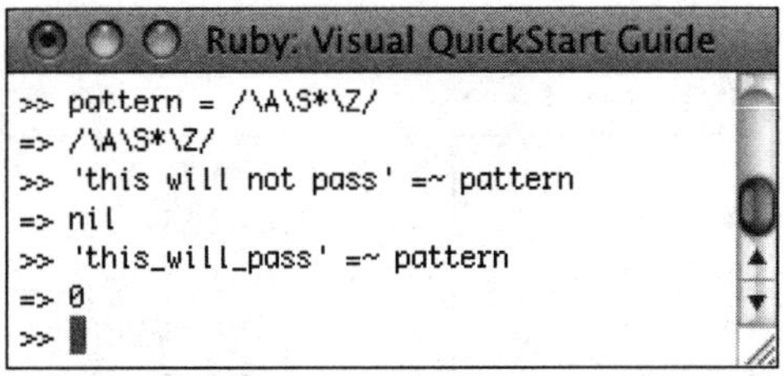

3. Validate an email address (**Figure 10.16**).

```
pattern = /\A[\w.+-]+@[\w.-]+\.
→ [A-Za-z]{2,6}\Z/
'larry@example.com' =~ pattern
'larry' =~ pattern
'larry.ullman@example.com.au' =~
→ pattern
```

The pattern **\A[\w.+-]+@[\w.-]+\.[A-Za-z]{2,6}\Z** provides for reasonably good email validation. It's wrapped in anchors, so the string must be a valid email address and nothing more. An email address starts with letters, numbers, and the underscore (represented by **\w**), plus a period (.), a dash, and a plus sign. This first block will match *larryullman*, *larry77*, *larry.ullman*, *larry-ullman*, and so on. Next, all email addresses include one and only one **@**. After that, there can be any number of letters, numbers, periods, and dashes. This is the domain

Figure 10.15 The no-white-space shortcut can be used to ensure that a submitted string is contiguous.

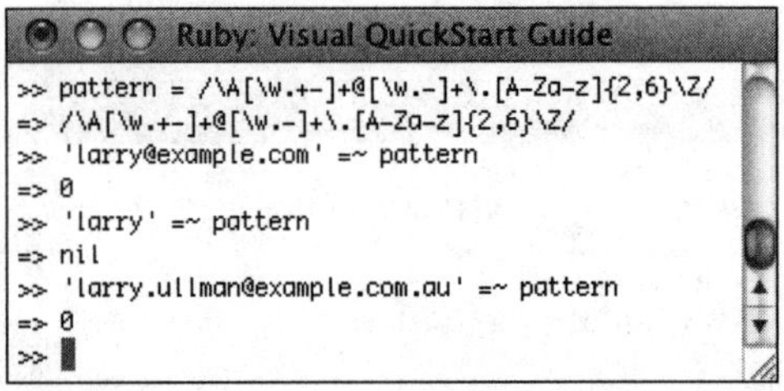

Figure 10.16 A pretty good and reliable validation for email addresses.

name: *dmcinsights*, *smith-jones*, *amazon.co* (as in *amazon.co.uk*), etc. Finally, all email addresses conclude with one period and between two and six letters. This accounts for *.com*, *.edu*, *.info*, *.travel*, etc.

✔ Tips

- This email address validation pattern is pretty good, although not perfect. It will allow some invalid addresses to pass through (like ones starting with a period or containing multiple periods together). However, a 100 percent foolproof validation pattern is ridiculously long, and frequently using regular expressions is really a matter of trying to exclude the bulk of invalid entries without inadvertently excluding any valid ones.

- Regular expressions, particularly PCRE ones, can be extremely complex. When starting out, it's just as likely that your use of them will break the validation routines as that it will improve them. That's why practicing like this is important.

USING CHARACTER CLASSES

Using Modifiers

The majority of the special characters you can use in regular expression patterns are introduced in this chapter. The final type of special character that I'll discuss is the *pattern modifier* (**Table 10.5**). Pattern modifiers are different than the other meta-characters in that they are placed *after* the closing delimiter.

Of these delimiters, the most important is *i*, which enables case-insensitive searches. For example, all of the examples using variations on *cat* would not match the word *Cat*. However, **/cat/i** would be a match.

The multiline mode is interesting in that its treats a newline (\n) as just another character. This means that the period will match it, and it also changes the effect of the caret and the dollar sign. By default, they match the beginning or end of the string, as well as the beginning or end of any line within the string. In multiline mode, where a newline is just another character, the caret behaves like \A and the dollar sign like \Z.

To use modifiers:

1. Recheck the title of this book for *star*, case-insensitive (**Figure 10.17**).

   ```
   book = 'Ruby: Visual QuickStart Guide'
   book =~ /star/i
   ```

   This was the very first test case in the chapter, but now it's been made case-insensitive, thanks to the *i* modifier.

Table 10.5

Pattern Modifiers	
CHARACTER	RESULT
i	Enables case-insensitive mode
m	Enables multiline matching
o	Perform interpolation once
x	Ignores most white space and allows comments

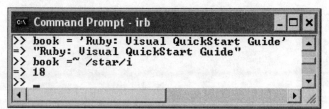

Figure 10.17 Thanks to the case-insensitive modifier, the regular expression **/star/i** will match a string that contains *Star*, *sTar*, *STAr*, etc.

2. Validate an email address in case-insensitive mode (**Figure 10.18**).

```
pattern = /\A[\w.+-]+@[\w.-]+\.
→[a-z]{2,6}\Z/i

'larry@example.com' =~ pattern

'larry' =~ pattern

'larry.ullman@example.com.AU' =~
→pattern
```

When using case-insensitive mode, the part of the pattern that checks the final extension—**[A-Za-z]{2,6}**—can be simplified to just **[a-z]{2,6}**.

✔ Tip

- Regular expressions in Ruby 1.9 and later have been changed to support Unicode. Simply put, this means that you can apply regular expressions to a broader range of languages and use Unicode characters in your patterns. A related change is the addition of the e, n, s, and u modifiers, which indicate the encoding.

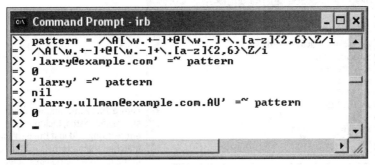

Figure 10.18 Another way of validating an email address (compare with Figure 10.16).

Finding Matches

The examples thus far have primarily focused on demonstrating the syntax used to create patterns. Each application of the pattern simply used the pattern matching operator to see if a match was made. Often, all a script will need to do is confirm whether or not a match was made, like when data is being validated. But in other situations, you'll want to know *what exact match* was made.

One way of accessing a match is to use the `match` method, which returns a `MatchData` object:

```
str = 'abc 43 def'
m = str.match(/\d+/)
```

Once you have that object, you can invoke its `string` method to see the entire string to which the pattern was applied. The object's `to_s` method returns a simple version of the matched values. You can also use a `MatchData` object like an array to find information about the match. The object's `size` (or `length`) method returns the number of elements in the array. The first element in the array will be the match found (**Figure 10.19**).

If you'd prefer to use the pattern matching operator, you still can. After a successful match, the special variable `$~` will be the `MatchData` object:

```
'abc 43 def' =~ /\d+/
puts $~[0] # 43
```

The `MatchData` object will contain more information when your patterns include groupings (or subpatterns). For instance, if you want to access a matched email address by its username, domain name, and extension (**Figure 10.20**):

```
pattern = /\A([\w.+-]+)@([\w.-]+)\.
→([a-z]{2,6})\Z/i
'larry.ullman@example.com' =~ pattern
$~.to_a
```

```
● ○ ○        Ruby: Visual QuickStart Guide
=> "abc 43 def"
>> m = str.match(/\d+/)
=> #<MatchData:0x34d1a4>
>> m.string
=> "abc 43 def"
>> m.to_s
=> "43"
>> m.size
=> 1
>> m[0]
=> "43"
>>
```

Figure 10.19 Information about a successful match, including the entire string and just the part that matched the pattern, is available in the returned `MatchData` object.

```
● ○ ○        Ruby: Visual QuickStart Guide
>> pattern = /\A([\w.+-]+)@([\w.-]+)\.([a-z]{2,6})\Z/i
=> /\A([\w.+-]+)@([\w.-]+)\.([a-z]{2,6})\Z/i
>> 'larry.ullman@example.com' =~ pattern
=> 0
>> $~.to_a
=> ["larry.ullman@example.com", "larry.ullman", "example", "com"]
>>
```

Figure 10.20 When a matched pattern contains groupings, the first element in the MatchData object will be the entire match. Each subsequent element will correspond to a subpattern match.

```
>> str = 'This has four words.'
=> "This has four words."
>> str.scan(/\w+/)
=> ["This", "has", "four", "words"]
>> words = str.split(/\s/)
=> ["This", "has", "four", "words."]
>>
```

Figure 10.21 Because this example uses scan to find words (letters, numbers, and underscores) but uses split to break on space characters, there is a slight difference in the result (note the period after *words* in the last line).

Being Less Greedy

A key component to Perl-compatible regular expressions is the concept of *greediness*. By default, PCRE will attempt to match as much as possible. For example, the pattern **<.+>** matches any HTML tag. When tested on a string like *<a href="page.php">Link</a>*, it will actually match that entire string, from the opening angle bracket (<) to the closing one. But that string contains three possible matches: the entire string, the opening tag (from *<a* to ">"), and the closing tag (*</a>*).

To overrule greediness, make the match *lazy*. A lazy match will contain as little data as possible. Any quantifier can be made lazy by following it with the question mark. For example, the pattern **<.+?>** would return two matches in the preceding string: the opening tag and the closing tag. It would not return the whole string as a match.

Another way to make patterns less greedy is to use negative classes. The pattern **<[^>]+>** matches everything between the opening and closing angle brackets except for a closing >. So using this pattern would have the same result as using **<.+?>**. This pattern would also match strings that contain newline characters, which the period excludes.

Whether you use the pattern matching operator or the match method, it's important to understand that both only ever find the *first match* in a string. If you were to test **(\w+)** against *abc def*, the match would only contain *abc*.

Another way you can find matches is to use the scan and split methods of the String class. Both can take a regular expression as an argument, and both will return arrays of matches. The scan method returns each match found. The split method uses the regular expression to break up the string into pieces (**Figure 10.21**).

```
str = 'This has four words.'
str.scan(/\w+/)
words = str.split(/\s/)
```

Because both methods return arrays, you could tie them to blocks:

```
str.scan(/\w+/) { |m| puts m.upcase}
```

When you start looking at matches, you may be surprised by the results. Perl-Compatible Regular Expressions are *greedy* by default, a topic discussed in the sidebar. The next series of examples will further differentiate between the pattern matching operator (or the match method), scan, and the greediness of regular expressions.

FINDING MATCHES

To find matches:

1. Create a test string:

```
str = 'This is a formulaic test for
→ informal matches.'
```

This string has three different uses of the characters *for* in it. It may not be proper English, but it's a good test subject for exploring boundaries, greediness, and multiple matches.

2. See if the letters *for* can be found within the string (**Figure 10.22**):

```
str.index('for')
str.scan('for')
m = str.match(/for/)
m.to_a
```

To just find if one literal piece of text is within another, you can use the `index` method, rather than a regular expression. To find every instance of one literal piece of text within another, use `scan`, but again providing it with a string, not a regular expression.

To contrast what happens with the `match` method, a regular expression is tested. As you can see in the figure, only one match is returned (compared to the three returned by the `scan` method).

```
● ○ ○          Ruby: Visual QuickStart Guide
>> str = 'This is a formulaic test for informal matches.'
=> "This is a formulaic test for informal matches."
>> str.index('for')
=> 10
>> str.scan('for')
=> ["for", "for", "for"]
>> m = str.match(/for/)
=> #<MatchData:0x4d6e8>
>> m.to_a
=> ["for"]
>>
```

Figure 10.22 When searching for literal text in a string, don't use regular expressions. When looking for every match in a string, don't use the `match` method, which will return only one.

```
●  ○  ○        Ruby: Visual QuickStart Guide
>> str.scan(/for.*/)
=> ["formulaic test for informal matches."]
>> m = str.match(/for.*/)
=> #<MatchData:0x3ea94>
>> m.to_a
=> ["formulaic test for informal matches."]
>>
```

Figure 10.23 Because regular expressions are greedy by default (see the sidebar), this pattern finds only one match in the string. That match happens to start with the first instance of *for* and continue until the end of the string.

```
●  ○  ○        Ruby: Visual QuickStart Guide
>> str.scan(/for\S*/)
=> ["formulaic", "for", "formal"]
>>
```

Figure 10.24 This revised pattern matches strings that begin with *for* and end on a word.

```
●  ○  ○        Ruby: Visual QuickStart Guide
>> str.scan(/\b[a-z]*for[a-z]*\b/)
=> ["formulaic", "for", "informal"]
>>
```

Figure 10.25 Unlike the pattern in Figure 10.24, this one matches entire words that contain *for* (*informal* here, *formal* in Figure 10.24).

3. Find *for* within its full context (**Figure 10.23**):

```
str.scan(/for.*/)
m = str.match(/for.*/)
m.to_a
```

For the second test, change the pattern to the regular expression **for.*** The result may surprise you; its cause is discussed in the sidebar, "Being Less Greedy." To make this search less greedy, the pattern could be changed to **for.*?**, whose results would be the same as those in Figure 10.22.

4. Find each occurrence of *for* within its context (**Figure 10.24**):

```
str.scan(/for\S*/)
```

Using **\S** in the pattern instead of the period has the effect of making the match stop as soon as a white space character is found (because the pattern wants to match *for* followed by any number of non–white space characters).

5. Find each occurrence of *for* within its proper and full context (**Figure 10.25**):

```
str.scan(/\b[a-z]*for[a-z]*\b/)
```

This pattern makes use of word boundaries, discussed earlier in the chapter. Note that if you use match or the pattern matching operator, only the first match—*formulaic*—will be returned.

Performing Substitutions

Sometimes you don't need to know what exactly matched a pattern but, instead, you need to replace that match with another value. To do so, use the sub, sub!, gsub, or gsub! methods. The sub and sub! methods will only make one replacement, on the first found match. The gsub and gsub! methods will replace every found match. The sub and gsub methods return a copy of the original string, with any replacements made. The sub! and gsub! methods alter the original string. All four methods take two arguments: the string or regular expression to match, and the value to use instead. Here's a simple string replacement:

```
str = 'Hello, World!'
str.sub!('Hello', 'Goodbye')
str.sub!('!', '?') # Goodbye, World?
```

Backreferencing

Backreferencing is the ability to refer to pattern groupings—sections within parentheses—later in the pattern or in replacement text. You can refer to matched subsections by using a backslash followed by a number. The entire match can be referenced using \0; \1 matches the first grouping; \2, the second; and so forth. For instance, this next example would replace @ in an email address with the letters *AT*, surrounded by spaces:

```
pattern = /\A([\w.+-]+)@([\w.-]+)\.([a-z]{2,6})\Z/i
email = 'larry.ullman@example.com'
email.sub!(pattern, '\1 AT \2.\3')
```

So \1 would refer to the characters matched by **([\w.+ -]+)**: *larry.ullman*. The \2 matches *example*, and \3 matches *com*. Of course, as I've said before, if you're looking for or replacing literal text, a String method would be better to use, but I wanted to show how to refer to parts of a pattern. Here's a more appropriate use of backreferencing:

```
link = email.gsub(pattern, '<a href="mailto:\0">\0</a>')
```

You can use backreferencing within a pattern, too, not just in a replacement string, as you'll see in Step 3 of this last exercise in the chapter. Do be careful when using double-quotation marks with backreferencing, as the backslash has special meaning. Within single quotes \0 refers to the entire match, but within double quotes, you'd need to use \\0 instead.

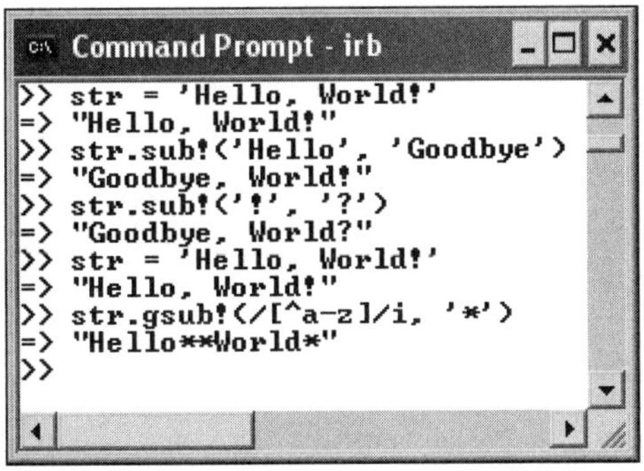

Figure 10.26 Various ways of substituting words and characters.

In this next example, every non-letter (case-insensitive) is replaced with an asterisk (**Figure 10.26**):

```
str = 'Hello, World!'
str.gsub!(/[^a-z]/i, '*')
```

Another way to use these methods is to provide the pattern or string to match, and then handle any found matches in a block. This next example has the same effect as applying the upcase! method to the entire string:

```
str = 'Hello, World!'
str.gsub(/[a-z]/) { |m| m.upcase! }
```

This next series of steps will show different ways you might perform substitutions. One example will also make use of *backreferencing*, discussed in the sidebar.

To perform substitutions:

1. Replace every occurrence of a bad word with asterisks (**Figure 10.27**).

   ```
   text = 'Oh, bleep! This text contains
   → a really bleeping bad word.'

   text.gsub!(/(bleep)(s|ed|er|ing)?/,
   → '****')
   ```

   A curse word can appear in many forms, often ending with an *s*, *ed*, *er*, or *ing* (in English, that is). This example will replace every occurrence of a particular bad word, in various forms, with four asterisks. I'm using *bleep* here, because there are certain things you just don't put into a technical book, but you could use an actual bad word if you'd prefer.

   continues on next page

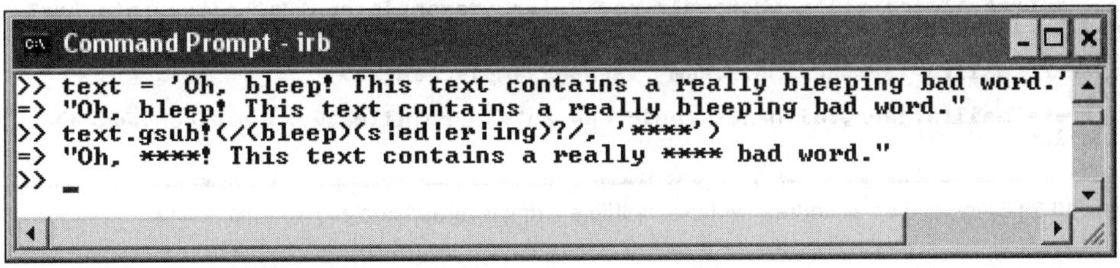

Figure 10.27 The resulting text has uses of *bleep*, *bleeps*, *bleeped*, *bleeper*, and *bleeping* replaced with *****.

2. Format every valid email address in a list
as an HTML *mailto* link (**Figure 10.28**).

```
pattern = /^[\w.+-]+@[\w.-]+\.
→ [A-Za-z]{2,6}$/
list = 'larry@example.com
larry
larry.ullman@example.com.au'
list.gsub!(pattern) do |m|
"<a href=\"mailto:#{m}\">#{m}</a>"
end
puts list
```

The email matching pattern used earlier
in the chapter is first altered so that it
works on a multiline string. By using
the caret and the dollar sign, the pattern
matches any valid email address found on
its own line. When applied to the gsub!
method, each match will be returned.
In this case, the first and third values in
the string are matches. Because a block
is associated with the method call, the
block will receive the match in the m variable. This value is used within another
string to create and return a properly formatted HTML link, which will be placed
in the string, replacing the original value
(see the figure).

```
>> pattern = /^[\w.+-]+@[\w.-]+\.[A-Za-z]{2,6}$/
=> /^[\w.+-]+@[\w.-]+\.[A-Za-z]{2,6}$/
>> list = 'larry@example.com
larry
larry.ullman@example.com.au'
=> "larry@example.com\nlarry\nlarry.ullman@example.com.au"
>> list.gsub!(pattern) do |m|
?>   "<a href=\"mailto:#{m}\">#{m}</a>"
>> end
=> "<a href=\"mailto:larry@example.com\">larry@example.com</a>\nlarry\n<a href=\
"mailto:larry.ullman@example.com.au\">larry.ullman@example.com.au</a>"
>> puts list
<a href="mailto:larry@example.com">larry@example.com</a>
larry
<a href="mailto:larry.ullman@example.com.au">larry.ullman@example.com.au</a>
=> nil
>> _
```

Figure 10.28 Every valid email address within a multiline string is turned into an HTML *mailto* link.

3. Change every paragraph tag in a string to a div tag (**Figure 10.29**).

```
pattern = /<p(\s*[^>]*)>(.*)<\/p>/
text = '<p>This is the text.</p>
<p id="article"><h2>Title</h2>This
↪ is more text.</p>'
text.gsub!(pattern, '<div\1>\2
↪ </div>')
```

The pattern starts by finding strings that begin with <p, which indicates the start of a paragraph tag. Because a tag could include attributes, like id="article", the pattern has to allow for that. By wrapping it in parentheses, the attributes can be reused by backreferencing this part of the pattern (see the "Backreferencing" sidebar). However, because regular expressions are greedy (see the sidebar "Being Less Greedy" earlier in the chapter), the pattern says that the tag's attributes can contain everything *except for* a closing angle bracket. If you didn't take that step, then the entire string would be a match, which would be bad. Next, the pattern finds the closing angle bracket, marking the close of the opening paragraph tag. Then, the pattern matches anything that's between the opening and closing tags, also grouped to allow for backreferencing. Finally, there's the closing paragraph tag, whose forward slash must be escaped so as not to conflict with the regular expression delimiter.

continues on next page

```
Command Prompt - irb
>> pattern = /<p(\s*[^>]*)>(.*)<\/p>/
=> /<p(\s*[^>]*)>(.*)<\/p>/
>> text = '<p>This is the text.</p>
<p id="article"><h2>Title</h2>This is more text.</p>'
=> "<p>This is the text.</p>\n<p id=\"article\"><h2>Title</h2>This is more text.
</p>"
>> text.gsub!(pattern, '<div\1>\2</div>')
=> "<div>This is the text.</div>\n<div id=\"article\"><h2>Title</h2>This is more
text.</div>"
>>
```

Figure 10.29 A practical example, showing how you can convert HTML from one tag type to another without affecting any of the attributes or other HTML.

PERFORMING SUBSTITUTIONS

The test string contains two different paragraphs. One is simple; the other has an `id` attribute and contains HTML within the paragraph's content.

To make the replacement, the `gsub!` method is called, replacing every match with an opening `div` tag, including any existing attributes (found in \1), the actual content (found in \2), and the closing `div` tag.

✔ Tips

- To find any matching pair of HTML tags, you could use backreferencing within the pattern: `/<([a-z0-9]+)(\s*[^>]*)>(.*)<\/\1>/i`.
  The \1 within the closing HTML tag says that for this to be a match, whatever value starts the opening tag—*a*, *p*, *h2*, etc.—must be the same as that in the closing tag.

- The `tr` and `tr!` methods can also be used to replace characters in a string with other characters.

DEBUGGING AND ERROR HANDLING

Whether you've just begun programming in a new language or have been using the language for years, you're going to have errors. Learning how to find and fix errors is an important skill, and one with which you'll no doubt get plenty of practice! Although experience is truly the best way to master debugging, there are tools and techniques that can expedite the learning process.

The first and last sections of the chapter discuss different Ruby libraries that help to root out bugs and other problems in your Ruby code as you write it. These are the kinds of issues that arise even when the script is being properly used. The specific topics range from basic debugging skills to *unit testing* and *profiling*. All of these approaches and add-ons help to find and squash bugs that inevitably crop up as you develop applications.

After you've found and fixed every bug in your code, you may be ready to release it into the wild (i.e., let other people take a crack at it). Before you do so, you ought to make sure that the code is written so well that it reacts accordingly *even when it's not properly used*. Toward that end, the middle of the chapter takes on the subject of exception handling.

Using the Ruby Debugger

A *debugger* is a special tool used to provide insight into an application while it's executing. Instead of merely running some code and outputting the result, a debugger can be used to pause the execution, move around within the execution logic, print the values of variables at any point, and so much more. Ruby comes with a debugger built into the Standard Library. To use that debugger, you can formally include it in a script:

```
require 'debug'
```

A more logical solution is to require the library on the fly, when you go to execute the script. You can do so by using the -r flag when invoking the Ruby executable, following it with the name of the library to include:

```
ruby -r debug scriptname.rb
```

That line tells Ruby to include the debug library, and then run *scriptname.rb*.

After following either of these approaches, you'll be within an irb-like interface in which you can examine and control the code. There, you use commands (**Figure 11.1**) to investigate, debug, and test the code. Besides these commands, you can also execute any expression, including changing the value of a variable or the definition of a method, to see the effect.

To navigate through a script, use step, next, and cont (short for *continue*). The last one just continues the execution of the code. The step command goes to the next line (or next *X* lines if you use step *X*), including into method definitions. The next command executes the next line of code (or the next *X* lines if you use next *X*), *not including* method definitions.

To see the values of variables, you can use var global and var local. To have the value of a specific variable shown whenever the debugger halts the execution of the code, use display *varname*. The list command shows the code around the current stopping point.

You can tell the debugger to stop execution at certain points by using break. You provide it with a line number, class name, or method name at which to halt the execution:

```
break 4
break some_method
```

The watch command sets a breakpoint when a given expression becomes true:

```
watch amount > 300
```

This is just a quick introduction to some of the debugger's commands. For more, type help at the debugger prompt (as shown in Figure 11.1). To practice using this, I'll take some code from Chapter 6, "Creating Methods," place it in a script, and run it through the debugger.

```
(rdb:1) help
Debugger help v.-0.002b
Commands
  b[reak] [file:|class:]<line|method>
  b[reak] [class.]<line|method>
                        set breakpoint to some position
  wat[ch] <expression>  set watchpoint to some expression
  cat[ch] (<exception>|off)  set catchpoint to an exception
  b[reak]               list breakpoints
  cat[ch]               show catchpoint
  del[ete][ nnn]        delete some or all breakpoints
  disp[lay] <expression>  add expression into display expression list
  undisp[lay][ nnn]     delete one particular or all display expressions
  c[ont]                run until program ends or hit breakpoint
  s[tep][ nnn]          step (into methods) one line or till line nnn
  n[ext][ nnn]          go over one line or till line nnn
  w[here]               display frames
  f[rame]               alias for where
  l[ist][ (-|nn-mm)]    list program, - lists backwards
                        nn-mm lists given lines
  up[ nn]               move to higher frame
  down[ nn]             move to lower frame
  fin[ish]              return to outer frame
  tr[ace] (on|off)      set trace mode of current thread
  tr[ace] (on|off) all  set trace mode of all threads
  q[uit]                exit from debugger
  v[ar] g[lobal]        show global variables
  v[ar] l[ocal]         show local variables
  v[ar] i[nstance] <object>  show instance variables of object
  v[ar] c[onst] <object>  show constants of object
  m[ethod] i[nstance] <obj>  show methods of object
  m[ethod] <class|module>  show instance methods of class or module
  th[read] l[ist]       list all threads
  th[read] c[ur[rent]]  show current thread
  th[read] [sw[itch]] <nnn>  switch thread context to nnn
  th[read] stop <nnn>   stop thread nnn
  th[read] resume <nnn>  resume thread nnn
  p expression          evaluate expression and print its value
  h[elp]                print this help
  <everything else>     evaluate
(rdb:1)
```

Figure 11.1 The available commands within the Ruby debugger, including their usage, purposes, and abbreviations.

To use the debugger:

1. Begin a new Ruby script in your text editor or IDE (**Script 11.1**):

   `# Script 11.1 - lucas.rb`

   The lucas method was defined in Chapter 6. It generates Lucas numbers, which are like Fibonacci numbers but start with 2 and 1. This script will contain that chapter's method definition so that it can be run through the debugger.

2. Define the method:

   ```
   def lucas(num)
       a = 2
       b = 1
       num.times do
           yield a
           c = a
           a = b
           b += c
       end
   end
   ```

   For a detailed description of how this method works, see Chapter 6.

3. Invoke the method:

   `lucas(10) { |x| puts x }`

4. Save the script as lucas.rb.

5. At a command prompt, run lucas.rb using the Ruby debugger (**Figure 11.2**):

   `ruby -w -r debug lucas.rb`

   You may need to move into the proper directory or change the reference to the file in order for this to work (see Chapter 2, "Simple Scripts"). If the reference to the script is correct, you should see something like that in Figure 11.2.

Script 11.1 This script defines and invokes a method to be used as a test case for the Ruby debugger.

```
1    # Script 11.1 - lucas.rb
2
3    # Method for calculating Lucas numbers.
4    # Argument is the quantity of numbers to
     return.
5    def lucas(num)
6        a = 2
7        b = 1
8        num.times do
9            yield a
10           c = a
11           a = b
12           b += c
13       end
14   end
15
16   # Call the method for the first 10 numbers:
17   lucas(10) { |x| puts x }
```

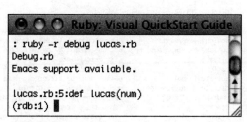

Figure 11.2 Starting to run a Ruby script through the debugger.

6. Enter next to go to the next non-method line of code.

This will move the debugger to the line that calls the lucas method, skipping the rest of the method definition.

7. Enter step to go to the next line of code (**Figure 11.3**):

This will move you into the method definition, which is the next line of executed code after the method has been called.

8. Show the current code block and the values of the local variables (**Figure 11.4**):

```
list
var local
```

The list command is very useful, showing where you are in the script (i.e., providing some context). Use the var command to show the values of any variables; var local will show only the local variables, like those defined within a method.

continues on next page

Figure 11.3 How the next and step commands move through the script.

Figure 11.4 The list command shows where the cursor is within the larger context. The var local command shows every variable local to the context.

USING THE RUBY DEBUGGER

9. Set a watchpoint for when the value of *a* is greater than 10, and then continue executing the script (**Figure 11.5**):

```
watch a > 10
cont
```

A watchpoint is a breakpoint that looks for a condition being true, like a variable having a certain value. The cont line says to continue executing the script up to the next breakpoint or until the program ends.

10. View the current context and local variable values (**Figure 11.6**):

```
list
var local
```

By setting watchpoints and other breaks, and following the values of variables, you can see "behind the scenes" to get a better sense of what happens in a script.

11. When you're done, type quit and enter *y* at the prompt to exit.

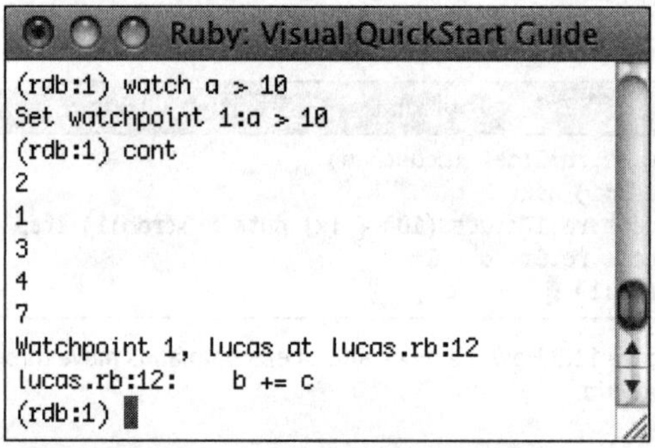

```
(rdb:1) watch a > 10
Set watchpoint 1:a > 10
(rdb:1) cont
2
1
3
4
7
Watchpoint 1, lucas at lucas.rb:12
lucas.rb:12:    b += c
(rdb:1)
```

Figure 11.5 A watchpoint is set and the program's execution continues.

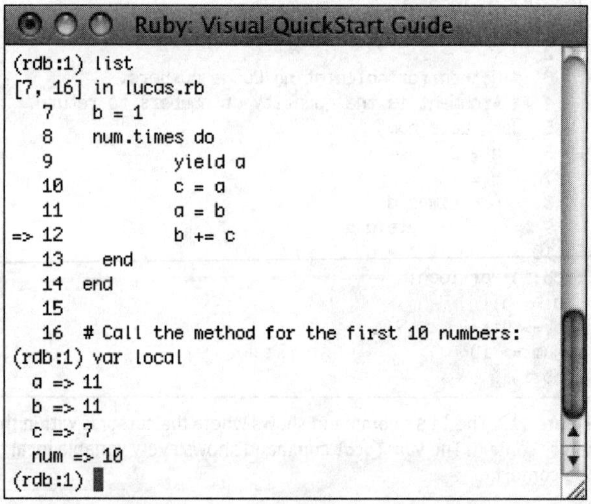

```
(rdb:1) list
[7, 16] in lucas.rb
   7      b = 1
   8      num.times do
   9             yield a
   10            c = a
   11            a = b
=> 12            b += c
   13     end
   14   end
   15
   16   # Call the method for the first 10 numbers:
(rdb:1) var local
  a => 11
  b => 11
  c => 7
  num => 10
(rdb:1)
```

Figure 11.6 This repetition of the steps in Figure 11.4 show the progression of the local variables' values.

USING THE RUBY DEBUGGER

✔ Tips

- This example doesn't really use the debug library for debugging, since the code actually works without problems. However, running the lucas method, which is a little bit complex despite its few lines of code, through the debugger can help you to comprehend both the code and how one might use the debugger itself.

- A popular alternative to the built-in Ruby debugger is the ruby-debug gem (http://rubyforge.org/projects/ruby-debug/). Because it's written in C, it's faster than the debug library (written in Ruby), particularly for more complex code.

General Debugging Techniques

Here are some general debugging techniques and best practices to keep in mind:

- Run scripts with the -w option to view all warnings.
- Use a consistent naming scheme for variables, methods, and classes.
- Remember operator precedence.
- Call to_s to get an object's value.
- Invoke the class method to see an object's class type.
- Pay attention to variable scope.
- Balance all parentheses, braces, and brackets.
- Don't forget to use end to conclude blocks and conditionals.

In my years of programming, regardless of the technology being used, the best piece of advice I can offer is to *take a break*! You'd be surprised how often stepping away from the computer and coming back to the problem with fresh eyes is exactly what was required.

Exception Handling

Even if you've never written a line of code in any language, you probably know that errors are inevitable. You should be very happy to hear, then, that you'll never see an error in Ruby! Instead, you'll see *exceptions*: errors in an object format. When a problem occurs, an exception is *raised*. A Ruby script will terminate when any exception occurs, but through exception handling, you can dictate what's to happen instead.

To handle exceptions, you write your code to keep an eye on potentially problematic processes. For example, it's unlikely that an exception occurs in the act of defining a class or a method, but likely that one occurs when taking user input, calling a method, creating an object, or working with files and databases (as just some common examples). The code in which an exception could occur is wrapped within a block created by the keywords begin and end. Within the block, the keyword rescue starts the code that handles an exception:

```
begin
    # Code
rescue
    # Do whatever upon exception.
end
```

It is important to understand that any code between where an exception is raised and the rescue clause will not be executed. The program will skip over those lines as if they were not there (you'll see this in some of the chapter's examples).

In most situations, you'll want to use the exception that was raised. To do so, add => *var_name* after rescue:

```
begin
    # Code
rescue => e
    # Do whatever with e.
end
```

The Exception Object

All exceptions in Ruby are objects of the Exception class or a derived subclass (also see Figure 11.7). The primary subclass you'll encounter is StandardError, which is further derived by (among others):

- ArgumentError, an incorrect number of arguments provided to a method

- NameError, of which NoMethodError is a child (if, for instance, you misspelled a method's name)

- TypeError, using an incorrect object type

StandardError exceptions, and its children, are the kinds of exceptions that scripts generally handle. More serious exceptions are normally indicative of a problem with Ruby or the environment as a whole, in which case a script won't, and often can't, handle them. For example, a syntax error in a script results in a ScriptError exception. Because the script has a syntax error, it can't be run and therefore can't handle that exception type.

EXCEPTION HANDLING

The e variable, which can be named anything, will be an object of whatever type of error was thrown (see the sidebar "The Exception Object" and **Figure 11.7**). The two most important methods defined in the `Exception` class, and inherited by the derived subclasses, are `message` and `backtrace`. The `message` method returns a string providing information about the error that occurred. If you've ever had an error in your code, you've seen this already. Referring to an exception object is the same as calling its `message` method:

```
puts e
puts e.message # Same as above.
```

continues on next page

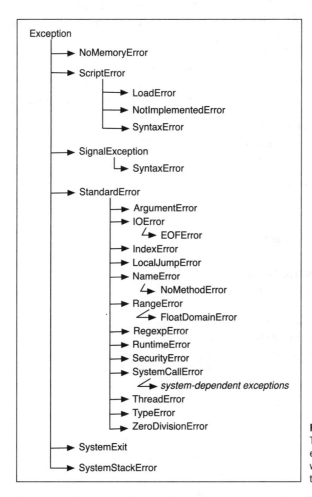

Figure 11.7
The hierarchy of Ruby exception objects, all of which are derived from the `Exception` class.

EXCEPTION HANDLING

The backtrace method returns an array of strings representing the files, lines, and (optionally) methods involved in the error.

To play around with raising and handling exceptions in Ruby, I'll turn to the Circle class defined in Chapter 9, "Modules and Includes."

To handle exceptions:

1. Begin a new Ruby script in your text editor or IDE (**Script 11.2**):

   ```
   # Script 11.2 - circles1.rb
   ```

2. Require the Circle library:

   ```
   require 'circle'
   ```

   The circle.rb file is defined in Chapter 9. You'll need to either save this file in the same directory where that one was saved, copy that file to this file's directory, or change this reference so that it's correct.

3. Start a code block:

   ```
   begin
   ```

   Any exceptions raised by the code following this, up to rescue, will be handled by the rescue clause.

4. Attempt to create and use two circles:

   ```
   c1 = Circle.new(5)
   c2 = Circle.new
   puts "c1 is greater than or equal
   → to c2: #{c1 >= c2}"
   ```

   When a Circle object is created, the new method must be provided with the radius for the circle. This is omitted when creating the second circle, so an exception will be raised. This also means that the comparison will never be executed.

Script 11.2 The intentional mistake in this code will be handled by the rescue clause.

```
1    # Script 11.2 - circles1.rb
2
3    # Require the Circle library:
4    require 'circle.rb'
5
6    # Start a block:
7    begin
8
9        # Create two circles, one erroneously:
10       c1 = Circle.new(5)
11       c2 = Circle.new
12
13       # Print a comparison:
14       puts "c1 is greater than or equal to
            c2: #{c1 >= c2}"
15
16   # Catch any exceptions:
17   rescue => e
18       puts "An exception occurred. Ruby
            reported: #{e}"
19
20   end
```

5. Handle any raised exceptions:

```
rescue => e
    puts "An exception occurred. Ruby
    → reported: #{e}"
```

Any type of exception that is raised by the three lines of code in the block will be handled by this clause. First, the exception will be assigned to the variable `e`. Then a `puts` statement prints a generic message, along with the specific exception text.

6. Complete the block:

```
end
```

7. Save and run the completed script (**Figure 11.8**).

You will see an exception, but this time it's intentional.

8. To see the result without using `rescue`, comment out or delete the `rescue` clause (lines 17 and 18), then save and re-run the completed script (**Figure 11.9**).

✔ Tips

■ Instead of assigning a raised exception to a variable using the construct `rescue => var_name`, you can just use the special variable `$!`, which always refers to the last exception that occurred.

■ A method definition is inherently the beginning of a block. Exceptions can be handled in a definition without overtly using `begin`:

```
def some_method
    # Method code
    rescue => e
end
```

■ Other programming languages use *throw* and *catch* to raise and handle errors. Ruby has these methods, but they are not used for exception handling. For this reason, I describe exceptions as being *raised* and *handled* in Ruby, not *thrown* and *caught*.

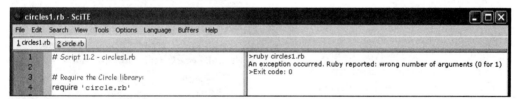

Figure 11.8 The user sees that an exception occurred and a basic message is then displayed.

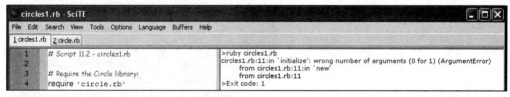

Figure 11.9 Without formal exception handling, this is how Ruby would have reported the same problem.

Handling Exceptions by Type

If you use `rescue` as in the preceding example, it'll handle any exception that occurs of type `StandardError` or of any child type. There are often times, however, where code should respond differently based upon the type of exception that is raised. For example, if a block of code opens a database connection and runs a query on that database, a problem with the first step is more serious than one with the second.

You can use `rescue` to catch different kinds of exceptions by following the keyword with the exception object type:

```
begin
    # Code
rescue SomeErrorType => e
    # Do whatever.
rescue SomeOtherErrorType => e
    # Do whatever.
rescue => e
    # Default.
end
```

The appropriate `rescue` block will handle the error, based upon its type. If there's not a `rescue` clause for an error type, the last `rescue` clause, if present, will act as the default (for all other `StandardError` exceptions).

else, ensure, and retry

Three other keywords that come into play with handling exceptions are `else`, `ensure`, and `retry`. An `else` clause can come after all `rescue` clauses. Its associated code will be executed if no exceptions are raised (i.e., if none of the `rescue` clauses take effect). Conversely, an `ensure` clause will always be executed, whether exceptions were raised or not (like a *finally* clause that some languages support). For example, you might open a file and attempt to write to it, but whether or not an exception is thrown, the file should be closed.

You can use `retry` when handling exceptions if you'd like the code that caused the problem to be executed again. Say you have a file that data should be written to but that could be locked if some other application is currently writing to it. If an exception is raised that the file could not be opened because it's locked, you might retry the code block, knowing that it will eventually become unlocked (although you would have to watch out for infinite loops in such situations).

Script 11.3 This update of Script 11.2 reacts differently to different kinds of exceptions that might occur.

```
1    # Script 11.3 - circles2.rb
2
3    # Require the Circle library:
4    require 'circle'
5
6    # Start a block:
7    begin
8
9        # Create two circles, one erroneously:
10       c1 = Circle.new(5)
11       c2 = Circle.new
12
13       # Print a comparison:
14       puts "c1 is greater than or equal to
         c2: #{c1 >= c2}"
15
16       # Print the addition:
17       puts c1 + c2
18
19   # Catch any exceptions:
20   rescue ArgumentError => e
21       puts "A method was misused. Ruby
         reported: #{e}"
22
23   rescue NameError => e
24       puts "You are attempting to use a
         class or method that does not exist.
         Check your spelling and any applicable
         documentation. Ruby reported: #{e}"
25
26   rescue => e
27       puts "Some other exception occurred.
         Ruby reported: #{e}"
28
29   end
```

To handle types of exceptions:

1. Open `circles1.rb` (Script 11.2) in your text editor or IDE, if it is not already.

   To apply the new information, this script will be touched up so that it can handle different types of exceptions.

2. After the first `puts` line, attempt to add the two circles (**Script 11.3**):

   ```
   puts c1 + c2
   ```

   This script now contains two problems. The first is the already existing failure to provide a radius when creating a new circle. This second problem is the use of the addition operator, which is not defined in the `Circle` class.

3. Before the existing `rescue`, add:

   ```
   rescue ArgumentError => e
       puts "A method was misused.
       → Ruby reported: #{e}"
   ```

   This `rescue` clause will only catch exceptions of type `ArgumentError` (and any derived subclasses). Such exceptions are raised when a method is called without the right number or type of arguments. So this clause will handle the exception raised by the creation of the first `Circle` object.

4. Add another `rescue` clause:

   ```
   rescue NameError => e
       puts "You are attempting to use
       → a class or method that does
       → not exist. Check your spelling
       → and any applicable documentation.
       → Ruby reported: #{e}"
   ```

   A `NameError` exception occurs when you call a method that does not exist (or reference a class or module that doesn't exist). In this script, use of the addition operator will raise this exception type. If you wanted to be more specific, you could watch for a `NoMethodError` exception, which is the applicable derived subtype.

continues on next page

5. In the original and now final `rescue` clause, change the message to read:

    ```
    puts "Some other exception occurred.
    ⇢ Ruby reported: #{e}"
    ```

    If a `StandardError` exception of a different type (besides `ArgumentError` and `NameError`) is raised, it'll be handled by this rescue.

6. Save and run the completed script (**Figure 11.10**).

    This script still has the original problem, but it will be handled in its own way now (i.e., with its own custom message).

7. Change the creation of the second `Circle` object so that it provides a radius:

    ```
    c1 = Circle.new(23.0)
    ```

    You can use any numeric value you'd like here. The goal is to stop seeing the `ArgumentError` exception so that the `NameError` exception can be raised and handled.

8. Save and re-run the script (**Figure 11.11**).

✔ Tip

- The exception messages and information as displayed in this chapter's examples are primarily for debugging purposes. You may want to have messages be informative yet less specific in applications to be used by the public.

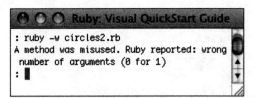

Figure 11.10 The message generated by the first rescue clause is printed along with the script's original exception.

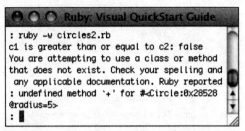

Figure 11.11 If an exception of a type other than `ArgumentError` occurs, a different message will be displayed. Notice that the circle comparison is actually made now, because now an exception occurs after that point.

Raising Exceptions

The preceding two sections of the chapter show how you can write code to handle exceptions that might occur. Well-written Ruby applications also raise exceptions themselves. To do so, use the `raise` method. You can provide `raise` with an error message:

```
raise 'error message'
```

When used like this, `raise` will generate a `RuntimeError` exception, which is likely not what you want. You can instead specify the type of exception to raise:

```
raise ExceptionType('error message')
```

You'll also see this written like so:

```
raise ExceptionType, 'error message'
```

Or even:

```
raise ExceptionType.new('error message')
```

One situation in which you'll want to raise exceptions is to make sure that the classes you define are properly used. For example, the `CreditCard` class defined in Chapter 8, "Inheritance and More," has a greater-than method defined. It should only be used to compare two objects that both have a `balance` method (for example, a credit card and a loan). You could define it like so:

```
def >(rh)
    raise TypeError.new('Both objects
→ must have a balance method.')
→ unless rh.respond_to?('balance')
    @balance > rh.balance
end
```

Let's turn to the `Circle` class one more time, raising exceptions as appropriate.

To raise exceptions:

1. Open circle.rb (Script 9.3) in your text editor or IDE.

   I'll start by updating the Circle class definition, and then update the script that uses the class.

2. Change the definition of the initialize method to (**Script 11.4**):

   ```
   def initialize(r = '')
       raise ArgumentError.new('The
       → radius must be a positive
       → number.') unless (r.is_a?
       → Numeric) && (r > 0)
       @radius = r
   end
   ```

   There are two changes here. First, the method's lone argument is given a default value of an empty string. I'll explain why in a moment. Second, an exception of type ArgumentError is raised unless the r object is a Numeric type—of which Integer and Float are derived types—and has a positive value. If both conditions are true, then no exception is raised and the submitted value is assigned to @radius as before.

   Returning to the default argument value, that's necessary in order to handle the exception in a customized way. If a method's arguments are not given default values, then they are required and a failure to provide a value will result in Ruby automatically throwing an exception (**Figure 11.12**).

Script 11.4 The Circle class definition now raises exceptions when its methods are improperly used.

```
1    # Script 11.4 - circle.rb
2
3    # Define the Circle class:
4    class Circle
5
6        # Include Comparable mixin:
7        include Comparable
8
9        # Accessors for the radius:
10       attr_reader :radius
11
12       # initialize method sets the radius:
13       def initialize(r = '')
14
15           # Radius must be a positive number:
16           raise ArgumentError.new('The radius
                 must be a positive number.') unless
                 (r.is_a? Numeric) && (r > 0)
17
18           @radius = r
19       end
20
21       # Define the comparison operator:
22       def <=>(rh)
23           raise TypeError.new('Both objects
                 must be Circles.') unless rh.is_a?
                 Circle
24           @radius <=> rh.radius
25       end
26
27   end # End of Circle class.
```

```
: ruby -w test.rb
test.rb:33:in `initialize': wrong number of arguments (0 for 1) (ArgumentError)
        from test.rb:33:in `new'
        from test.rb:33
:
```

Figure 11.12 Ruby's default message when a required method argument is omitted.

Script 11.5 More problems are introduced in this version of the script, to see how the Circle class's exceptions are raised.

```
1    # Script 11.5 - circles3.rb
2
3    # Require the Circle library:
4    require 'circle'
5
6    # Start a block:
7    begin
8
9        # Create three circles and a string:
10       c1 = Circle.new(5)
11       c2 = Circle.new('cat')
12       c3 = Circle.new(-23.45)
13       c4 = 'Hello, World!'
14
15       # Print a comparison:
16       puts "c1 is greater than or equal to
         c2: #{c1 >= c2}"
17
18       # Print an invalid comparison:
19       puts "c2 is between c1 and c4:
         #{c2.between?(c1, c4)}"
20
21   # Catch any exceptions:
22   rescue ArgumentError => e
23       puts "A method was misused. Ruby
         reported: #{e}"
24
25   rescue NameError => e
26       puts "You are attempting to use a
         class or method that does not exist.
         Check your spelling and any applicable
         documentation. Ruby reported: #{e}"
27
28   rescue TypeError => e
29       puts "You are using an invalid type
         somehow. Ruby reported: #{e}"
30
31   rescue => e
32       puts "Some other exception occurred.
         Ruby reported: #{e}"
33
34   end
```

3. Change the definition of the comparison operator to:

```
def <=>(rh)
    raise TypeError.new('Both objects
    → must be Circles.') unless
    → rh.is_a? Circle
    @radius <=> rh.radius
end
```

This method now raises a TypeError if the right-hand operand isn't also a Circle. If you wanted to be able to compare different kinds of objects, for example, a Circle and a Rectangle (perhaps by area), you could use *duck typing* to make the condition more lenient. Duck typing is also discussed in Chapter 8.

4. Save the file.

5. Open circles2.rb (Script 11.3) in your text editor or IDE, if it is not already.

6. Change the creation of the Circle objects to (**Script 11.5**):

```
c1 = Circle.new(5)
c2 = Circle.new('cat')
c3 = Circle.new(-23.45)
c4 = 'Hello, World!'
```

The first Circle object remains the same, using a radius of 5. The next two Circle objects have inappropriate radius values. Then a string is defined, which will be used in an invalid comparison.

continues on next page

RAISING EXCEPTIONS

7. Add an invalid comparison:

```
puts "c2 is between c1 and c4:
→#{c2.between?(c1, c4)}"
```

This line will cause an exception because the comparison operator insists that the right-hand operand is a `Circle`. The `between?` method, available here thanks to the `Comparable` module (see Chapter 9, "Modules and Includes"), will make two comparisons: one using `c2` and `c1`, and another using `c2` and `c4`. That second comparison will fail.

8. Remove the use of the addition operator.

Since I already know that line creates an exception, I'll get rid of it.

9. Add another `rescue` clause:

```
rescue TypeError => e
    puts "You are using an invalid
    →type somehow. Ruby reported:
    →#{e}"
```

To handle the `TypeError` exception raised by the comparison operator, another `rescue` clause is added. This is optional, as the final `rescue` clause would handle it by default.

10. Save and run the completed script (**Figure 11.13**).

The first exception will be raised by the creation of the second `Circle` object.

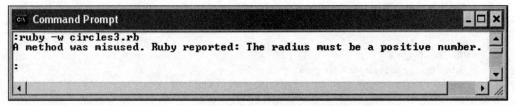

Figure 11.13 Trying to create a `Circle` object with a radius of *cat* generates this result.

11. Change the creation of the second `Circle` object so that it provides a valid radius:

```
c2 = Circle.new(45)
```

You can use any numeric value you'd like here. The goal is to stop seeing the `ArgumentError` exception so that the `NameError` exception can be raised and handled.

12. Save and re-run the script.

The result will be the same as in Figure 11.13, this time caused by the negative radius in the creation of the third `Circle`.

13. Remove the creation of the third `Circle` object, save, and re-run the script (**Figure 11.14**).

✔ Tips

■ To make the exceptions more informative, they could indicate the value provided for the radius (in the `initialize` method) and the class type of the right-hand operand (in the comparison operator).

■ When defining your own modules and classes, you might consider also defining your own `Exception` object types to be used by your code. To do so, derive your custom exception class from `StandardError`:

```
class MyExceptionClass < StandardError
    # Other methods, if needed.
end
```

■ If you use `raise` by itself as the last line in a rescue block, the exception that was raised will be re-raised.

```
begin
    # Do whatever.
rescue => e
    # Do whatever.
    raise
end
```

```
:ruby -w circles3.rb
c1 is greater than or equal to c2: false
You are using an invalid type somehow. Ruby reported: Both objects must be
Circles.
:
```

Figure 11.14 Trying to compare a `Circle` and a `String` generates this message.

Unit Testing

Test-driven programming is as much a philosophy as it is a debugging and development tool. Test-driven programming starts with a series of tests that reflect what an application should do. The software is then written for the purpose of passing those tests. *Unit testing* is a subset of this approach, where the focus is on testing an application's parts: its classes, methods, interfaces, etc. Even if you program more conventionally—writing code first, testing it second—you can still apply unit tests to your work.

The Ruby Standard Library's `Test::Unit` module is a framework for creating tests. Start by including that library:

```
require 'test/unit'
```

Next, define a class that extends the `Test::Unit::TestCase` class:

```
class TestThis < Test::Unit::TestCase
    # class code
end
```

Within the class, define methods that begin with *test*.

```
def test_write_to_file
    # method code
end
```

Each method in the class represents a separate test to be run on your application. For example, the preceding method, when fully defined, would confirm that a script could properly write to a text file. A second method might test a script's ability to read from a file.

Various methods defined in the `Test::Unit` class are used to confirm passage or failure of a test. The `assert` method takes a Boolean expression as an argument:

```
assert(something.empty?)
```

If the expression evaluates to `true`, the code passed that particular test.

The `assert_nil` and `assert_not_nil` methods take an object as their lone arguments. The code passes the test if the provided object is or is not `nil`, accordingly.

The `assert_equal` and `assert_not_equal` methods take two arguments: the expected result and the actual result. These are perhaps the most commonly used assertion methods. As an easy-to-understand example, say that the `something` method should return `true` so long as it's called with at least one argument. To test the method, you would write:

```
def test_something
    assert_equal(true, obj.something
    → ('hello'))
    assert_equal(true, obj.something
    → (456))
    assert_not_equal(true, obj.
    → something)
end
```

In each example, the expected result is the Boolean value `true`. The actual result is generated by the use of the hypothetical class method.

Some of the other methods you might use include `assert_match` and `assert_no_match`, which take regular expressions as their first arguments and strings as their second. The `assert_instance_of`, `assert_kind_of`, and `assert_respond_to` methods test objects by type, to various levels of strictness. The `assert_nothing_thrown`, `assert_nothing_raised`, `assert_thrown`, and `assert_raises` methods confirm that the code does or does not throw or raise exceptions. The latter two methods take blocks of code to be executed and look for exceptions of specific types.

This knowledge could be applied to the `Circle` class again, but instead I'll define and test a `Rectangle` class. This class was introduced in Chapter 7, "Creating Classes," and will be expanded to raise exceptions here.

UNIT TESTING

To test code:

1. Begin a new Ruby script in your text editor or IDE (**Script 11.6**):

```
# Script 11.6 - testing.rb
class Rectangle
    attr_reader :height, :width
```

The script begins with the definition of the Rectangle class. It has attribute reader methods for the class' @height and @width instance variables.

2. Define the initialize method:

```
def initialize(h = 0, w = 0)
    raise ArgumentError.new('The
  → height must be a positive
  → number.') unless (h.is_a?
  → Numeric) && (h > 0)
    raise ArgumentError.new('The width
  → must be a positive number.')
  → unless (w.is_a? Numeric) &&
  → (w > 0)
    @height, @width = h, w
end
```

The method takes two arguments, both of which must be positive numbers. If either does not meet this criterion, an ArgumentError exception is raised as was the case in the Circle class' initialize method.

3. Define the perimeter method:

```
def perimeter
    (@height + @width) * 2
end
```

This method returns twice the sum of the two dimensions.

Script 11.6 The creation of the second class will be used to run tests to confirm that the Rectangle class works as it should.

```
1   # Script 11.6 - testing.rb
2
3   # Define the Rectangle class:
4   class Rectangle
5
6       attr_reader :height, :width
7
8       def initialize(h = 0, w = 0)
9           raise ArgumentError.new('The height
            must be a positive number.') unless
            (h.is_a? Numeric) && (h > 0)
10          raise ArgumentError.new('The width
            must be a positive number.') unless
            (w.is_a? Numeric) && (w > 0)
11          @height, @width = h, w
12      end
13
14      def perimeter
15          (@height + @width) * 2
16      end
17
18      def is_square?
19          if @height == @width then
20              true
21          else
22              false
23          end
24      end
25
26   end # End of Rectangle class.
27
```

(script continues on next page)

Script 11.6 *continued*

```
         ⬤ ⬤ ⬤              📄 Script
28   # Require the testing library:
29   require 'test/unit'
30
31   # Define a testing class:
32   class TestRectangle < Test::Unit::TestCase
33
34      def test_is_square
35         assert(Rectangle.new(6, 6).is_
           square?)
36         assert(!Rectangle.new(3.58, 1234).
           is_square?)
37      end
38
39      def test_perimeter
40         assert_equal(48, Rectangle.new
           (20, 4).perimeter)
41         assert_equal(48, Rectangle.new
           (4, 20).perimeter)
42      end
43
44      def test_create_rectangle
45         assert_instance_of(Rectangle,
           Rectangle.new(1, 2))
46         assert_equal(5, Rectangle.new
           (5, 8).height)
47         assert_equal(8, Rectangle.new
           (5, 8).width)
48         assert_nothing_raised do
49            r = Rectangle.new(3, 4)
50            puts r.height
51            puts r.width
52            puts r.perimeter
53            puts r.is_square?
54         end
55         assert_raise(ArgumentError) {
           Rectangle.new(3) }
56         assert_raise(ArgumentError) {
           Rectangle.new(-1, 2) }
57         assert_raise(ArgumentError) {
           Rectangle.new('cat', 6) }
58      end
59
60   end
```

4. Define the `is_square?` method and complete the class:

```
def is_square?
   if @height == @width then
      true
   else
      false
   end
end
end # End of Rectangle class.
```

This method just returns a Boolean value, indicating whether or not the rectangle is also a square.

I've omitted the definition of the *area* method, for brevity sake. See Chapter 7 if you'd like to implement that here.

5. Require the Test/Unit library and begin defining a new class:

```
require 'test/unit'
class TestRectangle < Test::Unit::
→TestCase
```

You can name the new class anything you'd like, just make sure it inherits from Test::Unit::TestCase.

6. Define the first testing method:

```
def test_is_square
   assert(Rectangle.new(6, 6).is_
   →square?)
   assert(!Rectangle.new(3.58, 1234).
   →is_square?)
end
```

This method tests the `is_square?` member of the **Rectangle** class. Remember that the method's name must start with *test*.

continues on next page

UNIT TESTING

Within the method, two uses of `assert` will constitute the tests. The first says that the `is_square?` method should return `true` if provided with a `Rectangle` whose dimensions are 6 and 6. The second `assert` call says that the `is_square?` method should return `false` if provided with a Rectangle whose dimensions are 3.58 by 1234.

These assertions may seem a bit silly because obviously the one is a square and the other is not, but the point of testing is to confirm that things work as they should.

7. Define the second testing method:

```
def test_perimeter
    assert_equal(48, Rectangle.new
    → (20, 4).perimeter)
    assert_equal(48, Rectangle.new(4,
    → 20).perimeter)
end
```

This method tests the `perimeter` method of the `Rectangle` class. Two uses of `assert_equal` confirm that the value returned by perimeter equals 48 when given a `Rectangle` with dimensions of 20 by 4 or 4 by 20. Since the same two numbers, used in either combination, should return the same result, these two tests will root out any existing bugs in the `perimeter` method.

8. Begin defining the last test method:

```
def test_create_rectangle
    assert_instance_of(Rectangle,
    → Rectangle.new(1, 2))
    assert_equal(5, Rectangle.new(5,
    → 8).height)
    assert_equal(8, Rectangle.new(5,
    → 8).width)
```

The first line within the method simply confirms that calling `Rectangle.new` creates a `Rectangle` instance. The next two lines confirm that if you create a

UNIT TESTING

Rectangle with dimensions of 5 by 8, the height method will return the value 5 and the width method will return the value 8. These simple tests rule out bugs is the assignation and recollection of the rectangle's attributes.

9. Test for exceptions with basic Rectangle usage:

```
assert_nothing_raised do
    r = Rectangle.new(3, 4)
    puts r.height
    puts r.width
    puts r.perimeter
    puts r.is_square?
end
```

The assert_nothing_raised method confirms that no exceptions are raised when an associated block of code is executed. This block creates a Rectangle object and then calls four of its methods, printing the results.

10. Confirm that ArgumentError exceptions will be raised when appropriate:

```
assert_raise(ArgumentError) {
→ Rectangle.new(3) }
assert_raise(ArgumentError) {
→ Rectangle.new(-1, 2) }
assert_raise(ArgumentError) {
→ Rectangle.new('cat', 6) }
```

These three uses of assert_raise confirm that ArgumentError exceptions are raised when invalid arguments are provided to the new method (and therefore initialize). The assert_raise method also takes an associated block of code, like assert_nothing_raised, but since the code is just a single line, I wrap each in curly braces. These lines show that testing isn't just a matter of seeing what happens when code is used properly, but also confirming the expected results—namely, exceptions—when code is used improperly.

continues on next page

Benchmarking

Along with unit testing, *benchmarking* is another approach often taken with code. Benchmarking is simply timing how long it takes to execute a script. You can then tweak the code and re-time it to see if the speed can be improved. To benchmark your Ruby code, use the Benchmark module defined in the Ruby Standard Library.

To take this concept one step further, you can profile your code. *Profiling* is detailed benchmarking, determining not just how fast a whole script executes but rather how much time individual parts of the script require. The profile module, also in the Standard Library, can be used for this.

Although benchmarking and profiling can be used to improve a script's performance, you can also use both to waste a lot time hunting down insignificant issues. Use both judiciously and never at the cost of making sure that the code works properly!

11. Complete the `test_create_rectangle` method and the `TestRectangle` class:

```
    end

end
```

12. Save and run the completed script (**Figure 11.15**).

That's all there is to it. You do not need to create an object of the `TestRectangle` class. The tests will automatically be run when the script is executed.

✔ Tips

- As you get in the habit of testing scripts, you'll likely want to use a separate file for the tests. That file would define the test class and methods and then include the file that contains the class being tested.

- Unit testing can also be done in Ruby using ZenTest (`http://zentest.rubyforge.org/ZenTest/`). *Behavior driven development*, which is slightly different, can be done using RSpec (`www.rspec.info`).

- Another series of tests can be run using the rcov Ruby gem. It generates statistics reflecting how frequently certain code in your scripts is executed. If it indicates failure to execute some code, that's likely a problem.

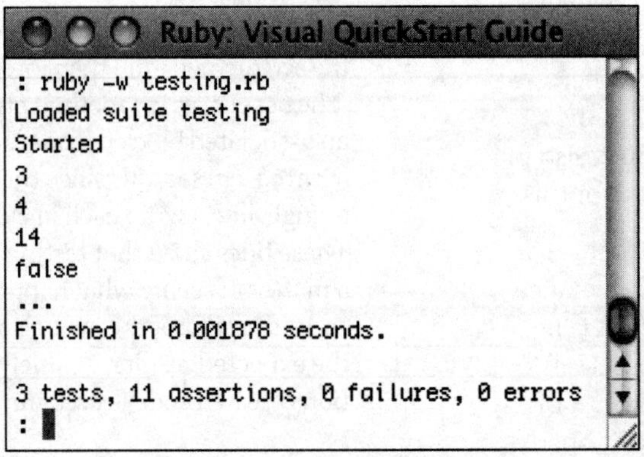

```
  ● ● ●    Ruby: Visual QuickStart Guide
: ruby -w testing.rb
Loaded suite testing
Started
3
4
14
false
...
Finished in 0.001878 seconds.

3 tests, 11 assertions, 0 failures, 0 errors
:
```

Figure 11.15 The testing results show both the output from any executed code as well as the test outcomes.

RUBYGEMS

Chapter 9, "Modules and Includes," talks about various ways that you can modularize and reuse existing code. The examples there show how to do this with code you create or with that in the Ruby Standard Library. Another option is to use *RubyGems*.

RubyGems is a package management system, which is to say that it's a way to bundle, distribute, and install libraries of related code, called *gems*. Most programming languages have similar capabilities, like PEAR and PECL in PHP or CPAN in Perl. By using a gem, you can quickly create powerful and professional applications.

This chapter starts by demonstrating how to install the RubyGems software and how to manage individual gems. From there, the chapter discusses how to use four different gems. One particular gem—Rails—is given its own full treatment in Chapter 16, "Ruby on Rails."

Installing RubyGems

Before you can install any individual gem, you need to install the RubyGems program, called gem. As of Ruby 1.9, RubyGems is automatically included in an installation of Ruby. In earlier versions, you'll need to install RubyGems separately, as is discussed in the next sequence of steps.

Before attempting to install RubyGems, you should first check if RubyGems isn't already on your computer, just to be safe. If you used the one-click installer on Windows, RubyGems will be included, and it may be pre-installed on some versions of Mac OS X and Unix/Linux as well. To see if RubyGems is installed, run this command within a command shell (**Figure 12.1**):

```
gem -v
```

If a version is returned by that command (see the figure), RubyGems is installed and you can skip to the next section of the chapter. If that command returns an error, likely along the lines of *program/command not found*, you'll need to install RubyGems. The following steps walk through generic instructions. Certain versions of Unix/Linux can install RubyGems using tools like the Red Hat Package Manager (rpm) or apt-get. For instance, RubyGems can be installed on Ubuntu Linux using sudo apt-get install rubygems (**Figure 12-02**).

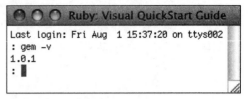

Figure 12.1 If RubyGems is already installed, the command gem -v will print the installed version.

To install RubyGems:

1. Download RubyGems.

   You can find it by going to either www.rubyforge.org/projects/rubygems or www.rubygems.org. The downloads link at the RubyGems Web site will just take you to the official project page at the RubyForge site.

   You should download the latest version, in either .zip (Windows) or .tgz (all other operating systems) format.

2. Uncompress the downloaded file.

   You should be able to accomplish this by just double-clicking the downloaded file. For Unix/Linux (and Mac OS X) users, the command-line option is:

   `tar -xzvf rubygems-version.tgz`

   Of course you must be in the same directory as the downloaded file and should replace *version* with the actual version, so that the filenames match (e.g., `rubygems-1.2.0.tgz`).

continues on next page

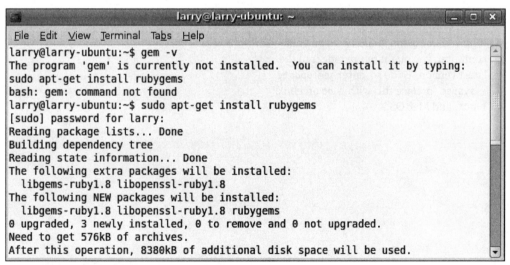

Figure 12.2 Because the *gem* command was not found on this Ubuntu Linux installation, RubyGems needs to be installed using `apt-get`.

INSTALLING RUBYGEMS

3. Move into the RubyGems directory within a command shell:

```
cd /path/to/rubygems-version
```

If you don't know what this means, see Chapter 1, "Getting Started," which discusses the similar steps that can be taken to install and test Ruby itself.

4. Type one of the following and press Enter/Return:

```
ruby setup.rb (Windows)
```

or

```
sudo ruby setup.rb (Unix, Linux,
→ and Mac OS X)
```

You use Ruby to install RubyGems, by executing the code in the `setup.rb` file. On Windows, you can execute this command without alteration. On Unix-based operating systems, which include Mac OS X, you must run the command as a superuser by prefacing it with `sudo`. You'll then need to enter the administrator's password at the prompt.

5. Confirm that RubyGems was installed by running:

```
gem -v
```

✔ Tip

■ If RubyGems came preinstalled on your computer, you ought to upgrade it to the latest version. To do so, enter `gem update --system` (preface this with `sudo` on Unix, Linux, and Mac OS X).

Managing and Installing Gems

The RubyGems software is used to manage and install individual gem packages. Its syntax is quite simple, but it must be run from the command line (a DOS or console window on Windows; a Terminal or similar application on Mac OS X, Unix, and Linux). In the next series of bullets, I detail basic RubyGem usage. Do note that any command that installs, updates, or uninstalls a package on Mac OS X, Unix, and Linux must be prefaced with sudo, so that the command is run as a superuser (**Figure 12.3**). On Windows, this is not required.

Also, you must be online in order to install or update any gem, as RubyGems will download the source code for the gem from an online server (specifically http://gems.rubyforge.org). If you're behind a proxy, you should first set that value as an environmental variable:

set HTTP_PROXY=http://proxy_url:port

Finally, when it comes to selecting which gems to install and use, factor in its:

◆ Development status (alpha, beta, stable)

◆ Activity level (the frequency of updates)

◆ Available documentation

This last consideration is particularly important, because if you can't figure out how to use a gem, then it won't be very useful to you.

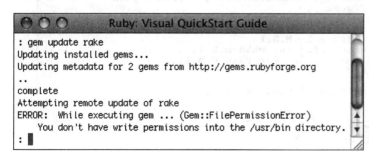

Figure 12.3 Failure to install, update, or uninstall a gem as a superuser (on Mac OS X, Unix, and Linux) may result in a permissions error.

To use RubyGems:

◆ To see a list of installed gems, type (**Figure 12.4**):

`gem list`

This command lists all of the locally available (i.e., installed) gems. If your computer came with RubyGems installed (or if it was installed as part of the one-click installer on Windows), you'll likely see something when you run this command. If you installed RubyGems yourself, you're not likely to see any.

◆ To install a gem, type:

`gem install gem_name -y`

The command `gem install gem_name` is all you need to do to install any gem. However, many gems make use of other gems, so once you install gem A, you might be notified that you also need to install gems B, C, and D. To have every required gem also be installed, add the -y (or longer --install-dependencies) option. As of version 0.9.5 of gem, -y is the default setting and does not need to be specified.

◆ To update an installed gem, type (**Figure 12.5**):

`gem update gem_name`

This command will update to the latest version any individual gem that you've already installed.

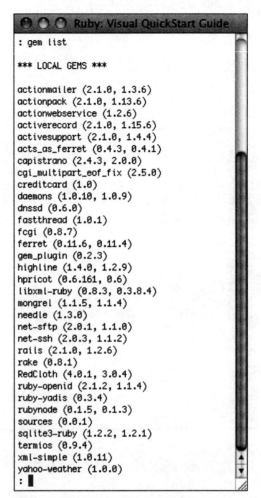

Figure 12.4 The list of gems currently installed on my Mac OS X machine.

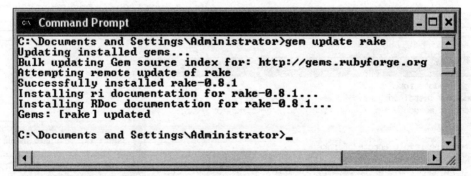

Figure 12.5 Updating a single gem.

MANAGING AND INSTALLING GEMS

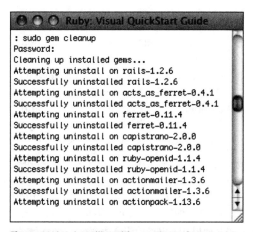

Figure 12.6 Uninstalling older versions of gems on Mac OS X (which is why sudo also has to be used).

◆ To update every installed gem, type:

`gem update`

◆ To update RubyGems itself, type:

`gem update --system`

◆ To remove an installed gem, type:

`gem uninstall gem_name`

◆ To uninstall older versions of gems, type (**Figure 12.6**):

`gem cleanup`

This command will have RubyGems remove all but the latest version of each gem when multiple have been installed. The ability to install multiple versions of the same gem is an interesting attribute of RubyGems, so understand that you may not necessarily want to remove older versions (see the sidebar "Multiple Gem Versions" for more).

◆ To search for available gems by keyword, type (**Figure 12.7**):

`gem search term --remote`

continues on next page

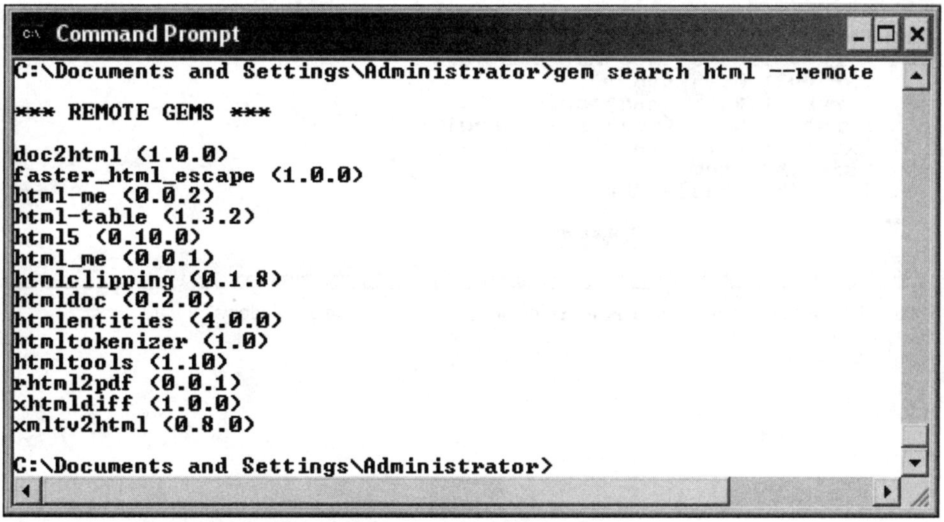

```
C:\Documents and Settings\Administrator>gem search html --remote

*** REMOTE GEMS ***

doc2html (1.0.0)
faster_html_escape (1.0.0)
html-me (0.0.2)
html-table (1.3.2)
html5 (0.10.0)
html_me (0.0.1)
htmlclipping (0.1.8)
htmldoc (0.2.0)
htmlentities (4.0.0)
htmltokenizer (1.0)
htmltools (1.10)
rhtml2pdf (0.0.1)
xhtmldiff (1.0.0)
xmltv2html (0.8.0)

C:\Documents and Settings\Administrator>
```

Figure 12.7 All of the available gems with the word *html* in their names.

The search command looks for gems whose name includes whatever term you provide (not in quotes). If you omit the --remote option, the search will look through the list of *installed* gems. If you use --remote, the search will look through every available gem, by searching the remote gem server (http://gems.rubyforge.org by default).

◆ To get help, type:

```
gem --help
```

This will return information on basic gem usage.

◆ To get help with a specific command, type:

```
gem help command
```

For example, to learn more about using the install command, type gem help install.

✔ Tips

■ Some gems will be available in multiple versions. If so, you'll be given a choice as to which version you want to install (**Figure 12.8**). Sometimes this occurs as older versions are kept available, and sometimes you'll be presented with operating system–specific options.

■ When a gem is installed, the documentation for it will also be installed so that it's viewable using RDoc and/or ri, assuming that the gem creator provides documentation in those formats.

■ You can create your own gems to build and distribute, but the subject is outside the scope of this book. For details, see www.rubygems.org/read/chapter/5.

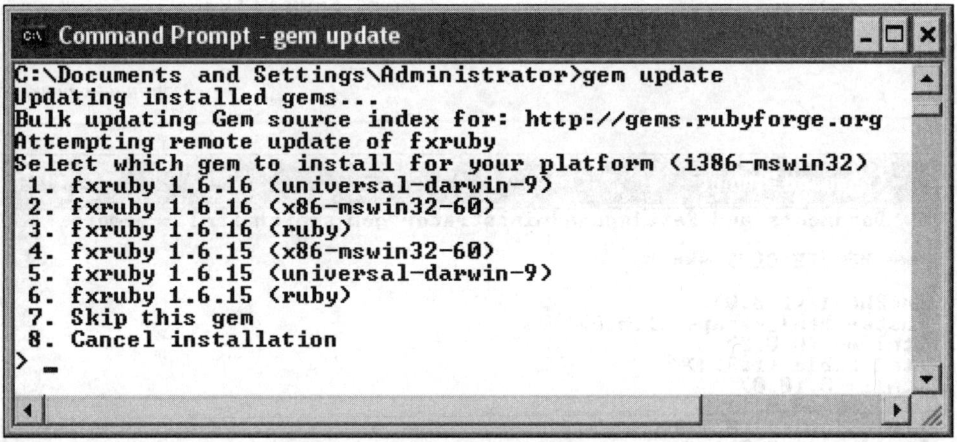

```
Command Prompt - gem update                              _ □ ✕

C:\Documents and Settings\Administrator>gem update
Updating installed gems...
Bulk updating Gem source index for: http://gems.rubyforge.org
Attempting remote update of fxruby
Select which gem to install for your platform (i386-mswin32)
 1. fxruby 1.6.16 (universal-darwin-9)
 2. fxruby 1.6.16 (x86-mswin32-60)
 3. fxruby 1.6.16 (ruby)
 4. fxruby 1.6.15 (x86-mswin32-60)
 5. fxruby 1.6.15 (universal-darwin-9)
 6. fxruby 1.6.15 (ruby)
 7. Skip this gem
 8. Cancel installation
> _
```

Figure 12.8 A list of options when it comes to installing the fxruby gem on Windows.

MANAGING AND INSTALLING GEMS

Using Gems

Once you've installed a gem onto your computer, you can make use of it in your Ruby code. How you do so depends in part on what version of Ruby you're using. In versions of Ruby before 1.9, you must first include RubyGems itself:

```
require 'rubygems'
```

Then you can require the specific gem you want to use:

```
require 'gem_name'
```

As of Ruby 1.9, RubyGems will automatically be included, so you don't need to require it, and can just include the specific gem.

In this next series of steps, I'll demonstrate how to use the yahoo-weather gem (http://rubyforge.org/projects/yahoo-weather/) within an irb session. It's a simple gem that uses Yahoo! to fetch the current weather conditions for a given U.S. zip code. (Needless to say, you must be online to use this gem.)

To use the yahoo-weather gem:

1. Install the gem (**Figure 12.9**):

   ```
   gem install yahoo-weather
   ```

   This one line will install the gem, as well as any gems it's dependent upon. If you're using an older version of RubyGems, add the -y option (it won't hurt if you use it regardless of the RubyGems version). On Mac OS X, Unix, and Linux, you must preface this command with sudo.

2. Start an irb session, if you have not already.

3. Include rubygems and yahoo-weather (**Figure 12.10**):

   ```
   require 'rubygems'
   require 'yahoo-weather'
   ```

   These two lines are required to use a gem in your Ruby code (you only have to use the second line as of Ruby 1.9). If you haven't installed RubyGems or the particular gem, you'll get errors from these lines.

   continues on next page

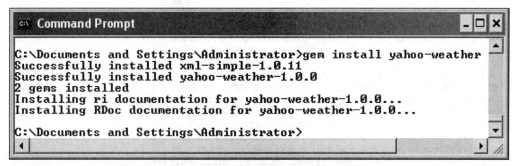

Figure 12.9 Installation of the two gems required to use yahoo-weather.

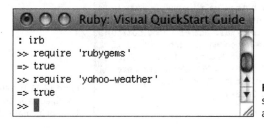

Figure 12.10 To use a gem, start by requiring rubygems and the specific gem.

USING GEMS

4. Create a `YahooWeather::Client` object:

`yw = YahooWeather::Client.new`

Different gems are used in different ways. Check the documentation for any given gem to see how to use it. Here, `yw` is an object of type `YahooWeather::Client` (where `YahooWeather` is a module and `Client` is a class defined within that module).

5. Look up the weather for a given zip code (**Figure 12.11**):

`info = yw.lookup_location('90210')`

This line performs the actual request. As you can see in the figure, the result will be a ton of data (if it worked).

```
>> >> yw = YahooWeather::Client.new
=> #<YahooWeather::Client:0x1290a58 @api_url="http://xml.weather.
yahoo.com/forecastrss">
>> info = yw.lookup_location('90210')
=> #<YahooWeather::Response:0x1279d44 @image_url="http://l.yimg.c
om/us.yimg.com/i/us/we/52/33.gif", @units=#<YahooWeather::Units:0
x12790c4 @speed="mph", @pressure="in", @distance="mi", @temperatu
re="F">, @longitude=-118.4, @request_location="90210", @condition
=#<YahooWeather::Condition:0x1278ef8 @code=33, @text="Fair", @tem
p=58, @date=Sun Oct 05 09:51:00 -0400 2008>, @location=#<YahooWea
ther::Location:0x1279c54 @city="Beverly Hills", @region="CA", @co
untry="US">, @latitude=34.08, @atmosphere=#<YahooWeather::Atmosph
ere:0x1278fac @visibility=8, @pressure=29.92, @humidity=87, @risi
ng=true>, @title="Conditions for Beverly Hills, CA at 6:51 am PDT
", @astronomy=#<YahooWeather::Astronomy:0x1279ca4 @sunset=Sun Oct
 05 18:32:00 -0400 2008, @sunrise=Sun Oct 05 06:51:00 -0400 2008>
, @description="\n<img src=\"http://l.yimg.com/us.yimg.com/i/us/w
e/52/33.gif\"/><br />\n<b>Current Conditions:</b><br />\nFair, 58
F<BR />\n<BR />\n<b>Forecast:</b><BR />\nSun - Partly Cloudy. High
: 72 Low: 59<br />\nMon - Sunny. High: 79 Low: 61<br />\n<br />\n
<a href=\"http://us.rd.yahoo.com/dailynews/rss/weather/Beverly_Hi
lls__CA/*http://weather.yahoo.com/forecast/USCA0090_f.html\">Full
 Forecast at Yahoo! Weather</a><BR />\n(provided by The Weather Ch
annel)<br/>\n", @wind=#<YahooWeather::Wind:0x1279010 @speed=3, @d
irection=320, @chill=58>, @page_url="http://us.rd.yahoo.com/daily
news/rss/weather/Beverly_Hills__CA/*http://weather.yahoo.com/fore
cast/90210_f.html", @request_url="http://xml.weather.yahoo.com/fo
recastrss?p=90210&u=f", @forecasts=[#<YahooWeather::Forecast:0x12
78354 @code=30, @low=59, @day="Sun", @text="Partly Cloudy", @high
=72, @date=Sun Oct 05 00:00:00 -0400 2008>, #<YahooWeather::Forec
ast:0x1278340 @code=32, @low=61, @day="Mon", @text="Sunny", @high
=79, @date=Mon Oct 06 00:00:00 -0400 2008>]>
>>
```

Figure 12.11 The creation of a new object type and invocation of one of its methods.

6. Print some of the returned information (**Figure 12.12**):

```
puts "#{info.title}:
#{info.condition.text} #{info.
→ condition.temp} degrees
Forecast for #{info.forecasts[0].
→ day}: #{info.forecasts[0].text}
→ #{info.forecasts[0].high} (High)
→ #{info.forecasts[0].low} (Low)"
```

You'll need to parse out the information you want from the returned result. Here, again, the gem's documentation will guide the way.

✔ Tips

- Many gems can be used independently of any Ruby code. For example, the RubyGems software, *gem*, is itself a gem.

- Windows users who installed Ruby 1.8 or earlier using the one-click installer don't technically need to require RubyGems either.

```
>> puts "#{info.title}:
#{info.condition.text} #{info.condition.temp} degrees
Forecast for #{info.forecasts[0].day}: #{info.forecasts[0].text}
#{info.forecasts[0].high} (High)
#{info.forecasts[0].low} (Low)"
Conditions for Beverly Hills, CA at 6:51 am PDT:
Fair 58 degrees
Forecast for Sun: Partly Cloudy
72 (High)
59 (Low)
=> nil
>>
```

Figure 12.12 The resulting weather report and forecast for the 90210 zip code.

Multiple Gem Versions

One of the interesting features of RubyGems is that it allows you to install multiple versions of the same gem. This is because installing a newer version of a gem does not actually replace an older version. One benefit of this feature is that you can try out new, beta versions of a gem while still keeping the older, stable version around. You can also write code that uses specific versions of a gem. To do that, invoke the `require_gem` method instead of `require`. Follow the name of the gem with an indicator or two of the version to use:

```
require_gem 'gem_name', '>=x.x'
require_gem 'gem_name', '>=x.x', '<=y.y'
```

The first line indicates that a version of *gem_name* greater than *x.x* should be included. The second line says that the version should be between *x.x* and *y.y*.

With respect to the gem versioning convention, the first number is the major version and is incremented when significant changes are made. Such changes may break existing code due to implementation differences. The second number is the minor version and reflects significant alterations while maintaining the interface (i.e., it should be backward-compatible). The third number, if one is used—*x.y.z*—is the build number, reflecting very minor changes and fixes.

The creditcard Gem

In order to provide a sense of what RubyGems has to offer, I decided to focus on three different gems in this chapter (not including yahoo-weather, which was just used for demonstration purposes). The first, creditcard (http://rubyforge.org/projects/creditcard/), provides basic credit card validation. It's very important to understand that this gem doesn't determine if a credit card is a working card or not; you'd need to use a payment gateway to determine that. Instead, this gem performs two basic tasks:

◆ Validates a number using the Luhn formula

◆ Returns or validates the card's type, based upon its number

If you're not familiar with the Luhn formula, a quick search online will provide all the details about it. In simplest terms, it's just a mathematical way to confirm that the numbers in a card match the specifications for that card's type. Let's practice using this gem within a Ruby script.

To use the creditcard gem:

1. Install the gem:

```
gem install creditcard
```

2. Create a new Ruby script in your text editor or IDE (**Script 12.1**):

```
# Script 12.1 - cc.rb
```

3. Include rubygems and creditcard:

```
require 'rubygems'
require 'creditcard'
```

Script 12.1 This script uses the creditcard gem to validate four different credit card numbers.

```
1    # Script 12.1 - cc.rb
2
3    # Include the gem:
4    require 'rubygems'
5    require 'creditcard'
6
7    # Create some credit card numbers as an
     array:
8    cc = Array.new
9    cc << '4111 1111 1111 1111'
10   cc << '5500 0000 0000 0004'
11   cc << '6011000000000004'
12   cc << '4111111111111117'
13
14   # Test each number:
15   cc.each do |n|
16       print "#{n}: "
17       puts n.creditcard? ? n.creditcard_type
         : 'invalid'
18   end
```

THE CREDITCARD GEM

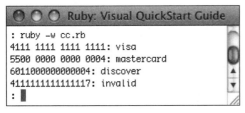

Figure 12.13 The result of validating the four potential credit card numbers.

4. Assign a couple of potential credit card numbers to an array:

```
cc = Array.new
cc << '4111 1111 1111 1111'
cc << '5500 0000 0000 0004'
cc << '6011000000000004'
cc << '4111111111111117'
```

The first three values are strings representing potentially valid Visa, MasterCard, and Discover numbers. Even though credit cards are numbers, you should create them as strings because the `creditcard` gem works by adding new methods to the `String` class. Plus, using a string, you can have spaces in the numbers, although those are optional. The last number represents an invalid credit card.

I've decided to place all of the numbers within an array so I can easily iterate through and validate them.

5. Print the validity and type of each card:

```
cc.each do |n|
    print "#{n}: "
    puts n.creditcard? ?
    → n.creditcard_type : 'invalid'
end
```

By calling the `each` iterator and using a block, each number in the array can be validated. Within the block, the number is first printed. Then either the associated credit card type, if it's a valid number, or the word *invalid* is printed.

6. Save and run the completed script (**Figure 12.13**):

✔ Tip

- The `creditcard?` method takes a card type as an optional argument. It will then return a Boolean value if the given number matches the formula for that card type:

```
'4111 1111 1111 1111'.creditcard?
→ 'visa' # true
```

THE CREDITCARD GEM

The Highline Gem

The next gem I want to demonstrate is called Highline (http://highline.rubyforge. org/). This gem helps make your Ruby scripts more professional by generating proper command-line interfaces (for those scripts that interact with a user). Highline takes basic puts and gets functionality, adds validation and then some, creating more reliable user input with little effort on your part. For example, if you need a *yes* or *no* response from the user, you could use the agree method:

```
agree('Reformat the hard drive? ')
```

This method will return true if the user entered *yes* (or *y*) and false if they entered *no* (or *n*), case-insensitive. Highline will continue to ask the question until an acceptable answer is inputted (**Figure 12.14**).

The agree method is a modified version of ask, which is the primary method for getting input from the user. Its first argument is the prompt, and its optional second argument is the type of data to allow (the default type is a string):

```
ask('Phone Extension: ', Integer)
```

You could also specify Date, DateTime, File, and Float, among others (all of this information is available in the gem's documentation).

You can associate blocks with ask, in which you establish validation parameters or otherwise adjust how the prompt works. Here's how you would set a default answer:

```
ask('Print? ') { |q| q.default = 'Yes' }
```

And here's how you could make sure that the input was an integer between 100 and 999:

```
ask('Phone Extension: ', Integer)
→ { |q| q.in = 100...999 }
```

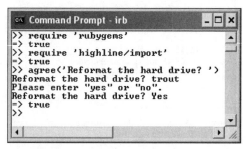

Figure 12.14 Using Highline to fetch a *yes*/*no* reply from a user.

This is how you would validate input against a regular expression:

```
ask('Email Address? ') { |q| q.validate =
→ / \A[\w.+-]+@[\w.-]+\.[a-z]{2,6}\Z/i }
```

To take input without showing what the user typed, use (**Figure 12.15**):

```
ask('Password: ') { |q| q.echo = '*' }
```

The `choose` method can be used to create menus, where you provide a list of options from which the user can select their choice.

```
choose('Replay Level', 'Next Level',
→ 'Exit')
```

You'll see an alternative way of using `choose` in this next example, which creates an interface for adding employee records. I'll define this interface as a module, so it's used without creating an instance. To keep things relatively simple, the example will implement the interface without actually doing anything with the inputted data.

```
▄▄ Command Prompt - irb                                          _ □ ✕
>> ask('Phone Extension: ', Integer)
Phone Extension: trout
You must enter a valid Integer.
?  390
=> 390
>> ask('Print? ') { |q| q.default = 'Yes' }
Print? |Yes|
=> "Yes"
>> ask('Phone Extension: ', Integer) { |q| q.in = 100...999 }
Phone Extension: 29
Your answer isn't within the expected range (included in 100...999).
?  390
=> 390
>> ask('Email Address? ') { |q| q.validate = /\A[\w.+-]+@[\w.-]+\.[a-z]{2,6}\Z/i
 }
Email Address? larry@example.com
=> "larry@example.com"
>> ask('Password: ') { |q| q.echo = '*' }
Password: ******
=> "thisis"
>>
```

Figure 12.15 Just some of the ways you can customize interactions and validate the input.

To use the Highline gem:

1. Install the gem:

```
gem install highline
```

2. Create a new Ruby script in your text editor or IDE (**Script 12.2**):

```
# Script 12.2 - employees.rb
```

3. Include rubygems and Highline:

```
require 'rubygems'
require 'Highline/import'
```

You could just require Highline, but by requiring Highline/import, ask and the other methods are brought into the current scope, making it easier to call them.

4. Begin defining the module:

```
module Employees
    def Employees.start
        Employees.create_menu
    end
```

The module will wrap up all the functionality for the employee interface example. This module will be used as a namespace, so each method must include the module's name (see Chapter 9 for details).

The start method begins the employee-input process and is the only one to be called directly outside of the module.

Script 12.2 The Highline gem can be used to create a proper command-line interface, including validation of user input.

```
1   # Script 12.2 - employees.rb
2
3   # Include the gem:
4   require 'rubygems'
5   require 'Highline/import'
6
7   # Define the module:
8   module Employees
9
10      # Method that gets the process started:
11      def Employees.start
12          Employees.create_menu
13      end
14
15      # Method that creates the menu of
        options:
16      def Employees.create_menu
17
18          # Add a spacer:
19          puts '---------------------'
20
21          # Create the menu:
22          choose do |m|
23              m.prompt = 'Select an option: '
24              m.choice(:'Add an Employee') {
                Employees.add_employee }
25              m.choice(:'View All Employees') {
                Employees.view_employees }
26              m.choice(:'Exit') { Process.exit }
27          end
28
29      end # End of create_menu
30
31      # Method for adding employees:
32      def Employees.add_employee
33
34          # Add a spacer:
35          puts '---------------------'
36
```

(script continues on next page)

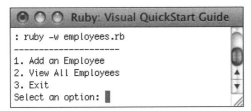

Figure 12.16 The application's menu.

Script 12.2 *continued*

```
37       # Get the info:
38       fname = ask('First Name? ') { |q|
         q.validate = /\A[a-z .'-]+\Z/i }
39       lname = ask('Last Name? ') { |q|
         q.validate = /\A[a-z .'-]+\Z/i }
40       id = ask('Employee ID? ', Integer)
         { |q| q.above = 0 }
41
42       # See if they want to add another:
43       Employees.add_employee if agree('Add
         Another? ')
44
45       # Create the menu:
46       Employees.create_menu
47
48     end # End of add_employee
49
50     # Method for viewing employees:
51     def Employees.view_employees
52
53       # Add a spacer:
54       puts '--------------------'
55
56       puts 'Here is where you would see all
         the employees.'
57       Employees.create_menu
58     end
59
60   end # End of Employees module.
61
62   # Start the ball rolling:
63   Employees.start
```

5. Define the `create_menu` method:

```
def Employees.create_menu
  puts '--------------------'
  choose do |m|
    m.prompt = 'Select an option:'
    m.choice(:'Add an Employee') {
    → Employees.add_employee }
    m.choice(:'View All Employees')
    → { Employees.view_employees }
    m.choice(:'Exit') { Process.
    → exit }
  end
end # End of create_menu
```

This method will generate a menu of options: *Add an Employee*, *View All Employees*, and *Exit* (**Figure 12.16**). It begins by creating a spacer line, just to visually break up the output. Then the `choose` method is used to create and manage a menu, using a slightly different syntax than already demonstrated. Within a `do` block, the `m` object will refer to the menu. First, its prompt is defined (see the bottom of Figure 12.16). Then three choices are presented. For each, a symbol is used. Because the symbol represents the printed choice the user will see, the values are wrapped in quotes so that spaces may be used (see Chapter 3, "Simple Types," for more on symbols). For each choice, an associated block indicates what should be done when the user selects that option. For the first two choices, other module methods will be called. For the last choice, the `Process.exit` method will be called, which terminates the script. In a complete application, the script would probably perform some post-input tasks instead, like storing the employees in a database or text file.

continues on next page

THE HIGHLINE GEM

6. Begin the method for adding employees:

```
def Employees.add_employee
  puts '---------------------'
  fname = ask('First Name? ') { |q|
→ q.validate = /\A[a-z .'-]+\Z/i }
  lname = ask('Last Name? ') { |q|
→ q.validate = /\A[a-z .'-]+\Z/i }
  id = ask('Employee ID? ', Integer)
→ { |q| q.above = 0 }
```

For each employee, three pieces of information will be requested: their first name, their last name, and their employee ID. The two names will be validated against regular expressions that allow for the letters *A* through *Z* (case-insensitive), spaces, periods, apostrophes, and hyphens. The user will be re-prompted until the submitted data passes the validation (**Figure 12.17**).

For the employee ID, the input must be an integer with a value greater than 0 (in Highline terms, this means the value must be *above* 0). The ID has no upper limit.

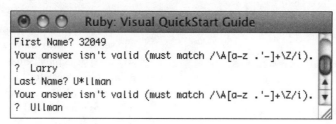

Figure 12.17 The employee's name is validated upon input.

7. Complete the `add_employee` method:

```
Employees.add_employee if
→ agree('Add Another? ')
Employees.create_menu
end # End of add_employee
```

After entering all of the information for an employee, the user is asked if they'd like to add another (**Figure 12.18**). If they answer *yes*, this same method will be called again. Once they answer *no*, the menu will be redisplayed.

Again, in a fully formed example, something would be done with the submitted input.

8. Create the `view_employees` method:

```
def Employees.view_employees
    puts '----------------------'
    puts 'Here is where you would see
    → all the employees.'
    Employees.create_menu
end
```

After printing a spacer and a message, this method calls the `create_menu` method again (**Figure 12.19**). If the submitted employees were actually stored somehow, this method would display that information instead.

9. Complete and use the module:

```
end
Employees.start
```

With the current structure of the module, this one line starts the process.

10. Save and run the completed script.

✔ Tip

■ Just as `ask` is a seriously upgraded version of `gets`, `say` is a modified version of `puts`. It takes a string as its lone argument. If the string ends with a space or tab, the string will be printed without an additional newline (as if you used `print`). Otherwise, a newline will be appended, as if you used `puts`.

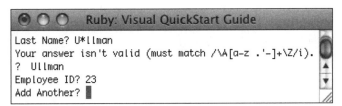

Figure 12.18 After entering an employee record, the user is given the choice of adding another.

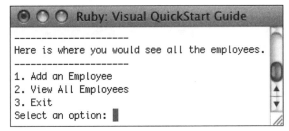

Figure 12.19 The result after selecting the *View All Employees* option.

The RedCloth Gem

The final gem this chapter spotlights is RedCloth (www.whytheluckystiff.net/ruby/redcloth/). RedCloth provides an interface for using *Textile* in Ruby. Textile (www.textism.com/tools/textile/) is a simple way to mark up text so that it can be later exported as HTML. With Textile, you get the benefit of having a document that's easy to create and read, but that can still be used to generate a relatively attractive Web page.

Table 12.1 lists some basic Textile formatting options. You can find many others at the Textile Web site or at www.redcloth.org/textile. Textile also supports CSS, creating tables, placing images, and more.

To output the text as HTML, use the RedCloth to_html method:

```
text = RedCloth.new(TextileText)
text.to_html
```

To use the RedCloth gem:

1. Install the gem:

   ```
   gem install RedCloth
   ```

   Note that RedCloth uses a capital *R* and *C*. Attempts to install or require *redcloth* will fail.

Table 12.1

Textile Conversions	
TEXTILE	HTML
h1. Header	<h1>Header</h1>
word	word
__word__	<i>word</i>
word	word
word	word
"Link":URL	<a href="URL">Link</a>
* list item	<ul><li>list item</li></ul>
# list item	<ol><li>list item</li></ol>
p. Text	<p>Text</p>

Script 12.3 This script creates some text marked up using Textile, which is then outputted as HTML thanks to the RedCloth gem.

```
        ●●●                      📄 Script
1       # Script 12.3 - html.rb
2
3       # Include the gems:
4       require 'rubygems'
5       require 'RedCloth'
6
7       # Create a string of marked-up text:
8       text = 'h1. The RedCloth Gem
9
10      p. The "RedCloth Gem":http://
        whytheluckystiff.net/ruby/redcloth/
        makes it possible to use _Textile_ in Ruby.
11
12      p. Textile has several benefits:
13      # Easy to write
14      # Easy to read
15      # Easy to generate valid HTML'
16
17      # Create the RedCloth object:
18      rc = RedCloth.new(text)
19
20      # Output as is:
21      puts rc
22      puts '------------'
23
24      # Output as HTML:
25      puts rc.to_html
```

2. Create a new Ruby script in your text editor or IDE (**Script 12.3**):

   ```
   # Script 12.3 - html.rb
   ```

3. Include `rubygems` and `RedCloth`:

   ```
   require 'rubygems'
   require 'RedCloth'
   ```

4. Define some marked-up text:

   ```
   text = 'h1. The RedCloth Gem

   p. The "RedCloth Gem":http://
   → whytheluckystiff.net/ruby/
   → redcloth/ makes it possible
   → to use _Textile_ in Ruby.

   p. Textile has several benefits:

   # Easy to write

   # Easy to read

   # Easy to generate valid HTML'
   ```

   Textile is nice, but you have to pay close attention to the syntax. For example, to place just *The RedCloth Gem* in header tags, it must be followed by a blank line.

5. Create the `RedCloth` object:

   ```
   rc = RedCloth.new(text)
   ```

   That's all there is to it! Now `rc` is an object of **RedCloth** type, which is really just a string with some added methods. This means you can still use any standard **String** methods on `rc`.

6. Output the original text and the text as HTML:

   ```
   puts rc
   puts '------------'
   puts rc.to_html
   ```

   Since `rc` is a string, it can be printed by just referencing the object. To convert the marked-up text to HTML, invoke the `to_html` method.

   continues on next page

7. Save and run the completed script (**Figure 12.20**).

When I was writing this book, there seemed to be a bug in the current version of RedCloth (4.0.1), resulting in lots of warnings when the to_html method is called. To avoid those, execute the script using just `ruby html.rb`, without the `-w` option.

8. To view the text as rendered HTML, load it in a Web browser (**Figure 12.21**).

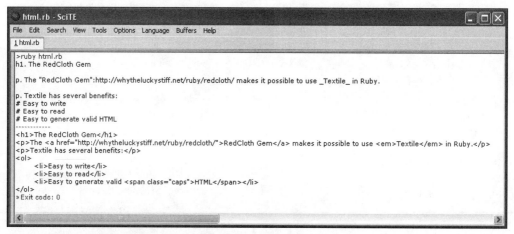

Figure 12.20 The original, marked-up text and its HTML equivalent.

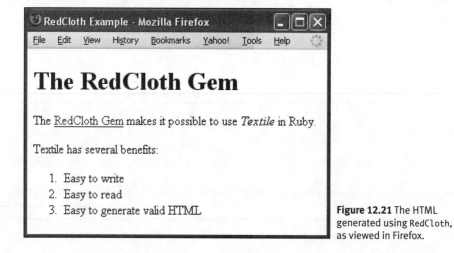

Figure 12.21 The HTML generated using RedCloth, as viewed in Firefox.

13

DIRECTORIES AND FILES

Interacting with the directories and files found on the computer is a standard use of nearly every programming language. As with many things in Ruby, once you're familiar with the basic concepts, directory- and file-related tasks are easily undertaken, with a minimum of code. And, of course, there are several ways you can go about most operations.

This chapter begins by covering the basic information you'll need to know to follow the examples herein. Next, you'll see how to view the contents of a directory. The following two subjects discuss various directory and file properties, like their size, modification times, and permissions. Then you'll see how to create, move, copy, and delete both directories and files. The final three sections of the chapter focus on reading from and writing to files.

The Basics

Working with directories and files in Ruby is not hard, but there are some basic terms and ideas that you must first know. Most of the functionality for working with directories and files is defined within the `Dir` and `File` classes. You can use either by creating an object of that type, that references a given directory or file, or by using the class' methods directly. Generally speaking, if you'll only perform a single task with a file or directory, invoking the class methods without creating an object is the norm. If you'll need to repeatedly refer to a file or directory, creating an object makes more sense:

```
f = File.new('somefile')
d = Dir.new('somedir')
```

A second consideration when deciding whether or not to create `Dir` and `File` objects is that many of the methods involved are *class methods*, not *instance methods* (see Chapter 8, "Inheritance and More"). Only instance methods can be invoked through an object.

There are two ways of referring to any file or directory on the computer: using an *absolute* or *relative* path. An absolute path begins at the root of the computer:

◆ `C:\ruby\somefile.rb` (Windows)

◆ `/Users/larry/somefile.rb` (Mac OS X).

A relative path will not start with the root of the computer—`C:\` or `/`. Instead it might be relative to the current working directory (**Figure 13.1**):

◆ `fileA.rb` (this directory)

◆ `dirB/fileB.rb` (inside `dirB`)

◆ `../fileC.rb` (inside parent directory)

◆ `../dirD/fileD.rb` (inside parallel directory)

Two periods together represent the current directory's parent folder. A single period by itself represents the current directory. If a *file's name* begins with a single period, the file is hidden (on Unix, Linux, and Mac OS X).

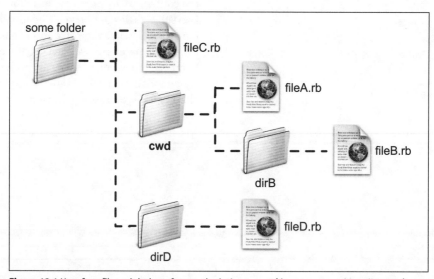

Figure 13.1 How four files might be referenced relative to `cwd` (the current working directory).

Table 13.1

Filename-Related Methods	
METHOD	RETURNS
basename	Just the filename
dirname	Just the directory name
extname	The file's extension
split	An array of the directory and file names

It technically doesn't matter whether you use a relative or an absolute path, so long as the path is accurate. In this chapter, I'll often use something like */path/to/file_or_dir* as a placeholder, which will need to be replaced with an actual and proper relative or absolute pathname in your Ruby code.

The last thing to know, before getting into some code, involves the separator used in paths. Windows uses a backslash (\ ) to separate files and directories, whereas Mac OS X, Unix, and Linux use a forward slash (/). But Ruby allows you to use a forward slash for all operating systems, including Windows (in fact, it's preferred). So `C:/ruby/somefile.rb` could be a valid reference, even on Windows Vista.

When it comes to files and directories, the first two methods to learn about are `pwd` and `chdir`. The first method, which is short for *print working directory*, returns the current directory (as does the synonym `getwd`). The second method, which is short for *change directory*, changes the current directory:

```
here = Dir.pwd
Dir.chdir('/path/to/directory')
```

With respect to files, **Table 13.1** lists four methods used to parse information from a file's path. All are class methods that take a string—an absolute or relative path to a directory or file—as an argument. The following set of steps will walk you through some simple uses of these within `irb`.

To practice the basics:

1. Open an irb session.

2. Print the current working directory:

   puts Dir.pwd

   The value printed will depend upon your operating system and environment.

3. Change the current working directory (**Figure 13.2**):

   Dir.chdir('/path/to/directory')

   This is a step you might take if there are a number of operations to be performed within another directory, saving you from adding that part of the directory's path to each command.

4. Create a string that contains the pathname for a file or directory on your computer:

   f = '/path/to/filename'

   On my computer, I'll use a reference to a Ruby script created in an earlier chapter (as you'll see in the next figure). This variable, f, is not a File object; it's just a string that will be used by the file methods.

5. Print some information about the file identified in Step 4 (**Figure 13.3**):

   puts File.basename(f)

   puts File.dirname(f)

   puts File.extname(f)

   puts File.split(f)

   These four methods are all invoked through the File class. The argument for each is the string that contains the path to a file, as defined in Step 4.

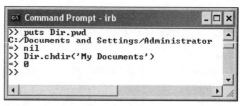

Figure 13.2 The current working directory is first printed, then changed.

Figure 13.3 A reference is first made to a file located within the ruby subdirectory. Then information about that file is returned using four different File methods.

✔ Tips

- If using backslashes within double quotation marks, you must use two backslashes. This is because a single backslash is the escape character. So a file path on Windows could be represented as 'C:/ruby/somefile.rb', 'C:\ruby\somefile.rb', or "C:\\ruby\\somefile.rb".

- The basename method takes an optional second argument, representing the string that appears at end of the file's name (like an extension). The method then returns the file's name without that string:

  puts File.basename('somefile.rb',
  → '.rb') # somefile

- The expand_path method returns an absolute path for a directory or file.

THE BASICS

Accessing Directory Contents

To list the files and directories found within a directory, you can use `entries` or `foreach`. The former returns an array of values; the latter is an iterator that you tie to a block (**Figure 13.4**):

```
puts Dir.entries('/Users/larryullman/
→ Desktop').inspect
Dir.foreach('/Users/larryullman/
→ Desktop') { |item| puts item }
```

An alternative way to access a directory's contents is to use the `Dir` class' array operator. You can use it to find items that match a pattern. This isn't a pattern in the regular expression sense, but rather a more minimal version, where `*` is a wildcard that matches any character or number of characters, `?` matches a single character, and `**` matches any number of directories:

```
contents = Dir['/Users/larryullman/*']
```

Now `contents` is an array of every visible item found within `/Users/larryullman`. Unlike the `entries` and `foreach` methods,

this approach can be used to return the absolute path of each found item (if an absolute path is provided to the method, as in the above). Also, this approach may omit any hidden files (like `.DS_Store` and `.localized` in Figure 13.4), and representations of the current (`.`) and parent (`..`) directories.

Another way you might use the array operator is to limit the returned items to those with a certain name. For example, if you want to find all of the PNG (Portable Network Graphics) files within a certain directory, you would use:

```
pngs = Dir['/path/to/folder/*.png']
```

The `glob` method achieves the same result but can be used with a block instead of returning an array:

```
Dir.glob('/path/to/folder/*.png') {
→ |item| puts item }
```

The `glob` method can also be applied to hidden files—those beginning with a period—if passed a second argument, the constant `File::FNM_DOTMATCH`.

```
Dir.glob('/path/to/folder/*.rb', File::
→ FNM_DOTMATCH) { |item| puts item }
```

```
Ruby: Visual QuickStart Guide

>> puts Dir.entries('/Users/larryullman/Desktop').inspect
[".", "..", ".DS_Store", ".localized", "Fig 13-02.tif", "Fig 13-03.tif",
 "Hide", "Picture 1.tif", "Shortcut to ruby.lnk", "Videos"]
=> nil
>> Dir.foreach('/Users/larryullman/Desktop') { |item| puts item }
.
..
.DS_Store
.localized
Fig 13-02.tif
Fig 13-03.tif
Hide
Picture 1.tif
Shortcut to ruby.lnk
Videos
=> nil
>>
```

Figure 13.4 The contents of my desktop, returned as both an array and as individual items.

To list directory contents:

1. Start an irb session, if you have not already.

2. List every item in a directory (**Figure 13.5**):

   ```
   Dir.foreach('/path/to/dir')
   → { |item| puts item }
   ```

   This is kind of the standard way to list an entire directory's contents. Change the path to something that would work for your computer.

3. List only the directories and visible files in the same directory as that in Step 1 (**Figure 13.6**):

   ```
   Dir.glob('/path/to/dir/*') { |item|
   → puts item }
   ```

   The glob method does not show hidden files (on non-Windows systems) by default, so it's sometimes a better choice than foreach. However, it expects to match a pattern, so to show everything (visible) within a directory, use the wildcard character. Using just '/path/to/dir' will return nil.

```
>> >> Dir.foreach('/Users/larryullman/Pictures') { |item| puts item }
.
..
.DS_Store
.localized
0013.jpg
Aperture Library.aplibrary
Art
Design
Desktop.ini
figures
Humor
iChat Icons
iPhoto Library
Katamari
Movies
Nature
Sample Pictures.lnk
trixie.jpg
trout.JPG
Ultrasounds
Urban
Web Site Test images
=> nil
>>
```

Figure 13.5 The contents of my Pictures directory, including hidden items and links.

```
>> >> Dir.glob('/Users/larryullman/Pictures/*') { |item| puts item }
/Users/larryullman/Pictures/0013.jpg
/Users/larryullman/Pictures/Aperture Library.aplibrary
/Users/larryullman/Pictures/Art
/Users/larryullman/Pictures/Design
/Users/larryullman/Pictures/Desktop.ini
/Users/larryullman/Pictures/figures
/Users/larryullman/Pictures/Humor
/Users/larryullman/Pictures/iChat Icons
/Users/larryullman/Pictures/iPhoto Library
/Users/larryullman/Pictures/Katamari
/Users/larryullman/Pictures/Movies
/Users/larryullman/Pictures/Nature
/Users/larryullman/Pictures/Sample Pictures.lnk
/Users/larryullman/Pictures/trixie.jpg
/Users/larryullman/Pictures/trout.JPG
/Users/larryullman/Pictures/Ultrasounds
/Users/larryullman/Pictures/Urban
/Users/larryullman/Pictures/Web Site Test images
=> nil
>>
```

Figure 13.6 The contents of my Pictures directory, without showing hidden items, a single period, or a double period (compare with Figure 13.5).

ACCESSING DIRECTORY CONTENTS

This approach will also return the full path for every item in the directory, unlike foreach.

4. Find all of the Ruby scripts within a given directory (**Figure 13.7**):

```
Dir.glob('/path/to/dir/**/*.rb') {
→ |item| puts item }
```

The glob method can navigate through subdirectories if you use ******, as in the figure.

5. Store that list of Ruby scripts in an array (**Figure 13.8**):

```
scripts = Dir['/path/to/dir/**/*.rb']
```

To return an array of values, you can use either **entries** or the array operator. But to match a pattern, you have to use the array operator.

✔ Tips

- Remember that you can shorten some of the paths used in the examples by calling Dir.chdir to move into a directory first.

- Odd as it may seem, the methods that return a directory's contents will not do so in any guaranteed order.

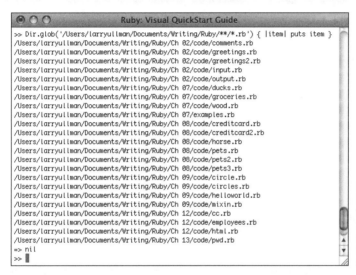

Figure 13.7 This is a listing of all of the files with an .rb extension found within my Ruby directory (the folder for this book) and its subdirectories.

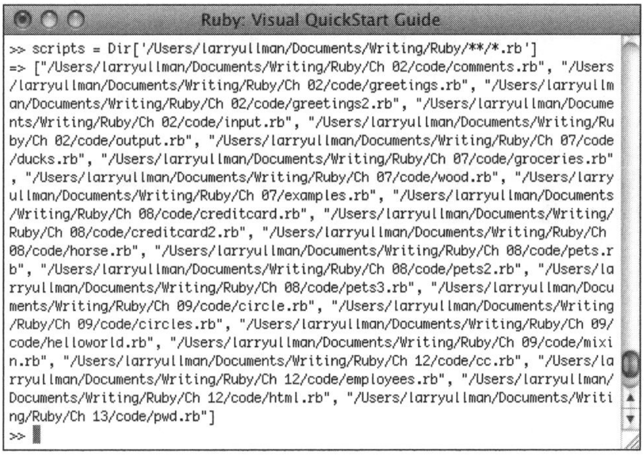

Figure 13.8 The same list as in Figure 13.7, returned as an array.

Directory and File Properties

There are a number of methods built into Ruby for returning information about a file or a directory. Some of these return Boolean values, indicating if the item has a certain property (**Table 13.2**).

Even though these are all `File` class methods, they can be applied to both files and directories alike:

```
File.directory?('/path/to/dir') # true
File.file?('/path/to/dir') # false
```

Along with these, there are two methods that return timestamps associated with a file or directory. The `mtime` method returns the last modification date and time, whereas `atime` returns the last time the file or directory was accessed. Both return a `Time` object (see Chapter 3, "Simple Types").

```
puts File.mtime('/path/to/dir')
puts File.atime('/path/to/file')
```

The `size` method returns a file's size in bytes. Although it can be applied to directories, it won't necessarily be accurate, as it doesn't compute the size of a directory's subfolders.

To find out all of this information for a file or directory in one action, use the `stat` method:

```
info = File.stat('/path/to/file_or_dir')
```

This method returns an object of type `File::Stat` (i.e., the `Stat` class defined within the `File` module). To such an object you can apply the `atime`, `directory?`, `file?`, `mtime?`, `size`, `symlink?`, `zero?` and other methods, but without any arguments:

```
puts info.directory?
puts info.size
puts info.mtime
```

Table 13.2

Condition Methods	
METHOD	RETURNS TRUE IF THE ITEM…
directory?	exists and is a directory
exist?	exists
file?	exists and is a file
symlink?	exists and is a symbolic link
zero?	is empty

To view file and directory properties:

1. Start an irb session, if you have not already.

2. Assign a file or directory's path to a string:

   ```
   item = '/path/to/file_or_dir'
   ```

3. Display some of the item's properties using the methods listed in Table 13.2 (**Figure 13.9**):

   ```
   puts File.directory?(item)
   puts File.file?(item)
   puts File.exist?(item)
   ```

   The first two method calls will return opposite results, depending upon whether the item in question is a file or a directory. The third method will return true if the item exists. You may find yourself referring to files and directories that don't yet exist because the code will create them at a later point.

4. Print the item's size and last modification date and time (**Figure 13.10**):

   ```
   puts File.size(item)
   puts File.mtime(item)
   ```

   Remember that if the item in question is a directory, size will return an invalid number.

continues on next page

```
>> item = 'C:\Documents and Settings\Administrator\My Documents\ruby'
=> "C:\\Documents and Settings\\Administrator\\My Documents\\ruby"
>> puts File.directory?(item)
true
=> nil
>> puts File.file?(item)
false
=> nil
>> puts File.exist?(item)
true
=> nil
>>
```

Figure 13.9 Some of the properties of my ruby directory on my Windows computer.

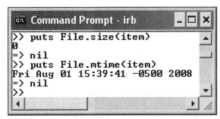

```
>> puts File.size(item)
0
=> nil
>> puts File.mtime(item)
Fri Aug 01 15:39:41 -0500 2008
=> nil
>>
```

Figure 13.10 The size method's returned value of 0 for this directory is incorrect, but the mtime value is right.

DIRECTORY AND FILE PROPERTIES

5. Invoke the stat method and then redisplay some of the item's properties (**Figure 13.11**):

```
info = File.stat(item)
puts info.file?
puts info.size
puts info.mtime
```

This is just another way of accessing the same information obtained by calling the individual methods separately.

✔ Tips

■ The size? method (with a question mark) returns a file's size in bytes or nil if the file is empty.

■ The lstat method, unlike stat, does not follow symbolic links. Instead, it will return all of the information about the link itself.

■ The ftype method returns a string—*link*, *file*, *directory*—indicating the type of thing that an item is.

■ The utime method can be used to set a file's or directory's access and modification times.

■ The identical? method returns true if the two named files both exist and refer to the exact same file. It even follows symbolic links and aliases:

```
File.identical?('C:/ruby/somedir/
→ somefile.rb', '../somefile.rb')
```

■ The compare method returns true if two named files have the exact same contents.

■ The File::Stat object returned by the stat method has a defined comparison operator (<=>). This means that, after creating File::Stat references to two files, you can compare them by their modification times.

DIRECTORY AND FILE PROPERTIES

```
>> info = File.stat(item)
=> #<File::Stat dev=0x2, ino=0, mode=040755, nlink=1, uid=0, gid=0, rdev=0x2, si
ze=0, blksize=nil, blocks=nil, atime=Tue Aug 12 14:44:38 -0500 2008, mtime=Fri A
ug 01 15:39:41 -0500 2008, ctime=Thu May 22 19:48:54 -0500 2008>
>> puts info.file?
false
=> nil
>> puts info.size
0
=> nil
>> puts info.mtime
Fri Aug 01 15:39:41 -0500 2008
=> nil
>>
```

Figure 13.11 Some of the same information for the directory as in Figure 13.10, retrieved via a File.stat call.

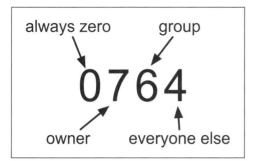

Figure 13.12 A file or directory's permissions can be represented by a four-digit number like this one.

Permissions

An important aspect of working with files and directories is the comprehension of *permissions*. Permissions dictate who can do what with an item on the computer. For files, it's a question of who can read from, write to, or execute them. For directories, it's a question of who can read from (i.e., view their contents), write to (alter their contents), or search them. Unix, Linux, and Mac OS X have a more defined and consistent permissions system, so I'll address those first.

A file or directory's permissions on these systems can be represented by an octal (base-8) number, which is four digits long and always starts with a 0 (**Figure 13.12**). The second number represents the permissions for the item's owner; the third number represents the permissions for the owner's group (of users); and the fourth number represents the permissions for everyone else (aka, the *world*). For a file or directory you create, the owner will be you, the group will be the group that your user account is a part of. For example, on Mac OS X, standard users are part of the *staff* group.

To determine the values of the second through fourth digits, you'll add up three significant numbers. The number 4 represents permission to read; the number 2 represents permission to write; and, the number 1 represents permission to execute (for files) or search (for directories). These three numbers can be added together to create values from 0, meaning no permissions are granted, to 7, meaning everything is allowed. For example, 4 means only reading is allowed and 6 (or 4 + 2) means reading and writing are allowed.

Taking all of this information together, then, the number 0744 means that the owner can do anything with a file or directory but other group members and everyone else can only read it. And the number 0666 means that

PERMISSIONS

anyone can read from or write to the item, but no one can execute or search it.

On Unix, Linux, and Mac OS X, you can set an item's permissions using the chmod (change mode) and chown (change owner) commands. On Mac OS X, you can also use the Finder's Get Info window (**Figure 13.13**).

Windows uses an alternative method for managing permissions, and it changes in different releases of the OS. It also depends upon whether you're using a "home" or "professional" release, what service pack you've installed, and whether you've enabled file sharing. For these reasons, it's impossible to go into detail on Windows permissions in this chapter. To learn more about the permissions system for your particular version of Windows, you can use your computer's help system for details, or search the Web. That being said, you should be able to follow all of the steps in this chapter without touching the Windows permissions system at all.

To manipulate the permissions that a file or directory has, you can use chmod:

```
File.chmod(mode, '/path/to/file')
```

The *mode* value is the octal four-digit number described already. Here's how Ruby would be used to make a text file writable by its owner and readable by everyone else:

```
File.chmod(0644, 'somefile.txt')
```

This will only work if Ruby, which is to say the user that is executing the Ruby code, has the authority to change the file's permissions. Because Windows doesn't use that permissions system, this method is not usable on that operating system.

To change the ownership of a file, use chown:

```
File.chown(owner_id, group_id, '/path/
→ to/file')
```

Again, this method is not available on Windows. The first two arguments are numeric values representing the owner and group.

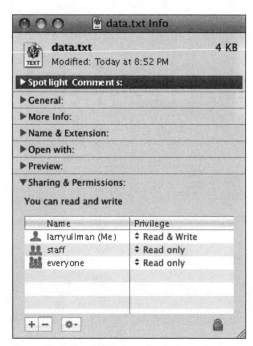

Figure 13.13 Mac OS X's Get Info window contains a Sharing & Permissions section in which a file or directory's privileges can be managed.

Table 13.3

Permissions Methods	
METHOD	**RETURNS TRUE IF THE ITEM…**
executable?	is executable
readable?	is readable
world_readable?	can be read by anyone
world_writable?	can be written to by anyone
writable?	is writable

Script 13.1 The data in this file will be read in by Ruby code later in the chapter.

```
1    4,Jack
2    8,John
3    15,Kate
4    16,Sawyer
5    23,Hugo
6    42,Charlie
```

The chmod and chown methods are available as both class and instance methods, so they can be used with or without an object. If applying either to a File object, omit the filename from the list of arguments:

```
f = File.new('/path/to/file')
f.chmod(0755)
f.chown(100, 1)
```

Most of the information in this section of the chapter only pertains to Unix, Linux, and Mac OS X, but there are some permissions-related methods in Ruby that are platform-independent (**Table 13.3**). Those methods can be used to test a file or directory's permissions before attempting to do something with it.

Finally, the File::Stat object returned by a stat method call has information regarding the file or directory's permissions. You can find the item's accessibility in the executable?, readable?, and writable? methods. The mode method returns an integer representation of the file's permissions.

To view file and directory permissions:

1. Using any text editor or IDE, create a blank text file.

   To practice working with a file's permissions, I'll create a test file.

2. Add a slew of information to the text file (**Script 13.1**):

   4,Jack

   8,John

   15,Kate

   16,Sawyer

   23,Hugo

   42,Charlie

   This is just a list of numbers and names, separated by commas, each on its own line. This data will be used by another example later in the chapter.

continues on next page

PERMISSIONS

3. Save the file as data.txt.

Save the file anywhere on your computer that it makes sense, perhaps in a directory where you also store your Ruby scripts.

4. In an irb session, run the stat method on the data.txt file:

info = File.stat('/path/to/data.txt')

As discussed in the preceding section of the chapter, File.stat returns a File:: Stat object which contains lots of information about a file or directory.

5. Display information about the file's permissions (**Figure 13.14**):

puts info.readable?

puts info.writable?

puts info.executable?

What you're hoping to see, in order to follow other steps later in the chapter, is that the file is both readable and writable.

6. If the results in Step 5 don't indicate that the file is writable, change its permissions so that it is.

On Unix, Linux, and Mac OS X, you should be able to change the permissions by typing:

File.chmod(0766, '/path/to/data.txt')

On Windows, if the file is indicated as being unwritable, you'll need to see your operating system's help files (or search the Web) for instructions.

✔ Tips

■ The File::Stat object also has gid and uid methods, which return the group and user ID, respectively, for a file or directory.

■ The chmod method can take any number of files as arguments:

File.chmod(0766, 'file1', 'file2', → 'file3')

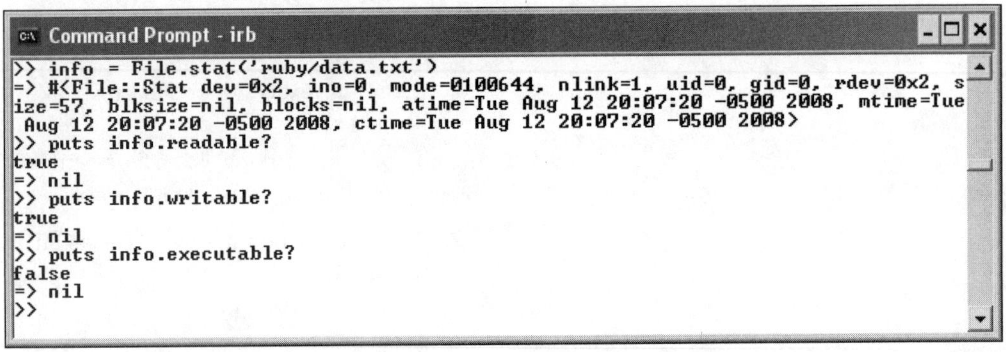

Figure 13.14 Some of the permissions for the just-created data.txt file (Script 13.1).

Creating, Moving, Copying, and Deleting

The `File` and `Dir` classes define methods for creating, moving, copying, and deleting files and directories. However, the `FileUtils` module in the Ruby Standard Library has the preferred methods for performing these tasks. To use those, start by including that module:

```
require 'FileUtils'
```

(See Chapter 9, "Modules and Includes," for more on the Standard Library and including files.)

To create a new directory, use the `mkdir` (*make directory*) method:

```
FileUtils.mkdir('/path/to/dirname')
```

To create a directory and possibly any parent directories that don't exist, use `mkdirs` or the synonymous `mkdir_p`:

```
FileUtils.mkdirs('/path/to/dirname')
```

That line will create the `dirname` directory as well as `to` and `path`, if they don't exist.

To create a file, you will normally use the methods outlined later in the chapter, but you can create one by invoking the `touch` method:

```
FileUtils.touch('/path/to/filename')
```

To move a file from one location to another, use the `mv` or synonymous `move` method:

```
FileUtils.mv(source, dest)
```

The first argument should be a file or an array of files. The second should be a file or a directory:

```
FileUtils.mv('somefile', '/path/to/
→ somefile')
FileUtils.mv('somefile', '/path/to/')
```

If you use the file/file combination, you'll move the file from the one location to the other, with the given name. You can also use this method to rename a file:

```
FileUtils.move('somefile', 'newname')
```

If you use file(s)/directory, the file(s) will be moved to the other directory, retaining the same filename(s).

To make a copy of a file, use the `cp` or synonymous `copy` method:

```
FileUtils.cp('somefile', '/path/to/
→ somefile')
FileUtils.cp('somefile', '/path/to/')
```

If the destination is a directory, you can use `cp` to copy a list of files.

To make a copy of a directory, use `cp_r` (short for *copy recursively*):

```
FileUtils.cp_r('somedir', '/path/to/')
```

To create a link to a file or a directory, use `ln` or `ln_s`. The former creates a hard link, the latter a symbolic link (this is a Unix convention with a somewhat subtle distinction).

```
FileUtils.ln('/path/to/dest', '/path/
→ to/link')
```

Finally, to remove an existing file, use `rm` or the synonymous `remove` method:

```
FileUtils.rm('/path/to/file')
```

To remove an existing directory, including all of its contents, use `remove_dir`:

```
FileUtils.remove_dir('/path/to/dir')
```

As a final note, understand that these methods will only work if Ruby has permission to make the requested change. Normally this means that the user executing the Ruby code must have write permissions on the directories involved (because, for example, creating, moving, or deleting a file is a way of "writing" to a directory).

To manipulate files and directories:

1. Start an `irb` session, if you have not already.

2. Create a new directory:

```
require 'FileUtils'
FileUtils.mkdir('/path/to/testdir')
```

To make use of a Standard Library, it must first be included. Then invoke the `mkdir` method to create the new directory. Create the directory in any logical place on your computer, but name it `testdir`, assuming you don't already have a directory with that name in that location.

3. Copy the `data.txt` file (Script 13.1) to the new directory:

```
Dir.chdir('/path/to/testdir')
FileUtils.cp('/path/to/data.txt',
→ '.')
```

To simplify the code in the remaining steps, I start by moving into the new directory by using `Dir.chdir`. Then I use `cp` to copy `data.txt` into the current directory, represented by a single period.

4. Confirm the contents of the new directory (**Figure 13.15**):

```
puts Dir.entries('.')
```

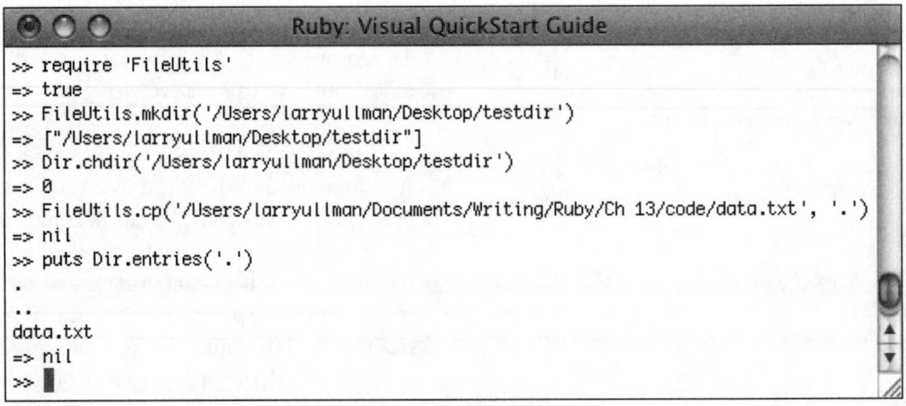

```
● ○ ○                Ruby: Visual QuickStart Guide
>> require 'FileUtils'
=> true
>> FileUtils.mkdir('/Users/larryullman/Desktop/testdir')
=> ["/Users/larryullman/Desktop/testdir"]
>> Dir.chdir('/Users/larryullman/Desktop/testdir')
=> 0
>> FileUtils.cp('/Users/larryullman/Documents/Writing/Ruby/Ch 13/code/data.txt', '.')
=> nil
>> puts Dir.entries('.')
.
..
data.txt
=> nil
>>
```

Figure 13.15 A new directory is created and the `data.txt` file is copied there.

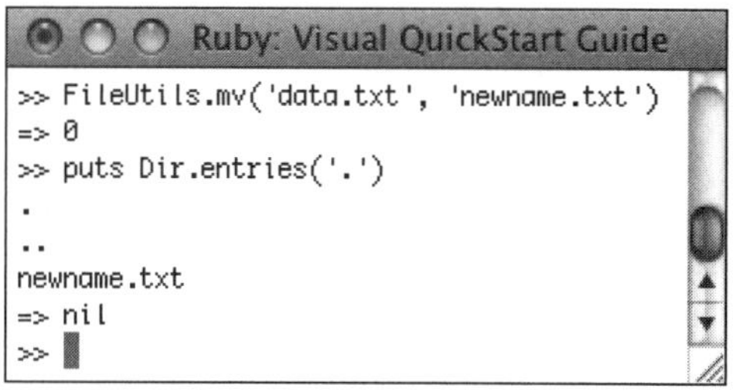

Figure 13.16 The data.txt file has been renamed to newname.txt.

Temporary Directories and Files

Operating systems use special temporary directories to store transient pieces of information. Such directories normally have wide-open permissions so that any application can write to them, and the platform has a garbage collection mechanism to automatically clean out deadwood. To find out the path to the operating system's temporary directory, include the Standard Library's tmpdir module, and then invoke the Dir.tmpdir method:

```
require 'tmpdir'
puts Dir.tmpdir
```

Similarly, temporary files are used by applications to briefly store information, such as session data. One way of creating temporary files is to use the Standard Library's Tempfile module:

```
require 'tempfile'
f = Tempfile.new('filename')
# Use the file as needed.
f.close
```

The Tempfile library will automatically delete the file when f object goes out of scope (at the latest, when the script stops running). Alternatively, you can use the close! method to delete the file immediately.

You can use Dir.entries or any of the other methods outlined earlier in the chapter to view the directory's contents. Since the first command in Step 3 made this the current working directory, you can use a single period to refer to it.

5. Rename data.txt and reconfirm the directory's contents (**Figure 13.16**):

```
FileUtils.mv('data.txt',
→ 'newname.txt')
puts Dir.entries('.')
```

The mv (or move) method can be used to rename a file.

6. Delete the directory:

```
Dir.chdir('..')
FileUtils.remove_dir('testdir')
```

First, I move out of the directory, into the parent, as attempts to delete the current working directory could be problematic. Then the remove_dir method is invoked to delete the directory and its contents.

✔ Tips

■ The FileUtils library includes other methods not mentioned already. For example, cd replicates chdir, plus there's chmod, chown, compare_file, getwd, pwd, and more.

■ The cp_r method will work with directories or files but cp only works with files.

Reading from Files

There are several different ways you can read from a file in Ruby. Which you choose depends upon what you'd like to do with the file's contents. To read in an entire file at once, use the read method:

```
contents = File.read('/path/to/filename')
```

If you'd like to read in an entire file in one step but have it broken into individual lines, use readlines, which returns an array:

```
contents = File.readlines('/path/to/
→ filename')
```

To access a file's contents one line at a time, use the foreach iterator, tied to a block:

```
File.foreach('/path/to/filename')
→ do |line|
    # Do whatever with line.
end
```

If you'll be referring to a file multiple times within some code, you may want to create a reference to the opened file. Do so by invoking open:

```
fp = File.open('/path/to/filename')
```

You could then use the each iterator to access each line:

```
fp.each do |line|
    # Do whatever with line.
end
```

A file opened like this should be formally closed once you're done with it:

```
fp.close
```

A benefit of the each method is that you can change the delimiter used to break up the returned data. By default it's a newline, but you could use a comma or tab instead:

```
fp.each("\t") do |line|
    # Do whatever with line.
end
```

Understand that when you use readlines, foreach, and each to return individual lines or parts from a file, the terminating character—the newline by default—will be part of each returned line. An exception may be the last line in a file if it does not end with a newline.

Another way to use the open method is to associate it with a code block. The block will receive a pointer to the opened file, which can then be used however you need:

```
File.open('/path/to/filename') do |fp|
    # Use fp, perhaps with each.
end
```

When using open in this way, the file is automatically closed after the code block has finished executing.

To practice using these different techniques, the next series of steps will read in the text from the data.txt file created earlier in the chapter (Script 13.1).

Understanding Streams

The process of reading from and writing to files involves *streams*, channels through which data can be sent. The base class for streams in Ruby is IO, short for *input/output*. The File class is derived from IO, as are those used to work with sockets (see Chapter 15, "Networking") and the standard input and output (see Chapter 2, "Simple Scripts"). This is important to know because all of the functionality for reading from and writing to files is defined within the IO class and inherited by File. Secondarily, the steps and methods used to read from and write to files will mimic those used to read from the standard input and write to the standard output, as well as sockets.

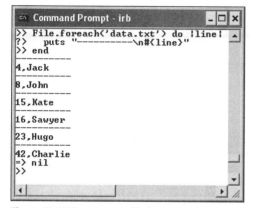

Figure 13.17 The contents of a text file, printed without any modifications.

```
>> File.foreach('data.txt') do |line|
?>   puts "----------\n#{line}"
>> end
----------
4,Jack
----------
8,John
----------
15,Kate
----------
16,Sawyer
----------
23,Hugo
----------
42,Charlie
=> nil
>>
```

Figure 13.18 The same text file (compare with Figure 13.17), with separators printed before each line.

To read from a file:

1. Start an `irb` session, if you have not already.

2. Change the working directory to the one that contains `data.txt`:

   `Dir.chdir('/path/to/dirname')`

   Instead of having to repeatedly enter the full pathname to the file, it'll be easier just to change the working directory.

3. Display the file's contents (**Figure 13.17**):

   `puts File.read('data.txt')`

   The `read` method is a quick and easy way to read in an entire file, but it is best used for shorter documents.

4. Display the file one line at a time, adding separators between each (**Figure 13.18**):

   ```
   File.foreach('data.txt') do |line|
       puts "----------\n#{line}"
   end
   ```

   By using `foreach`, you can access each line individually, doing whatever needs to be done with each.

   continues on next page

READING FROM FILES

305

5. Display the contents of the file in a different format (**Figure 13.19**):

```
fp = File.open('data.txt')
fp.each do |item|
    data = item.split(',')
    puts "#{data[1].chomp}
    ⇢ (#{data[0]})"
end
fp.close
```

For this final example, I'll formally open the file and later close it. After the file has been opened, the each iterator is called, which will send one line at a time to the block, where it's assigned to item. Then item is split into its two parts on the comma, which is assigned as an array to data. The separate values are then used within a puts statement.

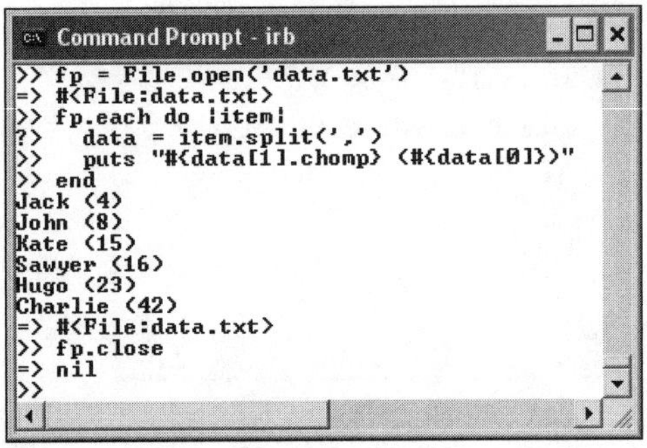

Figure 13.19 The text file's data, parsed and displayed in a different order and format.

✔ Tips

- You can read a single line from a file using gets. Unlike each and foreach, this is not an iterator, so it'll only return one line with each invocation. The getc method reads in a single character (in a non-iterative way).

- You can read in a single byte at a time using the each_byte iterator.

- Ruby scripts can read in data placed at the end of the same script after the keyword __END__:

```
# Ruby code.
__END__
this is data
```

The Ruby code (before the __END__) can read in the data by referring to DATA:

```
DATA.each { |line| puts line }
```

READING FROM FILES

Table 13.4

File Modes	
MODE	OPEN FOR…
r	Reading
r+	Reading and writing, but the file must exist
w	Writing, create a new file if it doesn't exist, overwrite existing file
w+	Like w, but allow for reading
a	Writing, append to the end of the file, if it exists
a+	Like a, but allow for reading
b	Binary mode

Writing to Files

The first step in writing to a file is to open the file in a *mode* that supports writing (**Table 13.4**). Then provide this mode value to the open method, as an optional second argument. By default, the mode is r, opening a file for just reading. All of the other modes support writing, but differ in:

◆ Whether they also support reading

◆ The result if the file does not exist

◆ Where new writing begins

Once a file has been opened for writing, you can write text to it the way that you "write" text to the standard output: primarily using print and puts. This works because both the standard output and a file are *streams* (see the "Understanding Streams" sidebar).

This next bit of code opens a file in appending mode and then adds *some text* as the last line in the file:

```
File.open('filename.txt', 'a') do |fp|
    fp.puts('some text')
end
```

Both print and puts write data to a file the same way they send output to the screen. The puts method will always make sure that a newline concludes each written string; print will not.

Writing plain text to a file is just that simple! In this next example, a script similar to Script 12.2 will be written that takes input from the user, this time adding it to data.txt. For a reliable interface and good validation, the Highline gem will be used, so see Chapter 12, "RubyGems," for a detailed discussion of that functionality.

To write to a file:

1. Begin a new Ruby script in your text editor or IDE (**Script 13.2**):

```
# Script 13.2 - lost.rb
```

I'm calling this one `lost.rb` because the names and numbers used (see Script 13.1) come from the television show *Lost*.

2. Start defining a new class and include the two gems:

```
class Lost
    require 'rubygems'
    require 'Highline/import'
```

This class will be called `Lost`. As it needs the `Highline` gem to work, that gem will be included within this class definition.

See Chapter 12 for more on these two lines. That chapter also shows how to install a gem, should you need that information.

3. Add an instance variable and the constructor:

```
attr_reader :fp
def initialize(file)
    @fp = File.open(file, 'a')
end
```

The instance variable `@fp` will represent a pointer to the file. The `initialize` method, called when an object of type `Lost` is created, takes a string as an argument, which is a path for the file to which the data will be written. The method then opens the file in appending mode, assigning the result to `@fp`.

See Chapter 7, "Creating Classes," for more on defining your own class. As an added feature, you may want to throw an exception (see Chapter 11, "Debugging and Error Handling") if the provided file argument isn't valid.

Script 13.2 This script creates a class for retrieving information from the user to be written to a file. The `Highline` gem manages the interface.

```
1   # Script 13.2 - lost.rb
2
3   # Define the class:
4   class Lost
5
6       # Include the gem:
7       require 'rubygems'
8       require 'Highline/import'
9
10      # Need a getter for the file pointer:
11      attr_reader :fp
12
13      # Constructor opens the file:
14      def initialize(file)
15          @fp = File.open(file, 'a')
16      end
17
18      # Method for adding records:
19      def add_record
20
21          # Get the info:
22          name = ask('Name? ') { |q| q.validate
                = /\A[a-z .'-]+\Z/i }
23          id = ask('ID? ', Integer) { |q|
                q.above = 0 }
24
25          # Write the data to the file:
26          @fp.puts "#{id},#{name}"
27
28      end # End of add_record
29
30      # Method for closing the file:
31      def close
32          @fp.close
33      end
34
35  end # End of Lost class.
36
37  # Create the object:
38  lost = Lost.new('data.txt')
39
40  # Add two more records:
41  2.times { lost.add_record }
42
43  # Close the file:
44  lost.close
```

4. Define a method for adding records:

```
def add_record
   name = ask('Name? ') { |q|
q.validate = /\A[a-z .'-]+\Z/i }
   id = ask('ID? ', Integer) { |q|
q.above = 0 }
   @fp.puts "#{id},#{name}"
end
```

The `add_record` method will be used to get information from the user, through the command line, and then write that information to the text file. The `Highline` gem is used to make sure that the submitted information fits certain parameters. The name input can contain only letters, spaces, periods, apostrophes, and hyphens. The numeric input has to be an integer greater than 0.

5. Complete the class:

```
def close
    @fp.close
end
end # End of Lost class.
```

The `close` method closes the opened file.

6. Create an object of the `Lost` type:

```
lost = Lost.new('data.txt')
```

When creating an object of this type, you must provide a reference to the `data.txt` file (Script 13.1). This code assumes that both this script and that file are in the same directory, so change the code accordingly if that will not be the case for you.

7. Add two new records:

```
2.times { lost.add_record }
```

A new record is added every time the `add_record` method is called. You can call it in many ways. I'll do so by using an iterator that calls the method within the block. Just changing the initial number alters how many records will be added.

continues on next page

WRITING TO FILES

8. Close the file:

```
lost.close
```

9. Save and run the completed script (**Figure 13.20**).

10. If you want, confirm that the new data was written to the file.

    You can do so by opening `data.txt` in any text editor or by using the Ruby code demonstrated in the previous set of steps.

✔ Tips

- The examples in this chapter read from and write to files in a linear fashion. You can randomly access files, although this is less often necessary. The `seek` method will move to a spot within a file and any subsequent reads and writes will begin at that point.

- The examples in this chapter also focus on reading and writing plain text data. You can manipulate binary data in Ruby, in which case you read and write bytes, not strings. Besides using different methods, the file must also be opened in binary mode. To do so, add a `b:binary`—the letter *b* plus the symbol `:binary`—to the mode. This is only necessary on Windows, which differentiates between binary and non-binary files.

Unicode and Files

One of the major changes in Ruby 1.9—not yet released at the time of this writing—is support for Unicode. Unicode and support for it is a huge subject, but I want to quickly demonstrate how Unicode can affect how one reads from or writes to files by indicating the file's encoding.

To identify the encoding to be used, add the appropriate symbol to the mode when using the `open` method:

```
fp = File.open('filename.txt',
→ 'w+:utf-8')
```

That line opens `filename.txt` for reading and writing, using the UTF-8 encoding. From this point on, you can read from and write to the file using the same methods you otherwise would.

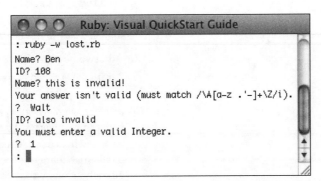

Figure 13.20 Execution of Script 13.2, including demonstrations of how the `Highline` interface and validation work.

WRITING TO FILES

Using FasterCSV

A common way to store multiple, discrete pieces of information in a text file is to use comma-separated values (CSV). Script 13.1 does this, separating a number from a name. If you'll be doing a lot of work with CSV data, it's worth your while to learn and use `csv`, from the Ruby Standard Library, or FasterCSV (http://fastercsv.rubyforge.org), a gem I'll discuss here.

To use FasterCSV, you must install the gem (see Chapter 12) and then require the necessary libraries:

```
require 'rubygems'
require 'fastercsv'
```

From there, you can read the data in different ways. To read in one string at a time, use `foreach`:

```
FasterCSV.foreach('/path/to/filename.
→ csv') do |line|
    # Use line.
end
```

Within the block, `line` will be an array, with one element for each comma-separated value. (I used the `.csv` extension in that example, but CSV files don't have to use `.csv`.)

The `read` method will return all of the lines as a multidimensional array:

```
contents = FasterCSV.read('/path/to/
→ filename.csv')
```

To write CSV data to a file, open the file using the same mode values as those listed in Table 13.4, and then invoke the `<<` operator:

```
FasterCSV.open('/path/to/filename.csv',
→ 'w') do |fp|
    fp << ['array', 'of', 'values']
end
```

That will write *array,of,values* \n to the file.

Besides being a fast and efficient way to work with CSV data, another benefit of using `FasterCSV` is that it'll automatically handle data with commas in it, quoting those values so as not to mess up the integrity of the CSV file.

As a demonstration of `FasterCSV`, let's update Script 13.2.

To use FasterCSV:

1. Install the `FasterCSV` gem.

   ```
   gem install fastercsv
   ```

   See Chapter 12 for instructions on how to install gems on your operating system.

2. Open `lost.rb` (Script 13.2) in your text editor or IDE if it is not already.

3. After including the other gems, include FasterCSV (**Script 13.3**):

   ```
   require 'fastercsv'
   ```

4. Change the `attr_reader` line so that it refers to `:file` instead of `:fp`:

   ```
   attr_reader :file
   ```

   This version of the class will behave a little bit differently to be in accordance with how `FasterCSV` works. Instead of automatically opening the file and assigning that to `@fp`, the constructor will assign the pathname to `@file`.

5. Redefine the `initialize` method:

   ```
   def initialize(file)
       @file = file
   end
   ```

   The class will use the file's full path a couple of different ways, so the `initialize` method just assigns it to an instance variable.

Script 13.3 This update of the Lost class uses the FasterCSV gem to both read and write CSV data.

```
1    # Script 13.3 - lost2.rb
2
3    # Define the class:
4    class Lost
5
6        # Include the gems:
7        require 'rubygems'
8        require 'Highline/import'
9        require 'fastercsv'
10
11       # Create the getters:
12       attr_reader :file
13
14       # Constructor opens the file:
15       def initialize(file)
16           @file = file
17       end
18
19       # Method for adding records:
20       def add_record
21
22           # Get the info:
23           name = ask('Name? ') { |q| q.validate
                 = /\A[a-z ,.'-]+\Z/i }
24           id = ask('ID? ', Integer) { |q|
                 q.above = 0 }
25
26           # Write the data to the file:
27           FasterCSV.open(file, 'a') do |fp|
28               fp << [id, name]
29           end
30
31       end # End of add_record
32
33       # Method for returning records:
34       def each
35           FasterCSV.foreach(file) do |record|
36               yield record[0], record[1]
37           end
38       end
39
40   end # End of Lost class.
41
42   # Create the object:
43   lost = Lost.new('data.txt')
44
45   # Add two more records:
46   2.times { lost.add_record }
47
48   # Print each record:
49   lost.each do |num, name|
50       puts "#{name} (#{num})"
51   end
```

USING FASTERCSV

6. Change the `@fp.puts` line so that it uses FasterCSV instead:

```
FasterCSV.open(file, 'a') do |fp|
  fp << [id, name]
end
```

This approach, already discussed, will open a file for appended writing and then add another line of comma-separated values. The values themselves come from the user input and need to be in an array.

7. Add an *each* method:

```
def each
  FasterCSV.foreach(file) do |record|
    yield record[0], record[1]
  end
end
```

There are many ways you could show all of the records within the associated file. You could create a method that reads them all in and returns them in a formatted way. However, that approach would be unnecessarily limiting. Instead, by defining an *each* method that returns every record as an array, the code that uses this class can determine, in a block, what's done with those records. To expand upon this, you could include the `Enumerable` module to provide even more iterators (see Chapter 9).

To create an *each* method, the `FasterCSV`'s `foreach` method will loop through every line in the file, assigning each line to `record`. That variable will be an array, whose two elements will be yielded (to the block associated with this method's invocation). See Chapter 7 for more on using `yield`.

continues on next page

YAML

Another common way to store data in a text file, besides using CSV, is to use *YAML* (YAML Ain't Markup Language, www.yaml.org). YAML can store more complicated data structures in a way that's human friendly (i.e., easy to read) and that can even be edited by hand.

Start by including `YAML`, which is part of the Standard Library. The `YAML::dump` method takes an object—your data—as an argument and returns it in a serialized format. You can then do whatever with the serialized data, including writing it to a plain text file. Conversely, the `YAML::load` method takes YAML data and translates it back to its original state. The `YAML` library must have access to the class definition for any object involved, however.

8. Remove the `close` method definition.

As the file is opened with a block, it'll automatically be closed, so the class doesn't need a separate `close` method.

9. After the class definition, remove the call to the `close` method, since it no longer exists.

10. Use the `each` method to display the file's contents:

```
lost.each do |num, name|
    puts "#{name} (#{num})"
end
```

The `each` method will yield two values with each iteration, assigned to `num` and `name` within this block. The block then prints the values.

11. Save and run the completed script (**Figure 13.21**).

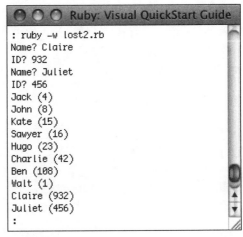

```
: ruby -w lost2.rb
Name? Claire
ID? 932
Name? Juliet
ID? 456
Jack (4)
John (8)
Kate (15)
Sawyer (16)
Hugo (23)
Charlie (42)
Ben (108)
Walt (1)
Claire (932)
Juliet (456)
:
```

Figure 13.21 Two more records are added, and then every record is displayed.

14

DATABASES

Database applications, such as MySQL, Oracle, and SQL Server, go hand-in-hand with programming languages. Applications often use directories and files to store information, but more sophisticated data warehousing requires a database. Ruby can use most of the popular database applications through associated gems and other libraries.

This chapter will cover everything you need to know to interact with the *SQLite* database application (`www.sqlite.org`). SQLite is a small, fast, sufficiently powerful, and open-source application that runs on most operating systems. While not as feature rich as MySQL, Oracle, and others, SQLite is easy to install and work with, and is perfectly suited for many purposes.

Before getting into the code, I should point out that this chapter does not teach *SQL* (Structured Query Language), the language used to communicate with databases, or the principles of relational database design. If you're not familiar with either, you'll still be able to follow along, but it's worth your time to learn both (discussed in my book *MySQL, 2nd Edition: Visual QuickStart Guide*, Peachpit Press, 2006).

Getting Started

To interact with an SQLite database, you'll need two things (aside from Ruby itself):

◆ The SQLite software

◆ The SQLite3 Ruby gem

The database software is available from www.sqlite.org. There are precompiled versions for Windows, Mac OS X, and Linux, or you can compile your own from the source code. Recent versions of Mac OS X come with SQLite3 pre-installed (it's used widely by the OS), so no steps need to be taken. On Windows, you just need to copy the `sqlite3.dll` file to the `WINDOWS\system32` directory.

Details for installing Ruby gems can be found in Chapter 12, "RubyGems," but it should just be a matter of running this command:

```
gem install sqlite3-ruby
```

On Unix, Linux, and Mac OS X, you need to preface this with `sudo`, and then enter the administrator's password.

One optional consideration would be to install a utility for interacting with SQLite databases. You can download a command-line one from the SQLite Web site, or there are plenty of freeware and shareware GUI tools available. Having one of these programs would allow you to manage and inspect SQLite databases without using Ruby. At the very least, using another interface to an SQLite database aids in debugging.

After you've installed everything, you can use SQLite in your Ruby code. Begin by including the gems:

```
require 'rubygems'
require 'sqlite3'
```

(On most Windows systems and in Ruby 1.9 and later, you can omit the first line.)

Next, create an object of type `SQLite3::Database`:
```
db = SQLite3::Database.new('/path/to/
→ file.db')
```

When creating this object, provide the path to the database file on the computer (SQLite stores entire databases in a single file). You can use any extension you'd like for the file, although `.db` makes sense. (Ruby on Rails, which uses SQLite as the default database, prefers the `.sqlite3` extension, in part because Windows uses `.db` for other purposes.) If the file does not exist, even if that means you have the wrong file or path name, it'll be created for you as an empty database without any tables.

Once you're done using the database, close the file:

```
db.close
```

Just to make sure everything is working before writing a script, this next sequence of steps will test the ability to open an SQLite database within `irb`.

To open a database:

1. Begin an `irb` session.

2. Move into the right directory:

   `Dir.chdir('/path/to/dir')`

   So as to simplify the next command, and to know exactly where the database file will be created, use the `chdir` method of the `Dir` class to change the working directory (see Chapter 13, "Directories and Files"). Later in the chapter, you'll write a couple of scripts that interact with this database, so you may want to create the database in the same directory as you'll place those scripts.

3. Include the gems:

   `require 'rubygems'`

   `require 'sqlite3'`

   Again, this assumes you've already installed both the SQLite gem and the SQLite software.

4. Open (and create) the database file:

   `db = SQLite3::Database.`
   `→ new('employees.db')`

   This line creates a new object of type `SQLite3::Database`, associated with the `employees.db` file found in the current directory.

   continues on next page

5. Close the database (**Figure 14.1**):

```
db.close
```

You should always close the database after you're done working with it.

6. Confirm the database file's existence (**Figure 14.2**):

```
puts Dir.entries('.')
```

You could use your operating system to check that the database file was created, but since you're already using `irb`, you can do so in Ruby. The `entries` method is also covered in Chapter 12.

Of course, you also know that the database file was created if you did not see an error in Step 3.

✔ Tips

■ The SQLite database file is cross-platform compatible, meaning that you can create an SQLite database on one computer, and then distribute and use it on another.

■ Since an SQLite database is just a file on the computer, it—and its contents—are accessible by other applications. SQLite does not have the same security layers that other database applications possess, so it should not be used to manage sensitive data.

■ The `closed?` method returns a Boolean value indicating if the database file has been closed.

■ The DataBase Interface (DBI) library provides a generic interface for multiple database applications (like `DBI` on Perl). If a script may switch to using a different database application at a later point, writing your code to use `DBI` could be prudent.

```
: irb
>> Dir.chdir('/Users/larryullman/Documents/Writing/Ruby/Ch 14/code')
=> 0
>> require 'rubygems'
=> true
>> require 'sqlite3'
=> true
>> db = SQLite3::Database.new('employees.db')
=> #<SQLite3::Database:0x5b44ec @results_as_hash=false, @driver=#<SQLite3::D
river::Native::Driver:0x5b43e8 @busy_handler={}, @authorizer={}, @callback_d
ata={}, @trace={}>, @transaction_active=false, @statement_factory=SQLite3::S
tatement, @closed=false, @handle=#<SWIG::TYPE_p_sqlite3:0x5a7ae4>, @translat
or=nil, @type_translation=false>
>> db.close
=> true
>>
```

Figure 14.1 The database file is successfully opened and closed, which means that support for SQLite is enabled and you can begin interacting with the database.

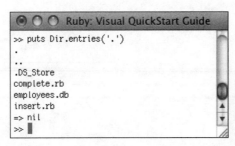

```
>> puts Dir.entries('.')
.
..
.DS_Store
complete.rb
employees.db
insert.rb
=> nil
>>
```

Figure 14.2 The new, empty database—`employees.db`—now exists in the current directory.

Table 14.1

SQLite Data Types	
NAME	**STORES**
INTEGER	A signed (plus/minus) integer
REAL	A floating-point number
TEXT	Any string
BLOB	Binary data

Intro to SQLite

From a technical standpoint, SQLite differs from the best-known database applications (Oracle, MySQL, SQL Server, etc.) in many ways. One big difference is that SQLite supports only four data types: It has no date or time type, and it doesn't constrain data by type (meaning that it'll let you store a string in a column defined as a real number). SQLite also has no system for managing users and permissions: A database is a file on the computer and all the data is readable and writable by any user or application (depending on the operating system's permissions on that file).

SQLite mostly adheres to the SQL92 standard and has a minimum of built-in functions. You can do pretty much whatever you normally do in other database applications, with a few exceptions: support for triggers, ALTER TABLE commands, views, and joins are incomplete. There are also no foreign key constraints. But for many database needs, SQLite will do just fine.

Executing Simple Queries

Once you have an SQLite3::Database object, the appropriately named execute method is used to run any SQL command. The method takes one argument: the string representing the query. This is where knowledge of SQL comes in.

As mentioned in the introduction, there's not enough room in the book to cover SQL in great detail, but the language is pretty easy to follow. To create a table, start with the clause CREATE TABLE, followed by the table's name, followed by the table's definition—which is to say the name and type of each column—within parentheses. Thus, the following string represents a query for creating a two-column table:

```
sql = 'CREATE TABLE testing (id INTEGER
→ PRIMARY KEY AUTOINCREMENT, something
→ TEXT)'
```

The id column is an automatically incrementing integer for each record's primary key. The something column just stores text.

If you've never used SQLite before, **Table 14.1** lists the available types you can use for table columns, and the sidebar "Intro to SQLite" provides a brief introduction to the software as a whole.

To create a table using Ruby, execute the command:

```
db.execute(sql)
```

(You don't have to, and often won't, create a separate variable to represent the query, but I did so here to distinguish the SQLite query from the Ruby code that executes it.)

As a final step in preparing a database to be used, let's create a table in the employees.db database. The specific example will store employee names and numbers in a single table. The table will be created using irb (as you only need to create a table once), but usage of this table will be demonstrated in scripts.

To open a database:

1. Begin an irb session and include the gems, if you have not already.

2. Open the database file:

   db = SQLite3::Database.
   → new('employees.db')

   You may need to change the argument to the new method here to provide a full and correct path to the database, if it won't be in the current working directory.

3. Define the SQL command:

   sql = 'CREATE TABLE employees (id
   → INTEGER INTEGER, first_name TEXT,
   → last_name TEXT)'

   Again, just to keep the query separate from its execution (for clarity sake), I'm assigning the SQL command to a variable, which will then be run on the database. This query will create a table containing three columns: id, a number, plus first_name and last_name, both text columns.

4. Execute the query:

   db.execute(sql)

5. Close the database (**Figure 14.3**):

   db.close

✔ Tips

■ Table names cannot begin with *sqlite_*, because that prefix is reserved for SQLite's use.

■ The data types supported by SQLite can be tricky (compared to other databases), so I'm glossing over the subject here. If you'll be using SQLite a lot, I recommend you read its simple manual at www.sqlite.org/docs.html. With respect to data types, check out the pages on *column affinity* for more information.

■ The execute method will only run the first SQL command in a string. If you need to execute multiple SQL commands at once, use execute_batch instead.

■ The complete? method returns a Boolean value indicating if an SQL command is syntactically complete:

   db.complete?('CREATE') # false

■ You can confirm the creation of the table by opening the database file in any application that can read SQLite databases.

```
Command Prompt - irb
>> Dir.chdir('My Documents/Ruby')
=> 0
>> require 'rubygems'
=> true
>> require 'sqlite3'
=> true
>> db = SQLite3::Database.new('employees.db')
=> #<SQLite3::Database:0x2ce3ae0 @closed=false, @translator=nil, @type_translati
on=false, @driver=#<SQLite3::Driver::Native::Driver:0x2ce3a40 @authorizer=<>, @c
allback_data=<>, @trace=<>, @busy_handler=<>>, @statement_factory=SQLite3::State
ment, @results_as_hash=false, @handle=#<SWIG::TYPE_p_sqlite3:0x2cdbed0>, @transa
ction_active=false>
>> sql = 'CREATE TABLE employees (id INTEGER INTEGER, first_name TEXT, last_name
 TEXT)'
=> "CREATE TABLE employees (id INTEGER INTEGER, first_name TEXT, last_name TEXT)
"
>> db.execute(sql)
=> []
>> db.close
=> true
>>
```

Figure 14.3 The creation of a table within the database.

Inserting Records

When you have a complete and working database, you can start doing what's important: storing data in it. This is accomplished using an INSERT query. The process of running an INSERT query is the same as that used to run a CREATE query: create the SQLite3::Database object and call the execute method.

An INSERT query adheres to one of two syntaxes:

```
INSERT INTO tablename VALUES (valueX,
→ valueY,…)
INSERT INTO tablename (column1,
→ column2,…) VALUES (valueX, valueY,…)
```

You can use the first syntax—where the table's columns are not named—so long as you provide a value for each column in the table. If there are four columns, there must be four values, and they must be in the proper order. By using the second syntax, you can populate only the columns for which you have values.

The values to be used in queries will likely come from variables. You *could* use variables in a query directly:

```
sql = "INSERT INTO testing (something)
→ VALUES ('#{some_var}')"
```

This is not advised, as that approach is vulnerable to SQL injection attacks. A more secure alternative is to use *bound parameters*.

To do so, use placeholders for the values, and then add the variables as extra arguments when executing the query:

```
db.execute('INSERT INTO testing
→ (something) VALUES (?)', some_var)
```

When the query is executed, the question mark will be replaced by the value of some_var. If you are using multiple bound parameters, use multiple question marks and variables:

```
db.execute('INSERT INTO tablename (col1,
→ col2) VALUES (?, ?)', var1, var2)
```

Using bound parameters is more secure than using variables directly because potentially problematic characters, like single or double quotation marks, will not break the query. Note, as well, that even if the value being inserted is a string, the question mark is not placed within quotes (as that would insert a literal question mark into the table).

The last thing to know about inserting records is that you can confirm that an insertion worked by invoking the changes method. This method returns the number of table rows affected by the previous query.

```
puts db.changes # Hopefully 1
```

To start populating the employees table, let's create a class for managing employees. The class will present a menu for the user (**Figure 14.4**), plus allow the user to add and view employees.

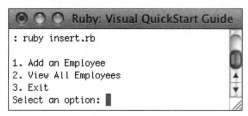

Figure 14.4 Some of the interface for an employee-management application.

To insert records:

1. Begin a new Ruby script in your text editor or IDE (**Script 14.1**):

```
# Script 14.1 - insert.rb
```

2. Begin defining the class and include the necessary gems:

```
class Employees
    require 'rubygems'
    require 'Highline/import'
    require 'sqlite3'
```

This class will use the already mentioned sqlite3-ruby gem for database purposes. It'll also use the Highline gem, introduced in Chapter 12, to manage the application interface.

3. Create a getter method for a @db instance variable:

```
attr_reader :db
```

The @db instance variable will represent the connection to the database. It needs to be accessible within every method.

4. Define the initialize method:

```
def initialize(file)
    @db = SQLite3::Database.new(file)
    create_menu
end
```

The initialize method will be called when a new object of type Employees is created. It expects one argument, a string representing the path to the database file. Within the method, the SQLite3::Database object is created, and then the create_menu method is called.

To flesh out this example, you'd likely want to add validation and exception handling to this method to make sure that the submitted file value points to an existing database.

Script 14.1 The Employees class defines an application for storing user-submitted values in a database.

```
1   # Script 14.1 - insert.rb
2
3   # Class for managing employees:
4   class Employees
5
6       # Include the gems:
7       require 'rubygems'
8       require 'Highline/import'
9       require 'sqlite3'
10
11      # db represents the database:
12      attr_reader :db
13
14      # Constructor opens the database and
        starts the menu:
15      def initialize(file)
16          @db = SQLite3::Database.new(file)
17          create_menu
18      end
19
20      # Method that creates the menu of
        options:
21      def create_menu
22
23          puts # Add some space
24
25          # Create the menu:
26          choose do |m|
27              m.prompt = 'Select an option: '
28              m.choice(:'Add an Employee')
                { add_employee }
29              m.choice(:'View All Employees')
                { view_employees }
30              m.choice(:'Exit') { exit_app }
31          end
32
33      end # End of create_menu
34
35      # Method for adding employees:
36      def add_employee
37
38          puts # Add some space
39
```

(script continues on next page)

Script 14.1 *continued*

```
                    Script

40          # Get the info:
41          first_name = ask('First name? ')
            { |q| q.validate = /\A[a-z ,.'-]
            +\Z/i }
42          last_name = ask('Last name? ') { |q|
            q.validate = /\A[a-z ,.'-]+\Z/i }
43          id = ask('Employee ID? ', Integer)
            { |q| q.above = 0 }
44
45          # Write the data to the database:
46          @db.execute('INSERT INTO employees
            (id, first_name, last_name) VALUES
            (?, ?, ?)', id, first_name,
            last_name)
47
48          # Print a message:
49          puts 'The employee has been added!'
            if @db.changes == 1
50
51          # Show the menu:
52          create_menu
53
54      end # End of add_employee
55
56      # Method for returning records:
57      def view_employees
58
59          puts # Add some space
60
61      # Print a caption:
62      puts "Current Employees"
63
64          # Show the menu:
65          create_menu
66
67      end
68
69      # Method for closing the application:
70      def exit_app
71          @db.close
72          Process.exit
73      end
74
75  end # End of Employees class.
76
77  # Create the object:
78  e = Employees.new('employees.db')
```

5. Define the create_menu method:

```
def create_menu
    puts # Add some space
    choose do |m|
        m.prompt = 'Select an option: '
        m.choice(:'Add an Employee') {
        → add_employee }
        m.choice(:'View All Employees')
        → { view_employees }
        m.choice(:'Exit') { exit_app }
    end
end
```

This method will be used to generate the application's interface. This code, which uses the Highline gem, is explained in detail in Chapter 12. A menu of three options is created (see Figure 14.4). When the user selects the first option, the add_employee method is called; when they select the second, view_employees is called; the third calls the exit_app method.

continues on next page

6. Start defining the `add_employee` method:

```
def add_employee
  puts # Add some space
  first_name = ask('First name? ')
  → { |q| q.validate = /\A[a-z
  → ,.'-]+\Z/i }
  last_name = ask('Last name? ') {
  → |q| q.validate = /\A[a-z ,.'-]+
  → \Z/i }
  id = ask('Employee ID? ', Integer)
  → { |q| q.above = 0 }
```

The method starts by creating a blank line, to separate this interface from the menu the user just saw. Then, using Highline, the user is prompted to enter the employee's first name, last name, and ID value. Each is validated: the names are checked against regular expressions, and the ID must be a positive integer (**Figure 14.5**).

7. Insert the record into the database:

```
@db.execute('INSERT INTO employees
  → (id, first_name, last_name)
  → VALUES (?, ?, ?)', id,
  → first_name, last_name)
```

The three question marks represent the three values to be used in the query, which are the second through fourth arguments to the **execute** method. Thanks to Highline, the values here are guaranteed to be appropriate to use in the query.

8. Complete the `add_employee` method:

```
  puts 'The employee has been
  → added!' if @db.changes == 1
  create_menu
end # End of add_record
```

The `puts` statement will only be executed if the INSERT query affected one row. You could add some exception handling routine here in case the query failed.

The `create_menu` method is then called so that the user can decide what to do next.

9. Define the shell of the `view_employees` method:

```
def view_employees
  puts # Add some space
  puts "Current Employees"
  create_menu
end
```

This method will be fleshed out in the next section of the chapter (because it requires a SELECT query). For now, it just creates a blank line, prints a caption, and then displays the menu.

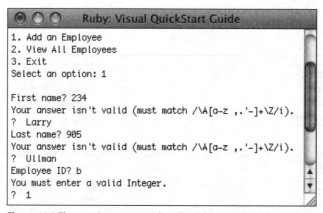

Figure 14.5 The user is re-prompted until valid input is keyed.

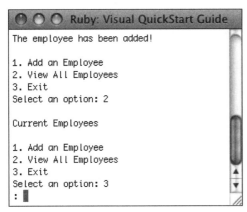

Figure 14.6 More usage of the employee-management application.

10. Define the exit_app method:

```
def exit_app
  @db.close
  Process.exit
end
```

This method is called when the user terminates the application. It first closes the database and then terminates the script itself.

11. Complete and use the class:

```
end # End of Employees class.

e = Employees.new('employees.db')
```

To use the class, just create an object of Employees type, passing it a reference to the database already created. The class code will take care of the rest.

12. Save and run the completed script (**Figure 14.6**).

✔ Tips

■ To retrieve the value of the automatically incremented primary key, call the last_insert_row_id method after executing the query:

```
db.execute(sql)

id = db.last_insert_row_id
```

■ SQLite does not support a syntax for inserting multiple records using one query:

```
INSERT INTO todo (item) VALUES
→ ('Something'), ('Something Else'),
→ ('A 3rd Thing')
```

This is possible within the popular MySQL database but is not part of the SQL standard.

■ The SQLite3::Database.quote class method can also be used to prepare strings for use in a query:

```
var = SQLite::Database.quote(var)
```

Retrieving Records

Records are retrieved from a database using a SELECT query. The basic syntax is:

SELECT *which_columns* FROM *tablename*

You can specify which columns are returned and in what order by naming them, separating each by a comma:

SELECT *col1, col2, col4* FROM *tablename*

Or you can use * to select every column. SELECT queries can also use WHERE clauses to limit which rows are returned, ORDER BY clauses to affect the order in which they are returned, JOINs to select information across multiple tables, and much, much more. The SELECT query is the workhorse of a database, so see a good SQL reference to learn more.

When retrieving records from a database, the query is executed just like any other but the result will differ. With a SELECT query, the execute method returns an array of rows that met the query's criteria. These rows can be assigned to a variable for later use:

rows = db.execute('SELECT * FROM
→ *tablename*')

Now rows is a multidimensional array. Each element in the array represents a returned row. Each returned row is also an array, of column values.

You can also execute SELECT queries by associating a block with the method's invocation:

db.execute('SELECT * FROM *tablename*')
→ do |row|
    # Use row.
end

Each returned record will be assigned to the row variable, one at a time.

By default, the selected columns will be returned as an array, indexed starting at 0. You can retrieve the results as a hash, if you'd prefer, by setting results_as_hash to true:

db.results_as_hash = true

By taking this step, you'll be able to refer to results using, for example, row['*column_name*'] instead of row[3].

Because of the way SQLite stores data—with little regard for type, all of the returned values will be strings, even if they have a numeric value like *"2"*. You can have all returned values translated into their proper Ruby types by setting type_translation to true:

db.type_translation = true

With that setting enabled, each selected value will be converted to the proper type based upon the column definitions.

To use this information, let's finish the view_employees method of the Employees class so that it retrieves and displays each stored employee (**Figure 14.7**).

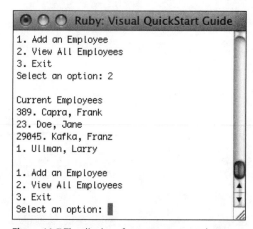

Figure 14.7 The display of every current employee recorded in the database.

Script 14.2 This script updates the Employees class so that it displays (i.e., selects) the records from the database.

```
1    # Script 14.2 - complete.rb
2
3    # Class for managing employees:
4    class Employees
5
6        require 'rubygems'
7        require 'Highline/import'
8        require 'sqlite3'
9
10       attr_reader :db
11
12       # Constructor opens the database:
13       def initialize(file)
14           @db = SQLite3::Database.new(file)
15           @db.results_as_hash = true
16           @db.type_translation = true
17           create_menu
18       end
19
20       # Method that creates the menu of
         options:
21       def create_menu
22           puts # Add some space
23           # Create the menu:
24           choose do |m|
25               m.prompt = 'Select an option: '
26               m.choice(:'Add an Employee')
                 { add_employee }
27               m.choice(:'View All Employees')
                 { view_employees }
28               m.choice(:'Exit') { exit_app }
29           end
30       end # End of create_menu
31
32       # Method for adding employees:
33       def add_employee
34           puts # Add some space
35           first_name = ask('First name? ')
             { |q| q.validate = /\A[a-z ,.'-]
             +\Z/i }
36           last_name = ask('Last name? ') { |q|
             q.validate = /\A[a-z ,.'-]+\Z/i }
37           id = ask('Employee ID? ', Integer)
             { |q| q.above = 0 }
38           @db.execute('INSERT INTO employees
             (id, first_name, last_name) VALUES
             (?, ?, ?)', id, first_name,
             last_name)
```

To select records:

1. Open insert.rb (Script 14.1) in your text editor or IDE, if it is not already.

2. Within the initialize method, after creating the SQLite3::Database object, set results_as_hash and type_translation to true (**Script 14.2**):

   @db.results_as_hash = true

   @db.type_translation = true

   These two settings make it easier to access and use the results returned by a SELECT query.

continues on next page

Script 14.2 *continued*

```
39           puts 'The employee has been added!'
             if @db.changes == 1
40           create_menu
41       end # End of add_employee
42
43       # Method for returning records:
44       def view_employees
45           puts # Add some space
46   puts "Current Employees"
47
48           @db.execute('SELECT * FROM employees
             ORDER BY last_name') do |row|
49               puts "#{row['id'].to_i}. #{row
                 ['last_name']}, #{row['first_
                 name']}"
50           end
51
52           create_menu
53       end
54
55       # Method for closing the application:
56       def exit_app
57           @db.close
58           Process.exit
59       end
60
61   end # End of Employees class.
62
63   # Create the object:
64   e = Employees.new('employees.db')
```

RETRIEVING RECORDS

3. Within the `view_employees` method, select and display every employee:

```
@db.execute('SELECT * FROM employees
→ ORDER BY last_name') do |row|
  puts "#{row['id'].to_i}.
  → #{row['last_name']},
  → #{row['first_name']}"
end
```

The query selects all three columns from the `employees` table. The rows will be returned in alphabetical order by last name. In the block associated with the query's execution, the employee's ID is printed, followed by a period, their last name, a comma, and their first name. The `to_i` method has to be called on the employee's ID so that it's displayed as an integer instead of a float (which is what it'd be returned as by default).

4. Save and run the completed script (**Figure 14.8**).

To distinguish this file from Script 14.1, I renamed it as `complete.rb`.

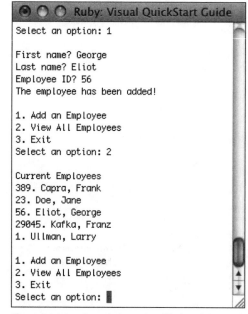

Figure 14.8 Another employee is added, and the entire list reprinted.

RETRIEVING RECORDS

✔ Tips

- If a query will only be returning a single row, use `get_first_row` instead of `execute`. This method is also usable if a query will return multiple rows but you only need the first one, but your queries should never ask for more information from the database than the application will use.

- If a query is only returning a single value, use `get_first_value` instead of execute:

  ```
  num = db.get_first_value('SELECT
  → COUNT(*) FROM tablename')
  ```

- The `execute2` method works exactly like `execute`, but the first returned record will be an array of column names. This method will always return at least one row, assuming the query does not have an error in it.

- You can access the column names and types returned by a query by referring to the `fields` or `types` method of any returned record:

  ```
  rows = db.execute('SELECT * FROM
  → tablename')
  puts rows[0].fields
  puts rows[0].types
  ```

  The `fields` method isn't usable when using the `results_as_hash` setting, though.

Exception Handling

In a fully realized application that interacts with a database, you'd need to add various types of exception handling. The concept as a whole is covered in Chapter 11, "Debugging and Error Handling," so read that for general principles.

There are about two dozen different types of exceptions defined within the `SQLite::Exceptions` class that you can watch for. A `CantOpenException` is thrown if the database file cannot be opened, and a couple of others are related to problems specifically with the database file. A `MismatchException` is thrown if an attempt is made to insert a non-integer value into an `INTEGER PRIMARY KEY` column; similar exceptions handle other SQLite-data issues. Generally, though, you'll see an `SQLException`, which occurs when there's an error in your SQL command (perhaps the most common problem when interacting with databases).

Performing Transactions

Transactions provide a different way of executing database queries. With the standard method used thus far in this chapter, a query's effects are made permanent as soon as the `execute` method is called. There is no way of undoing these executed queries! An alternative approach is to run queries within a *transaction*. By doing so, you can create checks that guarantee everything worked as expected. Then you can either make the queries permanent or undo their collective effects, depending on the overall result.

To start a transaction, call the `transaction` method:

```
db.transaction
```

From that point onward, every query will have only a temporary impact until the `commit` method is called:

```
db.commit
```

The other option would be to undo all the queries by calling `rollback`:

```
db.rollback
```

For example, you might do this within a `rescue` clause if an exception occurred.

An alternative way of performing transactions is to use a block:

```
db.transaction do |db2|
    # Execute queries
end
```

When performing transactions within blocks, the transaction will automatically be committed when the block terminates or will automatically be rolled back if an exception is raised. The block receives the database object as a parameter, which is assigned to a local variable, so within the block, you might run queries using:

```
db2.execute(sql)
```

From a programming perspective, using these functions is really straightforward. The trick is being able to determine when it's appropriate to commit a transaction and when it should be rolled back. To practice this, the next example will transfer funds from one bank account to another. Transactions are necessary in such situations because a transfer involves two steps:

1. Updating the "from" account to subtract the amount being transferred from the balance.

2. Updating the "to" account to add the amount being transferred to the balance.

If either of these steps fail, the entire transaction should be undone.

To use transactions:

1. Begin an irb session and include the gems, if you have not already.

   To best be able to follow what happens with transactions, this example will be executed entirely within irb.

2. Open the database file:

   ```
   db = SQLite3::Database.new('bank.db')
   ```

   The database file for this example will be called bank.db. It'll be created within the current working directory.

3. Create the table:

   ```
   db.execute('CREATE TABLE
   → accounts (id INTEGER PRIMARY KEY
   → AUTOINCREMENT, balance REAL)')
   ```

   The accounts table has just two columns: one for the account number and another for the balance. The account number will be an automatically incrementing primary key. With this definition, no value should be provided for this column when adding a new record. SQLite will automatically give this column a value one higher than the current highest id value.

continues on next page

PERFORMING TRANSACTIONS

4. Add at least two accounts (**Figure 14.9**):

```
db.execute('INSERT INTO accounts
→ (balance) VALUES (4890.23)')

db.execute('INSERT INTO accounts
→ (balance) VALUES (1234.56)')
```

Because one of the table's two columns is an automatically incremented primary key, only the other column requires a value when inserting new records.

5. Begin a transaction with a block:

```
db.transaction do |db2|
```

From this point forward, all queries will be part of the transaction until the end of the block or an exception occurs. And you don't need to handle the exception yourself (unless you want to customize the response), as Ruby will automatically rollback the transaction should one occur.

6. Perform a transfer (**Figure 14.10**):

```
db.execute('UPDATE accounts SET
→ balance=balance+100 WHERE id=1')

db.execute('UPDATE accounts SET
→ balance=balance-100 WHERE id=2')

end

db.execute('SELECT * FROM accounts')
→ do |row|

  puts row

end
```

Two execute calls will change the database, adding 100 (dollars or whatever) to account number 1 and subtracting 100 from account number 2. If no exceptions occur, the transaction will be committed when the end is reached. If an exception occurs with either query, the transaction will be rolled back and no changes will be made.

To confirm the values in the database, a SELECT query is then run.

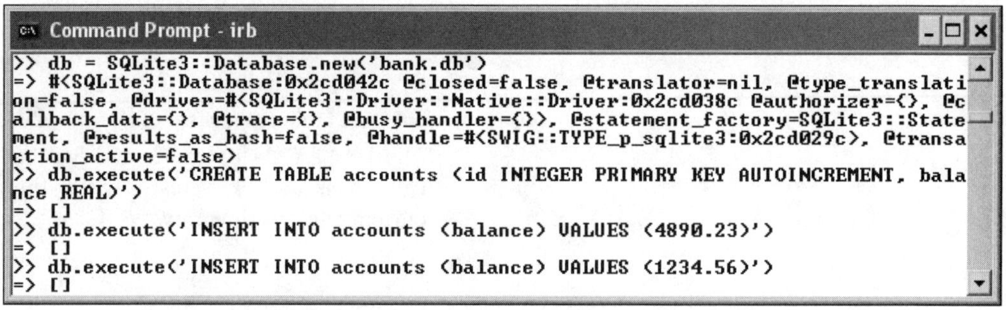

Figure 14.9 A new database is created, containing one table, into which two records are inserted.

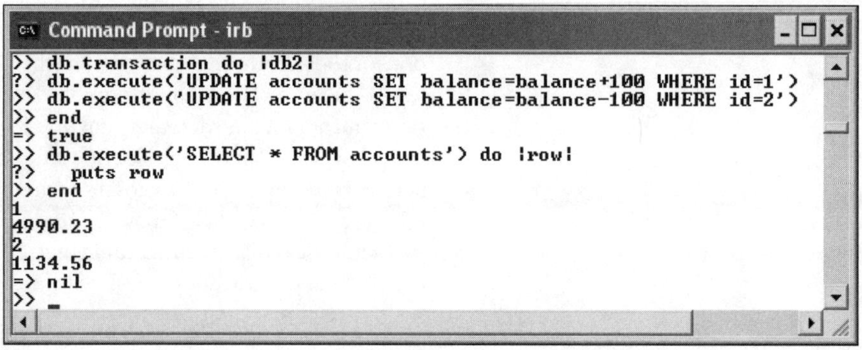

Figure 14.10 The success of the transfer (and the transaction) is reflected in the updated balances.

7. Create a failed transfer (**Figure 14.11**):

```
db.transaction do |db2|
db.execute('UPDATE accounts SET
→balance=balance+100 WHERE id=1')
db.execute('UPDATE accounts SET
→balnce=balance-100 WHERE id=3')
end
db.execute('SELECT * FROM accounts')
→do |row|
  puts row
end
```

This code is exactly the same as that in the previous two steps except that in the second query, the column name `balance` is misspelled. This will cause an exception and no changes will be made to the database.

8. Close the database:

```
db.close
```

PERFORMING TRANSACTIONS

```
Command Prompt - irb

>> db.transaction do |db2|
?> db.execute('UPDATE accounts SET balance=balance+100 WHERE id=1')
>> db.execute('UPDATE accounts SET balnce=balance-100 WHERE id=3')
>> end
SQLite3::SQLException: no such column: balnce
        from C:/ruby/lib/ruby/gems/1.8/gems/sqlite3-ruby-1.2.2-x86-mswin32/lib/s
qlite3/errors.rb:62:in `check'
        from C:/ruby/lib/ruby/gems/1.8/gems/sqlite3-ruby-1.2.2-x86-mswin32/lib/s
qlite3/statement.rb:39:in `initialize'
        from C:/ruby/lib/ruby/gems/1.8/gems/sqlite3-ruby-1.2.2-x86-mswin32/lib/s
qlite3/database.rb:154:in `new'
        from C:/ruby/lib/ruby/gems/1.8/gems/sqlite3-ruby-1.2.2-x86-mswin32/lib/s
qlite3/database.rb:154:in `prepare'
        from C:/ruby/lib/ruby/gems/1.8/gems/sqlite3-ruby-1.2.2-x86-mswin32/lib/s
qlite3/database.rb:181:in `execute'
        from (irb):36
        from C:/ruby/lib/ruby/gems/1.8/gems/sqlite3-ruby-1.2.2-x86-mswin32/lib/s
qlite3/database.rb:564:in `transaction'
        from (irb):34
        from C:/ruby/lib/ruby/site_ruby/1.8/rubygems/requirement.rb:129
>> db.execute('SELECT * FROM accounts') do |row|
?>   puts row
>> end
1
4990.23
2
1134.56
=> nil
>>
```

Figure 14.11 The syntax error in the second SQL query causes the transaction to be rolled back.

✔ Tips

- Understand that an exception is just one (obvious) reason why you'd roll back a transaction. In this example, if one query referred to an `id` value that didn't exist, no exception would occur but the transfer still shouldn't be committed. You would need to use program logic, like checking the value of `db.changes`, to determine whether or not to commit such transactions.

- When using transactions within blocks, do not ever call `commit` or `rollback` within the block. The block will take care of calling both as appropriate.

- You can only perform one transaction (aka group of queries) at a time. You cannot nest one transaction within another.

- SQLite and the `sqlite3-ruby` gem support many other, somewhat more advanced, techniques not discussed in this chapter. Topics to consider looking into include triggers, constraints, prepared statements, user-defined functions, and storing binary data (blobs).

Deleting Records

This chapter does not include examples of deleting database records, but doing so is no more complicated than running an `UPDATE` query. The SQL command involved would start with `DELETE` and would still be run using the `execute` method. As with `INSERT` queries, the `changes` method returns the number of rows affected by `DELETE`. However, if `DELETE` is used to completely empty a table (`DELETE FROM tablename`), the `changes` method returns nothing.

NETWORKING

Networking is simply the act of two computers communicating. The computer requesting information is the *client*, and the computer that receives requests and returns responses is the *server*. Often, clients send data as part of the request, which dictates the server's response. For example, a Web browser is a client that requests a Web page from a server. The server sends the HTML, images, and other content in response. That's the basic idea behind networking, but it can be implemented in any number of ways.

Ruby's networking functionality can be found in the Standard Library and in gems (the most popular of which, Ruby on Rails, is discussed in the next chapter). A lot of the functionality is easy to use and can be applied to many different needs.

This chapter starts by discussing basic client-server communications over *sockets*. You'll learn how to use a Ruby script in both the client and server roles. Between those discussions, there'll be a quick tangent into the subject of *threads*. Threads are not networking-specific but are often used in server situations. The chapter concludes with discussions of two more specific networking concepts. One involves making HTTP (Hypertext Transfer Protocol) requests; the other is on handling RSS (Really Simple Syndication) feeds.

Creating a Socket Server

The most primitive type of networking uses *sockets*: gateways for communication. Applications create sockets to allow for interactions; for example, the MySQL database server creates a `mysql.sock` file when it's running; any client that needs to communicate with a database uses that socket.

A socket consists of a *protocol*, an *IP address*, and a *port*. The two most common protocols are TCP (Transmission Control Protocol) and UDP (User Datagram Protocol). Ruby can make use of either protocol; in this chapter I'll demonstrate TCP, which is more common. The IP address identifies a computer. Servers available on the Internet use a meaningful IP address, whereas those on local networks have dummy ones. A socket's port is an integer between 1 and 65,535. Many ports are associated with specific applications or processes: 80 is commonly used for Web serving, 25 for SMTP (Simple Mail Transfer Protocol), and 3306 for MySQL. For your purposes, you'll likely want to choose something random and not otherwise in use.

Socket functionality is defined in the `TCPServer` and `TCPSocket` classes. To use either, include the `socket` library:

```
require 'socket'
```

To create a simple socket server, use the `open` method (equivalent to `new`):

```
server = TCPServer.open(port)
server = TCPServer.open(11000)
```

Once a socket server has been created, it can accept client connections, using the `accept` method. The server can then interact with the client, closing the connection once its finished. In theory, that code is just:

```
client = server.accept
# Do whatever.
client.close
```

However, that code will run once and eventually the Ruby script will terminate. If a connection isn't made exactly while the script is running, the client will miss its opportunity. Instead, have the script continually listen for clients, by using a loop:

```
loop {
    client = server.accept
    # Do whatever.
    client.close
}
```

Or you can use a `while` loop:

```
while client = server.accept
    # Do whatever.
    client.close
end
```

Once a client-server connection has been made, it can be used like a file, as a socket is another type of IO (input/output) object. This means a server can read input from the client using `gets` and send output to the client using `puts`. Conversely, a client can read the server's output using `gets` and send input to the server using `puts` (see Chapter 13, "Directories and Files," for more on IO and its methods).

Before walking through an example of this, there's one more thing to mention. The `puts` and `gets` methods, when called without referencing an object, are applied to the standard input and output. By default, these are the keyboard and the screen. Because network communications also involve reading from and writing to other sockets, it's a good idea to be explicit when using the standard input and output. To do so, use the special constants `STDOUT` and `STDIN`:

```
STDOUT.puts 'Enter your name: '
name = STDINPUT.gets
```

This next example will create a socket server, which you can then connect to using *telnet* (a command-line TCP client). A socket server could be used for all sorts of purposes, like

Script 15.1 This Ruby script creates a socket server that simply sends a hello greeting to the connected client.

```
        Script
1    # Script 15.1 - server.rb
2
3    # Include the library:
4    require 'socket'
5
6    # Create the object:
7    server = TCPServer.open(11000)
8
9    # Print a message:
10   STDOUT.puts 'The server is running.
     Press Control + C to terminate.'
11
12   while client = server.accept
13
14       # Send the client the message:
15       client.puts 'Hello, Socket World!'
16
17       # Close the connection:
18       client.close
19
20   end
```

```
      Ruby: Visual QuickStart Guide
: ruby -w server.rb
The server is running. Press Control + C to terminate.
```

Figure 15.1 The result when this script is executed.

reporting on an application's status or the health of the server itself (e.g., the amount of available disk space). To keep the particulars of this script simple, this server will just return a greeting.

To make a socket server:

1. Begin a new Ruby script in your text editor or IDE (**Script 15.1**):

   `# Script 15.1 - server.rb`

2. Include the socket library and create the socket server:

   `require 'socket'`

   `server = TCPServer.open(11000)`

   `STDOUT.puts 'The server is running.`
   `→Press Control + C to terminate.'`

   This server will run on the arbitrarily chosen port 11,000. A message then indicates to the person that started this script that the server is running and they have to press Control+C to stop the execution of the script and the server (**Figure 15.1**).

   Unfortunately, using Control+C on Windows will not successfully terminate the execution of the script. See the sidebar for an alternative if you're using Windows.

   continues on next page

CREATING A SOCKET SERVER

Control+C and Windows

Pressing Control+C will normally terminate a running process on Windows (within a console window). In the two server examples in this chapter, that doesn't work, for rather complicated reasons. A proper solution would require Ruby code beyond the scope of this book (and, to be frank, would detract from what's important in these examples). So instead of pressing Control+C when you need to terminate the script, bring up the Windows Task Manager by pressing Control+Alt+Delete. Then select ruby.exe in the list on the Processes tab, and click End Process. Click Yes at the prompt. That will terminate the Ruby script and return the console window back to the prompt. The scripts in this chapter will continue to include the Control+C message, but feel free to change it if you'd prefer.

3. Start a loop:

```
while client = server.accept
```

This loop will continue to run as long as it can accept client connections, which will be forever. Within the loop, the `client` variable represents the connected client.

4. Send something to the client:

```
client.puts 'Hello, Socket World!'
```

Use the `puts` method, applied explicitly to `client`, to send any text.

5. Close the connection and complete the loop:

```
    client.close

end
```

6. Save and run the completed script.

Figure 15.1 shows what you should see when you start the socket server.

7. Use telnet to contact the server (**Figure 15.2**).

You'll need to access your computer from a command-line interface, like a console window on Windows or a terminal application on Mac OS X, Linux, or Unix. Then execute this command:

```
telnet localhost 11000
```

The second argument to telnet is the IP address; the third is the port. You can

specify the IP address of your computer, or of the computer running the Ruby script if it's different, but you can also just use *localhost*, if running both the script and the telnet client on the same machine.

If you see an error saying something along the lines of "command not found," then you do not have a telnet client installed. Search the Internet for an alternative client application to download and use, such as the popular PuTTY for Windows (`www.chiark.greenend.org.uk/~sgtatham/putty/`).

8. Press `Control+C` to terminate the execution of the server script.

Again, if you're using Windows and `Control+C` doesn't work, see the sidebar for instructions on terminating the script.

✔ Tip

■ I state in the introduction to this chapter that networking is communication between two (or more) computers, but the first three examples are run on just one. In these cases, the same computer is acting as both the server and the client, which is fine, and the end result is the same as if you were using two separate machines.

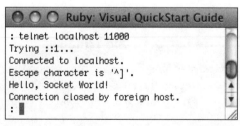

Figure 15.2 Using telnet, a server connection was made (your results might vary slightly, depending upon the operating system and telnet client in use).

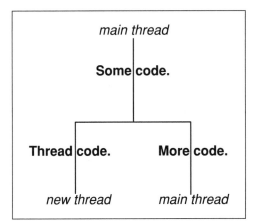

main thread

Some|**code.**

Thread|**code.**   **More**|**code.**

new thread   *main thread*

Figure 15.3 When a new thread is created, the execution of the script continues, while simultaneously executing the new thread's code.

Using Threads

As mentioned in the introduction to this chapter, threads are not networking-specific but can be used with network-related code, like a socket server. With a non-threaded Ruby script, the Ruby interpreter executes the commands in the script sequentially and then terminates. By using threads, you can have the interpreter run sets of commands at the same time (i.e., in parallel). Ruby threads aren't perfect (see the sidebar "Thread Issues") but are perfectly fine for many situations.

To create a new thread, use Thread.new, following it with a block of code to be executed:

```
# Some code.
Thread.new { # Thread code }
# More code.
```

As **Figure 15.3** illustrates, a new thread executes the code in the block while the existing thread continues executing the rest of the script. Unlike in a non-threaded script, the code is not run in a single, sequential line.

One thing to watch out for is that the script will terminate when the main thread has finished running. When this happens, any still running threads will be killed off. Because it's not possible to know whether the main thread or a secondary will finish running first, you can use the join method to make the script wait for a thread to finish:

```
some_var = Thread.new { # Thread code. }
# Main thread code.
some_var.join
```

This next script will create a socket server that allows for multiple simultaneous connections by creating a new thread for each. Unlike the server in Script 15.1, this server will also be interactive: maintaining a connection, taking input from the client, and sending information back. To do so, the script will use a loop to read in the input, as if it were reading data from a text file.

To create a threaded server:

1. Begin a new Ruby script in your text editor or IDE (**Script 15.2**):

   ```
   # Script 15.2 - server2.rb
   ```

2. Create the server object:

   ```
   require 'socket'
   server = TCPServer.open(11000)
   STDOUT.puts 'The server is running.
   → Press Control + C to terminate.'
   ```

   This code is exactly like that in Script 15.1. This socket server will again run on port 11,000.

3. Start a loop:

   ```
   loop do
   ```

   Because this script uses threads, the infinite loop will be written differently. This loop takes no conditions and just runs until the loop is explicitly broken.

4. Create a new thread for each connection:

   ```
   Thread.new(server.accept) do |client|
   ```

   The new method takes any number of optional arguments. By providing it with the value of server.accept, every time a new client connects to this server, a new thread will be created, associated with that connection. That association is passed to the thread block, where it is assigned to client.

5. Print some messages:

   ```
   client.puts 'Connected!'
   client.print 'Enter a command
   → ("quit" to terminate): '
   ```

   The first line indicates to the user that they have successfully connected to the server. The next line prompts the user. The print method is used so that the user types on the same line as the prompt (**Figure 15.4**).

Script 15.2 Using threads, this script can handle multiple client connections at one time. This server also interacts with the client, instead of immediately terminating the connection.

```
1   # Script 15.2 - server2.rb
2
3   # Include the library:
4   require 'socket'
5
6   # Create the object:
7   server = TCPServer.open(11000)
8
9   # Print a message:
10  STDOUT.puts 'The server is running. Press
    Control + C to terminate.'
11
12  # Run continuously:
13  loop do
14
15      # Each connection is a new thread:
16      Thread.new(server.accept) do |client|
17
18          # Greet the client:
19          client.puts 'Connected!'
20          client.print 'Enter a command
            ("quit" to terminate): '
21
22          # Get the input:
23          while input = client.gets
24
25              # Drop the newline:
26              input.chomp!
27
28              # Terminate?
29              break if input == 'quit'
30
31              # Print some messages:
32              STDOUT.puts "#{client.peeraddr[2]}
                :#{client.peeraddr[1]} entered:
                '#{input}'"
33              client.puts "You entered
                '#{input}'."
34              client.print 'Enter a command
                ("quit" to terminate): '
35              client.flush
36
37          end # End of while loop.
38
39          # Close the connection:
40          client.puts 'Terminating the
            connection...'
41          client.flush
42          client.close
43
44      end # End of Thread.new
45
46  end # End of loop.
```

USING THREADS

6. Read in the user input:

```
while input = client.gets
  input.chomp!
```

This is a simple way to read in what the client submits (i.e., what the user types at the client prompt). The terminating newline character also read in by `gets` is permanently removed using the `chomp!` method.

7. If the user enters *quit*, terminate the connection:

```
break if input == 'quit'
```

The server should have some command that the user can enter to close the connection. If the user enters just *quit*, then the `while` loop will be broken. The thread will then execute the code after the `while` loop begun in Step 6.

8. Have the server print something to the standard output:

```
STDOUT.puts "#{client.peeraddr[2]}:
#{client.peeraddr[1]} entered:
→ '#{input}'"
```

This is a kind of way of having the server report activity (you could also write it to a log). The server will send to the standard output (i.e., the screen) whatever the user entered. To identify the different connections, the client's `peeraddr` method is called. It returns an array of information about the connection. The third element, indexed at 2, will be the host name of the client; the second element will be the port of the client (which will be a different port than the server uses). **Figure 15.5** shows the result.

9. Print some messages to the client:

```
client.puts "You entered
→ '#{input}'."
client.print 'Enter a command
→ ("quit" to terminate): '
client.flush
```

First, what the client entered at the prompt is reported back to the client. Then the client is re-prompted. The `flush` method is called to immediately send the messages to the client, so they don't linger in the buffer (see the first tip if you're not familiar with the concept).

continues on next page

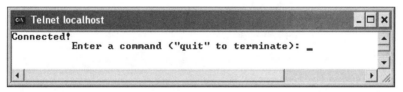

Figure 15.4 What the client sees after they've connected to the server.

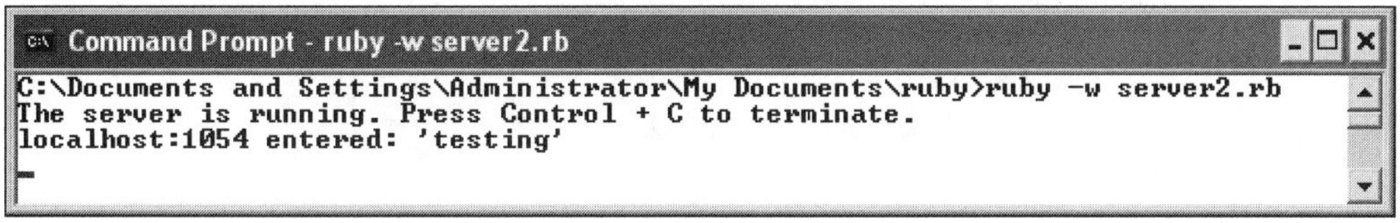

Figure 15.5 The client activity is reported by the server script.

10. Complete the `while` loop and close the connection:

```
end # End of while loop.
client.puts 'Terminating the
→ connection...'
client.flush
client.close
```

The script gets to this point after the client has entered *quit*. A message is sent indicating that the connection will be closed, the buffer is flushed, and the connection is actually closed.

11. Complete the script:

```
    end # End of Thread.new
end # End of loop.
```

12. Save and run the completed script.

13. Simultaneously connect to the server using multiple clients.

Just create two console sessions, and execute `telnet localhost 11000` in both.

14. Type any random text in both sessions to test the server (**Figures 15.6**, **15.7**, and **15.8**).

Note that you may see some odd formatting—extra spaces and the like—in the client window, depending upon the operating system and telnet software being used.

15. Press `Control+C` to terminate the execution of the Ruby script.

Or use the Windows Task Manager on Windows.

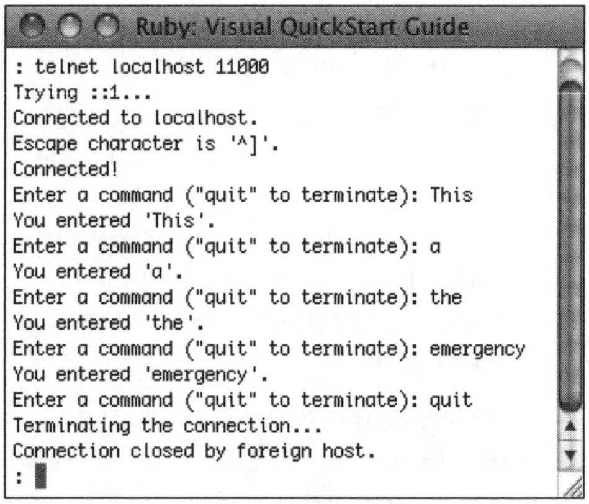

Figure 15.6 One client interaction with the server.

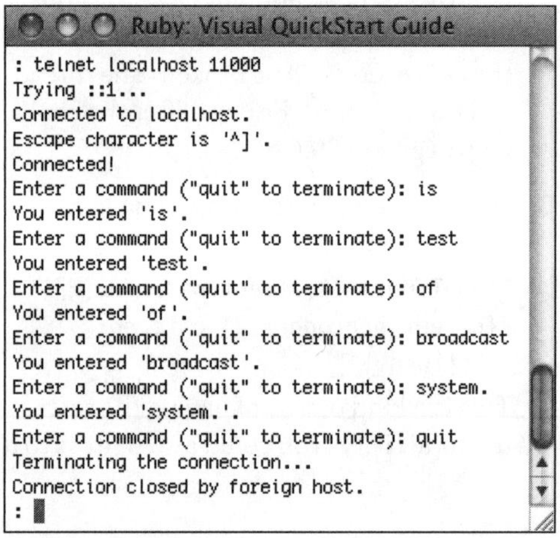

Figure 15.7 A second, simultaneous client interaction with the same server.

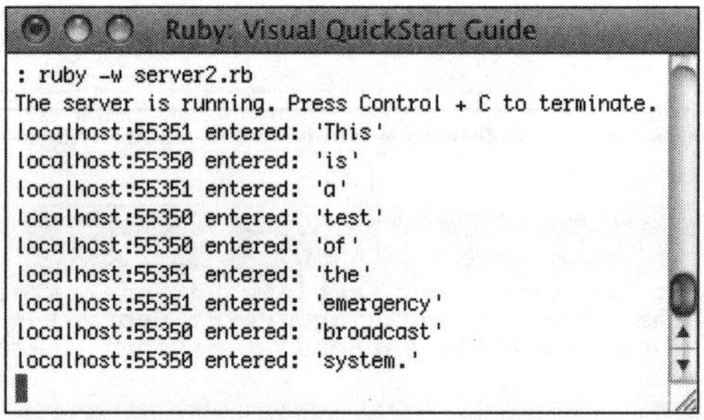

Figure 15.8 The results in the server's console window.

Thread Issues

Threads as discussed in this section of the chapter are implemented entirely within Ruby. This makes them usable on any operating system, but they do have their drawbacks. For starters, parallel code execution may really be interwoven: some of this thread is executed, then the other, then the first again, etc. Second, Ruby threads can't take advantage of computers with multiple processors or multiple cores. In short, Ruby threads won't always be fast or efficient.

One alternative to Ruby threads is to use *forks*. A fork is also a parallel execution of some code, but using another instance of the Ruby interpreter. Metaphorically speaking, think of Ruby threads as having two people in the same car instead of just one: twice as many people are traveling but their fates are tied together. Conversely, forks are like sending two people in two separate cars. Unfortunately, forks cannot be used on Windows, so this is not a cross-platform option.

Another alternative is being added in Ruby 1.9: *fibers*. Fibers implement *coroutines*, which are a more advanced topic than threads. See the Ruby documentation on the `Fiber` class for details.

✔ Tips

■ Input/output interactions, like using the keyboard and screen, files, or sockets, make use of a *buffer*. The buffer is memory where input and output are temporarily stored. For instance, reading from a file starts with the data being read into the buffer, followed by the buffer being read in by the Ruby code. Any delays created by the buffer are normally imperceptible, but to forcibly empty the buffer, thereby immediately enacting an input/output occurrence, call the `flush` method.

■ There is a lot more to the topic of threads than is covered here. For more information, like how to access and control threads, see the Ruby documentation.

■ `GServer`, part of the Ruby Standard Library, can be used to create multi-threaded servers. It manages threads, logs activity, and can even create servers running on different ports at the same time.

Creating a Socket Client

The first two examples demonstrate how to create a socket server; now it's time to look at the client side of things from a Ruby perspective. To create a socket client, again turn to the socket library, but this time, create an object of type TCPSocket. Provide it with the IP address or host name of the server, and the port. When you're finished with the server, close the connection:

```
require 'socket'
server = TCPSocket.new(hostname, port)
# Use server.
server.close
```

The open method is used like new but can take a block. The block will be passed the connection, which will automatically be closed at the end of the block (like using blocks with file connections):

```
TCPSocket.open(hostname, port) do
→ |server|
    # Use server.
end
```

As in Scripts 15.1 and 15.2, you can treat the connection as you would any IO object, using gets for input—reading data from the server—and print or puts for output—sending data to the server. But using gets will be problematic. That method reads only one line at a time. If the server sends multiple lines of text, there's a conflict. Also, gets is a *blocking* method, halting all other activity while it waits to read in a line. If it attempts to read in a line when none is forthcoming, the script will just wait and wait. The solution will be to use the read_nonblock and readpartial methods. The former never blocks other activity, and the latter only does so in certain circumstances. Both should be provided with the maximum number of bytes to read in. As 4,096 bytes is a common buffer size, it makes sense to use that value.

Script 15.3 This script sends user-typed input to a server and displays the server's response in the console window.

```
                            Script
1    # Script 15.3 - client.rb
2
3    # Include the library:
4    require 'socket'
5
6    # Create the object:
7    TCPSocket.open('localhost', 11000) do
     |server|
8
9        # Print what the server initially says:
10       sleep(1)
11       STDOUT.print server.read_nonblock(4096)
12
13       # Loop continually:
14       loop do
15
16           # Get input from the user:
17           input = STDIN.gets
18
19           # Send it to the server:
20           server.puts input
21           server.flush
22
23           # Print the server's response:
24           STDOUT.print server.readpartial
             (4096).chomp
25
26           # Terminate?
27           break if input.chomp == 'quit'
28
29       end # End of loop.
30
31   end # End of TCPSocket block.
32
33   # Add a newline:
34   puts
```

To create a socket client:

1. Begin a new Ruby script in your text editor or IDE (**Script 15.3**):

```
# Script 15.3 - client.rb
```

2. Create the server object:

```
require 'socket'
TCPSocket.open('localhost', 11000)
→ do |server|
```

The client will connect to the server created by Script 15.2, running on this computer and using the port 11,000.

3. Retrieve the server's initial response:

```
sleep(1)
STDOUT.print server.read_nonblock
→ (4096)
```

The script first uses the `sleep` method to wait one second before continuing. This gives the server time to do whatever it needs to do and respond to the client. Then up to 4,096 bytes, or 4 kilobytes, are read in and immediately displayed in the standard output.

4. Start a loop:

```
loop do
```

This script should run so long as the user wants to continue communicating with the server. So an infinite loop is used, exactly as in Script 15.2.

5. Read input from the keyboard and send it to the server:

```
input = STDIN.gets
server.puts input
server.flush
```

A line of text is read in from the standard input (the keyboard by default) and then sent to the server using `puts`. The server's buffer is flushed so that it receives the message without delay.

continues on next page

6. Print the server's response:

```
STDOUT.print server.readpartial
→ (4096).chomp
```

Here, the `readpartial` method is used to read up to 4 kilobytes of the server's response. The response is then sent to the standard output so that the user can see it.

7. If the user enters *quit*, terminate the script:

```
break if input.chomp == 'quit'
```

If the user enters *quit*, that message will be sent to the server (in the code up to this point), and the server will terminate the connection. But this script is also running an infinite loop, so it should also watch for this command. When it's entered, this script's infinite loop will be broken.

8. Complete the script:

```
    end # End of loop.
end # End of TCPSocket block.
puts
```

The final use of `puts` just adds a newline to the output so that the next prompt, after the script terminates, appears on a subsequent line.

9. Make sure that Script 15.2 is running.

10. Save and run this script (**Figure 15.9**).

✔ Tip

■ I've cheated a little bit here with my use of `puts` and `print`. Because I know how the Ruby script server sends its messages—sometimes adding newlines, sometimes not, I've manipulated the use of `puts`, `print`, and `chomp` here to make the end result appear as I want it to. This is really just a cosmetic issue and doesn't affect the functionality of the script.

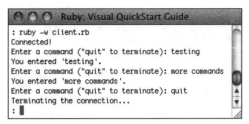

Figure 15.9 This client application, written as a Ruby script, is being used to interact with the server (Script 15.2).

Table 15.1

Open-URI Methods
METHOD
base_uri
charset
content_encoding
content_type
meta
last_modified
status

CGI and eRuby

Among the networking-related tasks you can perform using Ruby but are not discussed in this chapter is the creation of dynamic Web sites. I omitted this topic largely because Chapter 16 adequately covers Ruby on Rails, by far the most popular way to develop Web applications using Ruby.

The alternatives to using Ruby on Rails include writing CGI (Common Gateway Interface) scripts and using eRuby (embedded Ruby). CGI scripts used to be a common way to handle forms and generate content on the fly, but they are more rarely seen these days. They can be written in many languages, including Perl, C, and, of course, Ruby. A CGI script is just pure Ruby code that includes the cgi library and is run from a special directory on the Web server.

If you'd rather use Ruby directly within HTML code, switch to eRuby. To use it, the Apache Web server must have mod_ruby enabled and the file must use the appropriate extension (such as .rhtml). Ruby code is then embedded within the HTML using special tags: <% and %>. Using eRuby instead of CGI scripts is both easier to program and faster to execute

HTTP Connections

HTTP, and its more secure sibling HTTPS, are used for interactions with Web sites (which is why most URLs begin with *http://*). Normally HTTP requests are made using a Web browser, but you can also use Ruby.

To establish an HTTP connection, you can use the Standard Library's net/http class. An example usage of that class can be found in Chapter 17, "Dynamic Programming," so I'll skip formal discussion of it here, as most of its functionality is part of the Open-URI class (along with other capabilities). Open-URI is also part of the Standard Library, so you need to include the library to use it in your code:

```
require 'open-uri'
```

To make the connection, use the open method:

```
http = open('http://www.example.com/
→ page.html')
```

At this point you can read from the object using any of the standard IO methods. Then you close the connection:

```
http.close
```

As with many other resources used in Ruby, you can assign a block to the established connection. This has the added benefit of automatically closing the connection at the end of the block. Within the block, you can access the server response as if you were reading data in from a file:

```
open('http://www.example.com/page.html')
→ { |http|
    puts http.read
}
```

Along with reading in the contents of the resource, you can use the methods listed in **Table 15.1** to see some of the resource's properties.

There's more to HTTP interactions than just requesting a page, however. Requests often involve sending data to the Web server, performing authentication, and more. In this next example, a request will be made of a page that requires the proper username/password combination. **Figures 15.10 and 15.11** show what those responses would look like if the page was accessed using a Web browser.

When accessing such a page in the Web browser, you'd be prompted for the user-name and password. To provide these values from a Ruby script, use the **open** method's second parameter. That optional argument can be used to customize the request in many ways. For example, that argument can provide authentication values or be used to have Ruby pretend to be a particular Web browser by setting the *user-agent* value.

To make an HTTP request:

1. Begin a new Ruby script in your text editor or IDE (**Script 15.4**):

   ```
   # Script 15.4 - http_test.rb
   ```

2. Include the Open-URI library:

   ```
   require 'open-uri'
   ```

3. Begin a block of code:

   ```
   begin
   ```

   In order to nicely handle any problems that might occur, for example, if the page could not be found, I'll apply exception handling to this example. For details, see Chapter 11, "Debugging and Error Handling."

Script 15.4 The Open-URI library is used to request an authentication-protected Web page.

```
1   # Script 15.4 - http_test.rb
2
3   # Include the library:
4   require 'open-uri'
5
6   # Start a block:
7   begin
8
9       # Open the resource, providing basic
        authentication:
10      open('http://www.dmcinsights.com/
        ruby/ruby_test.php', :http_basic_
        authentication => ['Chicago', 'Bears'])
        { |http|
11
12          # Display some information about
            the page:
13          puts "Content-type:
            #{http.content_type}"
14          puts "Status: #{http.status[1]}"
15          puts '--------------'
16
17          # Display the page's content:
18          puts http.read
19
20      }
21
22   rescue => e
23       puts "The connection could not be
         made: #{e.message}"
24   end
```

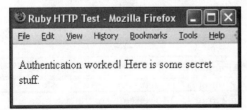

Figure 15.10 If the page is requested in a Web browser by a properly authenticated user, this will be the result.

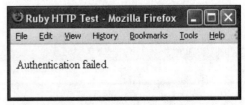

Figure 15.11 Without proper authentication, the page looks like this (again, in a Web browser).

HTTP CONNECTIONS

4. Open a connection to the URL:

```
open('http://www.dmcinsights.com/
→ ruby/ruby_test.php',
→ :http_basic_authentication =>
→ ['Chicago', 'Bears']
) { |http|
```

The specific URL is a PHP script on the Web site associated with this book. The authentication values passed along with the request are a username of *Chicago* and a password of *Bears*.

Within the block, the open resource will be assigned to the `http` variable.

5. Display some information about the resource:

```
puts "Content-type:
→ #{http.content_type}"
puts "Status: #{http.status[1]}"
puts '--------------'
```

Just to see these values, I'll print out the resource's content type and its status. The last line creates a separator for the page content to follow.

6. Display the page's content:

```
puts http.read
```

The `read` method will read in the page's content, as if it were reading from a file.

7. Complete the `open` block:

```
}
```

8. Handle any exceptions:

```
rescue => e
    puts "The connection could not
    be made: #{e.message}"
end
```

If a problem occurred, this message will be printed, along with the specific error (**Figure 15.12**).

continues on next page

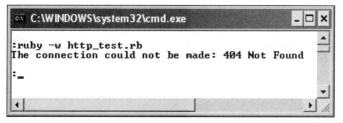

Figure 15.12 If the URL could not be accessed, for whatever reason, the exception will be handled and displayed.

HTTP CONNECTIONS

9. Save and run the completed script (**Figure 15.13**).

10. Change the authentication values, then save, and rerun the completed script (**Figure 15.14**).

✔ Tips

■ The Open-URI library can handle most HTTP, HTTPS, and FTP-related tasks. If you need to perform more elaborate procedures, such as sending cookies to a URL, use the specific *net* library instead, such as net/http. Again, there's a quick use of this library in Chapter 17.

■ The Hpricot Ruby gem can be used to parse HTML. You might use it to read in a Web page and then access specific parts of it.

■ You can generate HTML from Ruby using the RedCloth gem, discussed in Chapter 12, "RubyGems," or Markaby (www.tfletcher.com), among others.

```
C:\WINDOWS\system32\cmd.exe                                              _ □ ×
:ruby -w http_test.rb
Content-type: text/html
Status: OK
----------------
<!DOCTYPE html PUBLIC "-//W3C//DTD XHTML 1.0 Strict//EN"
        "http://www.w3.org/TR/xhtml1/DTD/xhtml1-strict.dtd">
<html xmlns="http://www.w3.org/1999/xhtml" xml:lang="en" lang="en">
<head>
        <meta http-equiv="content-type" content="text/html; charset=utf-8" />
        <title>Ruby HTTP Test</title>
        <meta name="generator" content="BBEdit 8.7" />
</head>
<body>
<p>Authentication worked! Here is some secret stuff.</p>
</body>
</html>

:_
```

Figure 15.13 The result when using the proper authentication values.

```
C:\WINDOWS\system32\cmd.exe                                              _ □ ×
:ruby -w http_test.rb
Content-type: text/html
Status: OK
----------------
<!DOCTYPE html PUBLIC "-//W3C//DTD XHTML 1.0 Strict//EN"
        "http://www.w3.org/TR/xhtml1/DTD/xhtml1-strict.dtd">
<html xmlns="http://www.w3.org/1999/xhtml" xml:lang="en" lang="en">
<head>
        <meta http-equiv="content-type" content="text/html; charset=utf-8" />
        <title>Ruby HTTP Test</title>
        <meta name="generator" content="BBEdit 8.7" />
</head>
<body>
<p>Authentication failed.</p>
</body>
</html>

:_
```

Figure 15.14 If the username and password are incorrect, but the URL was accessible, you'll see this.

Table 15.2

FeedTools:: Feed Methods
METHOD
abstract
author
base_uri
categories
copyright
description
entries
id
images
items
language
link
published
rights
source
subtitle
time
title
updated

Handling RSS Feeds

Another of the many ways that a Ruby script or any client might interact with a server is to handle RSS feeds. RSS, short for Really Simple Syndication (in the current implementation, it has older meanings, too), is a format Web sites can use to provide information about the site's content. For example, news-related sites and blogs use RSS feeds to list recent articles and postings.

The RSS client (and not to confuse the point, but many Web browsers can now handle RSS as well) retrieves the feed as XML data. The data reflects the feed's title, description, URL, copyright, and more. Secondarily, but just as important, the XML file contains a list of items, which is the feed's content. For each item, the RSS feed provides its title, description, author, posting date, direct URL, and more.

You can handle an RSS feed in a Ruby script by just reading and parsing the XML file, but using the FeedTools gem (www.rubyforge. org/projects/feedtools/) is an easier option. To start, install the gem, and then include it:

```
require 'rubygems'
require 'feed_tools'
```

Next, call the Feed class' open method, providing it with a URL for the feed:

```
feed = FeedTools::Feed.open('http://www.
→ example.com/feedpage/')
```

Table 15.2 lists some of the methods you can invoke on the feed object. The value each returns is clearly implied by the method's name, for the most part.

Of these methods, one of the most important is items, used to access each item in the feed:

```
feed.items.each do |i|
    # Use i.title, i.description, etc.
end
```

For this next example, a Ruby script will access an RSS feed provided by this book's supporting Web site. Specifically, it's an RSS feed of recent postings in the site's supporting forums.

To handle an RSS feed:

1. Install the FeedTools gem (**Figure 15.15**):

   ```
   gem install feedtools
   ```

   That is the basic command for installing the gem. You'll need to preface this with sudo if using Mac OS X, Linux, or Unix. For more on gems, see Chapter 12.

2. Begin a new Ruby script in your text editor or IDE (**Script 15.5**):

   ```
   # Script 15.5 - rss.rb
   ```

3. Include the gems:

   ```
   require 'rubygems'
   require 'feed_tools'
   ```

   As I state in Chapter 12, if you're using Windows or a version of Ruby 1.9 or higher, you can omit the first line but there's no harm in keeping it in. Also note that the library is called *FeedTools* (with capital letters), it's installed by referring to *feedtools* (all lowercase), but it's included using *feed_tools* (all lowercase plus an underscore).

Script 15.5 The FeedTools gem is used to read in and display an RSS feed.

```
1    # Script 15.5 - rss.rb
2
3    # Include the gems:
4    require 'rubygems'
5    require 'feed_tools'
6
7    # Start a block:
8    begin
9
10       # Open the feed:
11       feed = FeedTools::Feed.open
         ('http://www.dmcinsights.com/phorum/
         feed.php?0,type=rss')
12
13       # Print the feed's information:
14       puts "Title: #{feed.title}"
15       puts "Description: #{feed.description}"
16
17       # Print each item
18       feed.entries.each { |item|
19           puts
20           puts "#{item.title}\n#{item.
             description.slice(0, 100)}...
             \n#{item.link}"
21       }
22
23   rescue => e
24
25       puts "The feed could not be read:
         #{e.message}"
26
27   end
28
```

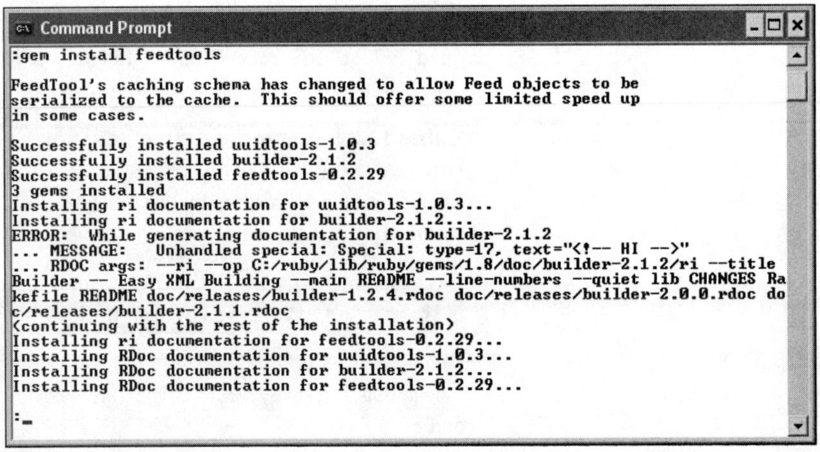

Figure 15.15 Installing the FeedTools gem on Windows.

4. Start a block and create the feed object:

```
begin
    feed = FeedTools::Feed.open
    → ('http://www.dmcinsights.com/
    → phorum/feed.php?0,type=rss')
```

As with the preceding script, this one will use a `begin-rescue-end` block to handle any exceptions that might occur. Then, the `FeedTools::Feed.open` method is called. The source for the feed is a PHP script on my server.

5. Print the feed's title and description:

```
puts "Title: #{feed.title}"
puts "Description:
→ #{feed.description}"
```

These two attributes apply to the feed as a whole.

6. Print each feed item:

```
feed.entries.each { |item|
    puts
    puts "#{item.title}\n#{item.
    → description.slice(0, 100)}...
    → \n#{item.link}"
}
```

This iterator will access every item in the feed, assigning each to `item` within the block. Then a blank line is printed by just calling `puts`. Next, the item's title, description, and link are each displayed on their own lines. The description returned by this feed can be quite long, so I slice it down to the first 100 characters.

7. Complete the script:

```
rescue => e
    puts "The feed could not be read:
    → #{e.message}"
end
```

If a problem occurred, this message will be printed, along with the specific error.

8. Save and run the completed script (**Figure 15.16**).

In version `0.2.29` of FeedTools, the most current one at the time of this writing, lots of warnings came up, so I ran the Ruby interpreter without the -w flag.

continues on next page

```
: ruby rss.rb
Title: Larry Ullman's Book Forums
Description: Forums primarily created to support Larry Ullman's books, but that can also be used to ask quest
ions about related technologies and topics.

have to log in twice in firefox (2 replies)
Hello.<br/><br/>I have built my first php/mysql website based very closely on examples in the book. ...
http://www.dmcinsights.com/phorum/read.php?19%2C38599%2C38599#msg-38599

Script 9.1 - view_users.php - id doesn't pass (14 replies)
Operating system: Windows XP, Apache Version: 2.2.8 , PHP Version: 5.2.6 , MySQL Version: 5.0.51b, W...
http://www.dmcinsights.com/phorum/read.php?19%2C38640%2C38640#msg-38640

connecting via PHP does nothing! (no replies)
Mac OS X 10.4.11 on an MDD G4 Mac<br/>MySQL 5.0.67 installed<br/>MySQL startup item installed<br/>PH...
http://www.dmcinsights.com/phorum/read.php?8%2C38674%2C38674#msg-38674

PHP vs RoR (4 replies)
In Newsletter #14, I saw Larry discussed how RoR was gaining popularity (which, after what I've unde...
http://www.dmcinsights.com/phorum/read.php?18%2C38653%2C38653#msg-38653

modified script 17.1, actors and movies (2 replies)
PHP version 5.2.5<br/>MySQL version 5.0.51a<br/>Apache version 2.2<br/>Mozilla Firefox version 3.01<...
http://www.dmcinsights.com/phorum/read.php?19%2C38572%2C38572#msg-38572

Pull-down shows vendor info.. doesn't post to products (7 replies)
```

Figure 15.16 The initial part of the feed.

✔ Tips

■ The FeedTools gem supports caching feed information in a local database. By using the cache, only new items will be downloaded from the feed site.

■ The FeedTools gem can also handle *Atom* feeds, an alternative format designed to fix some problems with RSS.

Other Networking Libraries

Most of the networking functionality that a Ruby script might require is defined within the Standard Library. Along with those mentioned in the chapter, there are net/ftp, net/http, net/imap, net/pop, net/smtp, and net/telnet. Each of these libraries provides an interface for using the indicated service type (e.g., FTP, IMAP, and so on).

You may also appreciate:

◆ Mail, used to break an email message into its respective parts.

◆ ping, used to ping a server.

◆ resolv, a DNS client that can return the IP addresses associated with a domain name.

◆ REXML, for parsing XML data.

◆ SOAP, for implementing the SOAP protocol.

◆ URI, for manipulating uniform resource identifiers.

◆ XMLRPC, used to invoke the XML-RPC protocol.

16

RUBY ON RAILS

Ruby on Rails (`www.rubyonrails.org`), sometimes abbreviated as *RoR* or just *Rails*, is a Web development framework, designed to hasten the creation of dynamic Web sites. Like all frameworks, you need to spend some time learning how to properly use Rails, but once you understand the structure, rules, and syntax, you can create impressive and bug-free sites in remarkably little time. Ruby on Rails is a powerful tool and is largely responsible for the increased visibility and popularity of Ruby itself.

Like all frameworks, Rails expedites matters by doing a lot of the grunt work for you, from creating files, directories, and databases, to generating code. Although coverage of Rails easily warrants its own book, in just this one chapter you'll use Ruby on Rails to create a complete and functional site. The specific example will be a Web-based interface for viewing, adding, editing, and deleting employees and departments in a generic company.

As a last note, this chapter uses version 2.1 of Ruby on Rails. The 2.*x* branch was released in December 2007, and while it's not a major overhaul of the framework, some things are done differently than they were in the 1.*x* branch, particularly in the areas of database migrations and scaffoldings.

A Rails Primer

Before getting into some code, I want to take a couple of pages to provide some context for how Ruby on Rails works. Rails uses the *MVC* approach, short for *Model-View-Controller*. This design breaks an application into three parts:

◆ *Model*, the data used by the application

◆ *View*, what the user sees

◆ *Controller*, primarily a functional agent between the other two

Rails has a fourth tool, called *helpers*, whose role falls between controllers and views.

Rails projects use a standardized layout. Within each application's (or site's) directory, you'll find ten subdirectories. **Table 16.1** provides a brief indication of what each is for; this chapter will focus on the first three.

A Rails application can be run in three different environments. By default, it starts in *development* mode. When you're ready to test an application, you switch to *test* mode. Finally, there's *production* mode for the realized and complete site. Each environment has its own set of error logs (with different levels of logging) and can use its own database. Development mode will be used exclusively in this chapter.

The Rails framework provides a *database abstraction layer*, so that different database applications can be used with minimal changes in the code (in fact, only one file would need to be altered). This abstraction is provided by *Active Record*, an *object-relational map (ORM)* design pattern. This means the *model* part of the application, which represents the data, defines classes that inherit from the `ActiveRecord::Base` class.

The *controller* and *view* parts of the application use *Action Pack* objects, subdivided into

Table 16.1

Directory Structure	
NAME	STORES
app	The logic, templates, and custom code
config	Configuration files
db	Database schema
doc	Application documentation
lib	Application libraries
log	Logs
public	HTML, JavaScript, CSS, etc.
script	Utilities
test	Testing tools
vendor	External libraries and plugins

Action Controller and *Action View*. Many of the methods used by the code in this chapter are defined in those classes, or in their derived subclasses. The documentation for all of the involved classes can be found at `http://api.rubyonrails.org`. It takes some effort to navigate the documentation, but you'll find that it's quite thorough. Alternatively, you can turn to `http://apidock.com/rails/` for more user-friendly documentation.

A philosophy that's integral to Rails is *convention over configuration*. This simply means that you if abide by given rules for how things are done (i.e., conventions), you don't have to spend as much time tweaking code (i.e., configuring). Perhaps the largest set of conventions has to do with the names given to files, tables, and classes. For example, in a Ruby on Rails application, you'll see that a controller called `Greeting` will go in a file named `greeting_controller.rb`. Within that file, there'll be a class named `GreetingController`. The class will have various methods, which are the controller's *actions*. If you have a method named `say_hello`, it'll correspond to a view file named `say_hello.rhtml`. If you use Rails to generate files and code for you, you'll automatically have everything set up properly. If you add things manually—and there'll be one example of that in this chapter—you'll need to maintain this structure.

✔ Tips

- All of the figures in this chapter will be taken using Windows (for my convenience), but the instructions will work just the same if you're using Mac OS X, Unix, or Linux.

- When doing Rails development, it's an excellent time to consider using an IDE, if you are not already. Aptana Studio (`www.aptana.com`), among others, supports Rails projects.

Getting Started

To use Ruby on Rails, you'll need to install Ruby, of course, and the Rails gem. If you've not yet installed the RubyGems system, see Chapter 12, "RubyGems," for details.

You'll also want a database application installed. In this chapter, I'll use SQLite, discussed in Chapter 14, "Databases." If you'd rather use, for example, MySQL (www.mysql.com), a common choice for Web applications, you only need to change one command and edit one file (assuming that you've already setup the MySQL server). Regardless of the database application you use, you'll need to install the associated gem.

To create a new Rails project, use the `rails` command, followed by the application's name:

```
rails application_name
```

With Rails version 2.0 and greater, the default is to use SQLite as the database. To tell Rails to use a different database application, use the -d flag when invoking the `rails` command:

```
rails -d mysql application_name
```

If you don't take this step, the same effect can be had by editing the database configuration file, discussed next in the chapter.

To create a Rails project:

1. Install the Rails gem:

   ```
   gem install rails
   ```

   Run this command in a console window or terminal application. On Unix, Linux, and Mac OS X, you'll need to preface this with **sudo**, and then enter the administrative password at the prompt. Again, see Chapter 12 for more information.

2. Install the associated database gem, if you have not already:

   ```
   gem install sqlite3-ruby
   ```

   This particular gem is for interacting with SQLite version 3 databases. If you have not already installed this gem, do so now. If you're using a different database application, install that gem instead.

   Remember that you must also install the database application itself. Chapter 14 has instructions for SQLite.

3. Move into the directory where you'll create the project:

   ```
   cd /path/to/dir
   ```

   The Rails project will be created within a folder on your computer. It should be one that you have permissions to use, like a folder within your home directory. It does not need to be a standard Web directory (like where Apache stores Web documents).

4. Create the Rails application (**Figure 16.1**):

```
rails employees
```

After you've installed the gem, this one command is all that's required to create the shell of the application. The application's name can be anything meaningful to you.

As in the figure, you'll see a bunch of information, referring to the directories and other resources created for this new project.

5. Move into the application's directory:

```
cd employees
```

6. Start the Ruby Web server (**Figure 16.2**):

```
ruby script/server
```

Rails comes with its own Ruby-based Web server, which will be used to run the application. This command starts that server.

Note that you will not get another command prompt in this session so long as the Web server is running. To stop the server, press Control+C. To run the other commands in this chapter, you'll need to open another console or terminal session.

continues on next page

```
┌── Command Prompt ──────────────────────────────────────────── _ □ X ┐
│ C:\Documents and Settings\Administrator>cd "My Documents"/ruby        │
│                                                                       │
│ C:\Documents and Settings\Administrator\My Documents\ruby>rails employees │
│         create                                                        │
│         create   app/controllers                                      │
│         create   app/helpers                                          │
│         create   app/models                                           │
│         create   app/views/layouts                                    │
│         create   config/environments                                  │
│         create   config/initializers                                  │
│         create   db                                                   │
│         create   doc                                                  │
│         create   lib                                                  │
│         create   lib/tasks                                            │
│         create   log                                                  │
│         create   public/images                                        │
│         create   public/javascripts                                   │
│         create   public/stylesheets                                   │
│         create   script/performance                                   │
│         create   script/process                                       │
│         create   test/fixtures                                        │
│         create   test/functional                                      │
└───────────────────────────────────────────────────────────────────── ┘
```

Figure 16.1 Creating a new Ruby on Rails project, named *employees*.

```
┌── Command Prompt - ruby script/server ──────────────────────── _ □ X ┐
│ :cd employees                                                         │
│                                                                       │
│ :ruby script/server                                                   │
│ => Booting WEBrick...                                                 │
│ => Rails 2.1.1 application started on http://0.0.0.0:3000             │
│ => Ctrl-C to shutdown server; call with --help for options           │
│ [2008-09-08 14:08:48] INFO   WEBrick 1.3.1                            │
│ [2008-09-08 14:08:48] INFO   ruby 1.8.6 (2007-09-24) [i386-mswin32]   │
│ [2008-09-08 14:08:49] INFO   WEBrick::HTTPServer#start: pid=2240 port=3000 │
└───────────────────────────────────────────────────────────────────── ┘
```

Figure 16.2 Start the Web server so that you can run the application in your Web browser.

GETTING STARTED

7. Visit `http://localhost:3000` in your Web browser (**Figure 16.3**).

By default, Rails runs on port `3000`, so the URL for the application is `localhost` (i.e., your computer), plus the port number. You can also use an IP address, like `http://0.0.0.0:3000` or `http://127.0.0.1:3000`.

8. Click where it says *About your application's environment* to see more information (**Figure 16.4**).

✔ Tips

■ To start the server on a different port, use `ruby script/server --port=XXX`

■ On some operating systems, commands that begin with `script`, for example, `script/server`, can be invoked without referencing the Ruby interpreter: just `script/server` or `./script/server`. In this chapter, I'll continue to use the more explicit invocation—`ruby script/server`, for cross-platform reliability.

■ Instant Rails (`http://instantrails. rubyforge.org`) for Windows and Locomotive (`http://locomotive. sourceforge.net`) for Mac OS X provide preconfigured Ruby on Rails packages. BitNami's RubyStack (`www.bitnami.org/ stack/rubystack`) also installs a preconfigured Rails environment but is available for Windows, Mac OS X, and Linux.

Figure 16.3 The default index page for a new Rails site.

Figure 16.4 Thanks to a little Ajax, clicking the link displays information about the Rails environment and the running application.

Script 16.1 The standard database configuration for the *employees* application, when using an SQLite database.

```
1    # SQLite version 3.x
2    # gem install sqlite3-ruby (not necessary
     on OS X Leopard)
3    development:
4      adapter: sqlite3
5      database: db/development.sqlite3
6      timeout: 5000
7
8    # Warning: The database defined as "test"
     will be erased and
9    # re-generated from your development
     database when you run "rake".
10   # Do not set this db to the same as
     development or production.
11   test:
12     adapter: sqlite3
13     database: db/test.sqlite3
14     timeout: 5000
15
16   production:
17     adapter: sqlite3
18     database: db/production.sqlite3
19     timeout: 5000
```

Database Configuration

Thanks to its *convention over configuration* approach, there's little configuration to be done in a Rails application. One exception to this is the database configuration, which needs to be established when you start a new project. The configuration parameters are stored in the `database.yml` file, found within the `config` directory. This file is automatically generated when you execute the `rails` command. Depending upon the database application in use, and your system setup, you may or may not need to edit this file, but I'll take a look at the file in these steps just so you're familiar with manual database configuration.

A Rails project can use up to three databases, one each for development, testing, and production. Each is identified and configured in the database configuration file. In the next series of steps, I'll show how to edit the configuration file to use a MySQL database. Do note that you only need to follow these steps if you need to change the default settings generated by the `rails` command.

To configure the database:

1. Open `config/databases.yml` in your text editor or IDE (**Script 16.1**).

The existing file contains the default database configuration. In earlier versions of Rails, the default was to use MySQL. In version 2.1, the default is to use SQLite.

continues on next page

2. If necessary, edit the three adapter lines to identify the database application (**Script 16.2**):

```
adapter: mysql
```

To use a MySQL database, set the adapter to *mysql*. You'll likely want to do this for all three settings—development, test, and production, although Rails does allow you to use different database applications for each stage.

3. Edit the three database: lines to identify the specific database:

```
development:
    database: employees_dev
test:
    database: employees_test
production:
    database: employees
```

When using SQLite, the database will be a file in the db directory, so a default value will be something like db/development.sqlite3 (see Script 16.1). For other database applications, use the name of the database instead. I'll call this one employees.

Your development and production databases can be the same, but be absolutely certain that the test database is different. When the application is tested, the test database will be deleted and rebuilt, so you'll lose any existing data.

Script 16.2 An edited database configuration for using a MySQL database.

```
1    # MySQL. Versions 4.1 and 5.0 are recommended.
2    #
3    # Install the MySQL driver:
4    # gem install mysql
5    # On Mac OS X:
6    # sudo gem install mysql -- --with-
     mysql-dir=/usr/local/mysql
7    # On Mac OS X Leopard:
8    # sudo env ARCHFLAGS="-arch i386" gem
     install mysql -- --with-mysql-config=/usr/
     local/mysql/bin/mysql_config
9    # This sets the ARCHFLAGS environment
     variable to your native architecture
10   # On Windows:
11   # gem install mysql
12   # Choose the win32 build.
13   # Install MySQL and put its /bin directory
     on your path.
14   #
15   # And be sure to use new-style password
     hashing:
16   # http://dev.mysql.com/doc/refman/5.0/en/
     old-client.html
17   development:
18       adapter: mysql
19       encoding: utf8
20       database: employees_dev
21       username: root
22       password: password
23       host: localhost
24
25   # Warning: The database defined as "test"
     will be erased and
26   # re-generated from your development
     database when you run "rake".
27   # Do not set this db to the same as
     development or production.
28   test:
29       adapter: mysql
30       encoding: utf8
31       database: employees_test
32       username: root
33       password: password
34       host: localhost
35
36   production:
37       adapter: mysql
38       encoding: utf8
39       database: employees
40       username: root
41       password: password
42       host: localhost
```

4. Add the username, password, and host values:

username: *actual_mysql_user*

password: *mysql_user_password*

host: *localhost*

SQLite doesn't use these values, so the default configuration doesn't include them. Add these to each of the three environments, using proper username/ password/hostname combinations for your MySQL setup.

5. Remove any unnecessary configurations. The default configuration for SQLite has a `timeout:` option, which you can delete.

6. Add any other configuration settings as necessary.

For MySQL, you can specify the port and socket, if using other than the standard values (`3306` and `/tmp/mysql.sock`, respectively). You can also indicate the encoding (see Script 16.2).

7. Save the file.

8. Restart the Ruby Web server.

Configuration changes require restarting the Web server to take effect. To do so, return to the command line interface where you started the server, enter `Control+C` to cancel the current operation (the running Web server), and then enter `ruby script/server` again.

✔ Tip

■ Rails also supports the PostgreSQL, SQL Server, DB2, Firebird, and Oracle database applications out of the box. You can add support for other database applications by writing your own Rails adapter for it.

Creating the Database

After you've edited the database configuration file, you can use the command-line `rake` utility—part of the Rails framework—to make the database itself. To do so, run

```
rake db:create
```

Besides creating the database files, running this command confirms that Rails can access and manipulate the database, given the parameters in the configuration file.

With the database created, you can then create its tables. You can use any third-party application to make those (also true for the database itself), but there's a better option. The Rails framework has a *migration* tool that can be used to define a database's tables. Its syntax is unlike a standard SQL `CREATE` statement (see Chapter 14). However, a migration can be used to recreate the database should you move the application to another server, update the database as needed for different versions of the application, downgrade the database if necessary, and more.

To make the migration, invoke RoR's workhorse: `script/generate`. This tool builds files and code for you. Some generated code will just be a bare outline; other code will be fully realized. To start, generate a *scaffold*:

```
ruby script/generate scaffold name
→ columns...
```

The topic of scaffolds is discussed more in the next section of the chapter. As for the syntax of this command, the name of the item being generated should be a singular version of whatever it is you'll be storing in a database: so *user* not *users*. The name is followed by the column definitions in the format *name:type*, each separated by a space. **Table 16.2** lists the available types.

Table 16.2

ActiveRecord Column Types
TYPE
binary
boolean
date
datetime
float
integer
string
text
time
timestamp

Table 16.3

departments Table Columns	
NAME	TYPE
id	INTEGER
name	STRING

Table 16.4

employees Table Columns	
NAME	TYPE
id	INTEGER
department_id	INTEGER
first_name	STRING
last_name	STRING
hire_date	DATE

For example, to generate the migration for a books table, you might use

```
ruby script/generate scaffold book
→ title:string author:string
→ description:text price:float
→ published:date
```

This step creates a file in the db/migrate folder. It'll have a name in the format *YYYYMMDDHHMMSS*_create_*tablename*.rb. You can open this file in any text editor to see, or tweak, its contents.

Once you've generated the migration file, you can create the table in the database by again using rake:

```
rake db:migrate
```

For this chapter's example, the database will contain two tables (**Tables 16.3** and **16.4**). In the departments table, the id column will be the primary key, an automatically incrementing integer. The name column is the name of the department: *Accounting*, *Marketing*, *Human Resources*, etc.

In the employees table, the first column is again the table's primary key. The second column is a foreign key to the departments table, reflecting the one-to-many relationship between employees and departments (each employee belongs to one department, but each department can have many employees). The third and fourth columns store the employee's name. The fifth column stores the date the employee was hired.

When creating the migration for these two tables in the next sequence of steps, note that you *don't* have to specify an ID/primary key column, as Rails will automatically assume that each table should have one. Also, case-sensitivity is irrelevant here, as Rails will manage that properly for you.

To create the database:

1. Access the application directory from a command-line interface.

   You'll likely want to open a new terminal or console window, as the Web server should still be running in the existing interface.

2. Create the database (**Figure 16.5**):

   `rake db:create`

   This command will create the database for the current environment. Since SQLite database files will be automatically created by the `rails` command,

you'll likely see a message like that in the figure (which is fine). If you see an error, your configuration details are properly incorrect. This would be more likely when using a different database application.

3. Create the `departments` scaffold (**Figure 16.6**):

   `ruby script/generate scaffold`
   `→ department name:string`

   The table's definition follows that in Table 16.1. Because Rails automatically creates the primary key column, you only need to identify the table's `name` column, which will be a string.

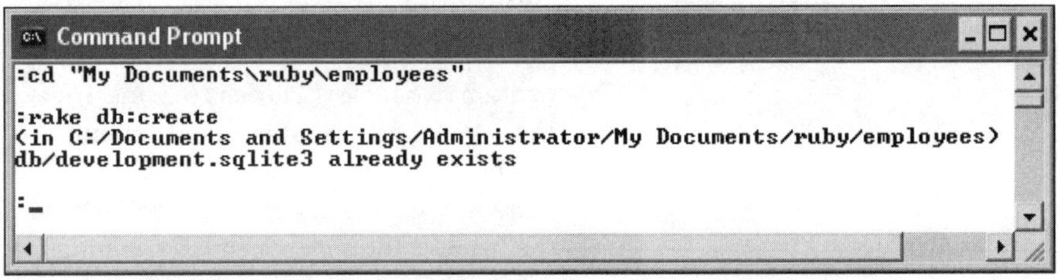

Figure 16.5 Use the `rake` command to create the database.

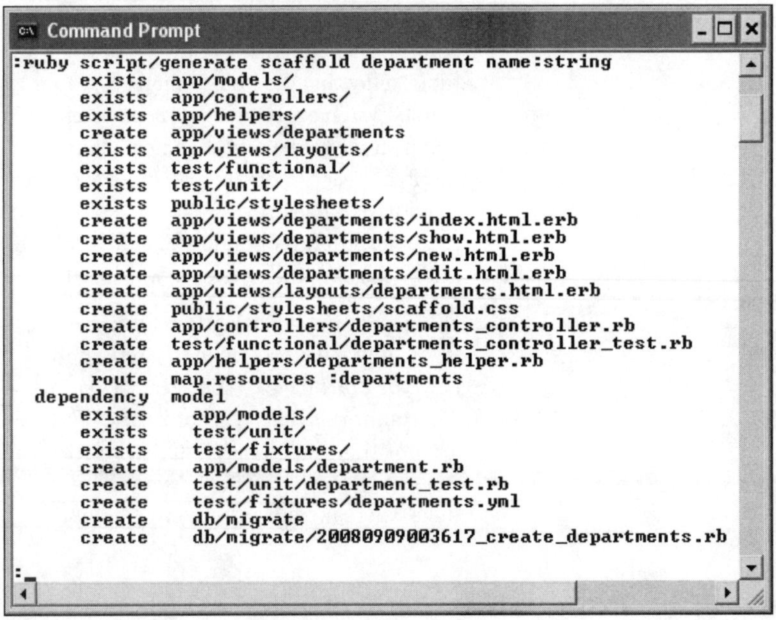

Figure 16.6 The definition for the departments table, plus lots of files, are generated by the scaffold command.

As you can see in the figure, this command creates not only the migration file, but also lots of other scripts. Those will be used and explained throughout the rest of the chapter.

4. Create the employees scaffold (**Figure 16.7**):

```
ruby script/generate scaffold
→ employee department:references
→ first_name:string last_name:string
→ hire_date:date
```

There's one little twist here: to generate the foreign key relationship to the departments table, the department column is identified as type references. In other words, this column refers to that other table.

continues on next page

```
:ruby script/generate scaffold employee department:references fi
last_name:string hire_date:date
      exists    app/models/
      exists    app/controllers/
      exists    app/helpers/
      create    app/views/employees
      exists    app/views/layouts/
      exists    test/functional/
      exists    test/unit/
      exists    public/stylesheets/
      create    app/views/employees/index.html.erb
      create    app/views/employees/show.html.erb
      create    app/views/employees/new.html.erb
      create    app/views/employees/edit.html.erb
      create    app/views/layouts/employees.html.erb
   identical    public/stylesheets/scaffold.css
      create    app/controllers/employees_controller.rb
      create    test/functional/employees_controller_test.rb
      create    app/helpers/employees_helper.rb
       route    map.resources :employees
  dependency    model
      exists       app/models/
      exists       test/unit/
      exists       test/fixtures/
      create       app/models/employee.rb
      create       test/unit/employee_test.rb
      create       test/fixtures/employees.yml
      exists       db/migrate
      create       db/migrate/20080909003840_create_employees.rb
:
```

Figure 16.7 The definition for the employees table, plus lots more files, are generated by this scaffold command.

5. Create the tables in the database
(**Figure 16.8**):

`rake db:migrate`

This step will use the migration files to
make the tables in the database.

✔ Tips

- If you reload the application's environment information in your Web browser
(as in Figure 16.4) after creating migrations and running `rake db:migrate`,
you'll see that the database schema version has been updated.

- Migration files don't just define how tables
should be created. Instead, they define
what changes should be made to the database for the next schema level. For example, you might later add an email address
to the `employees` table. The migration file
for this new feature would just make that
one change and would only work as an
extension of the previous migrations.

- You can open the database in any third-
party application to confirm the existence and definition of the two tables.

- If you want, open the migration files,
found within the db folder, in your text
editor or IDE to see what those look like.

- You can enhance the migration particulars by specifying other column attributes. For example, they can be defined
as `NOT NULL`, have default values, be
`UNSIGNED` (i.e., positive numbers), and so
forth. The syntax for adding these attributes can be found in the Rails documentation.

- The `rake db:create` command only
makes the database for the current environment: development, test, or production. The `rake db:create:all` command
will make all three.

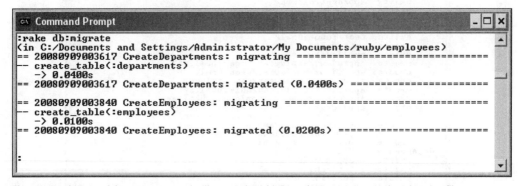

Figure 16.8 This use of the `rake` command will create the tables per the instructions in the migration files.

Figure 16.9 The initial page for the departments (there are currently no departments to show).

Figure 16.10 The form for adding a new department.

Figure 16.11 The result after submitting the form.

Trying the Site

If you're reading this chapter sequentially (and I really hope you are), you might think some pages are missing. How can you try the site out when you've only executed a couple of commands and haven't written a line of code? The answer is part of what makes Rails so great.

The `generate scaffold` command issued twice in the preceding set of steps doesn't just generate the functionality to create a given table (i.e., the database migration file). That command also manufactures all the code and files needed to manage that table's data. This includes controllers, helpers, models, views, and tests. After generating a scaffold, you will already be able to insert, view, update, and delete the table's records. Together, these four features are called *CRUD*: Create, Read, Update, and Delete.

Let's take a walk through the application as it is now, before learning how to customize it.

To try the application:

1. Start the Web server, if you have not already:

   `ruby script/server`

2. Load `http://localhost:3000` or `http://0.0.0.0:3000` in your Web browser, if you have not already.

3. Add `/departments` to the URL and load the page (**Figure 16.9**).

   This will load the initial page for CRUD interactions with the `departments` table.

4. Click *New department*.

   This link takes you to a page where you can begin adding departments.

5. On the resulting page, add a new department (**Figure 16.10**).

   Figure 16.11 shows the result.

continues on next page

6. Click *Back* to return to the main departments page (**Figure 16.12**).

The *Back* link on every departments page will always take you back to the initial departments page.

7. Use the other links to see what they do.

The *Show* link shows the record and provides a link to the edit page. The *Edit* link takes you directly to the edit page, where you can change the department's name. The *Destroy* link deletes the department record, after a JavaScript confirmation (**Figure 16.13**).

8. Change the URL to `http://localhost:3000/employees` and load the page (**Figure 16.14**):

This will take you to the initial page for managing the employee records.

9. Click *New employee* (**Figure 16.15**).

Because the `employees` table has a column that relates to the `departments` table, you'll see an error. So Rails doesn't do everything for you! Keep reading to see how to fix this.

Figure 16.12 The new department is reflected in the list.

Figure 16.13 The JavaScript confirmation appears when the user goes to delete a record.

Figure 16.14 The initial page for employees (there are currently no employees in the database).

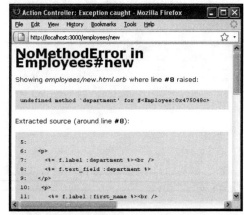

Figure 16.15 New employees cannot be added until some additional code is written.

Script 16.3 The `Employee` model needs to be updated to reflect its relationship to the `Department` model, and to enforce employee form validation.

```
1    class Employee < ActiveRecord::Base
2
3        # Relationships:
4        belongs_to :department
5
6        # Validations:
7        validates_presence_of :first_name,
         :last_name, :hire_date
8
9    end
```

Customizing Models

The work that the Rails framework has already done, just by executing a `generate scaffold` command twice, is rather impressive. But some of the site's functionality is not yet there (see Figure 16.15), and there's plenty of tweaking that can be done. To start, let's touch up the *models*.

As stated in the beginning of the chapter, models represent the application's data. In this example, that means there is one model for departments and another for employees. The `scaffold` command created shell files for both, which you can open and edit. The contents are pure Ruby code: both models are defined as classes, derived from the `ActiveRecord::Base` class. In this next sequence of steps, I'll show you how to add site functionality by augmenting the Ruby code.

By editing the models, I'll address three concerns:

◆ Form validation

◆ The employees-departments relationships

◆ A desired new feature

To customize the models:

1. Open `app/models/employee.rb` in your text editor or IDE.

   This file was generated by the `scaffold` command. As you can see when you open it, the script initially just declares the `Employee` class, which is derived from `ActiveRecord::Base`. It has no methods as written, which means that all of its functionality is inherited from `ActiveRecord::Base`.

2. Within the class definition, declare the employee relationship to department (**Script 16.3**):

   `belongs_to :department`

   continues on next page

To indicate the relationship, use the appropriate method, providing it with a symbol for the related object. The associated methods are: has_one, has_many, belongs_to, and belongs_to_many. This line says that Employee belongs to Department, which is to say that each employee is in a department. Note that the department symbol is in all lowercase and is singular (because an employee belongs to only one department).

If you were to save the file and attempt to create a new employee now, you would see the form, although it still has a problem (**Figure 16.16**).

3. On the next line, add validation routines:

```
validates_presence_of :first_name,
→ :last_name, :hire_date
```

Validation routines are used to ensure the necessary and proper data is submitted for an object's properties. With the code

Figure 16.16 An improved version of the new employee form (although the department input needs to be fixed).

Validations

There are several validation routines built into the Rails framework. The most basic of these is validates_presence_of, for ensuring that a model's attribute has a value. You would use this validation for any table column that can't be NULL. The validates_length_of method restricts a string to a certain length: a maximum, a minimum, or both. The validates_acceptance_of method checks that a user gave the proper value to something, like clicking a check box. The rather smart validates_confirmation_of routine is used to compare a re-entered value against an existing one, in cases where users should confirm something like an entered password or email address.

The validates_uniqueness_of routine makes sure that the item in question has a unique value for all of the data of that model type. The validates_numericality_of method ensures a numeric value. The validates_format_of method is more adaptable, comparing values against regular expressions (for example, to compare a string against the proper format for a URL or email address). The validates_inclusion_of and validates_exclusion_of routines confirm that a value is within or outside of a defined range.

Each of these validations can be customized in terms of when they apply: when creating records, updating them, or both. Each can also be written to provide a custom error message. You can also define your own validation routines to be applied to data. For example, a routine you create might validate that a date actually exists or is in the future.

Script 16.4 The Department model is updated to reflect its relationship to Employee, to enforce non-NULL and unique department names, and to add new functionality.

```
1    class Department < ActiveRecord::Base
2
3        # Relationship:
4        has_many :employees
5
6        # Validations:
7        validates_presence_of :name
8        validates_uniqueness_of :name
9
10       # Method for returning the number of
         employees in the department:
11       def employees_count
12           employees.count
13       end
14
15   end
```

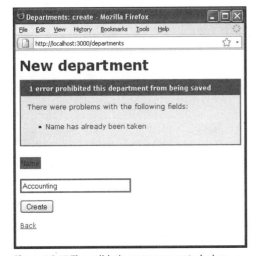

Figure 16.17 The validation error generated when I try to submit a department name that's already been recorded.

as originally written (or as generated), empty departments and employees can be created. To prevent this, the validates_presence_of routine will be added to the model. After it, each required item is listed as a symbol, separated by columns. The sidebar discusses validation options.

4. Save the file.

5. Open app/models/department.rb in your text editor or IDE.

As with the employee.rb file, this is also just a shell, automatically generated as part of the scaffold.

6. Within the class definition, indicate the relationship to employees (**Script 16.4**):

has_many :employees

This is the other side of the one-to-many relationship between employees and departments: each department can have many employees.

7. On the next line, add validation routines:

validates_presence_of :name

validates_uniqueness_of :name

The departments table only has one column to be filled with user-supplied data: the department's name. The first routine confirms that the submitted value isn't empty. The second routine ensures that each department has a unique name (**Figure 16.17**).

continues on next page

8. Define a new method:

```
def employees_count
    employees.count
end
```

To add functionality to a model, define another method, exactly as you would add a method to a class. This particular method will return the number of employees in a department. To do so, the `employees` model is referenced, then the `count` method (part of the `ActiveRecord` class) is invoked.

To understand why this returns only the employees in a specific department, instead of every employee, you need to think about how it is used. On a page that shows a department's record—say, `http://localhost:3000/departments/1`, there will be a `Department` object referencing the department record in the database with an `id` of 1. So when that object's `employees_count` method is called, the count is only applied to that department (or database record); just like any time you invoke a method through an object, it only applies to that class instance, not to the class as a whole.

9. Save the file, and then continue testing the site.

You still can't add an employee because of the missing tie-in to the `departments` table (see Figure 16.16), but you can now load the new employee page, as well as test the department validation routines.

✔ Tip

- By default, validation routines apply whenever model data is created or updated. This means, for example, that both the form for adding new departments and the form for editing existing departments will validate the user-supplied information.

Customizing Views

In the MVC approach, views are the interface with which a user interacts: i.e., everything you see in the Web browser. Rails use a template system to assemble a complete HTML page. You'll find the scaffold-generated view files within the `app/views` directory. Every file uses a `.html.erb` extension. The final *erb* is short for *embedded Ruby*—Ruby code placed within HTML, which is how the dynamic content is generated. Within the `views` directory, there's a `layouts` folder, where each model has an associated file: `departments.html.erb` and `employees.html. erb`. The layout files provide templates for the model as a whole.

If you open either of the two existing layout files, you'll see how simple embedded Ruby can be. Ruby code is placed with special tags: `<%` and `%>`. If the opening tag has an equals sign after it, that's an indication to print the result of the following Ruby code:

`<%= method_invocation %>`

You'll also see this construct:

`<%=h expression %>`

The `h` is a special helper method that encodes the expression's result so that it's

safe to display in the Web browser (it's an alias for `escape_html`). Using it prevents user-submitted HTML from mucking up a template or worse: creating cross-site scripting (XSS) attacks.

The final thing to point out in the layout files is this line:

`<%= yield %>`

When that code is encountered, the action-specific template file is included at that spot. Those files can be found within the `views/model_name` directory, for example, `views/employees`. Many of the actions one takes with a model have their own templates. For example: the `index.html.erb` template displays the list of departments (i.e., it corresponds to the URL `http://localhost: 3000/departments`); `new.html.erb` displays a form for adding a new department (`http://localhost:3000/departments/new`); `show.html.erb` shows the information for a specific record (`http://localhost:3000/ departments/1`); and `edit.html.erb` displays an edit form (`http://localhost:3000/ departments/1/edit`). As you'll see in the next section of the chapter, each of these templates directly relates to a method defined in a controller file.

Customizing Public Files

You can adjust the user interface by customizing the files in the `app/views` directory as well as by editing those found within the `public` directory. This other folder contains default HTML pages, CGI scripts, JavaScript, and CSS, all created by the `rails` command.

The `index.html` file is the default home page. You can edit it, or identify another home page using *routes*, a subject there's not room to cover in this one chapter. There are also HTML files to handle common server responses, like 404 errors (indicating a resource wasn't found).

The `javascripts` folder comes with lots of usable libraries for adding Ajax and other features to a site. The `stylesheets` directory contains the CSS files used by the application. Edit it to establish the fonts and colors used, and how error messages are displayed.

To customize the user experience, these next steps will make quite a few changes. A couple will be rather general, like adding navigation links to the bottom of every page. Other changes will be more significant:

1. Changing the new and edit employee forms so that they show the departments

2. Indicating the number of employees in a department on the individual department page

3. Reflecting which department an employee is in on the individual employee pages

To customize the views:

1. Open app/views/layouts/departments.html.erb in your text editor or IDE.

2. Just before the closing body tag, add (**Script 16.5**):

   ```
   <br><p>Navigation: <%= link_to
   → 'Employees', employees_path %>
   → | <%= link_to 'Departments',
   → departments_path %></p>
   ```

   This line will add two navigation links to the bottom of every department-related page (**Figure 16.18**). To generate them, the link_to method is called (it's defined within the ActionView class). Its first argument is the text value for the link; its second consists of configurable options. For both links, the only option provided is the href value (i.e., the URL to which the link should be tied). Those values come from the special employees_path and departments_path methods created by the scaffold command. Each identifies the base page for the associated model.

Script 16.5 The template for all of the department pages. It's updated to provide links to both the employees and departments areas of the site.

```
1   <!DOCTYPE html PUBLIC "-//W3C//DTD XHTML
    1.0 Transitional//EN"
2   "http://www.w3.org/TR/xhtml1/
    DTD/xhtml1-transitional.dtd">
3
4   <html xmlns="http://www.w3.org/1999/xhtml"
    xml:lang="en" lang="en">
5   <head>
6       <meta http-equiv="content-type"
        content="text/html;charset=UTF-8" />
7       <title>Departments: <%=
        controller.action_name %></title>
8       <%= stylesheet_link_tag 'scaffold' %>
9   </head>
10  <body>
11
12  <p style="color: green"><%= flash[:notice]
    %></p>
13
14  <%= yield%>
15
16  <br><p>Navigation: <%= link_to 'Employees',
    employees_path %> | <%= link_to
    'Departments', departments_path %></p>
17
18  </body>
19  </html>
```

Figure 16.18 Links to the employees and departments main pages have been added to the bottom of every department page.

3. Repeat Step 2 for `employees.html.erb`.

To reduce clutter, this script isn't displayed at this point in the chapter, but you'll see it in the *Customizing Controllers* section of the chapter.

4. Open `app/views/departments/show.html.erb` in your text editor or IDE.

This file contains the template for displaying information about a single department. To it I'll add the functionality that shows the number of employees in that department.

5. After displaying the department name, but before the links, add (**Script 16.6**):

```
<p>
    <b>Number of Employees:</b>
    <%= @department.employees_count %>
</p>
```

Within the template, `@department` is an instance variable: an object of type `Department` representing a particular record from the database. Call its `employees_count` method to return the number of employees in this department.

Script 16.6 The `show.html.erb` template now invokes the `employees_count` method added to the `Department` class (Script 16.4).

```
1   <p>
2       <b>Name:</b>
3       <%=h @department.name %>
4   </p>
5
6   <p>
7       <b>Number of Employees:</b>
8       <%= @department.employees_count %>
9   </p>
10
11  <%= link_to 'Edit', edit_department_path
        (@department) %> |
12  <%= link_to 'Back', departments_path %>
```

6. Open `app/views/employees/index.html.erb` in your text editor or IDE.

7. On line 13, change the reference from `employee.department` to `employee.department.name` (**Script 16.7**):

```
<td><%=h employee.department.name
→ %></td>
```

continues on next page

Script 16.7 The initial employees index page needs to be slightly updated so that it displays each employee's department name.

```
1   <h1>Listing employees</h1>
2
3   <table>
4       <tr>
5           <th>Department</th>
6           <th>First name</th>
7           <th>Last name</th>
8           <th>Hire date</th>
9       </tr>
10
11  <% for employee in @employees %>
12      <tr>
13          <td><%=h employee.department.name
            %></td>
14          <td><%=h employee.first_name %></td>
15          <td><%=h employee.last_name %></td>
16          <td><%=h employee.hire_date %></td>
17          <td><%= link_to 'Show', employee %>
            </td>
18          <td><%= link_to 'Edit',
            edit_employee_path(employee) %></td>
19          <td><%= link_to 'Destroy', employee,
            :confirm => 'Are you sure?', :method
            => :delete %></td>
20      </tr>
21  <% end %>
22  </table>
23
24  <br />
25  <%= link_to 'New employee',
        new_employee_path %>
```

You haven't really seen this template being used fully because there are no employees in the database. Within this template, a `for` loop accesses the `@employees` array—representing each employee listed in the database, printing each in a table row. Within the loop, `employee` refers to the current employee record. Therefore `employee.department` represents the employee's related department object, which is not what should be displayed. Changing it to `employee.department.name` will display the employee's actual department name instead.

8. Repeat Step 7 in `show.html.erb`, too (**Script 16.8**):

   `<%=h @employee.department.name %>`

9. Open `app/views/employees/new.html.erb` in your text editor or IDE.

Script 16.8 The individual employees page must also be updated to show the department name.

```
1    <p>
2        <b>Department:</b>
3        <%=h @employee.department.name %>
4    </p>
5
6    <p>
7        <b>First name:</b>
8        <%=h @employee.first_name %>
9    </p>
10
11   <p>
12       <b>Last name:</b>
13       <%=h @employee.last_name %>
14   </p>
15
16   <p>
17       <b>Hire date:</b>
18       <%=h @employee.hire_date %>
19   </p>
20
21
22   <%= link_to 'Edit', edit_employee_path
           (@employee) %> |
23   <%= link_to 'Back', employees_path %>
```

Figure 16.19 This part of the source code for the new employees form shows the naming scheme used for the form's elements.

Script 16.9 The template for adding new employees is finally complete, after the department element is edited to be a SELECT menu displaying every department.

```
⬤ ⬤ ⬤                    📄 Script
1    <h1>New employee</h1>
2
3    <% form_for(@employee) do |f| %>
4        <%= f.error_messages %>
5
6        <p>
7            <%= f.label :department %><br />
8            <%= select_tag('employee
             [department_id]', options_for_select
             (Department.find(:all).collect { |d|
             [d.name, d.id] })) %>
9        </p>
10       <p>
11           <%= f.label :first_name %><br />
12           <%= f.text_field :first_name %>
13       </p>
14       <p>
15           <%= f.label :last_name %><br />
16           <%= f.text_field :last_name %>
17       </p>
18       <p>
19           <%= f.label :hire_date %><br />
20           <%= f.date_select :hire_date %>
21       </p>
22       <p>
23           <%= f.submit "Create" %>
24       </p>
25   <% end %>
26
27   <%= link_to 'Back', employees_path %>
```

10. Change line 8 to (**Script 16.9**):

```
<%= select_tag('employee
→ [department_id]',
options_for_select(Department.
→ find(:all).collect { |d| [d.name,
→ d.id] })) %>
```

In the original form, the employee's department was a text field, which won't work. Instead, it needs to be a pull-down menu of the available departments. To create that, use the select_tag method. Its first argument is the name of the HTML form element. In this case, it'll be employee[department_id], which is the syntax Rails uses for forms (**Figure 16.19**).

The second argument should be the array of values to use as options in the select menu. To find those, call the find method of the Department object (inherited from ActiveRecord), providing it with an argument of :all. In other words, Department.find(:all) retrieves every department from the database. Apply the collect method, which takes a block, to the array. As the collect method accesses each array element, each individual department will be assigned to the d variable within the block. The block then returns the department's name and ID values.

In the end, this construct creates the HTML seen in **Figure 16.20**.

continues on next page

Figure 16.20 The dynamically generated source code of departments in the pull-down menu.

CUSTOMIZING VIEWS

11. Open app/views/employees/edit.html.erb in your text editor or IDE.

12. Change line 8 to (**Script 16.10**):

```
<%= select_tag('employee
→ [department_id]',
→ options_for_select(Department.
→ find(:all).collect { |d|
→ [d.name, d.id] },
→ @employee.department_id )) %>
```

Script 16.10 The template for editing an employee record is modified so that it also uses a pull-down menu of departments.

```
000                      Script
1    <h1>Editing employee</h1>
2
3    <% form_for(@employee) do |f| %>
4        <%= f.error_messages %>
5
6        <p>
7            <%= f.label :department %><br />
8            <%= select_tag('employee
             [department_id]', options_for_select
             (Department.find(:all).collect { |d|
             [d.name, d.id] }, @employee.
             department_id )) %>
9        </p>
10       <p>
11           <%= f.label :first_name %><br />
12           <%= f.text_field :first_name %>
13       </p>
14       <p>
15           <%= f.label :last_name %><br />
16           <%= f.text_field :last_name %>
17       </p>
18       <p>
19           <%= f.label :hire_date %><br />
20           <%= f.date_select :hire_date %>
21       </p>
22       <p>
23           <%= f.submit "Update" %>
24       </p>
25   <% end %>
26
27   <%= link_to 'Show', @employee %> |
28   <%= link_to 'Back', employees_path %>
```

Figure 16.21 The first employee has been added to the database.

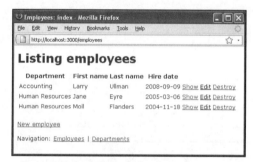

Figure 16.22 The employees home page now shows all recorded employees, including what department they are in.

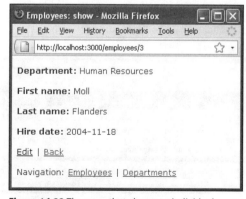

Figure 16.23 The page that shows an individual employee record also reflects their department.

Figure 16.24 The page for editing an employee's record.

Figure 16.25 The page that shows an individual department also indicates how many employees are in that department (thanks to the `employees_count` method added to the `Department` class).

As with the form for adding a new employee, the edit an employee form must be updated to show a pull-down menu of departments. This code is exactly like that added to `employees/ new.html.erb`, except that it has a second argument to the `options_for_ select` method. That argument is `@employee.department_id`, which indicates the option in the select menu that should be preselected.

13. Save all files and test the site (**Figures 16.21**, **16.22**, **16.23**, **16.24**, and **16.25**).

   You can now add, view, and edit new employees (Figures 16.21, 16.22, 16.23, and 16.24). Then check the department pages to see the number of employees in a department (Figure 16.25).

✔ Tips

■ There's obviously a lot to learn about customizing views, in particular discovering what methods are available and where variables come from. For more, see a full text on the Rails framework or any of the online tutorials available.

■ Strictly speaking, in the MVC approach, views should contain presentation and no logic. But views will inevitably contain some logic, so whether you would place, for example, the code for generating the select menu of departments in a view or a controller is really a matter of style.

Customizing Controllers

The preceding two sections of the chapter show how to edit models and views, thereby adding functionality and improving the user interface. The last aspect of the MVC model is the *controller*, to be addressed here. Controllers are go-betweens for models and views: much of your application's logic will go into a controller.

The potent and venerable `generate scaffold` command created one controller for each model. You'll find these files in `app/controllers`, named `departments_controller.rb` and `employees_controller.rb`. Unlike the models generated by the Rails framework, these controller files will already contain lots of code, specifically defining how to handle *CRUD* actions.

In this section of the chapter, I want to update the employees controller to add a simple search. The user will be able to enter a last name, or part of one, in a search box and the page will only show users that match that value (**Figure 16.26**). To accomplish this, the search form needs to be added to a view file, and then the logic for handling that form must be added to `employees_controller.rb`.

Figure 16.26 The added search box at the bottom of the page, with the results above it (compare with Figure 16.22).

Script 16.11 The template for every employees page is updated so that a search box appears at the bottom (after the navigation links added earlier in the chapter).

```
1   <!DOCTYPE html PUBLIC "-//W3C//DTD XHTML
    1.0 Transitional//EN"
2   "http://www.w3.org/TR/xhtml1/
    DTD/xhtml1-transitional.dtd">
3
4   <html xmlns="http://www.w3.org/1999/xhtml"
    xml:lang="en" lang="en">
5   <head>
6       <meta http-equiv="content-type"
        content="text/html;charset=UTF-8" />
7       <title>Employees: <%= controller.
        action_name %></title>
8       <%= stylesheet_link_tag 'scaffold' %>
9   </head>
10  <body>
11
12  <p style="color: green"><%= flash[:notice]
    %></p>
13
14  <%= yield %>
15
16  <br><p>Navigation: <%= link_to
    'Employees', employees_path %>
    | <%= link_to 'Departments',
    departments_path %></p>
17
18  <% form_tag employees_path, :method =>
    'get' do %>
19  <%= text_field_tag :term, params[:term] %>
20  <%= submit_tag 'Search', :name => nil %>
21  <% end %>
22
23  </body>
24  </html>
```

To customize a controller:

1. Open app/views/layouts/employees.html.erb in your text editor or IDE.

   The search form will be added to every employees page by placing it on the main template.

2. Use the form_tag method to begin a form (**Script 16.11**):

   ```
   <% form_tag employees_path, :method
   => 'get' do %>
   ```

   The form_tag method, part of the ActionView::Helpers::FormTagHelper class, generates opening and closing form tags. Its first argument is the *action* attribute: to what page the form should be submitted. For this form, that value is represented by employees_path, which is the root of the employees part of the application. The second argument is where you can add options, like the method—GET or POST—to use. Then a block is begun using do. Within the block is where the form's elements will be created.

   You could add literal HTML here to create the form, but that wouldn't be in keeping with using the Rails framework.

continues on next page

CUSTOMIZING CONTROLLERS

3. Add a text field for the search term:

```
<%= text_field_tag :term,
→ params[:term] %>
```

The `text_field_tag` method creates a text input. The input's name value will be *term*, represented here as the first argument to the method, the symbol `:term`. The preset value of the input will be the value of `params[:term]`. The `params` hash stores values sent to the page in the URL. If the form was submitted, `?term=XXXX` pair will be appended to the URL, so `params[:term]` will have a value of *XXXX*, which should be reflected in the search box, the normal behavior for most searches (see Figure 16.26).

4. Add the submit button:

```
<%= submit_tag 'Search', :name =>
→ nil %>
```

The `submit_tag` method creates a submit button. Its value—what appears on the button—will be *Search*. Its name will be empty, so that it doesn't appear in the URL (just to make the URL a little tidier).

5. Complete the form:

```
<% end %>
```

This completes the block begun by the `do` keyword in Step 2.

6. Open `app/controllers/employees_controller.rb` in your text editor or IDE.

This is the controller for the employees model. The logic for handling searches must be added to this.

7. Within the `index` method, check for the existence of `params[:term]` (**Script 16.12**):

```
def index
    if params[:term]
```

Script 16.12 The first 18 lines of the edited `employees_controller.rb` file reveals the modification to the `index` method.

```
1   class EmployeesController <
    ApplicationController
2       # GET /employees
3       # GET /employees.xml
4       def index
5           if params[:term]
6               @employees = Employee.find(:all,
                :conditions => ['last_name LIKE
                ?', "%#{params[:term]}%"])
7           else
8               @employees = Employee.find(:all)
9           end
10          respond_to do |format|
11              format.html # index.html.erb
12              format.xml    { render :xml =>
                @employees }
13          end
14      end
15
16      # GET /employees/1
17      # GET /employees/1.xml
18      def show
19
20  # Note: rest of the script omitted for
    brevity!
```

To understand what's happening here, you need to look at the whole file and understand how it works (admittedly, it is a little complicated). Controllers define methods, each of which is associated with an *action*. The methods generated by the scaffold are: `index`, `show`, `new`, `edit`, `create`, `update`, and `destroy`. Each of these reflects something to be done with an employee record. The first four methods are also tied to templates in the `views/employees` directory. The last three methods aren't tied to templates but apply when the second step of an action is requested: for instance, you go to the page for adding a *new* employee, and then submit that form to *create* the employee.

For the search feature, it makes sense to tie it into the *index* action. That action displays every employee on the initial employee home (which uses the `views/employees/index.html.erb` template). To add the search logic to the index action, I just need to edit what the `index` method does.

The method as originally defined creates an `@employees` array by invoking `Employee.find(:all)`, which will return every employee record. If there is a search term in the URL, because the form was submitted, then `params[:term]` will have a value and I need to limit which employees should be assigned to `@employees`.

8. Use the search term in the selection of the employees:

```
@employees = Employee.find(:all,
→ :conditions => ['last_name LIKE
→ ?', "%#{params[:term]}%"])
```

continues on next page

Other Topics

As I say in the introduction to this chapter, entire books can be devoted to the subject of Ruby on Rails. I could only hope to present the highlights of the framework here, while still striving to create a real-world example. The chapter does successfully do that, I hope, as well as provide you with a road map for the basic terms and ideas.

The next steps from here would begin with improving your knowledge of the MVC approach: seeing how to further customize these parts of an application and learning more about the *Active Record*, *Action View*, and *Action Controller* classes they rely upon. New topics to look into include using Ajax with Rails projects (a common feature), making use of sessions, and employing plug-ins. Along the way, you'll want to read up on what *routes* are, and what it means that version 2.*x* of the Rails framework creates *RESTful* sites. Finally, when it's time to take an application live, you'll need to know how to test and deploy it.

For more on any of these topics, see a complete book on the framework, visit the online documentation, and check out whatever useful tutorials you can find on Web sites like www.railscasts.com, www.thinkrefresh.com, and www.peepcode.com.

CUSTOMIZING CONTROLLERS

To limit which employees are returned, a second argument is provided to the find method. It defines a condition to be applied, namely that the last_name value should be LIKE ?, with the question mark being replaced by %#{params[:term]}%. If you understand SQL, you will recognize that the end result here is this query:

```
SELECT * FROM employees WHERE
→ last_name LIKE '%term%'
```

Using the question mark as a placeholder here, to be replaced by the result of "%#{params[:term]}%", is a security technique, preventing SQL injection attacks should malicious characters be entered into the search box.

9. Complete the if conditional:

```
else
    @employees = Employee.find(:all)
end
```

If params[:terms] was not set, then every employee should be retrieved, as the method originally did.

10. Save both files.

11. Test the search feature in your Web browser.

✔ Tip

■ If no search term is entered, the result will be the same as if you went directly to the employees page, where every employee is listed.

DYNAMIC PROGRAMMING

17

All programming languages are capable of some flexibility, whether it's responding to user input or merely using basic control structures. Ruby excels in this area, though, as Ruby scripts can be dynamic in ways that most other programming languages cannot. Through *metaprogramming*, *reflection*, *functional programming*, and the like, Ruby code can be truly dynamic. While thorough examination of these topics is well beyond the scope of a beginner's guide to Ruby (and, to be fair, not every Ruby programmer needs to use these techniques), this chapter will introduce these and other topics in this same vein.

To start, the first subject shows how you can write code that behaves differently, depending upon the operating system on which it is being run. The second and third topics address security related issues, in particular, how Ruby treats data based upon its source and the *safe level*. The chapter concludes with coverage of *procs* and *lambdas*: two slightly advanced techniques that are part of the functional programming approach.

OS Integration

Ruby is a cross-platform language, meaning it runs on most operating systems. Ruby is not unique in this regard, but Ruby goes a step further in being generally operating-system independent as well. With comparatively few exceptions, code written for one system will work on another, without modification. The primary exceptions involve files and directories. This should be expected, as Windows, Mac OS X, Unix, and Linux all organize files and directories in different ways.

To determine the operating system in use, look at the RUBY_PLATFORM constant. It's a string that indicates both the operating system and the hardware on which it's running. This value won't be as simple as just *Windows* or *Mac*: on my Intel Mac, it's

universal-darwin9.0, on my Ubuntu Linux, it's *i486-linux*, and on my Windows installation, it's *i386-mswin32*. Knowing this, you can use string searches or regular expressions to see if the platform is a particular type:

```
puts 'Windows' if RUBY_PLATFORM.index
→ ('mswin')
```

More operating system factors can be found in *environmental variables*. These are system and user settings that affect how applications and scripts run. For example, the PATH variable stores the directories in which the computer will look for executable files. All of the environmental variables are available in a Ruby script through the ENV hash (**Figure 17.1**):

```
ENV.to_hash.each_pair do |k, v|
    puts "#{k}\t#{v}"
end
```

igure 17.1 A partial list of environmental variables, and their values, on Windows.

Script 17.1 This script uses the RUBY_PLATFORM constant and the appropriate environmental variable to determine the user's home directory for the computer on which the script is running.

```
1   # Script 17.1 - os.rb
2
3   # Determine the Home directory based upon
    the OS:
4   if RUBY_PLATFORM.index('mswin') then
5       puts "I think you're using a version of
        Windows."
6       home = ENV['HOMEPATH']
7   elsif RUBY_PLATFORM.index('darwin') then
8       puts "I think you're using a version of
        Mac OS X."
9       home = ENV['HOME']
10  elsif RUBY_PLATFORM.index('linux') then
11      puts "I think you're using a version of
        Linux."
12      home = ENV['HOME']
13  else
14      puts "I'm not sure what operating system
        you're using."
15  end
16
17  # Print the home directory:
18  puts "Your home directory is #{home}" if
    home
```

To identify the operating system:

1. Begin a new Ruby script in your text editor or IDE (**Script 17.1**):

   `# Script 17.1 - os.rb`

2. Begin an if conditional:

   ```
   if RUBY_PLATFORM.index('mswin') then
       puts "I think you're using a
       → version of Windows."
       home = ENV['HOMEPATH']
   ```

   Similar to the code already shown, this condition will be true if the RUBY_PLATFORM constant contains the substring *mswin*. Since a case-sensitive search for a string should work, the code uses a string method—index—instead of a regular expression.

   If the condition is true, a message is printed and the HOMEPATH element of the ENV hash is assigned to the home variable.

3. Add a condition for Macs:

   ```
   elsif RUBY_PLATFORM.index('darwin')
   → then
       puts "I think you're using a
       → version of Mac OS X."
       home = ENV['HOME']
   ```

   The identifier for the Mac OS X platform contains the keyword *darwin* (Darwin is an offshoot of FreeBSD Unix). If that substring is found, a message is printed but this time the ENV['HOME'] element is referenced, as Macs don't have an ENV['HOMEPATH'] environmental variable.

   continues on next page

OS INTEGRATION

389

4. Add a condition for Linux:

```
elsif RUBY_PLATFORM.index('linux')
→ then
    puts "I think you're using a
    → version of Linux."
    home = ENV['HOME']
```

This code looks for the string *linux*, which could mean Ubuntu or many other distributions. As with Macs, the proper environmental variable to refer to is ENV['HOME'].

5. Complete the conditional:

```
else
    puts "I'm not sure what operating
    → system you're using."
end
```

6. Print the presumed home directory:

```
puts "Your home directory is
→ #{home}" if home
```

Other scripts might use this variable to know where to read from or write files to.

7. Save and run the completed script (**Figure 17.2**).

8. If you can, run the script on another computer (**Figure 17.3**).

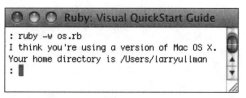

Figure 17.2 The result of running the script on my Mac.

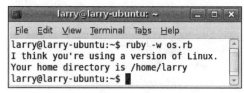

Figure 17.3 The result on Ubuntu Linux.

✔ Tips

- If you'd like to make a script behave differently based upon the version of Ruby in use, refer to the `RUBY_VERSION` constant.

- To have a Ruby script make use of some standard Windows behavior—like creating alert windows and dialog boxes, use `Win32API`, found within the Ruby Standard Library.

- For more sophisticated Windows interactions, check out `WIN32OLE`, also part of the Standard Library. Using it, you can interact with GUI applications like Internet Explorer and Microsoft Excel, and work with the Windows Registry.

Executing Other Programs

Sometimes it's necessary to execute commands directly on the computer as if you were typing them at a command prompt. For example, you may do this so that your Ruby script could make use of the functionality provided by an existing utility. One way to do this is to place the command between backticks:

```
result = `command`
```

The result of the command—what you would otherwise see in the console window—will be returned (and, in the preceding code, assigned to the `result` variable). If you don't like using backticks, or don't have them on your keyboard, this is equivalent:

```
result = %x{command}
```

If you don't care about the result of executing a command, use the `system` method instead:

```
system 'command'
```

This method only returns a Boolean value indicating its ability to execute the given command.

Finally, you can use the `exec` method to run a command. It behaves completely differently in that it terminates the execution of the Ruby code, giving complete control over to the command execution. You might use `exec` if a Ruby script's primary role is to start a command or process.

You can learn more about all of these commands in the Ruby documentation. Each method is found within the `Kernel` module. Within the `IO` module, you'll find the `popen` method, which can be used for actual interactions between Ruby code and an external application.

Tainted Data

Well-written scripts need to be both functional and secure. The first quality is relatively easy to check for, especially if you apply unit testing (see Chapter 11, "Debugging and Error Handling"). The second quality takes more effort, in part because it requires that you think about using your script maliciously, something that's fortunately not natural for most people. Thankfully, Ruby helps in this regard through the identification of *tainted data*. Every object in Ruby is either *tainted* (potentially unsafe) or *untainted* (presumably safe). Ruby will automatically flag an object as one or the other, depending upon its origin.

Literal values in code are the most obvious type of untainted object:

```
name = 'Larry'
```

Tainted objects are everything else: data from external sources. Tainted data may come from (among other places):

- Files
- Command-line arguments
- User input
- Environmental variables
- Network communications

Furthermore, the "taintedness" of an object is inherited: an object derived from a tainted object will be tainted as well (with few exceptions, see the first tip).

You can change the tainted status of an object, depending upon the safe level in use (discussed next in the chapter). To mark an object as tainted, apply the `taint` method:

```
my_obj.taint
```

Script 17.2 This script will be read in by Script 17.3 twice: once from the local file system and once over a network connection.

```
1    VERY SCARY COMMAND!
```

Script 17.3 To explore where tainted data comes from, four objects are created from different resources.

```
1    # Script 17.3 - data.rb
2
3    # Literal object:
4    literal = 23
5
6    # Environmental variable:
7    env = ENV['USER']
8
9    # User input:
10   print 'Enter something: '
11   input = gets
12
13   # File:
14   fp = File.open('data.txt')
15   local = fp.read
16   fp.close
17
18   # Network communication:
19   require 'net/http'
20   url = URI.parse('http://www.dmcinsights.
     com/ruby/data.txt')
21   response = Net::HTTP.get_response(url)
22   online = response.body
23
24   # Indicate the "taintedness":
25   puts "The literal object--#{literal}--is
     tainted: #{literal.tainted?}"
26   puts "The environmental variable--#{env}--
     is tainted: #{env.tainted?}"
27   puts "The user input--#{input.chomp}--is
     tainted: #{input.tainted?}"
28   puts "The file data--#{local}--is tainted:
     #{local.tainted?}"
29   puts "The network communication--
     #{online}--is tainted: #{online.tainted?}"
```

To see if an object is tainted, use the `tainted?` method, which returns a Boolean value:

```
my_obj.tainted?
```

To mark a tainted object as not tainted, use `untaint`:

```
my_obj.untaint
```

Note that by invoking this method, you're overruling one of Ruby's main security features, so only use it with due diligence, for instance, after thoroughly validating the object's value.

This next example will simply display the tainted status of different types of data. The subsequent example will show how the data's origin impacts how it can be used.

To test for tainted data:

1. Begin a new Ruby script in your text editor or IDE (**Script 17.2**):

   ```
   VERY SCARY COMMAND!
   ```

   That's all this file needs to contain. It will be read in by the next script.

2. Save the file as `data.txt`.

   You should save it in the same directory where you'll put the next Ruby script.

3. Begin a new Ruby script in your text editor or IDE (**Script 17.3**):

   ```
   # Script 17.3 - data.rb
   ```

4. Create a literal object:

   ```
   literal = 23
   ```

   This object's value is hard-coded into the script, so it is not tainted.

5. Reference an environmental variable:

   ```
   env = ENV['USER']
   ```

   You might think that an environmental variable is safe, but it's not, as will be demonstrated. If you're using Windows, change `USER` to `USERNAME`.

continues on next page

TAINTED DATA

6. Get some user input:

```
print 'Enter something: '
input = gets
```

The user will be prompted to enter something, which will be read in and assigned to `input`.

7. Read some data from a file:

```
fp = File.open('data.txt')
local = fp.read
fp.close
```

These three lines, which come from Chapter 13, "Directories and Files," will read in the contents of `data.txt` (Script 17.2), assigning those contents to `local`.

8. Read some data from a network:

```
require 'net/http'
url = URI.parse('http://www.
→ dmcinsights.com/ruby/data.txt')
response = Net::HTTP.get_response(url)
online = response.body
```

This code reads in the contents of a file found online (Script 17.2, placed on my server). The specific code has not previously been discussed in this book, so I'll explain it quickly (Chapter 15, "Networking," uses the `open-uri` library instead, see the second tip for an explanation for the switch).

First, the `net/http` library is included. Then a `URI::HTTP` object is created by providing the `parse` method with a URL. The `Net::HTTP.get_response` method requests the URL and returns the response. The response's body, which is the contents of the text file in this case, is then found in the `body` method.

9. Indicate the value of each object and if it is tainted or not:

```
puts "The literal object--
→#{literal}--is tainted:
→#{literal.tainted?}"

puts "The environmental variable--
→#{env}--is tainted:
  →#{env.tainted?}"

puts "The user input--
→#{input.chomp}--is tainted:
→#{input.tainted?}"

puts "The file data--#{local}--is
→tainted: #{local.tainted?}"

puts "The network communication--
→#{online}--is tainted:
→#{online.tainted?}"
```

For each of the five objects, they are printed out, along with a simple Boolean indication of their status.

10. Save and run the completed script (**Figure 17.4**).

✔ Tips

■ Untainted objects can contain tainted values. For example, if you create an array that contains the env, input, local, and online objects from Script 17.3, the array itself will not be tainted, but its individual elements will be.

■ Chapter 15 uses the open-uri library to read in data from a network resource. I chose not to use it in this example because that library marks the data it returns—the contents of Script 17.2—as not tainted (it calls the untaint method to accomplish this). I didn't want that result to confuse the underlying point that all external data is tainted.

■ The environmental variable PATH may or may not be tainted, depending upon the properties of the directories listed therein. If the PATH contains a directory whose security is questionable, then the entire PATH is considered to be tainted.

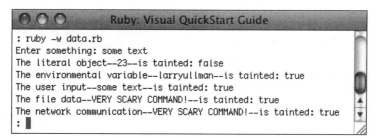

Figure 17.4 Of the five objects from different origins, the only one that is not tainted is the literal number.

Safe Levels

The other half of the Ruby security model, along with the notion of tainted data, is the *safe level*. Ruby code runs at a specific safe level, represented by the integers 0 through 4. For each level, different operations are or are not permitted, depending upon the potential for harm implicit in a given action (and, where applicable, the "taintedness" of the data involved).

With the default safe level of 0, no safety precautions are taken. There are no restrictions as to what can be done with any kind of data.

At safe level 1, some restrictions are instituted. For example, you cannot use tainted data when:

◆ Executing system calls

◆ Evaluating code (see the sidebar)

◆ Including libraries

◆ Opening a file

◆ Establishing a network connection

Safe level 2 adds to the restrictions found in safe level 1. Altering directories and files, generating forks and processes, and including external Ruby files are all restricted, whether or not they involve tainted data.

Safe level 3 takes the restrictions in safe level 2 and treats all objects as being tainted (except for some predefined global objects). This means that even hard-coded literals in the code are flagged as tainted. And you cannot use the untaint method to change the status.

Safe level 4, which is the highest level of security, greatly restricts access to and changing of most objects. Environmental variables cannot be altered, file input/output is prohibited, and *metaprogramming* methods are denied. (Metaprogramming is code that

The eval Method

Ruby, like many programming languages, has the useful but dangerous eval method. This method takes a string as an argument and executes it as Ruby code. For this reason, one should be very, very careful about using eval, if not avoiding it altogether. The string provided to the method—the code to be executed—must be validated and safe, lest a malicious user take advantage of the security hole and try to have their code executed. With this in mind, use of eval is restricted in safe levels 1 through 3 (in safe level 4, other restrictions make using eval safe again).

Ruby has three variants on eval: class_eval, module_eval, and instance_eval. Each is used to evaluate code within a specific context: as part of a class, a module, or an instance. For all of these methods, especially eval, you should use them only if absolutely necessary, and preferably not with external data.

Script 17.4 Two common tasks—reading information about a file and changing directories—will be tested against different safe levels using this script.

```
1    # Script 17.4 - levels.rb
2
3    # Literal object:
4    file = 'os.rb'
5
6    # User input:
7    print 'Enter a directory: '
8    dir = gets
9
10   # Print a heading:
11   puts "At safe level: #{$SAFE}"
12
13   # Reference a file:
14   puts "Attempting to stat #{file}..."
15   File.stat(file)
16
17   # Test directory change:
18   puts "Attempting to change to
     #{dir.chomp!}..."
19   Dir.chdir(dir)
```

generates or updates other code, which is what Ruby's `attr_reader` and `attr_accessor` methods do.)

The `$SAFE` global variable stores the current safety level. You can change it within a script to increase the amount of security:

`$SAFE = 1`

This only works one way: you cannot assign a lower value to the variable (i.e., you cannot make code run in a less safe manner).

Alternatively, you can change the safe level when executing a Ruby script by using the `-T` flag, immediately following it with a number:

`ruby -w -T1 scriptname.rb`

If you attempt to do something not allowed by the safe level, a `SecurityError` exception will be raised. To see this in action, the next script will attempt two common Ruby tasks. It'll be run under three different safe levels— 0, 1, and 4—so you can see the impact that the safe level has on a script.

To test the safe levels:

1. Begin a new Ruby script in your text editor or IDE (**Script 17.4**):

`# Script 17.4 - levels.rb`

2. Create a literal object:

`file = 'os.rb'`

This is a hard-coded string, so it will not marked as tainted from the outset. It refers to `os.rb` (Script 17.1), found in the same directory as this script.

continues on next page

SAFE LEVELS

3. Get a directory value from the user:

```
print 'Enter a directory: '
dir = gets
```

This user input will represent a directory on the computer, either an absolute path or relative to this script. Because it's user input, the value will be considered tainted from the start.

4. Display the current safe level:

```
puts "At safe level: #{$SAFE}"
```

This script will be run three times, at three different safe levels. To change the levels, the command-line flag will be used. This caption just prints the numeric level value.

5. Invoke the stat method on the file:

```
puts "Attempting to stat #{file}..."
File.stat(file)
```

The file and directory methods are restricted in the different levels, so they make good test subjects for this script. Here, the stat method is called on the untainted file object, which should be a comparatively safe endeavor (see Chapter 13 for more on this method).

6. Change the current working directory:

```
puts "Attempting to change to
→ #{dir.chomp!}..."
#Dir.chdir(dir)
```

You may not think that just changing the working directory is a dangerous step, but it could lead to unsafe results. Here, the current directory is being changed to whatever the user entered, which is even less secure.

The chomp! method must be applied to remove the newline character from the end of the user's input.

7. Save and run the completed script (**Figure 17.5**).

When run in the default safe level of 0, everything works without a hitch.

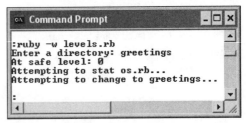

Figure 17.5 The script as executed under the default safe level.

8. Run the script at level 1 (**Figure 17.6**):

   `ruby -w -T1 levels.rb`

9. Remove the directory parts of the script (lines 7, 8, 18, and 19), and then save the script.

   Since you already know that the `chdir` method cannot be called at safe level 1 and above, there's no reason to prompt the user for this value or try to use it.

10. Run the script at level 4 (**Figure 17.7**).

    Levels 1 and 4 are arguably the most commonly used safe levels. The former applies some reasonable amount of security to a script; the latter locks it down entirely.

✔ Tip

- The safe level is thread-specific, meaning that different threads in the same script can be run under different security levels.

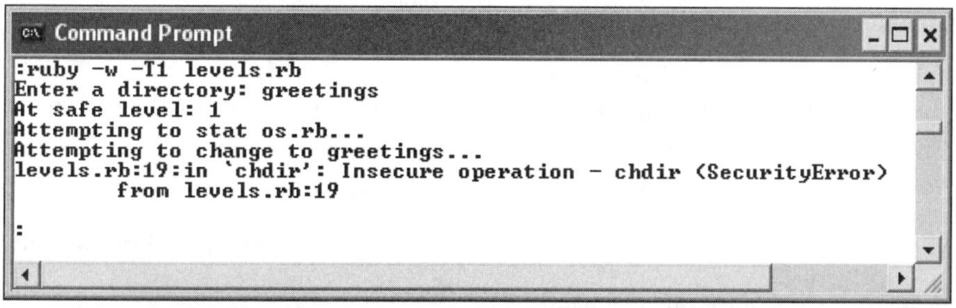
Command Prompt
:ruby -w -T1 levels.rb
Enter a directory: greetings
At safe level: 1
Attempting to stat os.rb...
Attempting to change to greetings...
levels.rb:19:in `chdir': Insecure operation - chdir (SecurityError)
from levels.rb:19
:

Figure 17.6 At safe level 1, the `chdir` line now fails because it uses tainted data.

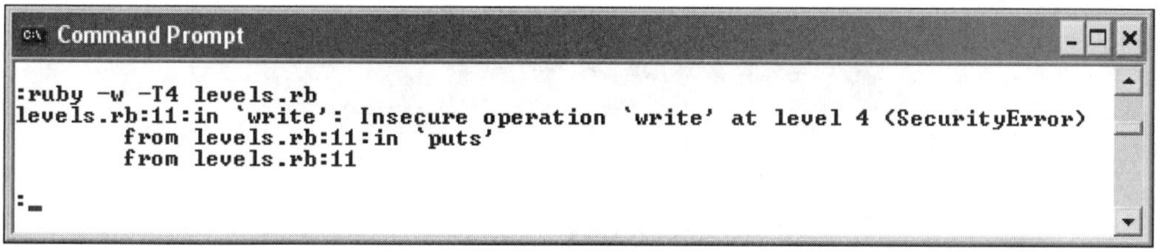
Command Prompt
:ruby -w -T4 levels.rb
levels.rb:11:in `write': Insecure operation `write' at level 4 (SecurityError)
from levels.rb:11:in `puts'
from levels.rb:11
:

Figure 17.7 At safe level 4, even the `puts` method cannot be used (because it's equivalent to writing to the standard output).

Procs and Lambdas

To understand *procs* and *lambdas*, you need to understand *blocks*. Chapter 5, "Control Structures," introduced blocks tied to iterators, in examples like:

```
10.downto(1) { |num| puts num }
```

The `downto` method goes from `10` to `1` by ones, passing each number to the block, which then prints it.

Blocks are also used with other types of methods in Ruby (and in this book). For example, when using `IO` objects, a block can be tied to the opening of the resource.

```
File.open('filename.txt') do |fp|
    # Do whatever.
end
```

In that example, after the file is opened, a reference to the opened file is passed to the block, where it is assigned to the `fp` variable. Inside the block, the code might read from or write to the file.

In both of these cases, what's really happening is that the block is also being passed to the method—`downto` or `open`—as an extra argument. The method then passes control to the block, using the `yield` keyword, when appropriate.

In those examples, the blocks are just useful syntactical structures. But what if you wanted to do more with blocks? Another

way blocks are used in Ruby is as objects. Creating a block as an object generates either a *proc* or a *lambda*. These concepts can be confusing, so I'll discuss them in some detail.

Both procs and lambdas are instances of the `Proc` class. Like any other object, they can be created on the fly, passed to methods, returned by methods, and so forth: these things you can do with a `Proc`, which cannot be done with blocks, is what makes them special. Despite the fact that both objects are of `Proc` type, there are some differences between procs and lambdas. A proc is simply a named version of the syntactic blocks you've already used, whereas a lambda is more like a method. To maintain this distinction, I'll use the lowercase *proc* and *lambda* to refer to the specific implementations, and the uppercase class name `Proc` to refer to the overall concept of blocks as objects.

The most overt way to create a proc is to call the `Proc.new` method, providing it with the block's code:

```
p = Proc.new { # block code }
```

To create a lambda, use the `lambda` method instead of `Proc.new`:

```
l = lambda { # block code }
```

To execute either type of `Proc`, use `call`:

```
p.call
l.call
```

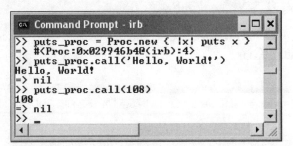

Figure 17.8 Creation, and two invocations, of a basic proc.

To hammer the point home, let's take a very simple example (**Figure 17.8**):

```
puts_proc = Proc.new { |x| puts x }
puts_proc.call('Hello, World!')
puts_proc.call(108)
```

Besides how they are created, another way in which procs and lambdas differ is in how their arguments are enforced. A proc won't complain if provided with the wrong number of arguments, whereas a lambda raises an exception if not called correctly (**Figure 17.9**):

```
p = Proc.new { |x, y| puts "Received:
→ #{x}, #{y}"}
l = lambda { |x, y| puts "Received:
→ #{x}, #{y}" }
p.call(1)
p.call(1,2,3)
l.call(1)
l.call(1,2,3)
```

continues on next page

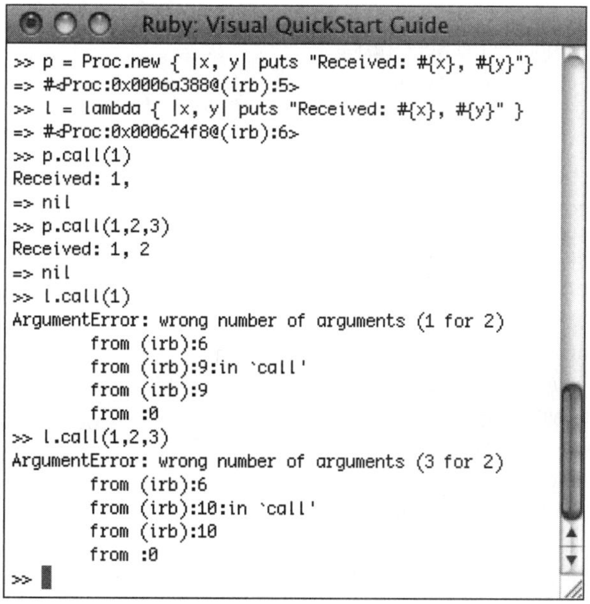

continues on next page

```
● ○ ○       Ruby: Visual QuickStart Guide
>> p = Proc.new { |x, y| puts "Received: #{x}, #{y}"}
=> #<Proc:0x0006a388@(irb):5>
>> l = lambda { |x, y| puts "Received: #{x}, #{y}" }
=> #<Proc:0x000624f8@(irb):6>
>> p.call(1)
Received: 1,
=> nil
>> p.call(1,2,3)
Received: 1, 2
=> nil
>> l.call(1)
ArgumentError: wrong number of arguments (1 for 2)
        from (irb):6
        from (irb):9:in `call'
        from (irb):9
        from :0
>> l.call(1,2,3)
ArgumentError: wrong number of arguments (3 for 2)
        from (irb):6
        from (irb):10:in `call'
        from (irb):10
        from :0
>> ▌
```

Figure 17.9 Improperly using a proc is allowed in Ruby, whereas improperly calling a lambda raises exceptions.

Yet another way in which procs and lambdas differ is in the effect that a `return` statement has. If a proc explicitly invokes `return`, the method in which the proc is executed will be affected as if the method called the return directly.

```
def ex1
    p = Proc.new { return }
    p.call
    puts "Won't be called."
end
ex1
```

If the proc is called outside of a method, or if the proc is passed from one method to another, the `return` will likely cause errors.

A `return` in a lambda only terminates that invocation of the lambda (**Figure 17.10**).

```
def ex2
    l = lambda { return }
    l.call
    puts "Will be called."
end
ex2
```

So when it comes to choosing between procs and lambdas, if you need to use `return`, create a lambda, thereby minimizing the potential for bugs. Further, use lambdas when you want to ensure that the proper number of arguments is provided to the `Proc`.

That covers enough of the basics for defining and using `Proc` objects. You may still be wondering what benefit there is to using a `Proc`, as opposed to a method. One benefit, already mentioned, is that you can do things with `Procs` that you can do with other objects, like passing them to methods, returning them from methods, etc. Conversely, actual methods cannot be returned by a method or passed to one. The other primary benefit comes from a `Proc`'s ability to remember the context in which it was defined. The next script will best demonstrate this concept.

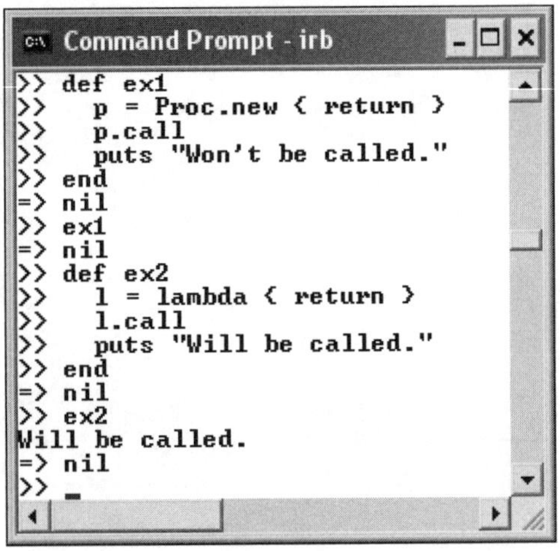

Figure 17.10 Two dummy functions demonstrate the effect of a `return` statement within a proc (top) and a lambda (bottom).

Script 17.5 The method returns a lambda, which is later used to calculate a range of numbers to the second and third powers.

```
                    Script
1    # Script 17.5 - lambdas.rb
2
3    # Method that returns a lambda:
4    def return_power_lambda(power)
5        lambda { |x| x ** power }
6    end
7
8    # Create two lambdas:
9    squared = return_power_lambda(2)
10   cubed = return_power_lambda(3)
11
12   # Apply the lambdas to some numbers:
13   2.upto(10) do |n|
14       puts "#{n} squared is #{squared.
         call(n)}"
15       puts "#{n} cubed is #{cubed.call(n)}"
16   end
```

To use Proc objects:

1. Begin a new Ruby script in your text editor or IDE (**Script 17.5**):

    ```
    # Script 17.5 - lambdas.rb
    ```

    This script will specifically use lambdas, not procs.

2. Create a method that returns a lambda:

    ```
    def return_power_lambda(power)
        lambda { |x| x ** power }
    end
    ```

    Since the value of the last executed statement in a method is the returned value of the method, this method returns a lambda. The lambda itself will calculate one number raised to a certain power. The power value will be fixed in the lambda when it's created.

3. Create two lambdas:

    ```
    squared = return_power_lambda(2)
    cubed = return_power_lambda(3)
    ```

    By invoking the return_power_lambda method with different arguments, and assigning the returned value to objects, two different lambdas are created. In the first, the power variable within the lambda will have the value 2; in the second, power will be 3.

continues on next page

4. Use both lambdas with a range of numbers:

```
2.upto(10) do |n|
  puts "#{n} squared is
  → #{squared.call(n)}"
  puts "#{n} cubed is
  → #{cubed.call(n)}"
end
```

To start, the `upto` method is used to increment from 2 to 10 by ones. This method uses a block (an unnamed block, not something created using `Proc.new` or `lambda`), to which it passes the number. So the `do...end` block will be executed nine times, assigning the numbers 2 through 10 to n.

Within the block, the two lambda objects are called within `puts` statements. The `squared` lambda represents the block `{ |x| x ** 2 }`, and `cubed` represents `{ |x| x ** 3 }`. This is what I mean when I say that `Proc` objects remember the context in which they were created: the `power` variable does not exist in this context (i.e., outside of the `return_power_lambda` method), but each lambda still knows what value it had.

With each `Proc` invocation, the value of n, used in the `call` method, will be assigned to x in the `Proc`'s code.

5. Save and run the completed script (**Figure 17.11**).

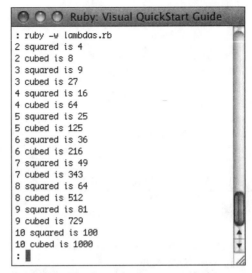

```
: ruby -w lambdas.rb
2 squared is 4
2 cubed is 8
3 squared is 9
3 cubed is 27
4 squared is 16
4 cubed is 64
5 squared is 25
5 cubed is 125
6 squared is 36
6 cubed is 216
7 squared is 49
7 cubed is 343
8 squared is 64
8 cubed is 512
9 squared is 81
9 cubed is 729
10 squared is 100
10 cubed is 1000
:
```

Figure 17.11 Nine lines of code, not counting comments and blanks lines, are able to churn out all these calculations, thanks to `Proc` objects.

✔ Tips

- Both procs and lambdas are examples of *closures*: blocks of code that recall the local variables that existed when they were created. Closures are a key part of *functional programming* (http://en.wikipedia.org/wiki/Functional_programming).

- Procs take on the safe level in effect at their creation. This will impact where and how the Proc can be used.

- Another way to create a Proc is to define a method that takes a block as an argument. To do so, preface the argument's name with an ampersand:

```
def some_method(&p)

end
```

The method would be called like so:

```
some_method { # block code }
```

The block's code will be assigned to the variable p in the method, and is therefore a Proc.

continues on next page

Ruby 1.9 Proc Changes

The creation and usage of procs and lambdas will change somewhat in Ruby 1.9. In Ruby 1.9 and later, the proc method is used like the lambda method but is equivalent to calling Proc.new:

```
p = proc { # block code }
```

In earlier versions of Ruby, the proc method is synonymous with lambda, which is rather confusing.

Ruby 1.9 also supports creating *lambda literals*. This Ruby 1.8 lambda:

```
greater = lambda { |x, y| x > y }
```

could be defined like so in Ruby 1.9:

```
greater = ->(x,y) { x > y }
```

By using this new, somewhat awkward syntax, you can set default values for the lambdas' arguments, making them even more method-like.

Ruby 1.9 also allows you to call Proc objects using parentheses:

```
p = proc { |x, y| x + y }
p.(1, 2)
```

- To pass a `Proc` to a method, you can create the `Proc`, and then use it in the method call as you would any other object type:

```
def double(num, block)
  block.call(num)
end
p = Proc.new { |x| x * 2 }
double(4, p) # Returns 8
```

- The `arity` method, defined in the `Proc` class, returns the number of arguments expected by a `Proc`.

- The `lambda?` method returns a Boolean value indicating if the object is a lambda (as opposed to a proc).

- `Proc` objects can also be called using square brackets in place of the `call` method. The lambda call in Script 17.5 could be written as:

```
puts "#{n} squared is #{squared[n]}"
```

Reflection

Ruby is a very flexible language. Unlike C programs, as an example, Ruby applications are not locked into set behavior when they're written. The book has many examples of this, like those in which existing classes—even major ones like `String`—can be altered in any Ruby code (as opposed to needing to rewrite the Ruby source code itself). More flexibility can be had by applying *reflection*. This is an advanced topic, not one that every programmer needs to use, but it's worth mentioning.

Reflection is a program's ability to inspect its own properties and modify its behavior accordingly. For example, the `methods` method returns all the methods that can be called using an object. Or you can break this list down by calling `public_methods`, `protected_methods`, and `private_methods`.

Chapter 7, "Creating Classes," demonstrates *duck typing*: where the use of an object is not limited by its type but rather by what it's capable of doing. If you'd rather look at an object's type, you can call the `class` method, which returns the object's class. The `superclass` method returns its parent class, if you need that information. The `ancestors` method returns an object's parents and mix-in modules.

These are just a few of the ways that code can inspect itself. Using this information to execute new code on the fly is beyond the scope of this book, but also something one really shouldn't ponder until they're thoroughly comfortable with the standard aspects of Ruby.

INDEX

A

\A anchors, 218–220
`Abbrev` modules, 196
absolute paths
    files or directories via, 288–289
    requiring files and, 204–205
abstract methods, 175
access. *See also* validation
    controlling in inheritance, 180–185
    to directory contents, 291–293
    to documentation, 1, 9–11
accessors, 141–143
Action Pack objects, 356–357
ActiveRecord
    column types in, 364
    models, customizing, 366–371
    in Ruby on Rails generally, 356
`add_record` method, 309
`agree` method, 278
aliases, 112
alternation, 215–217
`ancestors` method, 406
anchors, 218–220
Apple's Xcode application, 4
`ArgumentError`, 246, 251–254
arguments
    command-line, 66
    default values, 121–122
    errors in, 246, 251–254
    methods taking, 118–120
    parameters as, 118
    variable-length, 125–128
arrays, 59–73
    adding elements to, 67–69
    associated, 77
    collection iterators and, 109

    command-line arguments and, 66
    common methods using, 63–66
    creating, 60–62
    extended conditionals adding to, 90–91
    hashes and, 77
    introducing, 59
    multidimensional, 62
    multiple interactions of, 70
    ranges and, 74–76
    removing elements from, 70–72
    strings and, 72–73
`ask` method, 278–281
`assert` methods, 258–264
associated arrays and keys, 77
Atom feeds, 354
`attr-accessor`, 141–143
attributes. *See* variables
`attr-reader`, 141–143, 312–313
authentication, 347–350. *See also* validation

B

\b anchors, 218–220
\B anchors, 218–220
backreferencing, 234
backslashes, 217
`backtrace` method, 246–247
`base` classes, 168–169
`basename` method, 290
behavior-driven development, 264
benchmarking, 263
binary data, 310
blocks
    lambdas vs., 400
    methods and, 129–132
    numeric iterators and, 104–106
    procs as, 400